John Notman, Architect

1810-1865

John Notman, Architect

1810-1865

Constance M. Greiff

The Athenaeum of Philadelphia

1979

THIS PROJECT IS SUPPORTED BY A GRANT FROM THE NATIONAL

ENDOWMENT FOR THE ARTS IN WASHINGTON, A FEDERAL AGENCY

Library of Congress Catalog Card No.:
ISBN: 0-916530-10-8

FIRST EDITION

*Published on the occasion of an exhibition at
The Athenaeum of Philadelphia
October 23, 1978-January 31, 1979.*

LIBRARY OF CONGRESS CATALOGING IN PUBLICATION DATA

Greiff, Constance M
    John Notman, architect, 1810-1865.
    "Published on the occasion of an exhibition at the
Athenaeum of Philadelphia, October 23, 1978-January 31, 1979."
    Bibliography: p.
    Includes index
    1. Notman, John, 1810-1865—Exhibitions. 2. Architects—
United States—Biography. I. Philadelphia. Athenaeum. II. Title.
NA737.N67A4   720'.92'4   79-18978
ISBN 0-916530-10-8

DUST JACKET
Guernsey Hall, Princeton, N. J.

Photograph by Otto Baitz

FRONTISPIECE
John Notman (1810-1865), *c.* 1845-50
by Samuel Bell Waugh (1814-1885)
Collection of Mrs. Davis S. Abbott

Foreword

THE PUBLICATION OF THIS BOOK by The Athenaeum keeps a trust with John Notman reaching back over one hundred thirty years. At the cornerstone ceremonies on November 1, 1845, Athenaeum President Samuel Breck remarked prophetically, "we stand here to participate in the commencement of a structure that will, we hope, do honour to our architect, and be an ornament to the town." Both these hopes have been more than realized. The diarist Sidney George Fisher called The Athenaeum "the handsomest edifice in the city" when it opened, and from 1848, when Louisa Tuthill published it in her *History of Architecture*, the building has been recognized as a seminal American work. Recently the restored and expanded Athenaeum was designated a National Historic Landmark by the Secretary of the U. S. Department of the Interior. This classification is reserved for those sites possessing "national significance in commemorating the history of the United States of America."

The modern Athenaeum's fascination with the life and works of its architect began with the pioneering essays of the late Robert C. Smith, for a quarter century a member of the Board of Directors, and in subsequent articles and books by no less than three of the society's Librarians. This research publicized the importance of The Athenaeum design and kept alive the name of its nearly forgotten architect at a time when Victorian architecture was rarely taken seriously. Now that mid-nineteenth century architecture is being reappraised, it is time for The Athenaeum to bring together in one place all that has been learned about this innovative talent.

Funding for the exhibition "John Notman, Architect"—for which this book is the catalogue—came in part from the National Endowment for the Arts. The production was made possible by The Athenaeum's revolving publication fund, established by the Ella West Freeman Foundation to publish significant works on American Victorian architecture and decorative arts. It is the first in a series of exhibitions and catalogues on major nineteenth century American architects. Just as *John Notman, Architect* went to press it was learned that the National Endowment for the Arts will also assist The Athenaeum to mount a similar exhibition on Thomas U. Walter (1804-1887) in the fall of 1979.

I want to take this opportunity to thank Constance M. Greiff for giving a year of her life to John Notman and his works. She documents for the first time an impressive number of his designs, and she sheds much light on both building practices and the emerging architectural profession of the mid-nineteenth century. By assembling and reproducing all of his drawings and discussing the nearly one hundred known designs, Mrs. Greiff's most important contribution will be to secure for John Notman his rightful place in American architectural history.

ROGER W. MOSS, JR.,
Secretary & Librarian

9

Preface

This volume was written to accompany an exhibition of drawings and other materials related to Notman's work held at The Athenaeum of Philadelphia from October 23, 1978 to January 31, 1979. Research and preparation for the exhibition and publication were funded by a grant from the National Endowment for the Arts and The Athenaeum. I am grateful for having had the opportunity to devote the better part of a year to John Notman. In the course of my work the staff of The Athenaeum was consistently helpful, particularly Lawrence F. Filippone, who ferreted out several important pieces of information from various Philadelphia archives, and Eileen Magee, who attended with patience and efficiency to numerous details. No words are adequate to acknowledge the constant support and encouragement of Dr. Roger W. Moss, Jr., Secretary and Librarian of The Athenaeum, who conceived this project, and served throughout as guide and editor.

John Notman is an architect of tenacious appeal. This catalogue is the outgrowth of research on his buildings in Princeton, expanded over a decade to embrace his work in New Jersey, in Philadelphia and its environs, and in other parts of the country. In preparing it I was fortunate that Notman engendered continuing interest on the part of others, notably the authors of two pioneering studies of his life and work. Francis James Dallett was kind enough to give me additional biographical information collected since his article "John Notman Architect" was published in the *Princeton University Library Chronicle* in 1959. Jonathan Fairbanks, whose 1961 Master

of Arts thesis, "John Notman: Church Architect," is an invaluable source of information on Notman's religious commissions, provided me with a transcript of the anonymous biographical sketch now vanished from the collections of the Historical Society of Pennsylvania, and first suggested to me the possibility that the Parish Building of Trinity Church, Princeton, was designed by Notman.

Neither the exhibition nor the publication would have been possible without the cooperation of the institutions and individuals that own Notman's drawings and other materials related to his career. They are recognized specifically in references to their holdings, and I am grateful for the contributions of all. In particular I wish to acknowledge the unfailing assistance of the staff of the Historical Society of Pennsylvania, especially Peter Parker and Lucy Hrivnak. Also helpful were Edwin Wolf 2nd and Kenneth Finkel, the Library Company of Philadelphia; Mrs. Drayton M. Smith for the Laurel Hill Cemetery Company; Alan Frazer and Howard Wiseman, New Jersey Historical Society; Earle Coleman, Princeton University Archives; and Charles Green, Rare Books and Manuscripts, Princeton University Library.

In Philadelphia, Sandra Thornton and Rev. James Trimble helped me gain access to the archives of Christ Church, and Charles Latham, Jr., to those of the Episcopal Academy. In Virginia, Connally Edwards, Calder Loth, Mary Mitchell, and Elise H. Wright were welcome guides through unfamiliar territory, as were Michael Langdon and David Walker in Edinburgh.

Over several years, numerous people have added to the mosaic of information about Notman and his work. I wish to thank William B. Bassett for first suggesting that Springdale was Notman's design, and Wanda S. Gunning for finding, and calling to my attention, material in the Hodge Collection in the Princeton University Library that confirmed the attribution, as well as shedding light on Notman's work for the Princeton Theological Seminary. Charles E. Peterson's observations on Notman's use of iron at Nassau Hall made me aware of its significance in the history of American building technology, and I am grateful to him for reading and making suggestions concerning the catalogue entry for the building. I also wish to thank William H. Short for sharing insight on Notman's residences, particularly Fieldwood (Guernsey Hall) and Ellarslie. Gary Wolf contributed ideas and provided research assistance at various stages of the project, and prepared the index to this volume.

The year's limit imposed by the terms of the grant from the National Endowment of the Arts was in one sense welcome. A deadline insures completion, although it also checks pursuit of those last promising leads. While the catalogue was in production, documentation of one additional building, the Hutchinson House in Bristol, Pennsylvania was found, too late to be included except by sketchy reference. Even later, my attention was called to another documented project, Spring Hill Cemetery in Lynchburg, Virginia, laid out on 2 Sept. 1855.

An important insight on a contemporary's view of Notman was provided by Robert B. Ennis from a letter in Thomas U. Walter's letterbook for 1854 to Gen. R[obert] Patterson of Philadelphia, 14 Apr. 1854.

You wish me to recommend some one to you in whose taste I have confidence. My own impression is that Mr. Notman (Spruce above Broad) is the best Archt in Philada. I am not personally acquainted with him, but his works, as The Athenaeum, St. Mark's Church, and other things I have seen of his, indicate taste, genius, and practical skill. After Notman I would suggest Mr. Jno. McArthur Jr. (cor. 5th & Library Sts) the Architect of the new building of the Presbyterian board of Publication—there is a host of Architects (so called) in Philada but I can't think of any others that I think would please you; these remarks are of course confidential, as the humblest in the profession would not take it kindly from me to be underrated. I am sorry to say that architectural talent in this country is not what it ought to be considering the vast field there is for its successful practice.

Undoubtedly other Notman projects and references will be discovered as contemporary records are searched. If a certain degree of haste has produced omissions and errors, the fault is mine.

Constance M. Greiff
Princeton, New Jersey
January 1979

John Notman, Architect

1810-1865

A Biographical Essay

JUST INSIDE the entrance gate of Laurel Hill cemetery stands a shaft of polished dark gray granite. Its face is inscribed:

John Notman
Born in Edinburg
Scotland
July 22, 1810
Died March 3, 1865
Martha Pullen
Wife of
John Notman
Died October 1870

The monument is not only plain, but undistinguished, far different from other memorials in Laurel Hill designed, as was the old part of the cemetery itself, by the man buried beneath.

When John Notman died, brief obituaries in the Philadelphia newspapers recalled him primarily as a designer of churches.[1] There was some justification for this: in the last decade of his life Notman was largely occupied with ecclesiastical work, serving as contractor as well as architect for Holy Trinity and St. Clement's Churches. These, along with St. Mark's Church and the facade of the Cathedral of St. Peter and St. Paul, have proven to be among his most enduring contributions to the Philadelphia townscape. His skill in church architecture was recognized outside his adopted city, bringing him commissions in Delaware, Maryland, New Jersey and western Pennsylvania.

But Notman, especially in the early period of his career, was far more versatile than the obituaries suggest. He introduced the Italianate villa to the United States at Burlington, New Jersey, and was recognized by the chief apostle of the picturesque, A. J. Downing, as one of the country's most skillful practitioners in that vein. For The Athenaeum of Philadelphia he designed an innovative Renaissance Revival building, a stylistic prototype for clubhouses for decades afterwards. He planned America's first architect-designed, park-like rural cemetery at Laurel Hill, Philadelphia, and, in Richmond, Virginia, the country's first major picturesque urban park. He designed the first psychiatric hospital embodying the advanced ideas of Dr. Thomas Kirkbride for the treatment of the mentally ill. Notman was, in sum, one of America's most innovative architects in the second quarter of the nineteenth century. Although not stylistically an originator, he was an importer of sophisticated design ideas from Britain, translating them skillfully for his American clientele. He also was quick

Gateway to Laurel Hill [see 2.3]

to utilize the technological developments that transformed the art of building in the nineteenth century, and he was alert to the availability of new materials and new techniques.

Facts about the life of John Notman are almost as sparse as the inscription on his tombstone. So far as is known, Notman left no diaries, no account books, no body of correspondence or other papers. An account of his career can only be pieced together by assembling widely scattered sources: a few brief memoirs, legal documents, newspaper and other contemporary accounts of building activities, and the family papers or institutional records of clients.

Part of what is known about Notman's early life is derived from a manuscript evidently written shortly after his death by a close friend or relative.[2] Other information is derived from family tradition, according to which Notman was descended from a long line of stoneworkers. His father, David, is said to have worked at a quarry adjoining an estate called "Fernieside" and to have been employed on the construction of the Bonally Reservoir, built as part of the Edinburgh Joint Stock Water Company in 1822.[3] The sketch indicates that John Notman studied drawing at "The 'School

of Arts' in Edinburgh, well known to all sojourners in that romantic city as the 'Royal Institution on the Mound.' " The Royal Institution for the Encouragement of the Fine Arts in Scotland, also often referred to as the Royal Academy of Scotland, was founded in 1819 and occupied its first Classical Revival building, designed by William Henry Playfair, in 1826.[4] Although some records of early matriculants are preserved in the Scottish Record Office at Register House in Edinburgh, Notman's name is not among them. If lists of those who taught at the Royal Institution were kept, or of those who attended classes without matriculating, they have not been preserved.

At a proper age he was apprenticed to a builder to learn the practical part of the profession of an architect for which he was destined—after serving four years apprenticeship he was engaged under an architect in a Castle he was erecting in the Highlands of Scotland, and afterward on a similar work in the north of Ireland—..."[5]

Unfortunately, no firm corroborative evidence for Notman's activities during his formative years in Edinburgh can be found. Neither his name nor his father's appears in city directories for the period, nor was his father entered in the roll of Burgesses. Again neither name appears in the Register of Sasines, the record of property ownership and other legal transactions (although the name of an older John Notman, a slater, appears in both places). By the early nineteenth century the medieval apprenticeship system was disintegrating, and it was becoming the exception rather than the rule for apprenticeship agreements to be recorded. It is therefore not surprising that Notman's name is not among those on the scanty roster of apprenticeships for the early 1820s preserved in the Edinburgh city archives.

Despite this lack of documentation the brief account in the Historical Society's sketch has a high degree of plausibility. The quarries in the vicinity of Edinburgh in the early nineteenth century were in the Parish of Liberton south of the city proper. The largest of these, the limestone quarry at Gilmerton, ran through the west side of Fernieside or Ferneyside Lodge.[6] Stone from the nearby quarry at Craigmillar was utilized for the Edinburgh Water Company's reservoir.[7] Employment at these coincides with the family tradition concerning David Notman's career.

The standard of elementary education in Scotland in the early nineteenth century was high. If, as the Historical Society's memoir indicates, John Notman was given "a fine education," he probably attended the parish school at Liberton, where he indeed would have received a sound fundamental training. Some idea of the breadth and quality of the curriculum can be derived from a report of an examination of pupils held in 1781:

On the 14th August, the parish school of Liberton was examined by the minister, in presence of a great many respectable gentlemen in the neighbourhood, upon the Greek, Latin, French and English languages, and likewise upon the English grammar, arithmetic, book-keeping and the principles of the Christian religion, when the children in their different classes acquitted themselves, very much to the satisfaction of all present, and discovered such proficiency as did much honour to the industry and abilities of Mr. Ferguson, the master of the school, and render him worthy of the greatest encouragement.[8]

The Greek, Latin and French may not have been of much use to an architect in later life,

but a thorough grounding in English grammar, arithmetic, and especially in book-keeping would prove invaluable.

It was customary for boys to leave school and commence their apprenticeships at the age of thirteen or fourteen. Although the Historical Society's sketch says simply that Notman was apprenticed to a "builder," his master was probably a carpenter. The guild system was declining in importance, but the building trades were still organized as carpenters, masons and slaters. Notman, until he began to call himself an architect ten years after he emigrated to the United States, listed himself as "carpenter" in official documents.

More important to his future career than his apprenticeship, however, was his reported employment in the office of an architect where he can be assumed to have learned the rudiments of his future profession. If he entered upon his apprenticeship at the age of thirteen or fourteen and served for four years, his architectural employment would have commenced when he was seventeen or eighteen, that is, in 1827 or 1828. At this period there were four architects with major practices in Edinburgh: William Burn (1789-1870); James Gillespie Graham (1776-1855); Thomas Hamilton (1784-1858) and William Henry Playfair (1790-1857).[9]

If Notman's anonymous biographer is to be believed, Notman could have served in the office of only one of these men. For in the last three years of the 1820s only William Henry Playfair was "erecting a Castle in the Highlands of Scotland, and afterward . . . a similar work in the north of Ireland." The former was probably Dumphail House in Morayshire, planned in 1827 and built in 1828-1829. The latter could only have been Drumbanagher House in County Armagh, planned in 1829.[10] Although Dumphail has been extensively remodeled and Drumbanagher demolished, the drawings, along with several thousand others by Playfair, survive at the University of Edinburgh Library. Both were substantial country houses in a style in which no other architect in Scotland, and indeed no architect in the British Isles, was then working—the fully developed picturesque Tuscan Revival, which Notman would introduce in the United States less than a decade later.

Although one of Playfair's letterbooks exists, covering at least part of the period Notman would have been in his office, it names none of his employees except his chief assistant, a Mr. McPherson.[11] Nevertheless, it makes clear that several "clerks," or draftsmen were employed and that they were engaged in the usual tasks of junior architects, the preparation of working drawings and the taking of measurements. Drumbanagher, especially, was a project that taxed the resources of the office. In a letter of 27 Aug. 1830, explaining why he had not prepared drawings for another client, Playfair wrote that 80 masons he had sent from Scotland to Ireland were idle and needed drawings immediately. A fortnight later he reported that his sketches were in the hands of his clerk being reduced to working shape. In a letter to another prospective client, a Mrs. Jeffrey, dated 15 Nov. 1830, he informed her that he intended to send two clerks to her property for the purpose of taking measurements.

Playfair was of a somewhat higher social class than most of his fellow practitioners in Edinburgh, who were the sons of builders or had started their careers as builders. The son of an architect, James Playfair, he came to live with his uncle, Professor John Playfair of the University of Edinburgh, after his father's death. He attended the university briefly, but left to train as an architect in the office of William Stark. Playfair's correspondence shows him to have been highly conscious of his status as a professional. He expected recognition of his authority from clients and demanded high standards and strict adherence to directions from contractors and his staff. The office was run on a businesslike basis, but his clerks would undoubtedly have had access to his library, which included works by Papworth, Robinson and Loudon. Playfair also owned a copy of G. L. Meason's *On the Landscape Architecture of the Great Painters of Italy*, the first English book to extol the virtues of Italianate architecture, published in London in 1828 in an edition of only 150 copies.[12]

Although the account of Notman's early life given by his anonymous biographer cannot be confirmed through contemporary records, each statement in it can to some degree be verified. This is not the case with another family tradition, cited by Dallett, which holds that Notman received some training from Michael Angelo Nicholson.[13] Nicholson, son of the architect and author of architects' and builders' manuals, Peter Nicholson, had a school for architectural drawing in Melton Place, Euston Square.[14] The tradition that Notman studied with him is based only on a statement made by Nicholson's grandson to Notman's grandniece almost a century later. No records covering a sojourn by Notman in London can be found.

Whatever formal training he may have received, a young man attuned to architecture could acquire sound grounding in fundamentals on the streets of Edinburgh. Through the late eighteenth century and on into the first decades of the nineteenth, James Craig's plan of 1776 for the New Town was being realized. Rows, squares, and crescents of decorous houses of an almost Roman severity were designed by Robert and William Adam and Sir William Chambers, and later by Playfair. Public buildings, among them Robert Adam's Register House and University, and Robert Reid's Parliament House, were constructed in both the New Town and the old. Later Thomas Hamilton's High School, based on the Propylaeum, and Playfair's unfinished National Monument on Calton Hill, modeled on the Parthenon, helped justify Edinburgh's sobriquet, "The Athens of the North." In the city and its environs, one could also see William Burn's early Gothic Revival work in the form of both churches and country houses.[15] Notman must have been alert to what he saw, for images of Edinburgh would haunt him throughout his career. They appear not only in references to specific buildings, but more tellingly, in the handling of materials, especially masonry. The heaviness and "stoniness" of his rustication, the stress on the thickness of the wall achieved through the strength of the openings, the solidity of proportion all have a Scottish air. Especially reminiscent of Edinburgh is the use of plain broad bands of masonry for belt courses and window surrounds.

A half-century of dazzling expansion came to a halt in the early 1830s. By 1833 the city of Edinburgh was, in fact, bankrupt.[16] Although building activity would eventually resume, it must have occurred to an ambitious young man that there were better opportunities elsewhere. John Notman set sail for America, on the ship *Thames*, out of London. Accompanied by his sister, Margaret, he arrived in Philadelphia in the fall of 1831. His name appears on the ship's manifest as "John Nutman," and his occupation as "carpenter." [17] Also on board was Robert Buist, "nurseryman," who, later, as treasurer of the Mount Vernon Cemetery Company, was probably instrumental in securing Notman a commission in the difficult years of the late 1850s. William D. Hewitt, whose brother George W. Hewitt had been a draftsman in Notman's office, believed that Notman's early years in this country were spent in Burlington, New Jersey.[18] However, all the available evidence shows that Notman settled in Philadelphia, although his name does not appear in the city directories until 1837. On 8 Feb. 1832, as a Philadelphia resident, he declared his intention of becoming a naturalized citizen.[19] In 1833 or 1834 Notman returned to Scotland, bringing back to Philadelphia his mother, his brother Peter, and his sisters Mary and Jane.[20]

How Notman earned his living during his first few years in his adopted city is uncertain. Presumably he worked as a carpenter, as he listed himself on this second ship's manifest and, indeed, in the Philadelphia city directories until 1841. His first known architectural work is a drawing for a small office building for the Library Company of Philadelphia [Fig. 1.1]. The drawing is undated, but the Library Company voted to erect the building on 1 Oct. 1835 and tenants paid their first quarter's rentals on 18 Nov. 1836.[21] Notman therefore, probably executed the drawing late in 1835 or early in 1836. He produced a design in no way unusual or distinguished. Of brick, three stories high, with hip roof, the building was adorned only by plain sills, a belt course and simple cornice. It provided rental offices on the first and second floors and a suite of rooms for the Library Company on the third, connected to the organization's existing building by a bridge. Notman appears to have received no compensation for his design. But the commission is nevertheless a significant one; it indicates that he had made the acquaintance of John Jay Smith.

Smith, Librarian of the Library Company, author and editor, was a descendant of families prominent in Philadelphia and Burlington County, New Jersey. Not himself a man of wealth, he was acquainted with those on both sides of the Delaware River who were, and he appears to have been the consistent link between Notman and the important patrons of his early career. Smith himself was the moving force behind Notman's first major commission, the rural cemetery at Laurel Hill. The concept of such a cemetery, detached from a church, outside the center of the city, and in a park-like setting, was not a new one. The Parisian suburban cemeteries, of which the most famous was Père-la-Chaise, were opened in the late eighteenth century, followed by similar developments in Frankfurt and Munich. In the New World the first rural cemetery was Mount Auburn in Cambridge, Massachusetts, begun in 1831.[22] This last example, laid out on irregular sloping ground and planned from the beginning to encompass picturesque landscaping, seems to have provided the most direct inspiration for Smith, an avid amateur horticulturist. The immediate impetus that led him to embark on the venture at Laurel Hill was the death of a young daughter. When he attempted to visit her grave in the burying ground of the Arch

Street Meeting, the cemetery was in such disorder that her place of interment could not be located.[23]

Smith initiated a meeting in November 1835 for the purpose of providing an alternative to burial in such city churchyards. Mount Auburn had been laid out by gentlemen amateurs. But from the beginning Smith seems to have intended to employ a professional designer, for William Strickland was one of those invited to the first meeting. However, Strickland withdrew from participation after his plan was rejected in favor of Notman's.[24]

Notman's plan for Laurel Hill appears to have owed little to either the well-known Père-la-Chaise or Mount Auburn. Rather it was influenced by a cemetery on the outskirts of northwest London, Kensal Green, planned in 1831-1832.[25] It is remotely possible that Notman saw Kensal Green when he returned to Great Britain in 1834, but more likely that his source was a pamphlet illustrating H. E. Kendall's designs for the project.[26] The most striking similarity between the plans is the use of a central circle to anchor the meandering, looping roadways and paths. Kendall divides his circle with radii, Notman with intersecting semi-circular sections, but the purpose of the device in affording a controlling focus to the scheme is the same. Nevertheless, the overall impact of both plans is picturesque. Indeed, Kendall labeled his plan with that epithet, and, in the foreword to his pamphlet, spoke of the grounds of Kensal Green as "on account of the elegant undulations of its surface, is capable, by the aid of judicious planting, interspersed with tombs, of being converted into a scene highly picturesque and beautiful. . . ."

That Notman knew the pamphlet is attested to by the dependence of his chapel for Laurel Hill on the chapel in the pointed style proposed by Kendall. Notman has simplified the design greatly, omitting the flying buttresses and much of the decorative detail, but the general forms and proportions are remarkably similar.[27] The small Gothic monument, also shown in Kendall's sketch, seems to have inspired Notman's monument for John Brown at Laurel Hill. In fact, the chapel and entrance lodge at Kensal Green were executed not in the Gothic style, but in a Greek Revival version of the Doric order. Notman may have been aware of this when he chose a classical revival mode for his entrance at Laurel Hill. Whatever their outer trappings, the entrances to both cemeteries adhered to the plan Kendall had suggested, in a Gothic version, in his scheme for the grounds of Kensal Green. This was essentially a Palladian five-part composition with a central building pierced by an archway, flanked on either side by a wall terminating in semi-circular quadrants. Notman, however, eschewed the heavy and severe forms utilized at Kensal Green. His central pavilion is reminiscent rather of the lightness and elegance of Decimus Burton's screen of 1827-1828 at Hyde Park Corner.

In the nineteenth century the rural cemetery was conceived as a place as much for the living as for the dead. These cemeteries, wrote Downing, "are the only places in the country that can give an untravelled American any idea of the beauty of many of the public parks and gardens abroad."[28] Laurel Hill was well publicized and became a public attraction. Tickets of admission were issued and between April and December 1848 there were 30,000 visitors.[29] Its spreading fame eventually brought Notman commissions to design cemeteries in Cincinnati, Ohio, and Richmond, Virginia. More importantly, it immediately brought him into intimate contact with men who would become patrons or otherwise advance his career.

John Jay Smith was undoubtedly the conceptual force behind Laurel Hill. But the man who provided the financial support to transform Smith's visions into reality was Nathan Dunn. Dunn, a prosperous merchant, who had spent much of his career in China, was active in Philadelphia affairs, but spent his summers in Mount Holly, New Jersey. While the work on Laurel Hill was going forward Notman designed for him a summer house called, in straightforward fashion, The Cottage [3]. This was indeed a "cottage orné," larger, but otherwise quite similar to the cottage designed for the superintendent at Laurel Hill. A two-story central section, bisected by a hall, was flanked by one-story wings terminating in semi-hexagonal bays crowned by conical roofs. The house had a strong flavor of the informal cottages illustrated in the popular English design books of the early nineteenth century, although no precise prototype can be found. Some attempt was made, however, to distinguish it from the generic type through the exterior detailing. Downing noted that, "The style of this building is mixed; the arcaded veranda has an oriental air while the main body of the cottage is in the English cottage manner."[30] The oriental motifs were superficial. They consisted of trellising on the veranda, more suggestive than replicative of anything visible in China, and small bulbous domes over the veranda posts, more reminiscent of the Near than the Far East.

In Europe orientalized buildings were often created to house importations of art and objects from the east.[31] The references to the orient in The Cottage were probably meant to serve the same purpose. Nathan Dunn had brought back from China a collection of at least 10,000 artifacts, some of which he undoubtedly displayed in his home, although the bulk of his collection was shown as a museum in Philadelphia from 1838 to 1841. He then decided to move the collection to London and called on Notman to provide plans for a building to house it [13]. In this case Notman provided, at least for the exterior, a truly oriental form, a pagoda reproducing a Chinese summer house.

It was probably also through the New Jersey connections of the proprietors of Laurel Hill that Notman met George Washington Doane. Doane was Bishop of New Jersey, but, because the diocese had no cathedral or seat, also served as rector of St. Mary's Church in Burlington. Wealthy through marriage, ambitious for himself and his church, and an

Anglophile, he was an ideal patron for a young architect wishing to carry out schemes that were then avant-garde even in Britain. For such a patron Notman was able to realize a fully-developed picturesque Italianate villa [4]. The cottages at Laurel Hill and Mount Holly embodied picturesque elements in the form of bays, oriel windows, colored glass and verandas, but their plans still followed the basic tenets of Palladian symmetry. At Riverside not only the forms, but the massing and the plan were determinedly picturesque. The irregularity of the rooflines led the eye to the dominating tower, placed off-center and to the rear. The plan, outflung to the landscape, conformed to the site and to the function of the interior spaces. In a motif that was to be more fully developed in his later villas, the hall became the central controlling feature. The stairs were removed to a separate stair hall. All major spaces within the building related to the hall, horizontally through access on the same level, or vertically through a semi-circular opening, enclosed by a rail at second-story level and lighted from above by a skylight.

Various English prototypes for Riverside have been suggested.[32] These include John Nash's Cronkhill of 1802 and Charles Barry's villa for Mr. Attree at Queen's Park, Brighton.[33] Also mentioned as sources for Riverside are English design books, particularly those of E. B. Lamb, John Claudius Loudon, Robert Lugar, J. B. Papworth, and Charles Parker. But except for some of Parker's designs, the English examples are Regency houses with Italianate trappings. The walls are taut skins and the openings emphasize their thinness, rather than confirming, as at Riverside, their substantiality. Both the vocabulary employed by Notman and the firmness and solidity with which it is handled relate not to these English examples, but rather to the Italianate houses designed by Playfair in the late 1820s and early 1830s. The square tower with the triple-arched windows appears at Drumbanagher and the farmhouse at Dalcrue. The powerful arched entrance is a feature of Belmont on the outskirts of Edinburgh. The grouping of tripartite flat-headed, heavily-enframed windows, with narrow lights flanking a wider central one, is a common motif in Playfair's designs. So robust a version of the picturesque Italianate or Tuscan Revival would not appear again on either side of the Atlantic until the following decade.

Notman's growing professional success was accompanied by evidence of improvement in his status as a private citizen. In 1837 he was listed for the first time in McElroy's *Directory*. His occupation was given as "carpenter," and two addresses were listed, one on Currant Alley, presumably his office or shop, and his home at 184 South 11th Street. In 1837 he became a member of the St. Andrew's Society, and in 1840, a shareholder in The Athenaeum.[34] Subsequently he joined other groups, the Historical Society of Pennsylvania, the Musical Fund Society, the Library Company, and Franklin Lodge, No. 134, Ancient York Masons.[35] He also was a life member of the Pennsylvania Institution for the Instruction of the Blind.[36] In 1841 he married Martha Pullen and then, or shortly thereafter, moved into the house at 1430 Spruce Street where husband and wife would live until their deaths.[37]

The Notmans appear to have lived comfortably, sharing an interest in music and art. Mrs. Notman owned a piano and had a "musical Library." Her paintings of Bothway Castle, Conway Castle, and a view near the Natural Bridge of Virginia, adorned the house, as did other pictures presumably by Notman: a "Prospective" of Holy Trinity and five "Pictures of Villas, etc." The Notmans also owned marble statues of lions; an engraving of George I reviewing his troops; an oil portrait of George Washington, a painting of an Italian peasant girl with a goat by Samuel Bell Waugh; and a portrait of Notman's three nephews, John Notman, Walter Gibson and James Catanach, by James Reid Lambdin.[38]

Both Notmans exhibited canvases from their collection at the Pennsylvania Academy of the Fine Arts. In addition to the Lambdin and Waugh paintings, which were shown in 1855, Notman displayed in 1848 "The Bridge Over the Clyde near Dumfries, Scotland," by Walter M'Pherson Bayne of Boston, and a "Street Scene, Third and Chestnut in 1810," by Bass Otis. Mrs. Notman showed "Ben Nevis," by Edward Moran, and "Prize Tuberose," by an artist named [John?] Williamson, in 1867.[39] In the course of his married life, Notman also accumulated a library, which when it was sold at auction following his death, netted the respectable sum of $709.65.[40] Unfortunately no copy of the catalogue prepared for the auction has been found. However, it may be presumed that Notman bought —and perhaps sold—books on architecture. A tantalizing note is the single clue to the books that interested him.

You kindly offered to loan to me the Vitruvius Brittanicus —at the time of buying.—Can you let me have it to peruse by the Bearer and oblige.[41]

Laurel Hill, The Cottage, and Riverside brought Notman a measure of recognition, if not, indeed, fame after Downing published the two latter in 1841 in the first edition of his *Treatise*. Marriage appears to have brought him a degree of security and status. However, Notman was not immune to the effects of the financial depression that followed the Panic of 1837 and the failure of the Bank of the United States. In the six years following the completion of Riverside Notman undertook only nine documented projects, of which only four are known to have been executed. Notman's lack of activity was not singular. A table of the numbers of buildings erected in Philadelphia between 1833 and 1851 shows how severe the decline was, and how slow and erratic the recovery until the boom years of the late 1840s.[42] Notman's financial difficulties during this period, as well as some of his projects, are revealed in a plea for extension of a loan.[43]

Notman's work in these lean years fulfills little of the promise shown in the designs for Laurel Hill and Riverside. Presumably the parlous financial times discouraged patrons willing to experiment. His own house [8] is indistinguishable from hundreds of other brick Philadelphia row houses. One design for Stephen Morris [Fig. 11.1] appears to be a conventional Federal hip-roofed house with an Italianate portico appended as an afterthought. The other [Figs. 11.2 and 11.3], more Regency in feeling, is simply a box with Italianate detailing minimally applied in the form of overhanging eaves, round-headed windows in the gable, and a favorite Notman device, window surrounds in which the architrave is continued below the sill. Perhaps it was for want of any more satisfying occupation that Notman produced during this period his only known "pattern-book" design. This appeared as Design IX in Downing's *Cottage Residences* published in 1842 [12]. It may be indicative of Notman's lack of interest in such activities that it is the only one of his designs that can be traced specifically to an English pattern book. Nevertheless, despite its symmetrical plan, the house, with its strong central tower, well-defined portico, and robust detailing, is more interesting than the project for Stephen Morris. It also, according to Downing's description, incorporated a relatively sophisticated feature, a central heating system, although it lacked indoor plumbing.

From what is known of Notman's public projects they do not appear to have been of much distinction either. The Assembly Building [6], for which he certainly served as contractor, and probably as architect, burned in 1852, and appears to have aroused so little interest that neither a picture nor a description of it can be found. Notman also was contractor, as well as architect, at least in name, for the Academy of Natural Sciences [7] at Broad and Sansom Streets. From the records of that institution it appears, however, that the design was by committee. If the one available illustration is to be trusted, this may well have been the case. A rectangular form, unadorned except for some weak pilasters on the Broad Street facade, the Academy too elicited little contemporary comment.

Notman's creativity and talent are revealed only in three unexecuted designs for The Athenaeum produced in 1840 [9 and 10]. The two versions of the later of these were prepared in July for a proposed juncture of The Athenaeum and the Library Company of Philadelphia. Unfortunately they survive only in plan. They show Notman's sensitivity to the programmatic requirements of his clients and his capability of planning on a grandiose scale, but provide few clues to the stylistic devices through which the buildings would be given form. For the earlier project of February 1840, for The Athenaeum alone, elevations as well as plans exist. The design provided a principal floor conceived as a series of octagons and other polygonal shapes. The octagon, a favorite motif in Notman's domestic designs, had already appeared at The Cottage and Riverside, and would reappear in several of his later residences. Its utilization in a public building echoes Playfair's Royal Institution of 1822-1826, where a grand staircase gives access to a suite of interlocking octagonal galleries on the *piano nobile*. However elegant the principal floor of The Athenaeum would have been, the polygonal shapes created awkward arrangements for the first floor offices. Notman, with good reason, abandoned the concept in his later designs for The Athenaeum. The chief interest of this unexecuted project lies, however, not in its plan, but in the style of its exterior. William Strickland and Thomas U. Walter, who also participated in 1840 in The Athenaeum competition, submitted designs in the Greek Revival mode that had dominated Philadelphia public building for over 30 years. Notman's astylar composition, with its strongly rusticated basement and dominating cornice, is clearly a break with tradition. It is in no sense as closely related to Renaissance precedents as his eventual design for The Athenaeum, but, like Riverside, it reveals the young architect ready to offer innovative proposals to a sympathetic client.

With the return of prosperity and the concomitant increase in building activity, Notman at last had opportunities for major commissions. The years between 1845 and 1852 would prove to be the most productive of his career. The Athenaeum, which had abandoned the idea of a new headquarters in 1840 because of economic conditions, again solicited proposals from Philadelphia's architects. In his response [16] Notman returned with more precision to the Renaissance forms he had tentatively utilized in 1840. His initial designs retain some features that smack more of the Regency than of the Victorian Renaissance Revival—the hip roof with its prominent bridged chimneys and, in particular, the delicate iron balconies. By the time he drew his fifth and final design, Notman had produced America's first full-blown Renaissance Revival building.

The precedents for Notman's Athenaeum are well established. Quite obviously he was influenced by the gentlemens' clubs of Sir Charles Barry, particularly the Travellers' Club in London, designed in 1829 and completed in 1832, and the Manchester Athenaeum, conceived in 1836 and constructed between 1837 and 1839. Both would have been available to Notman through publication.[44] Certainly Notman was conscious of his purposes in choosing a Renaissance model. In his own description of The Athenaeum, he referred to it as an "excellent specimen of the Italian style of architecture" of which "the beautiful proportions of its parts, the fine details and massive crowning cornice, give it an air of stateliness and grandeur."[45] His words echo the first English book to espouse the Italianate, a volume by G. L. Meason, with which Notman may have become familiar in Playfair's office. Meason characterizes Italian architecture of the quattrocentro as "the most manly, firm, imposing, and on the large scale the most allied to grandeur and stateliness."[46] It was a sentiment shared by the clubmen of the United States. Well into the twentieth century the example of The Athenaeum would be followed in downtown clubs based on the palazzi of Rome and Florence.

It was not, however, the new style of The Athenaeum that caught the attention of Philadelphians so much as its new material. The comparative virtues, both aesthetic and practical, of sandstone versus brick or marble were hotly debated. The *Public Ledger*, a proponent of sandstone, commented that "the rich gray and brown stone of every shade, from our native quarries, . . . impart an air of quiet gentility to private buildings, of philosophical gravity to those of a public character." Supporting this view in the same issue of the newspaper, "An Architect" wrote:

But there are other and greater reasons for the adoption of a substitute for marble—its perishable nature, its great cost, and the inconvenience of reflection to those living opposite. None of which objections can be used against the sandstone. When we see a row of stately buildings like the Athenaeum erected in our streets at one third the cost of marble, it will then be time to drag the "ugly stone to judgment."[47]

When the commentary appeared, Notman was already producing another "stately building." This was the Bank of North America [29], with a facade that was a more elaborate version of that of The Athenaeum, capped by a lionheaded cornice based on that of The Travellers' Club. It too was brownstone, according to one contemporary critic "one of the best materials for architecture which this country affords."[48] It made so strong an impression that Thomas U. Walter, in submitting one of the several mid-nineteenth century proposals for new City and County buildings on Independence Square, called for the use of stone similar to that employed in the bank. "With the view of making the exterior of the State House building (Independence Hall) harmonize," it would be covered with mastic to match.[49]

While Notman was preparing his preliminary proposals for The Athenaeum in April 1845, he was also engaged on a public project of greater magnitude, the New Jersey State House at Trenton [15]. Pressed for additional space, the legislators of New Jersey intended to erect two detached office buildings to supplement the provincial Federal State House erected in 1794. This idea was abandoned quickly. Unfortunately, there is no record of the discussions leading to a different approach, discussions in which Notman probably played an important role. Instead of erecting dependencies, the existing structure would be encompassed in a new edifice, with colonnaded porticos and an imposing dome. Use of these elements, following the example of the United States Capitol, had become a hallmark for State Houses by the mid-nineteenth century.[50] But Notman departed, although not so far as to offend his clients, from the Classical Revival vocabulary and composition of previous capitols. Despite the correct Roman Doric ordonnance of the north portico, the Corinthian columns on the south, and its symmetry, the building relates not to the antique prototypes that had inspired the architects of the previous three decades, but to an earlier view of antiquity. Once again Notman's inspiration was Italy. This time, however, his precedent was not the romantically interpreted villa of the Tuscan hills or the palazzo of the quattrocento or early cinquecento; rather it was the Renaissance as seen through British Georgian eyes. His south front related to such public buildings as Sir William Chamber's Somerset House or Playfair's museum front for the University of Edinburgh. The dome, different from that on any previous capitol, was based on Sir Christopher Wren's dome for St. Paul's.

More importantly, Notman's total design is also strongly infused with elements of the picturesque. Classical Revival architects using the colonnaded portico and dome had appended them to simple rectangular volumes. The separate elements of the building were clearly defined. In contrast Notman by confining his office additions to low pavilions, achieved a dramatic massing, culminating in the crowning dome. His retention of the polygonal ends of the existing building, and the expression of the octagonal rotunda beneath the dome on the exterior, produced a romantic irregularity of outline already clearly visible in the flank elevation of his preliminary proposal.

The building was greeted with almost universal approbation and even considerable comprehension. One astute observer praised

the extraordinary ingenuity of the artist in framing his plan so as to take in the original building with all its peculiarities of forms.... Tested by scientific rules, the plan may be an egregious sin against classic models. But we are not sure whether the picturesque is not more pleasing than frigid conformity with ancient rules.[51]

Official New Jersey opinion was also favorable. "... we believe," the State House Commissioners reported, "the plans of our architect have given us a state capitol that will not suffer in comparison with that of any other state in the Union, ..."[52]

Even before the State House was completed, this satisfaction found material expression in the offer of another major commission, the New Jersey State Lunatic Asylum [18] up the Delaware River from Trenton. Again Notman chose to effect a marriage of the classical and the picturesque. The central pavilion was a temple form, with a pedimented Tuscan hexastyle portico and a shallow dome. It was flanked by a system of receding wings and cross pavilions, the latter crowned by Italianate towers. The dome and towers served practical as well as aesthetic functions. The former housed water tanks for the plumbing; the latter served as essential components of the ventilating system. This was appropriate, for in fact the programmatic needs dictated the forms of the building. Nevertheless, the architectural problem was no more difficult than that of the State House, with its requirement of incorporating an existing building. But at the asylum the solution is not as successful. The wedding of classical and romantic imagery and forms is not a happy one. The rigid formality of the central section does not climax the more picturesque disposition of the wings, but seems to stand in opposition. Still the building is of interest for its sophisticated heating, ventilating and plumbing systems.

1845 also saw Notman launched on the aspect of his career on which much of his future reputation would rest—church architecture.

One of his previous patrons, Bishop Doane, ordered the design of a chapel for a girls' school in Burlington, New Jersey. The commission was a small one, but not without significance. The Chapel of the Holy Innocents [17] was the first building in the United States designed in at least partial accord with the tenets of the Cambridge Camden Society.

The 1830s and 1840s were a time of ferment in English Anglican circles.[53] Although engaging several groups with varying opinions, the reform movement was in agreement on its central purpose. Spirituality was to be revived, and the rationalism of the eighteenth century confounded, by a return to the old ritual of the Anglican Church. One of the major means of achieving this was through physical expression in a revival of medieval English architecture and the associated decorative arts. The ecclesiologists espoused this revival with missionary fervor. The word was disseminated largely through a publication of the Cambridge Camden Society (later the Ecclesiological Society), *The Ecclesiologist*. In its first issue of November 1851 *The Ecclesiologist* listed George Washington Doane as the sole patron member of the society in the United States. Doane, who had been named Bishop of New Jersey in 1832, was to become one of the foremost American exponents of the ecclesiologists' canons. Like his English counterparts, Doane expressed his views through tracts, and through support of "correct" architecture.

The Chapel of the Holy Innocents has a modest, even plain, exterior. Of sandstone, it is of simple rectangular form, broken only by a gabled projection on the west wall containing the organ chamber. There is a steep gable roof, originally adorned at the south end with a small bell turret. Inside, the building, while still spare, is somewhat richer. Dark-stained beams contrast with the plaster ceiling, now unfortunately covered with acoustic tile, and the original Minton tile floor remains, enriched with decorative tiles in the sanctuary. *The Ecclesiologist* criticized some aspects of the chapel, but found much to praise.[54] The arrangement of the seating, with the benches be-

tween the organ and sanctuary facing the aisle, was particularly pleasing because it was "the first instance . . . of an *exclusively* female community to be sitting in choir to be found in the community of Canterbury for the last three centuries." The large triplet window of the north wall of the sanctuary was also noted. The tracery, copied from the east window of the church of Stanton St. John, Oxfordshire, is perhaps the first example of the authentic reproduction of an English medieval detail in an American church.[55] Nevertheless, when Bishop Doane decided, while the chapel was under construction, to essay a more ambitious church, he did not turn to Notman. For St. Mary's Church, also in Burlington, he chose the New York architect Richard Upjohn. It was not until two years after the cornerstone of the Chapel of the Holy Innocents was laid that Notman would be commissioned to design a large church in the authentic Gothic Revival style approved by the ecclesiologists.

In the meantime his New Jersey connections were proving fruitful. In 1846 Richard Stockton Field, jurist, horticulturist, Episcopal layman, and friend of Bishop Doane, brought Notman to Princeton. Notman's early commissions in Princeton were not major, but it was a town to which he would return repeatedly over a period of ten years, designing a series of suburban villas, as well as buildings for the college. Because Princeton has suffered less change than most of the areas where Notman worked, all but three of the dozen projects he executed there have been preserved. Notman's first commission for Field was probably a building for the short-lived law school of the College of New Jersey [24]. Long known as Ivy Hall, it is in a simplified, non-archaeological version of the Tudor Gothic style, in the vein popularized by such authors as Loudon. Later in the year, Notman produced a landscape design in picturesque style for Field's estate [21]. By the time Field's house was built, almost a decade later, the details of the landscaping had been changed, but the major principles of the design were retained—the woodland in the south-eastern quadrant, the meandering walks and drives, and the artfully disposed groupings of trees and shrubbery. The Princeton Theological Seminary was another client in 1846. For that institution Notman produced a combined refectory and infirmary, a functional but rather bare building with spare Italianate detailing [23].

In other locales, Notman was less successful. He lost a competition for the repair and expansion, after a fire, of the Pennsylvania Academy of the Fine Arts [20]. Notman's descriptions of his drawings, and a sketch for the interior of the main gallery, survive, but supply little information about the appearance of his proposed building. They indicate that he intended to provide a more dramatic focus by opening the restored rotunda to the basement. The rendering of the gallery, with its entrances formed by arches carried on paired square piers, suggests that the building was to be Italianate. The most interesting feature of the gallery, however, is the exposure and transformation into a decorative device of the iron structure of the roof.

At the end of the year Notman submitted, also unsuccessfully, his entry in one of the most prestigious competitions of the mid-nineteenth century, for the new Smithsonian Institution [22]. With hindsight it appears obvious that the building committee, or at least its influential chairman, Robert Dale Owen, had predetermined that the Smithsonian would be a building of picturesque character in the Norman style, and that one of the architects from whom plans were solicited, James Renwick, Jr., was aware of this preference.[56] The other architects, and indeed Renwick himself in an alternative design, submitted schemes in the Gothic mode.

Notman chose to utilize a variant of the Gothic which was unfamiliar in the United States, what he termed in his submission letter the "collegiate style." Collegiate or Tudor inspiration occasionally had been used previously, most notably by A. J. Davis at New York University. As in many buildings of the early Gothic Revival Davis's design is suggestive of an historic form, not an attempt to reproduce it. Notman's version is more authentic in detail, although, with one noticeable exception, not derived from the precedents he rattled off. Indeed, their very number indicates that no reference to a specific Tudor building was intended. They included "Oxford and Cambridge Universities, the Inns of Law, Westminster Hall, the Palaces of Hampton Court, Eltham, Linlithgow, Falkland, St. James, and many halls and mansions in Great Britain" as well as "the town halls on the continent of Europe." What did serve Notman as a prototype is suggested in his comment that the style "expresses large rooms and halls well lighted for public purposes." The largest public building then under construction in the English speaking world was Sir Charles Barry's Houses of Parliament. The similarities between the original design for the St. Margaret's Street facade of that edifice and the north front of Notman's design for the Smithsonian are striking. Both employ a square central tower, buttressed by octagonal turrets, and flanked by six bays defined by ranks of mullioned windows, separated by buttresses crowned by pinnacles. Both feature subsidiary towers at the end, although Notman, dealing with the termini of his building, has substituted a multiplicity of towers for the single square tower of Barry's design. The large bell tower over the central octagon also appears at the Houses of Parliament, although Notman's is more closely based on Tom Tower at Christ Church, Oxford. The plan also is derived from that of the Houses of Parliament, focusing on the central octagon. From this "point of distribution," as in the Barry building, long corridors provided access to the wings and broader hallways to the stairs and entrances.

Notman was at pains to explain his aesthetic and functional purposes. His central hall, open to the tower, and stairs, set in a projecting semi-octagon, would have "a picturesque and highly architectural effect," viewed from any level. The composition would give an impression of "grandeur," but "the richness of the whole is produced by form and proportion, not by costly labor." The arrangement was also practical.

In arranging the Plan concentration is an object, as affording obvious and easy access from point to point of the interior, gives command of the whole building for a general system of heating and ventilation by interior wall flues, is a sounder construction with less material, and greatly cheaper....[57]

Indeed, despite its seeming symmetry, Notman's plan offered as great a degree of flexibility for the purposes of the institution as the almost equally symmetrical plan lurking behind Renwick's more picturesquely irregular exterior. To modern eyes Notman's designs do not look unusual, because the building style became a common one on American campuses in the waning years of the nineteenth century and early years of the twentieth. Innovative as the style was in its own time, it was not published and seems to have had no contemporary influence.

The following year Notman was given the opportunity to demonstrate his talent at another form of the Gothic, a full-blown version of the ritually and architecturally "correct" revival of fourteenth-century ecclesiastic architecture. St. Mark's Church [32] on Locust Street, between Sixteenth and Seventeenth Streets, in Philadelphia, was commissioned by a High Anglican congregation. The vestry seems to have accepted the authoritarian view of the ecclesiologists that church architecture was not just a matter of taste, but of religious integrity. They were perhaps uncertain of their own ability to judge what was faithful to the form and spirit of the fourteenth-century English Gothic approved by the ecclesiologists, and anxious to do the proper thing, they wrote to England for advice. The Ecclesiological Society responded by sending tracings of Richard Cromwell Carpenter's All Saints Church, Brighton. Ultimately, however, the vestry determined to accept Notman's designs and All Saints was not utilized as a source. Unlike the Church of St. James the Less, begun a year earlier than St. Mark's, the Locust Street church was not a copy of a specific model, medieval or contemporary. The designs

did, however, embrace some features of two English churches, which may have reassured the vestry. One was Augustus Welby Pugin's St. Oswald's, Old Swan, Liverpool, published in 1843 in Pugin's *The Present State of Ecclesiastical Architecture in England*; the other, St. Stephen's, Westminster, London, by Benjamin Ferrey, appeared in the *Illustrated London News* for 24 July 1847.[58] Although the influence of English churches may be discerned, St. Mark's is by no means derivative in conception. It is admirably suited to its urban site, particularly in the treatment of the south or Locust Street front. Considering the site, the assymmetrical placement of the soaring tower becomes not a variant on the basic St. Oswald's scheme, but almost an imperative. The shift, made between the preliminary and final design, of the main entrance door from the west front to the tower, reinforces the relationship of St. Mark's to the streetscape.

St. Mark's conformed to the ecclesiologists' view in more than design. The revivalists' credo included the concept that honesty of materials, soundness of craftsmanship, and the attitude of the workmen were inextricably woven into the fabric of religious belief. Accordingly the workmen were admonished: "A church is the House of *God*: and therefore, any work that has to do with a church is a holy work. Every stone you lay, and every beam you hew is lain and hewn for the honor of *Almighty God*—" They were to refrain from cursing, "lightness of speech," or any act that "may *seem* irreverent," such as singing, or whistling, or eating within the walls.[59]

St. Mark's echoed not only the forms of medieval architecture, but its methods of construction. At the Chapel of the Holy Innocents and at St. Thomas's, Glassboro [25], built in 1846-1847 in the style of an English parish church, the interior walls are plastered and the wooden members are too thin to be more than decoration evocative of the Gothic period. At St. Mark's the stonework is fully exposed and the timbering is structural. Later additions of carved woodwork and elaborate furnishings to the interior have obscured what is still obvious on the exterior: Notman had designed a stone building made beautiful not by decoration of the material, but by the precision of its placement. St. Mark's was a successful building in its congregation's terms because it was a correct expression of a particular set of beliefs. In architectural terms it also succeeded because of the fine proportions of its components separately and in relation to one another. The impact of its mid-block statement, crowned by its soaring tower, has fortunately been preserved through the scale of the neighboring buildings, several of which were probably also designed by Notman [93].

With the design of St. Mark's the *leitmotifs* for Notman's career were complete. He was a versatile architect, capable of originality within the framework of several of the popular styles of the era, and of producing designs well-suited to the functional needs of a variety of programs. His reputation, however, largely rested on his skills in three fields—landscape design (particularly for cemeteries), Italianate villas, and churches. These were the categories within which most of his commissions of the next five years would fall, especially those from outside the Philadelphia area.

Nationally it was undoubtedly the popular acceptance of Laurel Hill that caused the proprietors of other rural cemeteries to seek Notman's services. In 1845 he provided a design for the Spring Grove Cemetery Company of Cincinnati, Ohio [14]. The nature of Notman's plan is unknown. No drawing for it has been found, and within a decade a resident landscape designer began to obliterate all traces of Notman's work. Presumably the proprietors had not found the Notman scheme satisfactory: they deplored the excessive cost of the many roads and walks. With the owners of Hollywood Cemetery [34] in Richmond, Virginia, Notman was more successful. Notman first visited Virginia in the fall of 1847.[60] It is uncertain whether this was a business or pleasure trip, although the latter seems likely. Mrs. Notman may have accompanied him; her reference to her painting of Natural Bridge implies that it was done from life. By the late '40s the couple seems to have attained sufficient financial security to travel. Notman is known to have attended the inauguration of President Zachary Taylor in 1849.[61] In any event, Notman offered to stop at the resort of Huguenot Springs [28] about 16 miles west of Richmond, with the view of preparing a plan for the improvement of its landscaping. There is no evidence that Notman ever provided a design for Huguenot Springs, although work on the grounds was carried out in 1847-1848. What remains visible there is a mid-nineteenth century landscape so conventional as to suggest that the proprietors decided to forego professional advice.

However, Notman's contact with Huguenot Springs proved productive in other ways. Thomas T. Giles, his correspondent on that project, gave Notman's letter describing his working methods to the founders of Hollywood Cemetery, to whom Notman submitted a plan in February 1848. The report accompanying the plan sets forth the entwined imperatives of functionalism and aesthetics underlying Notman's design philosophy.[62] It begins with the choice of the position of the entrance as "most convenient to the city," and "very favorable to an extensive view of the grounds," as well as "the most desirable point to get the first glance of the beautiful variety of hill and valley." Probably Notman was aware of the complaints about the cost of the roads at Spring Grove. Dealing with a group of businessmen, he realized that "beauty must be secondary to use, if circumstances will not admit of their being united." He carefully explained that a multiplicity of roads was necessary, so that carriages could get near the lot at a funeral. He also pointed out that because the roads followed the contours of the ground, and gravel was plentiful on the site, the cost of construction would not be great. At the same time aesthetics would be served because the routes would "best display and view all the beauty of the grounds." The irregularity of the plan "produces many angles and corner lots, which are sought for, as you will find." The sales potential of his plan was stressed repeatedly. His arrangement allowed "the perfect opening up or exposing the whole of the grounds to the casual visitor. The pleasure of a drive over a variety of surface with such charming views, will induce visitors. . . . Many are interested by the novelty and beauty and become purchasers of lots—thus one class of the public are with you."

Laurel Hill, although essentially picturesque, employed a number of classical elements, notably the rigid geometry of the central circle and the Palladian design of the entrance. Hollywood, in contrast, is a fully developed example of picturesque romanticism. Contours, views, and natural features, such as watercourses, were utilized and enhanced. The recommended planting scheme employed trees and shrubs native to the area, rather than exotics. Where construction was necessary Notman recommended natural materials. The five bridges to cross the watercourses were to be made of tree trunks felled on the site, laid on abutments of drywall masonry, for which "granite on the ground might be easily quarried." Railings would be formed from the untrimmed branches of the felled trees, "in better keeping with the place and purpose than the most expensive railing planed and painted."

Notman's design for the grounds of Hollywod was executed, although his suggested gate house was not erected. His predictions of its popular appeal proved correct, and Hollywood became Richmond's most fashionable burying ground. The directors of the company had good reason to be satisfied with their architect. In 1851, two of them, William H. Haxall and Gustavus A. Myers, along with Thomas T. Giles, Notman's contact at Huguenot Springs, were appointed a committee to improve Richmond's Capitol Square [45], the setting for Jefferson's Virginia State House. It was only natural that they should turn again to Notman.

The documentation suggests that they had consulted Notman prior to their official appointment, perhaps as early as the summer of 1850. The impetus for the redesign of the square was not only its general improvement, but to provide a proper setting for the monument to George Washington that was about to be erected. The design problem, therefore, was quite different from that at Laurel Hill or Hollywood. There Notman had bent art to the dictates of natural contours and features. At Capitol Square he planned a major rearrangement of the terrain to enhance the manmade monuments. The site was highly irregular, with steep inclines and precipitous ravines. The state provided convict labor, which was employed to level some hills and fill some declivities, forming "gentle natural undulations, rising gradually to the base of the capitol and to the monument." [63] The purpose of this large-scale exercise in earth moving was to form a broad plateau as a base for the Capitol, a fitting podium for that chastely classical edifice. The soothing of the terrain also rendered it "picturesque" rather than "sublime." Once this was achieved, the romantic effect was heightened through the usual accouterments of meandering paths, splashing water, and irregularly disposed plantings. Again these were composed largely of materials native to the area. Planned even before Washington's Mall, New York's Central Park, or Philadelphia's Fairmount Park, Capitol Square was the first large urban park to be developed according to principles that previously had been applied to rural cemeteries and gentlemen's seats. It was the last of Notman's known major landscape projects.

Notman continued to supply, as he had done at Riverside and Nathan Dunn's Cottage, landscape designs as well as house plans for his residential clients. This was certainly the case at the John P. Stockton House [36], and probably at Springdale [49] and Prospect [50] as well. Others of his patrons, such as the Pearsons at Glencairn [40], preferred to handle this aspect of planning themselves; some, such as Harry Ingersoll at Medary [30] and Joshua Francis Fisher at Alverthorpe [47], preferred the services of that preeminent practitioner, A. J. Downing.

As the reputation of Laurel Hill probably

garnered Notman landscape commissions outside of the Delaware River Valley, so St. Mark's was presumably responsible for the demand for his services from High Episcopal congregations elsewhere. The first of his major churches outside the Philadelphia area, designed in 1849, is Emmanuel Protestant Episcopal Church in Cumberland, Maryland [46]. Like St. Mark's, Emmanuel posed difficulties in siting that Notman again resolved by the skillful grouping of the building's elements. Because Emmanuel stands on a hill with its east front facing the town, Notman placed the tower adjacent to the chancel, an arrangement for which R. C. Carpenter's St. Paul's, Brighton, may have served as precedent. Broad transepts anchor the building to what otherwise might have appeared to be a dangerously precipitous site. The vestry must have proved an unusually sympathetic patron, thoroughly comprehending what their architect had achieved. They commented that "the singular beauty of the site, the fine proportions of the building, the variety and happy grouping of its different parts, chancel, tower, nave, transepts and south porch and its lofty and very graceful tower and spire render the new Emmanuel Church an uncommonly picturesque structure." [64]

In the fall of 1850, while Emmanuel Church was under construction, Notman prepared plans for another High Episcopal Church, St. Peter's, Pittsburgh [52]. Similar to St. Mark's in design and construction, it won high praise from *The Ecclesiologist*, despite the fact that it was not properly oriented. Dealings with other parishes were less satisfactory. Notman entered into lengthy negotiations with the vestry of St. Luke's, Baltimore [43], which occupied most of 1849 and extended into 1850, for designs which never were constructed, and in the meantime lost the opportunity to plan a church for an unidentified parish in Savannah, Georgia.[65] In 1851-1852 Grace Church, Baltimore was constructed as a virtual replica of St. Mark's. Credit for the design, however, went to the local firm of Niernsee and Nelson.[66]

In 1848 the New York Ecclesiological Society was founded. Like its English counterpart, the society had a didactic mission, especially in regard to the proper architecture for Anglican churches. It, too, published, at least briefly, a journal devoted to architectural criticism, the *New York Ecclesiologist*. Notman was added to its list of approved architects in 1853, its last year of publication.[67] Whether the listing brought him new clients is unknown. After this period, he was responsible for only one other church to follow ecclesiological dicta, although others may be identified as parish records are explored.

Unlike Pugin or Richard Upjohn, Notman was no ideologue. Presumably he was born and brought up in the Church of Scotland. He married at the Episcopal Church of St. Luke's and the Epiphany, but is not known to have been a communicant of that or any other church. His funeral was held from his house.[68] His success as a designer of churches that met ecclesiological requirements was due not to religious conviction, but to professional competence. Given clients who could express the needs of their ritual, Notman could produce a building to satisfy the programmatic requirements. Fairbanks infers that Notman chose certain styles for his churches in accordance with his knowledge of the religious beliefs of his patrons. In fact, he was prepared to provide alternative stylistic claddings, as can be seen in the case of the Church of the Ascension [26], with the design of which he was involved from 1846 to 1850, and later at St. Clement's [62]. His theological ignorance was demonstrated when he presented the College of New Jersey with a chapel [27], which, while acceptably Italianate rather than Gothic, was cruciform. This so horrified that institution's Presbyterian trustees that they almost ordered its demolition when two-thirds of the walls had been erected.[69]

If Notman's apparent lack of religious commitment meant that he depended on his clients for guidance, it also rendered him flexible in undertaking commissions for a variety of denominations. Shortly before beginning work on St. Mark's, Notman was retained, after convoluted negotiations, to design the Green Hill Presbyterian Church on Girard Avenue in Philadelphia [32]. Like St. Thomas's, Glassboro, and the slightly later St. Paul's, Trenton [37], the church is in the Early English style. It, too, has a dominating square, buttressed central tower. At Green Hill the second stage of the tower is almost filled with a single large window with Perpendicular tracery. Use of this detail would, according to Fairbanks, relate to the historical period of the Reformation, and thus be appropriate for a dissenters' church.[70] The facade is a somewhat unusual five-part composition, similar to one Notman drew in 1852 for a transept church [fig. 70.5]. At Green Hill the composition is not as functional, since the end bays do not give access to a transept. They do, however, serve as a counterfoil to the almost overwhelmingly powerful tower. In terms of exterior style, Green Hill differs little from the two New Jersey churches designed for Episcopal congregations, except in the use of Perpendicular tracery. The interior, however, is very different in treatment. Beyond the vestibule is a broad light-filled hall, clearly intended for preaching rather than liturgical purposes. Unbound by ecclesiological requirements that only materials available in the medieval era could be utilized, Notman was free to carry hammer-beams on cast-iron columns. The effect is at once disconcerting and exciting in its expression of the strength of the columns; they appear unusually slender in relation to the heavy timbering.

The following year Notman designed a modest Presbyterian church in Princeton [37]. His sole essay in board and batten construction, it had pointed diamond-paned windows, wooden buttresses, and a weak central tower. Masonry, not wood was Notman's metier, unlike Upjohn, whose sense of form and proportion imbues his small wooden churches with style and grace. The adjacent stuccoed-brick manse in Loudonesque cottage style is far more successful.

Notman's largest church for a dissenting congregation was Calvary Presbyterian Church [51] on Locust Street, west of Fifteenth, in Philadelphia, and thus a near neighbor of St. Mark's. Begun in 1851 and completed in 1853, Calvary was what the nineteenth century would have termed "costly," both because of its large size and its lavish detail. The building has been demolished, but judging from the surviving illustrations the facade was virtually aquiver with decoration. There was a multiplicity of openings, filled with elaborate tracery, arcades, statuary niches, and arched paneling; the turrets and towers were elaborated with crocketting and crowned with finials. For all the carving, the facade has a curiously flat effect. Calvary in no sense equaled the forceful, yet serene, beauty arrived at in St. Mark's through sureness of proportion and massing. The principal floor of Calvary, the sanctuary, was in the second story. As at Green Hill, this was essentially a large hall, rising 40 feet to the ridge of the roof, broken only by a gallery over the vestibule and a niche for the pulpit. According to a contemporary description, it too was richly decorated.

At the same time that Calvary was under construction, Notman was probably engaged as superintending architect of the Roman Catholic Cathedral of St. Peter and St. Paul [54]. The history of the cathedral is cloudy. Construction began early in 1847 and spanned almost two decades. Responsibility for the design has been variously assigned to two priests and Napoleon LeBrun. It is known that LeBrun was the original supervising architect, was replaced by Notman, and was reinstated after Notman's dismissal. The dates at which these events transpired have not been established. However, a description of the façade, as conceived by Notman, was published in 1852, and presumably his tenure had begun sometime previously. Notman's design, once again, seems intended to refer to Italy, although in this instance his inspiration is, appropriately, Baroque church architecture rather than the Renaissance palazzo. The individual motifs, however, may have been based on sources more directly familiar to Notman. The dome as projected in particular, taller and slimmer than that of the New Jersey State House, was remarkably similar to one of the outstanding features of the Edinburgh skyline, Robert Reid's St. George's Church (1813-1814) on Charlotte Square. Whatever his immediate sources, Notman captured the spirit of the Baroque in the plasticity and rich chiaroscuro of his facade. How much Notman's designs depended for effect on form and massing, rather than decorative detail, may be seen by comparing the Cathedral to the contemporary West Arch Street Presbyterian Church by Joseph Hoxie.[71] The two share several elements: the Corinthian order, the central dome, and the subsidiary towers. But Hoxie's building, despite its far more lavish detailing, lacks the vitality and dramatic impact of Notman's.

In addition to public buildings and churches, Notman was occupied during the late 1840s and early 1850s with commissions for residences. Most were suburban villas, although he is known to have designed at least one group of city rowhouses [39]. In general his large houses reprise the Italianate vein first explored at Riverside. Occasionally, however, he made a foray into Gothic variants, presumably because it suited his client's taste. In 1851 he designed for Richard Stockton of Princeton, Springdale [49], a Gothic cottage of rather conventional form. With diamond-paned and cusped bay windows, a deep concave hood over the front entrance, broad overhanging eaves, and a verandah across the back, it followed the pattern set by the superintendent's cottage at Laurel Hill. A large and irregular castellated addition to the west, put on a decade later and probably also designed by Notman, somewhat obscures the modest symmetry of the original. A Gothic proposal for Henry Pratt McKean [fig. 48.1] is more pretentious. The choice of Tudor Gothic for a residence is, so far as is known, unique in Notman's work. His unsuccessful entry for the

Smithsonian competition was his most elaborate venture in the style. More typical is its application in modest educational buildings: Ivy Hall [24] in Princeton and the parish school for St. Mark's Church [42] and the Episcopal Academy [41] in Philadelphia. The house for McKean, with its projecting bays, lively skyline, and somewhat eccentric round-arched verandahs, would undoubtedly have been a structure of more theatrical vitality than Notman's executed buildings in this style. The facade, however, suggests that the plan, like that of Nathan Dunn's Cottage or Springdale, would have been a fairly conventional one.

It is in his Italianate houses that Notman's development as a designer is most clearly visible, although similar architectural concepts also inform his churches and public buildings. Notman introduced to America, most obviously in his domestic designs, a new functional and aesthetic rationale for interior planning, based on a dramatic and free interplay of spaces. Through the mid-nineteenth century, American house plans, with some notable exceptions, were largely based on a central hall, containing a stair, with rooms more or less symmetrically disposed on either side. By mid-century many architects were breaking the box form in which this arrangement was contained, most often by the use of protruding bays, or by masking the form by the addition of verandahs. But the basic organization remained the same: a plan with a central hall, containing the stair, serving as a single axis, a linear passageway for circulation, and a simple vertical connector between the building's levels. Notman's planning was far more sophisticated and far more open. It utilized the Palladian concept of a central core, to which the other spatial units were related. The Palladian sense of organization was achieved by maintaining these units as discrete and tightly enclosed within a cube. Notman on the other hand maintained central control in buildings which were irregularly disposed both on the ground and in elevation, and utilized dramatic spatial contrasts and interpenetrations in the interior. For his purposes the Italianate style was the perfect vehicle. Its highly volumetric masses provided the control; their free placement provided the drama. Notman's plans allowed for an irregular distribution of rooms, varied in size according to function, placed to take advantage of natural cooling and heating, and light and air, picturesquely outflung to the landscape, and at the same time held down to a central core. The means through which he achieved this were first expressed at Riverside. In this earliest of his Italianate villas the hall was the controlling factor to which all the major rooms related horizontally through direct access. At the same time the circular opening in the hall, rising to the roof, provided a vertical connection with the floors above. The stairs, set off from the hall, were also top-lit, although their placement did not reinforce the core as it would in some of his later plans. These openings of the interior from the ground floor to the sky sounded a note also developed further in Notman's later work, the interplay of a variety of forms and shapes, and of sources of light, articulated not only in plan, but in three dimensions.

In view of what was achieved at Riverside, Notman's next documented villa is a disappointment. Medary [30], designed in 1847, from the surviving plan and exterior view seems to have been a rather dull house inside and out. The front consisted of three rectangular blocks in receding planes; the rear was flat, relieved by a semi-hexagonal bay and a window of the same shape. The plan used the hall, L-shaped to accommodate the stair, merely as an entry. The John P. Stockton House [36] of 1848, although better proportioned, is intrinsically little more interesting in plan. Essentially this is an American Georgian center hall arrangement, with the rooms to the right of the hall thrust out front and rear by the insertion of the stair between them.

At Ellarslie [35] on the outskirts of Trenton, probably designed in 1848 or 1849, Notman further developed the sophisticated spatial organization he had employed at River-

side. This is immediately apparent on the exterior, where irregularly disposed masses culminate in an offset tower. The carriage approach is symmetrical and rather formal; the river front, in contrast, is dramatically broken in outline. Entrance could be achieved at many points on this facade, so that the house is closely related in an informal manner to the treed lawn falling away to the Delaware River. The major entrance, on the opposite side, leads the visitor through a sequence of spaces, varied in size, form, and lighting. The sequence leads from the generous and shadowy porte-cochere, to a small, rather dark vestibule, to the more capacious and brighter hall, and finally to the somewhat eccentric central space, lit from a variety of sources. This space is highly irregular in plan, defined in part by an S-curved wall, in part by the angled entry to the drawing room, and opened to one side by the stair. The stair, culminating in a rectangular dome, penetrates the space of the tower at the level of the first landing, where it is lit by a large round-headed window. Again, as at Riverside, and here with tighter organization, Notman has created a dramatic core to which the other spatial units relate both horizontally and vertically.

When Henry Pratt McKean rejected Notman's plan for a Tudor mansion, he elected to build an Italianate villa at Fern Hill [48]. Here Notman, perhaps at his patron's request, appeared not as an originator, but almost as a copyist. His model was Richard Upjohn's Newport villa of 1845 for Edward King, which had been published in 1850.[72] The general distribution of masses, the oversized tower, and the arcaded loggias at Fern Hill clearly all were derived from the Upjohn design. In plan, however, the two buildings were dissimilar. Upjohn's plan, as Downing noted, "is nearly square." The outline of Fern Hill, although not as irregular as that of Riverside or Ellarslie, is more open. Within there is also a freer distribution of space than in the near symmetry of Upjohn's scheme. At Fern Hill, as at Riverside, the hall was opened to the roof, the opening defined at ground level by

"4 elliptic arches with carved brackets and pilasters," a motif repeated on the second floor, where the opening was enclosed "with neat Iron railing." Even more strongly than at Ellarslie, a contrapuntal effect was provided by the broad staircase rising at right angles to this core area.

The full flowering of Notman's concepts of spatial organization was achieved in the three villas of the 1850s, Alverthorpe [47] in Jenkintown, and Prospect [50] and Fieldwood or Guernsey Hall [59] at Princeton. Alverthorpe was probably the earliest of these, although the dates of all are uncertain. In concept it was a curious admixture of the classical and the picturesque. There were the usual romantic hallmarks of the tower, the varied rooflines, the plethora of grouped chimneys, the multiplicity of window types, and the verandahs and balconies. These obscured, but did not disguise, the basic contained quality of the composition, which consisted of two rectangles, the family's quarters and servants' wing, linked by a hyphen. The plan of the main block seems almost classical in its strong axiality, established by the entrance and stair halls. Yet a closer look reveals that the apparent simplicity and clarity of the scheme were deceptive. It was impossible to define many of the major spaces, which, through such barriers as screens of columns and sliding doors, flowed into one another. Was the space behind the semi-circular portico part of the hall or of the library? Or was the space opposite the stair part of the stair hall or of the drawing room? These shifts in space occurred not only horizontally but vertically. The west section of the house was three stories, the east only two, although the roofs were not very different in height. The stair crossed from the end of the hall to rise from the second to the third stories above the central section, the spaces being both separated and united by arcaded openings.[73]

In the almost contemporary Prospect Notman combined the looser outline of Riverside or Ellarslie with the axial organization of Alverthorpe to create one of his finest com-positions. Fortunately in the case of Prospect both preliminary and final plans for the first floor survive [figs. 50.1 and 50.3]. From these it is possible to judge just how conscious his effects were. The interior changes consisted primarily of slight adjustments in the size and proportion of spaces and in the placement of openings. These changes, while maintaining the original irregular outline, heightened the pull of the central core, the domed vestibule rising through the full height of the house. Between the first and final plan Notman enlarged this area at the expense of the entrance hall. He also altered and improved the proportions of the drawing room and pulled this space closer to the core. The size of the tower, and therefore of the room within it, was reduced, with the result that the volume of the tower is expressed more clearly in plan and elevation. By reducing the tower room and enlarging the lobby he also achieved a more satisfying sequence of spaces. The openings in this cross-axial passageway were subtly shifted off-center, so that from the stair there is a vista to the outdoors through the west window of the tower room. At the same time the substitution of two windows for three on the south front of the drawing room provides a more cohesive alignment of these openings with those of the library and entrance hall. Alverthorpe's ambiguous shifts of space give way at Prospect to a totally controlled and smooth flow.

The centripetal force of Notman's plans is most clearly expressed at Fieldwood. This last of Notman's major villas was probably not completed until 1855. Its great octagonal stair hall has become the dominating factor, deriving enormous vitality from the stair that swoops and spirals upward with an almost Baroque vigor. The rooms clustered around it, varied in size and shape, orginally included an octagonal drawing room and two other major rooms terminating in semi-octagonal bays. Because the tower served Judge Field as law library and office, with a separate entrance, it was comparatively isolated from the family's living quarters.

Consideration of the complexities of form and space in Notman's plans should not obscure the fact that they were highly functional. His villas were carefully arranged to take advantage of the climate, natural light, and vistas.[74] Rooms were disposed and varied in size according to use. The frequent creation of "split-level" plans, with the major rooms rising through two stories, while the minor ones were encompassed in three, had obvious utilitarian purposes. As can be seen to some extent at Prospect, these functional considerations came first; the organizational refinements followed. Function and form may have determined the design, but decorative effects were not slighted. Unfortunately few of Notman's domestic interiors have survived intact, those of Prospect and the stair hall at Fieldwood being the happy exceptions. From descriptions in insurance surveys and specifications, as well as old photographs, however, Notman's decorative vocabulary can be reconstructed. It sometimes included columns, piers and pilasters, in some cases finished in scagliola. Richly molded plaster consoles are employed at Prospect and Fieldwood and also appeared at Fern Hill. Deep friezes and cornices were used to articulate the junction of wall and ceiling. In the more elaborate villas ceilings might be deeply coffered or paneled. Marble mantels were usual in the major rooms and cast iron was the favored material for railings on stairs and around openings between floors. Although the exteriors were uniformly Italianate, the interiors were often eclectic. This was especially the case at Riverside, where the interiors were Greek Revival, rococo and, in the library, Gothic. Fern Hill had an Egyptian mantel in the dining room and a "French" mantel in the library. The library at Prospect, like that at Riverside, is Gothic, at least in respect to its ceiling, paneled in ribs and bosses. To some extent the use of Gothic motifs for libraries was the product of the nineteenth-century predilection for defining function symbolically. As an influential British periodical put it, "The style of all others the most appropriate and effective for a library is the

Elizabethan, or the Gothic."[75] A degree of eclecticism in interior architectural ornament was probably in accordance with the taste of Notman's patrons, as the furnishings of Prospect attest [figs. 50.4-50.7].

Notman thus shared in the boom years of the 1840s and 1850s. If the reports of other architects' commissions in the Philadelphia newspapers are to be relied on, his was not the busiest office in the area. Certainly he did not participate to any great extent in the expansion of Philadelphia's commercial property and middle-class housing stock. But his clients were solidly prosperous and he seems to have received a good proportion of the available commissions for major free-standing buildings.

In 1853, however, Notman became embroiled in a controversy that was, in retrospect, a watershed in his career. The dispute arose around a competition for a new Masonic Hall for the Grand Lodge of Pennsylvania.[76] Notman was always wary of competitions, especially those in which, upon award of a premium, the drawings became the property of the sponsor rather than of the architect. Although he was persuaded to submit designs by his fellow Masons, he sent a letter accompanying his drawings in which he clearly stated that he was not proffering them in accordance with the terms of the competition. Of the six designs submitted, all evidently in the Gothic style, the Committee on Plans preferred three, those of Samuel Sloan, John Collins, and Notman. When these were sent out for estimates, Notman's "grand and sublime" design proved the most expensive, Collins's the least. Accordingly the committee recommended adoption of Collins's plan, but was overruled by the Grand Lodge. Their selection of Notman was probably influenced by his Masonic membership.

When the bids from contractors came in, the lowest was over 50 per cent more than the building committee's $85,000 estimate. Notman attributed the discrepancy to the internal arrangements required by the committee, the architectural competition having been confined to the design of the exterior. The Masons responded by reopening the competition. Notman, who believed that he had already been selected as their architect, indignantly refused to participate. His position was that, as their architect, he would make, without charge, whatever alterations were necessary to enable his scheme to be constructed within the budget, by this time raised to $100,000. If they reopened the competition and another architect were selected he, having produced working drawings and specifications, expected to be paid a minimum of three per cent of the construction costs. The Masons responded to what they considered Notman's "extraordinary and unjust" position with outrage. In their opinion $150 for the front and "a liberal compensation for his time, skill and services as an architect, in assisting the Committee in arranging and modifying the details and for his drawings and specifications" was a fair settlement. Bitter words were exchanged. In the end Samuel Sloan received the commission and it is not known whether Notman was ever compensated for his efforts. At the time his spirits could not have been too depressed. Later in the year he and Mrs. Notman are said to have left Philadelphia for a visit to Scotland and tour of the Continent.[77]

After returning to Philadelphia his career never recovered its previous momentum. In the last decade of life he was responsible for only eleven projects that can be documented, several of which were minor. It was not that the styles in which he worked had gone out of fashion, nor that his creative powers were diminished. Indeed in these years he produced some of his finest work, including Fieldwood and St. Clement's Church. In part the deterioration of Notman's practice may simply have coincided with a general falling off in construction activity that began to be apparent in 1854.[78] This decline was exacerbated by the depression that followed the panic of 1857 and only ended with the Civil War. But it is likely that to some extent clients shunned Notman because of the contentiousness that surfaced in the Masonic Hall episode. Although Notman's personality remains elusive, a testiness emerges in his correspondence with the Masons and, a few years later, with John Maclean in reference to Nassau Hall. Then, too, his fondness for ardent spirits may have begun to limit his effectiveness. Joseph Jackson, probably depending on information from William Hewitt, noted that Notman's death "probably was hastened by having brought with him the Scotch custom of drinking immoderately. It is said of him that he was a one-bottle man; that is, that he could empty a bottle of brandy at a sitting."[79] That alcoholism may have begun to cause problems is suggested by his signature on four receipts for Nassau Hall. In two the signature is strong and firm; in the others shaky and uncertain. His signature on several of the drawings for St. Clement's, some of which are not in his hand, is erratic. Whether caused by alcoholism or not, a form of physical disability was undermining the quickness and sureness of his hand. But Notman's powers as a designer did not fail and, indeed, his late works have a vigor and forcefulness that show him in full command as an architect. Nor was he content to rely on old formulae. Indeed, given the opportunity, Notman remained capable of introducing new architectural modes and utilizing new materials.

During the mid-fifties, Notman designed one of his rare commercial structures, a slim four-story building for Dr. C. M. Jackson, a purveyor of patent medicines [61]. As in the Bank of North America, Notman turned to Renaissance Italy for inspiration. By this time taste favored the richly seductive forms of the Venetian Renaissance over the restrained classicism of Florence or Rome. Such arcaded fronts were then simultaneously making an appearance in the cities of both Great Britain and the United States.[80] With their structural elements reduced to a skeletal web enframing large areas of glass, these arcaded buildings of the mid-nineteenth century prefigure the development of the modern office building later in the century. Many, probably the majority, had cast-iron fronts. Notman, however, with one notable exception, the cupola and cornice of Nassau Hall, did not use cast iron in imitation of other materials. For the Jackson building, he adhered to stone, introducing to Philadelphia a new material, highly amenable to decorative carving, Caen stone.

Closely related to the Jackson Building are his designs for an office building for the Pennsylvania Railroad [55], produced sometime between 1852 and 1856. In one version the building is divided into three bays, and the masonry and openings are equal in importance; in the other the upper stories have become open bands of windows held lightly in place by the masonry. More striking in many respects, however, is the accompanying design for a freight depot. Its upper stories also are arcaded. The first story, however, is composed of a series of great arched openings of almost Syrian form, opening like cavernous maws to admit or disgorge train and wagon traffic. Their strong and forceful expression of masonry construction prefigures that of Henry Hobson Richardson three decades later.

Although Notman's skill in handling masonry is a hallmark of his most successful buildings, he was not averse to using iron both structurally and decoratively. His most extensive utilization of this material was in the rebuilding of Nassau Hall [63] for the College of New Jersey [Princeton University] in 1855. Since the building had burned twice, fireproofing was an imperative. Notman had already constructed what was considered a fireproof flooring system for the Academy of Natural Sciences, consisting of cast-iron joists spanned by brick arches. He had proposed a similar system for the Smithsonian, and probably suggested it for consideration at The Athenaeum, for he sketched joists and an arch in the margin of one of his drawings for that project. [fig. 16.1] The proposed interior for the Pennsylvania Railroad's offices probably also called for some iron structural members, as the design for the Pennsylvania Academy of the Fine Arts certainly did. Cast iron, however, while highly efficient in compression, is far less so in tension and therefore not satisfactory for horizontal bearing members. When Notman received the commission for Nassau Hall, the firm owned by Peter Cooper and Abram Hewitt was producing a far more suitable material for fireproof flooring. This was wrought-iron rail, manufactured in their rolling mill at Trenton. By 1855 the firm was experimenting with new structural shapes akin to modern ones in form. As the triangular correspondence among Cooper and Hewitt, Notman, and John Maclean, the president of the college, makes clear, neither the structural properties of the new shapes nor their manufacturing costs were fully understood. Instead of the new beams, Maclean and Notman conservatively chose a shape, the properties of which were already known because it had been extensively used for railroad rail. Their conservatism should not be overstressed, however, for Nassau Hall was among the first buildings in the country to use wrought iron in this manner.[81] In the roof Notman may have been more adventurous. The documents refer to "heavy beams," by which Cooper and Hewitt meant I-shaped members, and "angle bars" for the roof. Unfortunately, the construction system of the roof of Nassau Hall has not been measured nor otherwise studied, and the manner in which iron was used is uncertain.

Notman also employed iron of other forms at Nassau Hall, although the surviving stone walls, hallowed by association, were sacrosanct. Notman, with his sensitivity to masonry, was delighted that stone from the original quarries was available for his added towers. The warm, yellow, local sandstone was, in any event, a material he evidently found attractive. All three of his Italianate villas at Princeton were built of this stone, laid up in rubble form. However, the stone was pointed to give the effect of random ashlar, and Nassau Hall was repointed to the same purpose. For new work, however, Notman used non-traditional materials. The cornice is made of galvanized iron, manufactured by R. S. Harris & Co. of Philadelphia.[82] The cupola utilized cast-iron elements fabricated by Bottom & Tiffany of Trenton.[83]

Nassau Hall was Notman's last public building. Although the college required that he respect the physical integrity of the walls, there was no suggestion that he restore the building to its mid-eighteenth century appearance. Accordingly he redesigned it to suit nineteenth-century taste. Tuscan towers at either end contain stone stairs, an improvement over the original circulation pattern, in which stairs rose in the center of each wing. This permitted removal of two of the original entries. The central entrance was made more prominent. Its massive rusticated arched opening is repeated in the large window above. This scheme, with its symmetrically placed towers, seems to be without precedent in Anglo-American Italianate architecture. It may, as Robert C. Smith suggested, have been the prototype for Eben Faxon's design for the rebuilding of the Wren Building at William and Mary after a fire in 1859.[84] Notman seems to have based the cupola on a type utilized on several early nineteenth-century English Church's, notably St. Mark's, Kennington in South London.[85]

Despite its eclecticism, Nassau Hall is an extremely cohesive composition, now somewhat marred by the truncation of the towers, the upper stages of which were removed in the early twentieth century. The much-enlarged cupola, in particular, provides a satisfying culmination to the building's bulk, lacking in the original design. Sensitive planning of the surroundng buildings has permitted Nassau Hall to retain its dominating position on Princeton's campus.

Although major commissions for other types of buildings eluded him, Notman's reputation as a church architect still appealed to Episcopalians in and out of Philadelphia. His last church was St. John's, Brandywine, now St. John's Cathedral in what has become a part of Wilmington, Delaware. Constructed in 1857-1858 it is a reprise of his ecclesiological designs of the late 1840s and early '50s. His two late Philadelphia churches, however, are buildings of extraordinary interest.

St. Clement's Church [62], at Twentieth and Cherry Streets, and Holy Trinity Church [65], on Rittenhouse Square, were under con-struction simultaneously, both being completed in 1859. Both employed what were understood in the nineteenth century as Romanesque forms. Romanesque architecture, however, did not inspire the passion for authenticity that was called forth by the Gothic, although Pugin published some Romanesque details.[86] The word Romanesque itself was rarely used. In the mid-nineteenth century the usual terms for pre-Gothic architecture were Norman or Lombard. These were applied without discrimination to buildings that utilized not the pointed arch of the Gothic but round-headed openings, combined with such details as corbeled cornices and chevron and lozenge moldings. Romanesque forms, while referring to the medieval era in which the Christian religion was believed to have reached its spiritual height, did not bear the weight of the imprimatur the ecclesiologists had placed on English Gothic. It was therefore a suitable alternative for other than Episcopal churches or for those Episcopalian congregations that did not follow High Church ritual.[87]

Perhaps because the style had been so little studied, most mid-nineteenth century essays in the Romanesque vein are neither convincing reinterpretations of the medieval style nor original creations utilizing Romanesque forms as reference.[88] Holy Trinity was the first American church with a facade composed in a manner similar to the medieval originals. Its general arrangement, with the triple arched entrances, rose window, and two flanking towers, may owe something to such English examples as John Gibson's Central Baptist Church, London, of 1845-1848, or the fine Romanesquoid churches of Thomas Henry Wyatt and David Brandon. But the skill with which such details as the blind arcading or deep moldings of the doors are handled shows that Notman had assimilated the spirit as well as the forms of the medieval prototypes. Holy Trinity is his Romanesque St. Mark's.

St. Clement's, on the other hand, is an original creation, which appears to owe little to either medieval or contemporary prototypes. It posed, as St. Mark's did, problems of siting that Notman once again solved with brilliance. Although St. Clement's was, like Holy Trinity, a Low Church congregation, the program called for a properly oriented church.[89] Therefore the apse occupies the main front of the street on Cherry Street. In the Gothic version Notman presented as an alternative, this was a rather weak feature, its basic form disguised by buttresses and broken by large pointed arched windows. In the executed building the theme of the rounded forms of the Romanesque arch is carried out with almost brutal force. The apse explodes onto Cherry Street, rising on a battered basement of massive courses of rusticated stone, finished with rounded profiles and graduated in size from bottom to top. Above, the rounded form of the apse is reinforced by a blind arcade.[90] The rustication is carried from the apse around the base of the tower in the northeast corner and serves to unite these two dominating features.

In contrast to the dramatic east end, the flanks of St. Clement's are conventional and even somewhat dull. The drawings give no indication of what was meant to be the main entrance, the north and south porches being inconspicuous and the west end indeterminate. This somewhat nebulous arrangement was finally resolved with Notman's last work, the addition of parish buildings [68] along the western end of the church's property. The swell of the apse had always carried the observer's eye to the courtyard along the south flank. Now this became the principal entrance, with a common portico giving access to both the vestibule of the church and the parish buildings. The portico is placed diagonally. It is deep, but narrow, consisting of a barrel vault carried on spiral columns. It thrusts into the open courtyard, creating an almost mannerist tension that is also present on the east front of St. Clement's.

At St. Clement's the drama and tension exist because there is a sense of contained force. In another of Notman's late works tension is also present, not because of its power, but because of its ethereal and dream-like quality.

This is the gate designed for Mount Vernon cemetery in 1856 [66]. It was a commission that, in those relatively lean years, probably came to him through Robert Buist, the cemetery's treasurer and a fellow emigrant a quarter of a century before. It is Notman's last known work in the Italianate style. The forms are familiar: the lodge is reminiscent of the servants' wings at Prospect and Alverthorpe, the tower strongly resembles that of the latter villa. But the tower, isolated and 100 feet high, has been greatly attenuated at Mount Vernon. Obviously it houses no human inhabitant. It is a setting for an Italian fairytale. The gate, too, with its trumpet-blowing angels, has an insubstantial, stage-like quality for all its weight.

The Mount Vernon gate demonstrates just how important materials were to Notman's effects. The cemetery company was offered the option of executing the gate in brownstone or marble. Fortunately, one suspects with encouragement from the architect, they chose the latter. The translucent quality of that material plays no small part in enhancing the otherworldly quality of the structure. Notman's drawings reveal that he always paid close attention to the disposition of each piece of stone. By the late 1850s his interest in stonework expanded to include the expressive potential of color. One of his obituaries cited him as having introduced stonework of mixed colors to Philadelphia.[91] If polychromy played any part in the design of Holy Trinity, time and the replacement of much of the stone has obliterated its traces. At St. Clement's, however, the use of polychromy, while restrained, is still evident. The contrast between the color, as well as the texture, of the rusticated stone of the apse with the smooth limestone above, is an important element in the design. The spire of St. Clement's, now removed, was covered with polychrome slates. For his Gothic version of the same church, Notman had suggested even more elaborate patterning.

Notman died at the age of 55. To the end of his life he was capable of creating powerful designs, and, indeed, of remarkable originality. If the body of his work is small, the cause must be something other than lack of talent. The reasons are to be sought not in the artistic, but in the business aspects of the practice of architecture. According to his anonymous biographer: "His success lay much in his native powers yet much also in the devotion he paid to his profession not merely as a means of living but as an art. He sacrificed much to his work. Had he loved his art less his pecuniary success might have been greater."

Notman's attitudes towards his profession, as well as aspects of his personality, are revealed in his relationships with his clients, which also shed a good deal of light on American architectural practices in the mid-nineteenth century. For a European-trained architect the United States offered the potential for economic improvement, but little comprehension of the role of the professional. It was a dilemma that men such as Pierre Charles L'Enfant and Benjamin Henry Latrobe had already encountered. Writing under the pseudonym "Z," a British builder-surveyor who tried his luck on this side of the Atlantic a few years after Notman, and decided to return home, described his experiences with some bitterness. Although he had fifteen years of experience, he found himself unable to find work in New York. Americans, he reported, had "some notion of what an architect was." However, one man he met, "who had lately had a first-rate house built for himself," assured him that

... there had been no drawings made for his house, and that the almost invariable practice is, to fix upon a house already built, as a model either to be copied exactly, or with such variations as the proprietor may think fit: an agreement is then drawn up, in few words, and, as you may suppose in very vague and general terms.... In consequence of this system prevailing to a great extent, I do not believe there is full time employment throughout the year for half a dozen working architects or surveyors.... The Americans are averse for anything which appears to them superfluities. There is as little to be done in the way of keeping accounts as in drawing; ... The master builders are practical men, and with very few exceptions, men who have gone over from their country as journeymen carpenters....[92]

Notman, probably younger and less experienced professionally than "Z," evidently had little difficulty in supporting himself as just such a "journeyman carpenter" until he received his first commission. As an architect his early association with John Jay Smith and his circle seems to have been a happy one. Smith, George Washington Doane, and Nathan Dunn each provided the young architect with more than one commission, and there is no record of anything but satisfaction with his work. A few years later Notman's dealings with important patrons were also cordial. In explaining delays in completing The Athenaeum to the Building Committee he wrote, "...I tender my grateful thanks for your courtesy, and the kind approval and encouragement you have given me during the progress of the work."[93] Smoothness and harmony also characterized Notman's relationship with the commissioners charged with enlarging the New Jersey State House. Having retained Notman to prepare the designs and superintend the work, they found themselves "bound to say that more efficient aid in their operations, from the commencement to the present time, they could not have desired."[94]

While work on the State House was accomplished with celerity, construction on Notman's other major commission for New Jersey, the Lunatic Asylum, dragged on for three years. Outsiders, such as the director of Boston's McLean Asylum and members of the building committee of the Smithsonian, were impressed by Notman's intelligence in fulfilling the needs of such an institution, but he garnered no official praise. Furthermore, in the published descriptions of the building, there is an undercurrent of tension about who actually was responsible for the design, Notman or Dr. Thomas S. Kirkbride. In Notman's version the plan was his, based on the "observations" of the commissioners and Kirkbride's "suggestions." According to Kirkbride his "general plan and form of building" were "embraced" in Notman's design.[95] In any event, when Kirkbride was next asked to serve as consultant for a similar institution, for the

State of Alabama in 1851, he chose to work not with Notman, but with the younger and presumably more malleable Philadelphia architect, Samuel Sloan.[96]

In the late 1840s Notman began to inform clients and prospective patrons, with some firmness, of his views on proper professional procedures. One issue of importance was the right of an architect, participating in a competition, to retain his drawings. It was a common practice for competition drawings to remain the property of the prospective client, with or without payment of a premium. Except in the case of the Smithsonian, Notman asked for their return, sometimes forfeiting prize money to achieve this end. A second issue was the establishment of rates for his work. This he held should be five per cent of construction costs in cases where he served as superintending architect. Some clients evidently felt these charges exorbitant and Notman had difficulty in collecting his fee within a reasonable time. The Refectory for Princeton Theological Seminary, which cost approximately $6,000, was begun in 1846 and completed in 1847. By the summer of 1848 Notman had still not been paid in full. Eli F. Cooley, a member of the building committee, and incidentally also one of the commissioners responsible for the erection of the New Jersey State Lunatic Asylum, wrote in a letter concerning bills still due: "I do not put in any thing about paying Notman—he has had $100. —an ample compensation for all he has done— however I suppose that he must ultimately be paid the other $200.—let him wait a little." [96] On 8 July 1848 Notman acknowledged receipt of another $100 from the seminary, but added:

...as to the further message from the Committee relative to charges—I superintended the building as well as made drawings &c and I had the responsibility of its propriety in accommodation and appearance. For this service my charge is 5 per cent and travelling expenses, which price I am gladly allowed where my services are understood, at the same time I will make a donation to the Seminary (as I promised Mr. Phillips) when the Committee pay me the balance which I respectfully beg may be at their earliest convenience. . . .[97]

He received his final payment five days later. Disagreement about fees was also responsible for the loss of a commission for St. Luke's Church in Baltimore.[98]

Misunderstandings, missed appointments, and miscalculations could also ruffle the relationship between architect and client. The best record of Notman's dealings with a client is the daily diary kept by Charles L. Pearson during the construction of his family's house, Glencairn, in Trenton, New Jersey. The diary shows Notman as a conscientious practitioner, responsible for laying out the ground, measuring the work to be sure the contractor's charges were properly calculated, and visiting the site frequently to check on the progress of construction. Notman often called on the Pearsons to discuss the project, and Charles Pearson visited Notman in Philadelphia. However, they never shared a meal under the same roof. Although their professional relationship was relatively cordial, Charles Pearson, admittedly something of a snob who kept an annual list of those with whom his family exchanged visits, obviously never considered the architect his social equal.

Some real difficulties arose; others were rumored. In May, when the foundations were being dug, it was discovered that the dimensions were incorrect. This was quickly rectified, but Pearson was later annoyed to discover that Notman had miscalculated the number of steps for the front portico. A month after construction started, Pearson began to worry about the possibility of trouble with Notman. He, himself, had nothing to complain of. "The house does not require my supervision, that is Mr. Notman's affair, & thus far, he seems inclined to do all in his power to please, even when it requires an additional expenditure on his part. . . ." Others, however, were warning of potential problems. "Phil[emon] Dickinson told Father some things of an unpleasant nature about overcharges of Mr. Notman, which caused us a good deal of uneasiness; however I hope nothing unpleasant will occur in our case, he seems fair and honest." Still Pearson listened when the contractor, John Grant, "told me to look over the specifications for our house, as Mr. Notman had forgotten some things already. I do hope that we will have no trouble with Mr. Notman, as the McCalls have, a suit is now pending between them." [99] A few days later Pearson noted "I imagine I see the glimmering of trouble with Mr. Notman about extra charges &c." In the long run, however, the only questions that arose were about whether installing a complete floor in the attic and a ceiling in the cellar were included in the contract, and the quality of door knobs to which the Pearsons were entitled. The final settlement was amicable. Notman was paid $1,000, with a balance due of $1,358, and the Pearsons felt relieved. "Our minds are considerably more at ease now, for Mr. N. has the reputation of having rather extensive bills of extras. With us his extras amounted only to 200 dollars, one hundred of which we had agreed upon long since." Still Pearson felt that if he were to build again he would dispense with the services of an architect.[100]

As the interconnections between Notman's patrons demonstrate, architects were highly dependent on clients' recommendations. Most of Notman's commissions came through prior personal contacts. A reputation for being difficult to deal with was a serious drawback. The houses for the McCalls and the Pearsons were the last buildings Notman was asked to design in Trenton. The disagreement over the design of a Masonic Hall for the Grand Lodge of Pennsylvania in 1853 was even more serious. The controversy involved several aspects of the client-architect relationship: participation in competitions, the nature of an employment agreement, and adequate compensation for services. The episode must have been talked about and, indeed, was reported, although in a guarded manner, in the Philadelphia newspapers. It appears to have been damaging to Notman, and his reputation could hardly have been enhanced when he was dismissed as superintending architect of the Cathedral of St. Peter and St. Paul. The client believed that Notman was abusing the five per cent fee by shipping raw stone to be cut on the site, rather than having it pre-cut at the quarry, thus raising its cost. Asked to modify his fee, Notman refused.

Even at Princeton, where, except for the seminary, Notman seems to have enjoyed pleasant relationships with his clients, he felt compelled to explain his proper role as architect. When Bottom & Tiffany, the contractors for some of the iron construction on Nassau Hall, presented a bill that was too high, Notman felt that he, rather than the client should settle the matter. "I ordered the work," he wrote to John Maclean, president of the College of New Jersey, "and directed it, and know the whole matter and am the only one to settle it on your part, . . ." [101]

The position of the architect in the United States in the mid-nineteenth century was a difficult one. Contractual agreements between builders and clients appear to have been understood. There are no records of controversy over those buildings, such as The Athenaeum, St. Mark's, Holy Trinity, and St. Clement's, where Notman acted as contractor as well as architect. But as "Z" found, Americans did not really comprehend architectural services. Pearson and Maclean obviously saw nothing wrong with dealing directly with contractors, rather than through the architect. Fees were questioned, and where they were not, Eli F. Cooley's "let him wait" attitude was evidently not uncommon. Notman often ended a job with money owing on account. At the end of his life, Notman was forced to beg the vestry of St. Clement's Church for payment for his work on their parish buildings. Although the standard fee of five per cent of construction cost had been agreed upon, the client, dissatisfied with Notman's performance, withheld payment.

Providing architectural services in a professional manner was not sufficient. The architect also had to educate his clients. Notman certainly had the knowledge to do this. His written descriptions of his buildings show him to have been intelligent and articulate. Charles Pearson found him interesting and pleasant in conversation. But his letters about business matters lack tact. Convinced of the propriety of his position he could be not only firm, but obstinate. The provocation may have been severe, but his letter to the Masons seems unduly offensive. His letters to John Maclean, who appears to have treated Notman with courtesy, border on being testy.

In Notman's case, problems with clients may have been exacerbated by his personality, which seems, in his later years, to have become inflexible and contentious. But the issues over which controversy arose were not unique to Notman's practice. Questions about the nature of competitions, the ownership of drawings, the scope of an architect's responsibilities, and, of course, adequate compensation were concerns of all architects. A professional discipline was being defined. In the process architects on both sides of the Atlantic began to band together. Professional organizations would provide the framework through which questions of procedure would be answered, not by individual disputes between client and practitioner, but by establishment of a set of regulations.

Between 1834 and 1837 the Institute of British Architects was founded and incorporated. In emulation, three American architects, Alexander J. Davis, William Strickland, and Thomas U. Walter founded the American Institution of Architects in 1836. Although this proved an abortive attempt, the concept of a professional organization of American architects did not die. It was revived in 1857 when a baker's dozen of New York architects, led by Richard Upjohn, held an organizational meeting to form the American Institute of Architects. The New Yorkers sent invitations to eleven prominent architects to join them; the two Philadelphians selected were Walter and Notman.[102] Notman was also a founding member, in 1861, of the Pennsylvania Institute of Architects, which evolved into the Philadelphia Chapter of the AIA.[103]

John Notman's career spanned the years from Andrew Jackson's presidency to the Civil War, a period of dramatic change in American architecture. Notman arrived in the United States at a time of transition in the manner in which buildings were designed. The practice of architecture was passing, albeit slowly, from the hands of the carpenter-builder and the gentleman amateur into those of the professional architect. By the time of his death architecture was recognized as akin to law and medicine in requiring standards for education and performance. Immigrant architects, such as Notman, professionally trained and committed to conducting their practices in a professional manner, played an important role in the transformation.

Beyond the struggles for professionalism, however, Notman and his contemporaries were faced by challenges new to architecture both as practical craft and as art. On the one hand the classical verities that had governed design from the Renaissance through the Greek Revival were replaced by a new, less rigid aesthetic; on the other, construction methods that had been utilized for centuries were rendered obsolete by technological developments in the form of new materials and mechanical devices. The architect began to emerge as a practitioner in the modern sense, responsible not only for the design and construction of a building, but for orchestrating the efforts of pipefitters, plumbers, metalworkers and heating specialists.

Abandonment of the classical orders and their accompanying rules of proportion, combined with the flexibility afforded by the new technology, provided an opportunity for architects to experiment with free and original forms. In assessing the period the symbiotic relationship between art and science should not be overlooked. The impact of open domestic planning, introduced by such architects as Notman and Davis, on the future development of American architecture has been acknowledged.[104] But it should not be forgotten that such designs would have been impractical in most of the United States without the concomitant development of central heating. There were fireplaces in the major rooms of Notman's villas, but, from Riverside on, furnaces for central heating were provided, and, as Charles Pearson noted, were capable of warming the entire house to a uniform 70 degrees. Sometimes Notman was fairly frank in expressing the union of design and technology. At the New Jersey Lunatic Asylum the Italianate towers not only provide a picturesque skyline, but function as the main outlets of the ventilating system.

One conceivable response to the abandonment of traditional forms and the development of new methods of construction might have been the invention of a new stylistic framework without historical reference. Instead the early nineteenth century developed an aesthetic of associative plurality. No longer restricted to classical antiquity, architects could choose from a number of past periods those considered most "fit" or "suitable" to a building's purposes. Within this envelope of historicism, the architect might design with a great deal of freedom; reference to the past gave innovation a degree of legitimacy. John Notman did not differ from his contemporaries in this respect. His churches are usually medieval; his suburban villas picturesque; his urban buildings variations on the palazzo mode. Although in some instances the choice probably was dictated by the client, Notman was certainly conscious of the message conveyed by each of the styles. However, the choice of a style was not a matter of simplistic symbolism. When Notman suggested Collegiate Gothic for the Smithsonian he undoubtedly was mindful of the value of its associative references for a quasi-educational institution. Of more importance, however, was his conviction that it "expresses large rooms and halls well lighted for public purposes." Style, in effect, followed function.

From Notman's statements about his projects, it is clear that the style or outer trappings of a building were incidental. What preoccupied him were such fundamentals of architecture as siting, proportion, and form. When he provided Downing with a description of Riverside, he did not mention its style at all, but rather wrote about the building's placement in the landscape and the effect of the

interior vistas he had created in relating it to the setting. The Athenaeum he cited, with evident pride, as "most impressive as a piece of street architecture." The New Jersey State Lunatic Asylum, although "in the simplest style of architecture" he believed would have a good architectural effect "from its great size, the well-arranged advancing and receding disposition of the wings, the variety in height, and the fine proportions of the several masses of the building." In the submission letter accompanying his Smithsonian designs he repeatedly stressed formal considerations, noting that "the richness of the whole is produced by form and proportion, not by costly labor." [105]

The period in which Notman worked was, for a long time, considered a sort of dark ages of American architecture.

When the Civil War broke, architecture in America had been sinking steadily for a generation. Order, fitness, comeliness, proportion, were words that could no longer be applied to it: construction was submerged in the morass of jerry-building, tedious archaicism, and spurious romanticism that made up the architectural achievement of the nineteenth century. [106]

More recent criticism has revised this harsh appraisal, but has tended to view America's Early Victorian era as a prelude to the country's architectural coming of age after the Civil War. This is perhaps a particularly appropriate time to view the period on its own merits. In many ways the nature of architecture then was analogous to the present situation. What had been the accepted vehicle for architectural expression for a generation, the Classical Revival was being rejected, just as in recent years the International Style and its descendants are no longer regarded as the ultimate solution. In the wake of the breakdown of a former certainty, architects, then as now, looked to a more distant past for reassurance, and at the same time sought a variety of alternatives. These were not just signposts for the future, but attempts to find answers to present needs.

Because the period in which he worked is relatively unexplored, it is difficult to assess John Notman's place in American architecture. Certainly he was an innovator. Some of his "firsts"—Laurel Hill, Riverside, The Athenaeum, and St. Mark's—were sufficiently publicized to bring him commissions from widely scattered parts of the country, and to be emulated even where his services were not employed. The ideas introduced by Notman, notably the open, fluid planning of Riverside, had continuing influence. Yet without more knowledge of the architects of his generation and their immediate successors, the manner in which such influences were transmitted remains undetermined. Notman's relative importance even within Philadelphia, for example, will be better understood when more is known about such contemporaries and competitors as Carver, Ferguson, Hoxie, Johnston, and Riddell.

On his own merits, John Notman stands as an architect of talent and skill. Because his intelligence was high and his grasp of the fundamentals of architecture was sound, he was able to demonstrate considerable versatility. Although his output was not large, he produced original and outstanding work in a variety of styles and to accommodate a wide range of functions. The invitation to join the founding members of the AIA attests to recognition of his stature by his peers. Over a century after his death his surviving works remain the best evidence of his excellence as a designer, serving old functions well and adapting to new ones with grace.

INVENTORY AND APPRAISEMENT OF THE GOODS AND CHATELS, RIGHTS AND CREDITS WHICH WERE OF MARTHA NOTMAN LATE OF PHILADELPHIA, TAKEN AND MADE IN CONFORMITY WITH THE ABOVE DISPOSITION:

Furniture
Dining Room

	Secretary		5.00
	Picture		5.00
	Mahogany Dining Table		4.00
	Prospective of Holy Trinity		.50
	Pine Table		2.00
5	Pictures of Villas, etc.		2.50
1	Sofa		5.00
1	Picture Group 1st at Waterloo		2.00
1	Easy Chair Hair cloth		3.00
1	Easy Chair cloth		2.00
3	Plain Chairs		.75
3	Shades		.30
23	yd Ingrain Carpet & Oilcloth		10.00
	Mantle Ornaments		.50
1	Brass Kettle		.50
	Watch & Chain		30.00

Parlor

6	Hair Seat Chairs	1.50	9.00
2	Shades		.25
2	Sofas		16.00
3	Pair Curtains & Cornices		25.00
1	Ottoman		3.00
19	Pictures		250.00
4	Plush Easy Chairs		30.00
2	Plate Glass Mirrors		40.00
2	Reception Chairs		5.00

1	Cloth Table Cover	2.00
2	Odd Easy Chairs	6.00
1	Upright Piano & Stool	50.00
2	Rose Wood Music Cases	15.00
1	Marble Top Table	20.00
1	Large Sofa Hair Cloth	15.00
1	Large Carved Table	6.00
2	Scagliola Pedestals	10.00
	Brussels Carpet	50.00
	Matting under Carpet	5.00
2	Ven Blinds	4.00
4	Small Stands	4.00

Main Hall

	Hat Stand, 1 Table Cover	5.00
2	Door Mats	.50
1	Picture	2.00
1	Pedestal Bust	2.00
1	Arm Chair	2.00
2	Cane Seat Chairs	1.00

Room over Dining Room

4	Cane Seat Chairs	1.00
	Oil Cloth on Floors	2.00
3	Odd Easy Chairs	3.00
1	Book Stand	1.00
1	L'kg Glass	1.50
1	Marble Top Table	1.00
3	Shades	.30

	Main Stairs & Hall	
	Brussels Stair Carpet & Rods	10.00
	Oil Cloth on Hall 1st Story	3.00
2	Maps N. J. & Phila.)	
	)	
2	Oil Paintings without frames)	3.00
1	Window Shade	.10
	Back Room 2 Story	
2	Wardrobes	8.00
1	Bureau	5.00
1	Secretary	5.00
1	Work Table	2.00
	Brussel Carpet	5.00
	Bed Stead old	2.00
1	Mirror	1.00
3	Paintings 2 without frames	5.00
1	Dressing Table & Glass	5.00
1	Tortise Shell Work Box	1.00
1	Small Stand	.50
	Hair & straw mattress Bolster—	
	Bed Bedding & Pillows	10.00
1	Silk Quilt	2.00
1	Rocking Chair	1.50
1	Chair	.25
	2nd Story Front	
1	Bureau	5.00
	Matting	4.00
	French Bedstead	5.00
2	Mattresses & Bed	10.00
1	Wash Stand	2.00
2	Chairs	.20
1	Table	1.00
3	Pictures	5.00
	Mantle Ornaments	1.00
	3rd Story Back	
	Bed & Table Linen	25.00
	Bedstead	1.00
	Feather Bed & Bedding	5.00
	Wash Stand	1.00
	Bureau	3.00
	Dressing Glass	1.00

	Table		1.50
	Chair		.10
	Carpet		1.00
	Wardrobe		3.00
	Lot Carpeting (not on floor) & Rods		15.00
	Stair & Entry Carpet 3rd story		2.00
	3rd Story Front		
	Matting		1.00
1	Chair		.25
	3rd Story Back Main Building		
	Bureau		3.00
2	Chairs		.50
1	Wash Stand		1.00
1	Towel Rack		.10
4	Pictures		1.00
1	Painting		2.00
	Mattress Feather Bed		15.00
	Lot Blankets		7.50
	4th Story Front		
	Contents of 4th story		5.00
	Andirons & shovel tongs		3.00
	4th Story Back		
	Bed stead		1.00
	Mattress & Bed		3.00
	Pair Stands for Drawing		2.00
	Wash stand		.25
	Chair		.25
	Table		.25
	Kitchen		
	Kitchen Utensils Dishes etc.		5.00
	Tables Bench Cloths Horse etc.		3.00
	Basement		
	Table & old lumber etc.		2.50
	Ladder		1.00
	Closet		
	China & Glass Ware		5.00
	Large China Bowl		2.00
	Waiter		.50
	Cash in Bank		197.00
	239½ oz. Silver	1.25	319.37
			$1,404.22

1. *The North American and United States Gazette*, 4 Mar. 1865, and Philadelphia *Public Ledger*, 3 Mar. 1865.

2. This manuscript, entitled "Short Sketch of John Notman," was once held by the Historical Society of Pennsylvania, but is now lost. However, its substance is recounted in Francis James Dallett, "John Notman, Architect," *Princeton University Library Chronicle*, XX, 3 (Spring 1959), 129, hereafter cited as Dallett, PULC, and Jonathan Fairbanks, "John Notman: Church Architect," unpublished master's thesis, University of Delaware, 1961, 11-12, hereafter cited as Fairbanks. Mr. Fairbanks has been kind enough to provide his transcript of the manuscript. Other important early sources of information about Notman's career are Joseph Jackson, *Early Philadelphia Architects and Engineers*, Philadelphia (1923) and *An Historical Catalogue of the St. Andrew's Society of Philadelphia 1749–1907*, Philadelphia (1907).

3. Dallett, *PULC*, 129.

4. A. J. Youngson, *The Making of Classical Edinburgh*, (1966), 162-164.

5. Quoted in Fairbanks, "John Notman," 12.

6. George Good, *Liberton in Ancient and Modern Times*, Edinburgh (1893), 160.

7. Tom Speedy, *Craigmillar and its Environs*, Selkirk (1892), 164.

8. Quoted in Rev. Campbell Ferenbach, *Annals of Liberton*, Edinburgh (1975), 24.

9. For an overview of the city's building activity see Youngson, *Classical Edinburgh*; for biographical information on the architects and lists of their works, see Howard Montagu Colvin, *A Biographical Dictionary of British Architects, 1600–1840*, London (1978).

10. Colvin, *Dictionary*, 647.

11. William Henry Playfair, Letterbook, 21 Aug. 1830-5 Aug. 1833, University of Edinburgh Library.

12. For information on Playfair's personality, practice and library I am indebted to Michael Langdon, Department of Architecture, University of Edinburgh, who is preparing a monograph on Playfair's career. The sale catalogue of the library is in the National Library of Scotland, KR. 16, f. 5 (1).

13. Dallett, PULC, 129.

14. *Dictionary of National Biography*, New York (1887), XLI, 23-25.

15. For Burn, see Youngson, *Classical Edinburgh* and David Walker, "William Burn: the country house in transition," in *Seven Victorian Architects*, London (1976).

16. Youngson, *Classical Edinburgh*, 262.

17. Report or Manifest of the Ship *Thames*, 2 Nov. 1831, Bureau of Customs, Collector of Customs, Port of Philadelphia, National Archives.

18. Joseph Jackson, *Early Philadelphia Architects and Engineers*, Philadelphia (1923), 215.

19. Declarations of Intention to be Naturalized, V (1828-1832), 515, Court of Common Pleas, Philadelphia City Archives. Notman's brother-in-law, Archibald Catanach, and his brother, Alexander Catanach, applied on the same day (513-514), having emigrated to Philadelphia a year before Notman.

20. Report or Manifest of the ship *Susquehanna*, 1 Apr. 1834, Bureau of Customs, Collector of Customs, Port of Philadelphia, National Archives.

21. Minutes of the Directors of the Library Company of Philadelphia, VI, 85 and Financial Records, 1836.

22. For the development of the rural cemetery, see James Steven Curl, *The Victorian Celebration of Death*, Newton Abbott (1972).

23. John Jay Smith, "Laurel Hill, Memoranda kept by Jno. J. Smith Jr." coll. Drayton M. Smith.

24. Thomas U. Walter also submitted plans. For the chronology of the foundation, design, and construction of Laurel Hill, see entry 2.

25. The similarities between Laurel Hill and Kensal Green were first pointed out by Fairbanks, "John Notman," 21, and expanded upon by Keith Morgan, "The Landscape Gardening of John Notman, 1810-1865," unpublished M.A. thesis, University of Delaware, 1973.

26. H. E. Kendall. *Sketches of the Approved Designs of a Chapel and Gateway Entrances intended to be erected at Kensall Green for the General Cemetery Company*, London (1832).

27. Phoebe, Stanton, *The Gothic Revival and American Church Architecture*, Baltimore (1963), 46, incorrectly postulates two designs for the chapel at Laurel Hill, one based on details from Hampton Court, the other on details from King's College Chapel, both derived from illustrations in Pugin's *Specimens of Gothic Architecture; Selected from Various Ancient Edifices in England*. Although Notman may have depended on sources other than Kendall for individual details, the overall resemblance between Kensal Green and Laurel Hill is too striking to be ignored. For a discussion of the relationship of Notman's drawing for the chapel at Laurel Hill to the executed building, see entry 2.

28. A. J. Downing, *Rural Essays*, New York (1853), 144.

29. *Ibid.*, 157.

30. A. J. Downing, *A Treatise on the Theory and Practice of Landscape Gardening...*, New York and London (1841), 345.

31. Clay Lancaster, "Oriental Forms in American Architecture," *Art Bulletin*, XXIX, 3 (1947), 183.

32. See Carroll L. V. Meeks, "Henry Austin and the Italian Villa," *The Art Bulletin*, XXX (June 1948), 145-149, and Clay Lancaster, "Italianism in Italian Architecture Before 1860," *American Quarterly*, IV (Summer 1952), 127-148.

33. The basement plan, in the collection of Barry drawings at the Royal Institute of British Architects, is dated 1830.

34. Notman is listed as a member, as of 1837, in *List of the Resident Members of St. Andrews Society of Philadelphia*, Philadelphia (1840), 9; master membership file, The Athenaeum of Philadelphia.

35. Dallett, *PULC*, 132, and Fairbanks, "John Notman," 42-44.

36. Last Will and Testament of Martha Notman, Will No. 608, 1870, Register of Wills, County of Philadelphia.

37. According to Dallett, *PULC*, 132n, the marriage was performed at the Church of St. Luke's and the Epiphany on 11 May 1841. The bride, seven years Notman's senior, was the daughter of Robert Pullen, an English-born auctioneer and nail manufacturer. Her previous marriage to Robert M. Anners, a jeweler was, according to Dallett, brief and unhappy, and she resumed her maiden name upon his death..

38. Information on the Notmans' possessions comes from the Last Will and Testament, Account, and Inventory and Appraisement of the Estate of Martha Notman, Will No. 608, 1870, Register of Wills, County of Philadelphia, John Notman having left his entire estate to his widow, it may be assumed that the inventory made after her death reflects the contents of the house during his life time. It is so revealing of the Notmans' style of life that it is quoted in full at the end of the introduction.

39. Anna Wells Rutledge, *Cumulative Record of Exhibition Catalogues: The Pennsylvania Academy of the Fine Arts*, 1807-1870, Philadelphia (1955), 22, 121, 145, 159, 245, 255, 319, 341.

40. Last Will and Testament and Account of John Notman, Will No. 145, 1865, Register of Wills, County of Philadelphia.

41. John Notman to Dr. (James) Rush, 4 Sept. 1850, Rush Papers, Library Company of Philadelphia.

42. 1833 - 492; 1834 - 361; 1835 - 465; 1836 - 369; 1837 - 248; 1838 - 243; 1839 - 383; 1840 - 379; 1841 - 452; 1842 - 275; 1843 - 325; 1844 - 420; 1845 - 552; 1846 - 492; 1847 - 512; 1848 - 531; 1849 - 571; 1850 - 630; 1851 - 655, Philadelphia *Public Ledger,* 2 Jan. 1852, 1.

43. In a letter to Joseph Cowperthwait, Cashier of the Bank of the United States, dated 28 Mar. 1840, Notman wrote: In explanation of my taking the freedom to call on you yesterday, I beg your attention to the following statement. My note to Ashmead & Croskey for $1400 becomes due on 10/13 April in the Bank of the United States, the original note of $1542 was given for lumber delivered and to be delivered and payable by renewal less ten per cent on each arrival at maturity, which was kindly done over (with continuation of Schuylkill Bank guarantee) by the Bank of the United States, during your late absence, but no farther renewal to be granted; thus unexpectedly called on to meet it, with deranged, and delayed, payments from sources depended on, I am compelled to ask your consideration of the acceptance of the enclosed warrant of Attorney to confess judgement by the Proprietors, for $5200, on the Assembly Buildings, corner of Chestnut & Tenth Sts. as a Collateral security. The claim is founded on my Lien as entered, and certified by Thos. I. Wharton and Joseph A. Clay Esquires, as good for the claim, without suit, on 1st November next. According to searches the Assembly Building stands, thus, original ground purchase $37,000, of which cash was paid 6000, leaving mortgage $31,000. The cost of the building was about $42,000, cash paid out about 22,000, leaving outstanding liens of $20,000, and it is believed there is a mortgage of 20,000 dollars after the liens. I will insure the claim, and make any farther searches required for security & satisfaction.

Should you be inclined to hold it, as collateral security, I would ask, besides paying the above note of $1400, a loan $2600, of which there would be an average balance in the bank of $1000 during the loan; should you take the claim entirely credit me with its whole amount. I will take $1200 of it in Schuylkill Bank funds. If you in kindness aid me in this exigency, you will greatly enhance my personal security, as this money advanced by you will enable me to release the [?] of Academy of Natural Sciences, which I am now building, and is due me above $8000, with little remaining to be done to it, and within a month, I will have a house finished, I own in Spruce St. just west of Broad St. where the claims do not amount near to its value, at the fallen prices for property of this year.

Almost a stranger to you, Sir, for the offense of thus familiarly addressing you, I plead necessity and your known friendship with those who have given me credit for integrity. If there is impertinence in my above statement and requests, place it rather to my ignorance of forms in business than presumption. If you approve it, I beg your best construction on it, to the Board of Directors. If objectionable your negative without going farther.

Will oblige Sir
with great Respect
Your Obedient Servant
(signed) John Notman

Manuscript collection, Henry F. duPont Winterthur Museum and Library.

44. That Notman probably did, in fact, know the Barry designs through published sources is evidenced by his use of square windows resting on a string course in The Athenaeum's attic story. This device appears in Barry's 1836 design for the Manchester Athenaeum, which was published in *Surveyor, Engineer and Architect* for 1843. (See fig. I-3 in Henry-Russell Hitchcock, *Early Victorian Architecture in Britain*, New Haven (1954).) In the executed Manchester building, the windows were replaced by a sculptured frieze. Full drawings of the London project were published in W. H. Leeds, *The Travellers' Club House*, London (1839).

45. [John Notman], "Architectural Description of The New Hall of the Athenaeum," *Thirty-Second Annual Report of the Athenaeum of Philadelphia*, Philadelphia (1847), n.p.

46. G. L. Meason, *On the Landscape Architecture of the Great Painters of Italy*, London (1828), 91.

47. Philadelphia *Public Ledger*, 26 Aug. 1847, 2.

48. Mrs. L[ouisa] C[aroline] Tuthill, *History of Architecture*, Philadelphia (1848), n.p.

49. Philadelphia *Public Ledger*, 7 Dec. 1848, 3. The idea of adaptive use and of designing new buildings compatible with the surrounding ones is obviously not a new one.

50. Henry-Russell Hitchcock and William Seale, *Temples of Democracy*, New York (1976).

51. *Trenton Sheet Anchor*, quoted in Trenton *State Gazette*, 9 May 1845, 2.

52. "Report of Commissioners to sell state property, build offices, etc., made to Legislature 16th February 1846." *Votes and Proceedings of the Seventieth General Assembly of the State of New Jersey*. Woodbury (1846).

53. For the English background and its effect on American church architecture, see Fairbanks, "John Notman" and Stanton, *Gothic Revival*; for the architectural impact of the ecclesiological movement in England, see Hitchcock, *Early Victorian Architecture in Britain*.

54. For the text of *The Ecclesiologist's* commentary, see entry 17. The description, based on one in Doane's publication, *The Missionary*, is somewhat confusing in that it conveys the impression that the longitudinal axis of the building is east-west. In fact, it is north-south.

55. Stanton, *Gothic Revival*, 49.

56. As early as 5 Feb. 1847 the Board of Regents authorized publication of Robert Dale Owen's *Hints on Public Architecture*, New York (1849), which was prepared in collaboration with Renwick; for a summary of their ideas, see Daniel D. Reiff, *Washington Architecture 1791-1861*, Washington (1971), 91-94.

57. John Notman, *Description and Estimate of Design . . . for the Smithsonian Institution*, Washington (1847).

58. Fairbanks, "John Notman," 79, says that the "only basic difference" between St. Oswald's and Saint Mark's is the assymmetrical placing of the tower. However, there are numerous other differences, as well, including the absence of a clerestory in the Pugin building. St. Oswald's did form a typological prototype of which St. Mark's is clearly a descendant. Stanton, *The Gothic Revival*, 117-124, details the similarities to St. Stephen's.

59. St. Mark's Church, Minute Book of the vestry of St. Mark's Church in the City of Philadelphia—A.D. MDCCCXLVIII to A.D. MDCCCLXIII, 27.

60. Morgan, "The Landscape Gardening of John Notman," 52. For the letter mentioning his visit, see entry 28.

61. Stanton. *The Gothic Revival*, 298.

62. John Notman, "Report Accompanying Plan of Holly-wood Cemetery, Richmond, Virginia," *Historical Sketch of Hollywood Cemetery*, Richmond (1875), 19-25.

63. "Report of the Committee on Capitol Square," *Richmond Daily Times*, 24 July 1851.

64. Quoted in Stanton, *The Gothic Revival*, 284.

65. *Ibid.*, 298-300.

66. *Ibid.*, 284.

67. *Ibid.*, 185.

68. *North American and United States Gazette*, 4 Mar. 1865.

69. The trustees' comments, quoted in full in entry 27, demonstrate the depth of emotion aroused by the ecclesiological movement. They regarded the symbolic use of the cross in architecture as "Puseyite," referring to Edward Bouverie Pusey, one of the chief Oxford Movement spokesmen for the Anglican revival, and "semipopistical."

70. Fairbanks, "John Notman," 80-81.

71. Illustrated in George B. Tatum, *Penn's Great Town*, Philadelphia (1961), Pl. 98.

72. A. J. Downing, *The Architecture of Country Houses*, New York (1850), Design XXVIII, figs. 143-144.

73. See Winslow Ames, "Alverthorpe *ex Tenebris*," *Nineteenth Century*, III, 3 (Autumn 1977), 68.

74. The buildings provide ample evidence of the importance of these factors in Notman's planning; his attitudes are expressed verbally in his description of Riverside, quoted in full in entry 4.

75. I. J. Kent, "Art. VII on the Dwelling Rooms of a House," *The Architectural Magazine*, II (1835), 404.

76. Documentation outlining the course of the competition and the dispute is given in detail in entry 56.

77. Dallett, *PULC*, 139.

78. Philadelphia *Public Ledger*, 13 Oct. 1854, 2.

79. Jackson, *Early Architects*, 225.

80. Henry-Russell Hitchcock, *Architecture Nineteenth and Twentieth Centuries*, Baltimore (1958), 236.

81. Other early buildings for which Cooper & Hewitt supplied wrought iron beams were Cooper Union (1852), Harper and Brothers (1853) and the United States Assay Office (1855) in New York.

82. "Messrs. Harris & Co. also make Patent Galvanized Cornices, which are cheaper and lighter, and more ornamental than stone, and more durable than wood. Specimens can be seen at the Academy of Music in Philadelphia, and at Nassau Hall, Princeton, N. J." Edward T. Freedley, *Philadelphia and its Manufactures*, Philadelphia (1859), 293.

83. The firm of Bottom & Tiffany cast the iron fronts for the Penn Mutual Building, the Pennsylvania Inquirer Building, the Manderson Building, the Davis & Co. Building, the Hoskins, Heiskill & Co. Building, and six storehouses on Arch Street west of Front Street, all in Philadelphia, and erected in Trenton a remarkable all-iron Gothic house.

84. Robert D. Smith, "John Notman's Nassau Hall," *Princeton University Library Chronicle*, XIV, 3 (Spring 1953), 133.

85. *Ibid.*

86. See, for example, *Gothic Architecture selected from various Ancient Edifices in England*, I, Plates 1-5.

87. See Fairbanks, "John Notman," 88-89, 92, and Hitchcock, "Early Victorian Architecture in Britain," I, 140-141. However, these were obviously not cut and dried rules. Although Notman presented three "Norman" designs for Holy Trinity, his alternative design for St. Clement's was Gothic.

88. There are, of course, notable exceptions, such as Renwick's "Castle" for the Smithsonian, which uses "Norman" forms for an entirely free, romantic composition.

89. St. Clement's subsequently became a High Church congregation and the building was altered to accommodate the liturgical differences. The apse of Holy Trinity is at the west end of the church.

90. The second blind arcade was added in the early twentieth century.

91. *North American and United States Gazette*, 4 Mar. 1865, 2.

92. 'Z,' "Emigration of Architects to North America," *The Architectural Magazine*, I (1834), 384-386. "Z's" experience in New York was similar to James Gallier's, who, rather than returning to England, moved on to New Orleans. See Talbot Hamlin, *Greek Revival Architecture in America*, New York (1944), 140-141.

93. John Notman, "Report of the Architect," *Thirty-Second Annual Report of The Athenaeum of Philadelphia*, Philadelphia (1847).

94. "Report of Commissioners to sell State Property, build offices, etc.," *Votes and Proceedings of the Seventieth General Assembly of the State of New Jersey*, Woodbury (1846), 387.

95. For Notman's and Kirkbride's full statements, see entry 18.

96. Harold Norman Cooledge, Jr., *Samuel Sloan (1815-1884), Architect*, University of Pennsylvania dissertation (1963), University Microfilms Inc., 18-19, 135-136, stresses the collaborative nature of the design of the series of hospitals produced by Kirkbride and Sloan.

96. Eli F. Cooley to Lewis W. B. Phillips Esq., 10 June 1848, Hodge Collection, PUL.

97. John Notman to Charles Hodge, 8 July 1848, Hodge Collection, PUL.

98. See entry 43.

99. Notman had recently completed Ellarslie, on the outskirts of Trenton, for the McCalls.

100. Charles L. Pearson, Diaries, 11 May, 11 June, 12 June, 21 July, 24 July, 13 Sept., 28 Nov. 1849, 3 Jan., 11 Mar. 1850, Coll. W. Houstoun Pearson.

101. For Notman's correspondence on this subject, see entry 63.

102. Accounts of the founding of the American Institute of Architects are in Stanton, *Gothic Revival*, and Everard M. Upjohn, *Richard Upjohn, Architect and Churchman*, New York (1939).

103. George C. Mason, "Professional Ancestry of the Philadelphia Chapter of the AIA," *Journal of the American Institute of Architects*, I (Sept. 1913), 370-386.

104. Vincent J. Scully, Jr., *The Shingle Style and The Stick Style*, rev. ed., New Haven (1971), xxiii-lix, deals with the transmission of mid-nineteenth century planning ideas through the publications of Downing and his followers.

105. For Notman's descriptions of his projects, see entries 3, 4, 16, 18, and 22.

106. Lewis Mumford, *The Brown Decades*, 2nd rev. ed., New York (1955), 109.

Catalogue of the Works of John Notman

Editorial Note

This catalogue of the work of John Notman is arranged in three sections. The first, and longest, covers his documented projects, built and unexecuted. Dates given are from initiation to completion where both are known. The entries are arranged chronologically based on the date of inception. The second category consists of buildings listed by Jackson, but not confirmed by additional documentation. The third lists buildings attributed to Notman by others, including the author.

For the documented projects, bibliographic information is divided into four categories. The first two cover graphic documentation in the form of drawings and other early illustrations, including a publication record. The third lists written documentation in the form of manuscripts and citations in newspapers and other contemporary publications. Abbreviations are used to refer to the following owners of major collections of material related to Notman:

HSP—Historical Society of Pennsylvania
LCP—The Library Company of Philadelphia
PUA—Princeton University Archives
PUL—Princeton University Library

Inclusion of Notman's work in three early listings is considered as supplementary documentation and given in abbreviated form following the citation of primary documents. These are:

AB—"Short Sketch of John Notman," formerly in the manuscript collection of the Historical Society of Pennsylvania

J—Jackson, Joseph. *Early Philadelphia Architects and Engineers.* Philadelphia (1923)
StA—*An Historical Catalogue of the St. Andrew's Society of Philadelphia 1749-1907.* Philadelphia (1907)

Finally, bibliographic references are to secondary sources. Publications cited in previous categories are not repeated, nor are mentions of Notman or his buildings in general books included. Two articles and two theses that form the basic bibliography on Notman are always cited first in abbreviated form. They are:

D—Dallett, Francis James. "John Notman, Architect." *Princeton University Library Chronicle*, XX, 3 (Spring 1959), 127-139
F—Fairbanks, Jonathan. "John Notman: Church Architect." Unpublished Master of Arts thesis, University of Delaware, 1961
M—Morgan, Keith. "The Landscape Gardening of John Notman, 1810-1865." Unpublished Master of Arts thesis, University of Delaware, 1973
S-PULC—Smith, Robert C. "John Notman's Nassau Hall." *Princeton University Library Chronicle*, XIV, 3 (Spring 1953), 109-134

Two other frequently cited references are also abbreviated:

T—Tatum, George. *Penn's Great Town.* Philadelphia (1961)
W—White, Theo B., ed. *Philadelphia Architecture in the Nineteenth Century.* 2nd rev. ed. Philadelphia (1973)

1.

OFFICE BUILDING

FIFTH STREET SOUTH OF CHESTNUT STREET,
    PHILADELPHIA
1835–1836
Client: Library Company of Philadelphia
Project: three-story rental office building

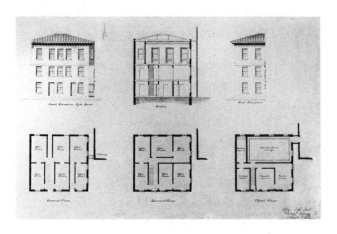

DRAWING: 1.1:
> *Title:* Offices. Fifth Street/Philada
> Library Lot
> *Signature:* John Notman
> *Date:* none
> *Scale:* none indicated (scales ⅛″ : 1′)
> *Other inscriptions:* Front elevation. Fifth
> Street./Section./End Elevation./Ground
> Plan./Second Floor./Third Floor.
> *Description:* elevations, section and plans
> *Medium:* ink and wash
> *Size:* 16 x 25¼ (40.7 x 64.2)
> *Owner:* Library Company of Philadelphia

OTHER EARLY ILLUSTRATIONS:
> Two early photographs, reproduced in
> Looney, Robert F. *Old Philadelphia in
> Early Photographs 1839–1914*, New York
> and Philadelphia (1976): Pl. 62 and 65,
> show that the building was erected approx-
> imately as planned.

DOCUMENTATION:
> Minutes of the Directors of the Library
> Company of Philadelphia, vol. 6 and Fi-
> nancial Records for 1836 and 1837, LCP
> Archives

IN THE SPRING OF 1835 the Library Company
began construction of a new building to house
its expanding collection. [Minutes, 7 May
1835: 79] This was located on the rear portion of a lot immediately north of their existing building on Fifth Street, now replicated
as the library of the American Philosophical
Society. By fall the board had decided to develop the front portion of the lot as rental
offices. Accordingly on 1 Oct. 1835 the board

Resolved, That the building committee be requested to
proceed with the erection of offices on the lots now occupied by the Fire and Hose Companies according to their
report this evening.   [Minutes: 85]

References to the offices and to the library's
own new building are intertwined in the min-
uts and accounts, but on 2 June 1836 an order
for $500 was drawn in favor of John C. Evans
"on account of building the offices on Fifth
Street." [Minutes: 99] On 18 Nov. 1836
quarterly rentals were received from Charles
Gilpin, Oswald Thompson and George W.
Wharton, and on 9 Sept. 1839 John C. Evans
was paid $1512.35 as the balance of his ac-
count for "building new Offices in Fourth
[sic] St." [Financial Records] Notman's
name does not appear in the records. Perhaps
he produced the designs without compensation as a means of launching his architectural
career.

The building appears from the photographs to have been constructed of brick with
a metal roof. It stood directly on the building
line, in contrast with the existing Library
Company building which was set back approximately 20 feet from the street. Designed
to accommodate two floors of rental office
space, it was linked to the existing building at
third floor level, providing a suite for use by
the Library Company.
PRESENT STATUS:
> Demolished

2.

LAUREL HILL CEMETERY
RIDGE AVENUE, PHILADELPHIA
1836–1839

Client: Laurel Hill Cemetery Company

Project: Plan of cemetery, designs for entrance gate, superintendent's cottage, shelter for statuary group "Old Mortality," chapel, several monuments

GENERAL VIEW OF LAUREL HILL CEMETERY.

Guide to Laurel Hill, 1844

DRAWING 2.1:

Title: Chapel Laurel Hill
Signature: John Not[man]
Date: none
Scale: none indicated
Other inscriptions: none
Description: flank elevation
Medium: ink
Size: 17⅝ x 25¼ (44.8 x 64.2)
Owner: Historical Society of Pennsylvania
Exhibition record: Two Centuries of Philadelphia Architectural Drawings, Philadelphia Museum of Art, 1964
Publication record: Stanton, Phoebe. *The Gothic Revival and American Church Architecture.* Baltimore (1968): 46. White, Theo B., ed. *Philadelphia Architecture in the Nineteenth Century,* 2nd rev. ed. Philadelphia (1973): Pl. 31

OTHER EARLY ILLUSTRATIONS:

"Plan of the Laurel Hill Cemetery near Philadelphia," Engraved by I. P. Hammond, Survey by Philip M. Price, 1836, Coll. Laurel Hill Cemetery Company. Another copy, divided into two sections, with some losses, is owned by LCP.

Plans of the gatehouse, chapel, cottage and stable yard, and a pre-existing house on the property are included in Perpetual Policy No. 1967, Franklin Fire Insurance Co. Records, HSP.

Other important views and illustrations of individual buildings and monuments appear in [Smith, John Jay]. *Guide to Laurel Hill Cemetery.* Philadelphia [1844]. Notman prepared the drawings for the lithographs used to illustrate this volume and carefully distinguished between those structures for which he had served as architect and those designed by others, signing the former as "archt" and "delt," and the latter as "delt" only. The designs illustrated for which Notman took credit are: the ground plan, general view of the cemetery chapel, mausoleum of E. W. Robinson, and monuments of Joseph S. Lewis and J. A. Brown; and those designed by others are monuments to Oscar Douglas and Commodore Hull.

Laurel Hill was a popular topic for illustration and reportage from its founding through the third quarter of the nineteenth century. Among the most important of the other early illustrations are: a plan of the cemetery and view of the central part of the entrance gate appearing in [Smith, John Jay]. *Statues of Old Mortality and His Pony....* Philadelphia (1838); "Lau-

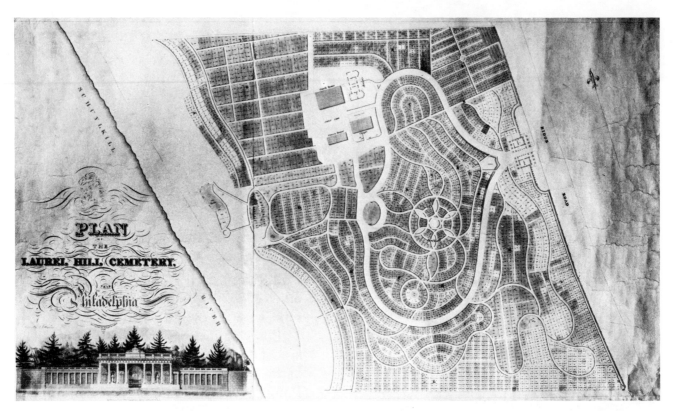

"Plan of the Laurel Hill Cemetery near Philadelphia." *Courtesy Laurel Hill Cemetery Company*

rel Hill Cemetery,/Philadelphia," J. C. Wild, printed by Wild and Chevalier, 1838, appeared in Wild & Chevalier's *Views of Philadelphia and its Vicinity*, reprinted 1838, copyrighted by J. T. Bowen, reprinted 1848; a view of Laurel Hill after a drawing of Augustus Koellner appears in *Views of American Cities*, lithographed by Deroy and published by Goupil, Vibert & Co. of New York and Paris between 1848 and 1851; "Laurel Hill Cemetery," printed by P. S. Duval, drawn from nature and aquatinted by Geo. Lehman expressly for Miss Leslie's, n.d.

DOCUMENTATION:

Cash Book I, Coll. Laurel Hill Cemetery Co.; Diary of Sidney George Fisher, HSP; Franklin Insurance Company Records, HSP; Memoranda (of John Jay Smith) Respecting the Foundation of Laurel Hill Cemetery, Coll. Drayton M. Smith; Minutes of the Managers of the Laurel Hill Cemetery Company, Coll. Laurel Hill Cemetery Co.; Philadelphia *Public Ledger; Poulson's Daily Advertiser; Regulations of the Laurel Hill Cemetery*. Phila-

adelphia, 1837; [Smith, John Jay]. *Recollections of John Jay Smith*. Philadelphia (1892); John Jay Smith Papers, Ridgway Collection, LCP, deposited at HSP; AB; J; St A

BIBLIOGRAPHICAL REFERENCES:

D: 130-31; F: 16, 24-26; M: 20-30, 84-85, 38n; S-PULC: 118; Curl, James Stevens. *The Victorian Celebration of Death*. London (1972); Downing, Andrew Jackson. *Rural Essays*. New York (1853); Harbeson, William. "Mediaeval Philadelphia." *Pennsylvania Magazine of History and Biography*, LXVII, 3 (July 1943): 227-253; Marion, John Francis. *Famous and Curious Cemeteries*. New York (1977); Smith, J[ohn] Jay. *Designs for Monuments and Mural Tablets: Adapted to Rural Cemeteries, Church Yards, Churches and Chapels*. New York (1846); Stanton, Phoebe. *The Gothic Revival and American Church Architecture*. Baltimore (1968); *The Stranger's Guide in Philadelphia*. Philadelphia (1862); *Philadelphia: Three Centuries of American Art*. Philadelphia (1976); T; W

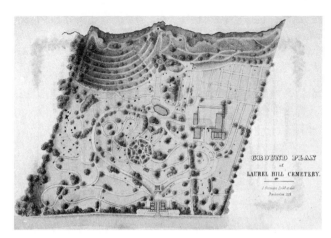

Guide to Laurel Hill, 1844

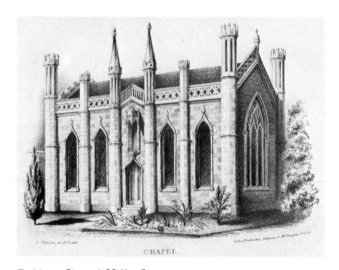

Guide to Laurel Hill, 1844

Guide to Laurel Hill, 1844

In Nov. 1835 John Jay Smith addressed letters to Frederick Brown, Nathan Dunn, D. W. Richards, William Strickland, and Thomas I. Wharton inviting them to meet at his office to discuss organizing a company to create a rural cemetery. All attended, Strickland bringing to the meeting John Struthers, a marble mason who would later carve some of the most elaborate monuments at Laurel Hill. All supported the conception, except Wharton who left the meeting, and throughout the remainder of the fall and winter a suitable site was sought. [Memoranda: 1-2] In March 1836, a meeting was held at which, after Dunn was appointed chairman and Smith secretary, it was reported that the property called Laurel Hill had been purchased for $15,000. [Minutes: 1 Mar. 1836]

Work began early in the spring. On 2 Apr. 1836, Smith noted that he had "contracted for a stone wall today to be placed along the entire front of the premises on the Ridge Road, and for a fence on the north and south sides." [Memoranda: 5] Although there is no record of a formal competition for designs for the cemetery, proposals were received from at least two architects other than Notman, William Strickland and Thomas U. Walter. Five drawings, three by Strickland and two by Walter, are preserved in the Library Company of Philadelphia; one of the Walter drawings is dated 14 May 1836. (These drawings, both sets featuring Egyptian Revival entrance gates, are discussed in M: 21-22.)

By June the Notman plan had been decided on, probably by Nathan Dunn. On 13 June Brown reported that Strickland had withdrawn from the board, probably because his plan had not been chosen. [Minutes: 13 June 1836] On 15 June, Smith noted that "Mr. Dunn contemplates some improvements of a costly kind and desiring to meet the company we were called together at my office this evening." [Memoranda: 6] Probably the group was shown a design that was about to be unveiled to the public. On 30 June *Poulson's Daily Advertiser* reported

There is now to be seen at the Exchange a very beautiful picture drawn by Mr. Walter, and designed by Mr. Notman, the architect, of the entrance adopted by the company to the new Rural Cemetery at Laurel Hill, near Philadelphia.... This entrance is to be erected at once.

On 1 July a correction was published in *Poulson's:*

... our paper yesterday respecting the entrance to Laurel Hill cemetery, contained an inadvertence, which we the more regret because it may appear to artists to convey a wrong impression of the part which Mr. Walter had in making the drawing now exhibited at the Exchange.... a plan, not entirely correct in its proportions, was handed to Mr. Walter, who, as a friend, politely agreed to remodel it ... without giving an opinion of the merit of the plan.

Morgan [24] suggests that the reports of this drawing may indicate a collaboration between Notman and Walter. However, Walter's name appears nowhere else in connection with Laurel Hill, except as designer of a monument for the Ball family.

John and Margaret Evans Tomb [see Public Ledger 1 Dec. 1849, 2] Gothic, 1849. *Author's photograph*

Work on laying out the lots evidently proceeded rapidly. On 19 July the first burial took place, Mercy Carlisle being interred in the lot of her son-in-law, Joseph Cowperthwaite. [Memoranda: 10] Construction of the buildings occupied most of the remainder of 1836 and continued into 1837. On 31 Mar. 1837 Smith recorded:

... the carpenters are busy with the chapel and the front fence on top of the wall (which I wish now had been iron) ; ... plasterers are occupied on the cottage and entrance; ...   [Memoranda: 25]

By the end of the year the first phase of building was complete. Sidney George Fisher noted in his diary for 6 Dec. 1837:

Stopped at the Laurel Hill Cemetery. They are going on with the improvements very rapidly ... They have built a pretty cottage, the plan and taste of which I admire much.

On 8 Dec. Smith noted "the entrance, enclosures, and cottage are completed; ..." [Memoranda: 45] These buildings are described in a survey made for the Franklin Fire Insurance Company on 20 Dec. 1839:

Charles Graff Monument, Classical, n.d.
Author's photograph

4th.   A Frame Cottage Consisting of a Centre two Story building and 2 Wing ends One Story; The Centre building is 36 by 19 feet, each Wing 15 feet Wide; the front ends are Octagonal and projecting in front of Centre building 5 feet to 1st offset, the South Wing projects Also 6½ feet West of Centre building: The Centre building is divided into 2 rooms & a Hall & Entry with Stair Way therein Across the Middle 8 feet Wide, the South Wing into 2 Rooms & the North Wing One room, (See Map) The Hall has a double Sash door outside 4 lights each 14 by 18 in glass with 3 transom lights Over. Also double panel inside doors. The Other Rooms are all 1¼ inch best frame with 6 inch p[i]lasters plain. Iron locks & brass knobs to doors; There is a bulk window to each Octagon end of Wing Centre Sash 12 lights each & 4 each side 9 by 15 glass; the Other Windows 12 lights 11 by 7 glass all having folding inside panel shutters plain 6 inch Moulds plain heads & panel under work, (except the Window in West end of South Wing & the one West Side of the Centre Room Adjoining which have panel outside shutters); The Fireplace to room on the right of Hall has a Marble Mantel, the room on the left of Hall plain Wood Mantel to fireplace; The Hall is partitioned off from the Stair Way by a lath and plaster partition. The Stairs are open to Entry and Winding to 2nd Story Mahogany rails & turned Mahogany posts. Banisters turned Yellow Pine, the partitions & Ceilings lathed & plastered with plaster Mould Cornice Rough Cast Outside, 1st Story 10½ feet in the Clear: The 2nd Story is 6 feet in the Clear divided into two rooms by board partitions planed ploughed & groved with like ledge doors, lath and plaster Ceiling 3 Windows West Side 12 light 8 by 10 glass. Cellar under the whole building. A Stair Way there to under the 2nd Story Stairs; A Portico in front of Centre building filling up the space between the wings painted tin roof Concave, 4 double small posts front laticed along under these eaves. Neat Cornice and dental drop eaves thereto, White Pine floors; The Centre building 2nd Story is panel work 2 ends and east side. The Wings have double pitch Cedar Shingle Roofs pitch to each Octagon end with drop Eaves in front and Sides, Cornice to West ends of Wings, Tin Gutters & conductors, rough cast outside; White pine floors best quality to the building, painted and finished in the best manner.

A two Story Stone Building With An Arch Way for an Entrance to Laurel Hill Cemetery from the Ridge Road.

Dimensions: The Whole front including the Arch is 68 feet; to wit, in the Centre is the Arch 12 feet Span, On each Side of the Arch Way is an Arch Piazza. Across the building 9 feet wide, the remaining 19 feet on each side of said arches is divided into lodge rooms, 2 each Story at each Side: the Width of Building 26½ feet with a Piazza on each Side Whole length of the Building; The Piazza in front next to the Road is 10 feet Wide the One next to the Cemetery is 8 feet wide. The front Piazza has 4 round frame Pillars in front on each side of the Arch which supports the roof which is a continued projection of the roof of the building, the pillars are fluted with solid turned bases & heads, and painted & sanded, & 7 feet circumference at base; there are the same number of Pillars on the Other Side Same Make & Size (but not fluted) and supporting the roof projecting the Same as in front. The floors to all the Piazzas are faced Sand Stone; The Piazza under the building on each side of the Entrance has 4 round Pillars, in front next the entrance 3½ feet circumference at the base & 8 feet high, materials and finish same as the others; The Arch to this entrance rises to the height of the 2nd Story of Building is Constructed of Frame and panel work painted and sanded, the Arches over the Piazzas along side of Entrance made in the same way & having block Cornices. There is a cast iron & a wooden laticed Gate to Entrance & a double panel door in front to each Piazza by the side of the large Arch, plain jambs painted & sanded: there is a similar door way at the other end of said Piazzas (but no doors hung) with panel jambs; there is one double panel blind door also in front to each front lodge room (1st Story) Near the extreme ends of building: The lodge rooms are 2 each Story on each Side of the Entrances; each a front and back room; from each Piazza by the Side of the Arch there is an entrance Door Midway to the lodge rooms 1st Story which leads directly to a Straight Boxed Stairway to 2nd Story. At the foot and head of Said Stairs is a small Entry from which there are doors to the rooms on each Side both Stories; There are also out doors at the extreme ends of building Midway leading into a Small Entry 3 feet deep and 5 feet Wide from which there is a door leading into each room. Also a door to Cellar way under the Stairs to 2nd Story, the entries in the lodges are all of the same size as the one described, the doors 1¼ inch best panel work, butt hinges, iron lock & brass Knobs; The rooms next the road have one Window at the ends farthest from the Arch each Story. There is also one other Window to each entry 2nd Story. The Windows are all 12 light 11 by 17 glass sash hung with weights, double folding inside panel shutters folding into the jambs with 6 inch pilasters and moulding the Windows 2nd Story Sash to the floor; Each room has a small fireplace, the backroom fireplaces 1st have Marble Mantels & side Slabs of Marble, the others are all plain Wood Mantels; corresponding to the front blind door is a back one inside of which is a dresser & Closet Over with Shelving & drawers to each front door & a large Closet to each back door, each back room 2nd Story has a Similar Closet directly Over the 1st Story One, There is a large Closet also to the South lodge rooms over the Stair Way, Over the Stairs to the North lodge rooms is a boxed stair way leading to trap door on roof; The partitions & Ceilings lath and plaster the back rooms 1st story having plaster Mould Cornice best heart pine floors & washboards ploughed & grooved. (Wood work all of the best materials) 1st Story 10 feet to Ceiling, 2nd Story the Same. Cellar under each end: The roof is double, pitch east and west & extending Over the Piazzas. Covered with tin and has turned colonading at each Side and end with a frame panel work Midway on each Side and end; The panel Work in front over the Arch Supports a large wooden urn, The eaves have deep dental bed Moulds & block Cornice and panel worked, The Ceilings to the Piazzas panel wainscoted, There is a wing wall on a range with the front of building extending 56 feet each Way, each having 8 round pillars in front in a row, frame painted & sanded, Also a Square one at each end, the roof to the Wall projects over the heads of the pillars and is covered with tin & has a row of turned Colonades on top like those on the building, there is also a Wall ranging with the West Side at each end About 20 feet long forming a Yard, A panel door in each; The whole building painted & finished in the best Manner.

One other structure, not called for in the original plan, had also been completed, the small shelter for the statuary group known as "Old Mortality." [Memoranda: 45] Based on a tale by Sir Walter Scott, the group became one of the major attractions of Laurel Hill.

> The figure of Old Mortality was cut by Mr. Thom in Scotland, and with its accompanying Pony and a plaster cast of Sir Walter Scott, was exhibited to admiring crowds in Edinburgh, London and elsewhere.
>
> [Smith, *Old Mortality*: n.p.]

Thom arrived in Philadelphia with an introduction to "his countryman Nottman [sic], the original architect of Laurel Hill." [Smith, *Recollections*: 255] The pony had been broken in transit, but Thom, having purchased a quarry in New Jersey, offered to recarve the pony and dispose of the group to Laurel Hill. He also carved the figure of Scott in stone. [Smith, *Old Mortality*: n.p.] The shelter, in which these statues, along with a bust of Thom, were placed, is a square structure with slender octagonal turrets at the corners. It has blind Tudor arches on its flanks and is opened at the front by a Tudor arch with waist-high cast iron railing.

Although these buildings had been completed, the chapel remained unfinished. Morgan [26-27] argues that the design was not even drawn until 1838 and that when it was, it represented a plan to remodel an existing building. The estate of Laurel Hill, before its sale to the cemetery company, had briefly been occupied as a Catholic boys' seminary, for

Mrs. George Leib Harrison Tomb, Gothic, c. 1850.
Author's photograph

which some sort of chapel would have been required. Morgan bases his conclusion that this chapel was a separate building on the observation that a group of four buildings appears at the right center in Strickland's and Walter's plans, as well as that of Notman, and that on Strickland's the lower left of these is labeled the chapel. He also quotes a description from the *United States Gazette* of 12 Mar. 1836:

> This superb place has lately been occupied by a Seminary, and there is on it, close to the large Mansion House, a handsome stone chapel which will be converted to the uses of a church for those who choose so to employ it.

The *Gazette* article, however, was undoubtedly inaccurate. In a letter of 17 June 1931 to Stuart Hunt of Laurel Hill Cemetery, A. C. Chadwick Jr., quotes a history of St. Bridget's Roman Catholic Church, written by Rt. Rev. Monsignor W. J. Walsh in 1923: "Father Jeremiah Kiely conducted classes, and a part of the mansion on the newly-acquired estate served both as a chapel for the school, and a place of worship." Furthermore, Smith, in describing Laurel Hill as a prospective purchase, noted: "They have converted the ball room [of the mansion] into a chapel where they have an altar in Catholic fashion." [Memoranda: 3] The buildings shown on all three plans were probably part of the program required by the cemetery's board.

The chapel was undoubtedly designed in 1836 along with the other buildings. Work was under way in 1837 when carpenters were employed on the chapel. [Memoranda: 25] However, construction was evidently suspended. Noting the completion of the first three buildings in December 1837, Smith added "the church, green house, stables, and alterations of house etc. are to be entered upon in the spring." [Memoranda: 45] The cause of the suspension of activity was perhaps reluctance on the part of the board to commit further funds. The country was in the grip of a financial panic and expenditures for Laurel Hill had already exceeded the estimates of $70,000 by $20,000. However, Dunn agreed to finance completion of the project at his own expense. [Memoranda: 45] But on 1 July 1838, Smith complained that "Mr. Dunn has not yet seen proper to commence the improvements, finishing the church etc. . . ." [Memoranda: 61] In August he pasted into his memorandum book a clipping from the *National Gazette* which, while generally praising Laurel Hill, remarked "that the Chapel or Church should be immediately completed." [Memoranda: 66] This article may have influenced the board, which "on motion of Mr. Smith, Resolved unanimously that it is expedient to finish the Chapel in a neat and substantial manner as soon as practicable and that Mr. Dunn be requested to have the same completed in as economical a manner as he may think proper." [Minutes: 24 August 1838] Just when this was done is not recorded, but the chapel is described as a finished building in the 1839 insurance survey.

Stanton [46] claims that there were two designs for the chapel, based on a comparison of Notman's drawing with the view reproduced in *Penn's Great Town* (the Deroy lithograph). However, the lithograph is deceptive. Comparison of the drawing with the lithograph in the 1844 *Guide*, as well as with old photographs, shows that the chapel was built as designed with some minor modifications. These were probably made in the interests of economy. The water table was omitted. To compensate for its absence the windows were lowered so that their finials no longer interrupted the cornice. The recessed panels were omitted from the lower intermediate towers, and the niche over the door was simplified. The most significant change was to the door itself. It was built without the portico, and the door frame was in the form of an ogival arch similar to that of the windows rather than the pointed arch shown in the drawing.

Joseph Saunders Lewis Tomb [see Memoranda, 60, 61, 75] Egyptian, 1838. *Guide to Laurel Hill*

The insurance survey described the building as:

3rd. Stone Gothic Chapel 50 by 24½ feet within the Walls has 6 half octagonal columns up the walls in front, the Same on the North Side. The Columns on each Side of the Door (which is in the Centre of front wall) have Spire tops, All the Others tower tops forming an Octagon above the roof; there is also a Small Spire on top of roof at each end; The Chapel has one Window in East end, 4 front & 5 in the North Side (all Gothic) The Window in East end is formed of a Centre and 2 Side Sash All together 10 feet wide the glass are diamond 5 inch Sq and Stained Various Colours; the Other Windows glass Same Size (Windows 3 ft Wide)

The door is double 2 inch panel with Countersunk brass lock & Knobs, the casings to Door & Windows painted & Sanded Outside (Stone Sill to door). The floor is heart Yellow Pine, Wash boards & Window boards and jambs best White Pine; The Roof is double pitch Cedar Shingle; Panel work along the eaves and at the ends up the roof painted and Sanded, Tin Gutters and Conductors, The building has plaster Mould Ceiling to Rafters, handsome Gothic Style; Building painted and finished in the best Manner & built of the best Materials.

For his work on Laurel Hill Notman received an unspecified sum between Feb. 1836 and Feb. 1837. [Statement of costs of real estate and improvements at Laurel Hill Cemetery from February 26, 1836 to February 26, 1837, Coll. Laurel Hill Cemetery Co.] Additional payments were made to him after completion of the work: $100 on 25 May 1839, $100 on account on 15 June 1839; $150 "on acct. of church" on 20 July 1839; and $150 "in full of all accounts" on 2 Jan. 1840. [Cash Book I: 20, 22]

In the fifteen years following the opening of Laurel Hill, Notman designed several monuments in a variety of styles. These have been identified, either by his taking credit for them in the 1844 *Guide* or because his name is carved into the monument's base.

Laurel Hill still belongs to the Laurel Hill Cemetery Company. Although it has been expanded several times, the main features of Notman's plan are preserved in that section of the cemetery known as North Laurel Hill. All the monuments designed by Notman are still standing (including the Robinson Mausoleum, contrary to F: 26), except the John A. Brown Monument, which was demolished in 1928. The Lavalett Monument has been moved from its original location. The chapel and the superintendent's cottage were also demolished in the early twentieth century, and the greenhouses and stabling were removed at an indeterminate date. The shelter for "Old Mortality" survives as built. The entrance gate also stands, although it has been altered. Major alterations include a second story on either side of the entrance in the piazza, removal of the colonnading and urn from the roof of the central portion, and glazing of the north pedestrian entrance to provide enlarged office space. Laurel Hill has been entered in the National Register of Historic Places.

John A. Brown Monument [also know as Monument of the Three Sisters] Decorated Gothic, prior to 1844. *Guide to Laurel Hill*

Edward William Robinson Mausoleum, Greek Revival, c. 1838. *Guide to Laurel Hill*

3.

THE COTTAGE
MOUNT HOLLY, NEW JERSEY
1837–1838
Client: Nathan Dunn
Project: residence and grounds

DRAWINGS: none
OTHER EARLY ILLUSTRATIONS:

A perspective view and ground floor plan appear in Downing, A. J. *A Treatise on the Theory and Practice of Landscape Gardening.* New York and London (1841); the perspective alone in 2nd ed., New York (1844) and 4th ed., New York and London (1849).

DOCUMENTATION:

In addition to Downing, Perpetual Policy #2033, Franklin Fire Insurance Co. Records, HSP; AB

BIBLIOGRAPHICAL REFERENCES:

D: 131; F: 31; M: 43; S-PULC: 119; Gowans, Alan. *Architecture in New Jersey.* Princeton (1964); Lancaster, Clay. "Oriental Forms in American Architecture." *Art Bulletin,* XXIX, 3 (1947): 183-93

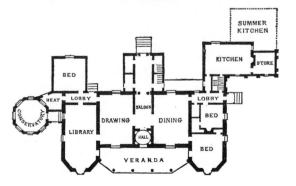

THE DESCRIPTION in the first edition of Downing quoted below definitively identifies Notman as the architect of "The Cottage," as well as providing one of the few surviving comments made on one of his buildings by Notman himself.

One of the most unique specimens of domestic architecture in the country, is the summer or cottage residence of Nathan Dunn, Esq., of Philadelphia, which is situated at Mount Holly, New Jersey, *figure* 42. The broad and highly elegant veranda is one of its striking features. This is covered, from the eaves one-third of its depth downward, by a screen of foliated apertures filled with coloured glass, giving a rich glow to the deep shade of the cool promenade beneath. The roof is ornamented by the graceful pendants of the eaves, and its bold projection insures the wall from dampness, while it gives a shaded appearance in summer.

This extensive cottage was designed by Mr. Notman of Philadelphia, who however, acknowledges his indebtedness to the elegant invention of the proprietor, for the suggestion of many of its most interesting features. The *facade* shown in the accompanying engraving, measures about 140 feet, and the domestic offices, etc., not shown, occupy about 80 feet more on the right. The style of this building is mixed; the arcaded veranda has an oriental air, while the main body of the cottage is in the English cottage manner. The aim in designing it being to produce something adapted to the American climate, in fitness, and expression of purpose, rather than to follow any one fixed style.

"From the veranda in front," says the architect in his description of the plan, figure 43, "you enter the *hall*, an elipsis of about 8 by 11 feet, with two niches on each side containing large and handsome flower vases: the ceiling is a pannelled dome. From this a door opens to the *saloon*, about 36 feet by 10, divided in length by scagliola columns in antae, and surmounted by an enriched pannelled ceiling with hatched gilding. On the right and left of the saloon, are the *drawing* and *dining-rooms*, each 26 by 18 feet. From the drawing-room opens the library, 34 feet by 18, and 16 feet high to the apex of the arched ceiling. This room is finished and furnished in a rich Gothic style: the ceiling is a Tudor arch; the rafters or ribs springing from corbels, and forming pannels in double series, foliated; and the effect, especially in the semi-octagon end, where the intersections of the tracery are numerous, is highly elegant. The·cottage-oriel window in this apartment is filled with a screen of Gothic pannel work, glazed with fine examples of landscapes painted on glass. From the library we enter, through a small lobby, an octagonal *conservatory* with glazed roof and sides, 20 feet in diameter. There is another reserve green-house from which this conservatory is kept constantly supplied with beautiful plants in full bloom.

From the dining-room a door opens to Mr. Dunn's *bed-room*, and from hence a lobby leads to the side entrance, to the kitchen, and to the back stairs; the latter conducting to a cool parlour on the cellar floor. Besides the bed-rooms on this floor, there are three in the second story, over the central portion of the house. An air furnace supplies heat to all the main body of the edifice shown in the engraving.   [Downing, 1st ed.: 345-47]

The date of "The Cottage" can be established by the insurance survey made 20 Dec. 1837, in which it is noted that " 'The Cottage' is not yet entirely completed...." The survey provides additional details about the design and construction of the house and about the disposition of other buildings on the estate.

Mount Holly Insurance Company   December 20th 1837

Make Insurance on the deposit or perpetual plan to the amount of Five Thousand dollars upon my dwelling house etc commonly called "the Cottage" situate on the West Side of the high or main street of Mount Holly, or as sometimes called "the Burlington Road" near Mt. Holly. The whole of said dwelling house and connected buildings being (with the exception of the conservatory & Gothic archway) of strong framed carpenter work, raised to their respective levels of first floor joisting on Brick Walls, varying from one foot to four feet and a half above the natural surface of surrounding grounds of which the following are more accurate details, Beginning on the South viz—

No. 1.   The conservatory, walls of brick built in the Octagon form with a window in each face—16 feet high and 17 feet from face to face. Glass & Tin Roof connected to No. 2 by three brick walls forming two entries of eight feet long and six wide, twelve feet high with tin roof.

No. 2.   The South wing forming a library, twenty one feet wide, thirty four feet deep and fourteen feet high, walls above joists of double framed work, lathed & plastered between the frames, lathed & rough cast outside and finished with lathe & plaster inside, covered with cedar shingles—back of the library & across the width and under the same roof runs a passage or Entry connecting No. 1 & 3 with door from Library, twenty one feet long, six feet wide and fourteen feet high, from which enters a bed room seventeen feet square, walls of single frame, ten feet high, lathed plastered & rough cast as before with covering of Cedar Shingles.

No. 3.   The Center building—forty eight feet front and twenty nine in depth forming on first floor, two parlors, vestibule & hall, the hall projects eighteen feet further back than the line of parlour, in which projections are likewise three closets and stair case to second story—height of walls fourteen feet above floor of double frame (excepting said projections) lathed & plastered between frames and

lathed and plastered outside and inside. Over the first story and in center of said forty eight feet front, rises a second story of thirty feet front twenty nine feet in depth and ten feet high forming three-chambers, store room & lobby, walls single frame lathed & plastered outside and inside roof covered with tin, the remainder of the forty eight on each side of said second story and the said projection of wall being covered with cedar shingles. A Verandah or open Portico extends the whole distance of the forty eight feet center, from wing to wing, twelve feet wide, fourteen feet high roofed & covered with tin.

No. 4.   The North wing of twenty one feet front and forty two feet in depth, forming two chambers, and entry with closet; the walls are fourteen feet high above floor, of double frame, lathed and plastered between framed and lathed and plastered outside and inside & covered with cedar shingles. Under No. 3 & 4 is excavated and built as a range of cellars, one room of which under No. 4 with lobby, closet and stair case are floored and finished with plaster.

No. 5.   The Kitchen buildings forming connecting piazza with No. 4 Kitchen, servants apartment, and Summer Kitchen of twenty six feet front on said Road with twelve feet behind No. 4. The piazza is eight feet by thirteen. Kitchen sixteen feet by twenty four feet. Servants apartment twelve by fourteen feet and summer kitchen twelve by twenty feet, the walls of single frame, lathed & plastered outside and inside, heighth above floor of back walls ten feet, front walls sixteen feet high—the whole is under one roof part covered with tin and part with shingles.

No. 6.   The Gothic Archway forming a carriage way of twelve feet wide and eighteen feet deep, a Bath House six feet by ten with covered entry six feet by eight, and a third passage to privy of six by eighteen feet, the walls of brick, eighteen feet high, roofed & covered with tin; thirty feet front and eighteen feet deep.

From No. 4 the buildings gradually fall back to No. 6, from the front, Nos. 2, 3 & 4 being at the distance of about one hundred feet from the road. From No. 6 to the North & West there is another range of buildings connected together & facing back from the front in a similar manner as the before mentioned buildings, but not intended to be covered by this Insurance. They consist of a Privy House, Wood House, Poultry House, and a Stable & Carriage House—are built of frame wood and plastered inside and outside.

It is the understanding by the parties to the Insurance that the Insured may effect other Insurance, either upon the premises insured at this office or the other range of buildings or both ranges. That this building called "the Cottage" is not yet entirely completed, that the insured has the right & privilege to employ workmen to finish the same....

A furnace is now erected under No. 3 for the purpose of warming the rooms above with heated air, and also to introduce heated air or steam into the conservatory by means of tin or iron pipes. The heat to be created by burning Anthracite Coal.

An addendum to the policy, dated 10 Dec. 1839, requests the extension of the policy to several recently erected outbuildings: a green house; "a Frame Paraphet [sic] or wall ... about thirty feet from the south side of the Conservatory"; and a frame building "for Storing ... Agricultural Products, and having an apartment for the use of the Gardener, and a roof for Pidgeons" about 50 feet west of the barn.

PRESENT STATUS:

As Fairbanks observed, the house is still standing, although so altered as to be virtually unrecognizable from the exterior. It has been transformed into an early twentieth century Colonial Revival house, presently sheathed in aluminum and imitation brick. On the interior, however, the spatial divisions and most of the architectural detail of the hall, drawing room and library have been preserved. The building is presently a Roman Catholic convent.

4.

RIVERSIDE
BURLINGTON, NEW JERSEY
1839
Client: Bishop George Washington Doane
Project: residence and grounds

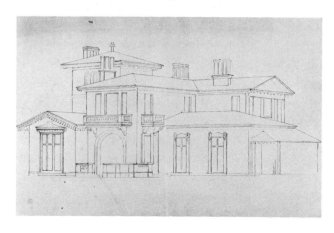

DRAWING 4.1:

Title: none
Signature: J. S.
Date: none
Scale: none indicated (scales approximately ⅛″ : 1′)
Other inscriptions: none
Description: tracing of perspective
Medium: pencil on tracing paper watermarked Whatman/Turkey Mill/1835/London Superfine
Size: 10⅝ x 17⅛ (26.9 x 43.5)
Owner: Henry F. duPont Winterthur Museum, #68 x 198.49

OTHER EARLY ILLUSTRATIONS:

Small watercolor perspective and plan, "Study on Bishop Doane," A. J. Davis Coll. II, #28-12, Avery Library, Columbia University; a general view appears in Collins, John. *Views of the City of Burlington, New Jersey.* Burlington (1847); the plan, perspective, and plan of the grounds are in Downing, A. J. *A Treatise on the Theory and Practice of Landscape Gardening.* New York & London (1841); 2nd ed. New York (1844); 4th ed. New York & London (1849); the Historic American Buildings Survey contains 44 sheets of measured drawings made in 1936 and eleven photographs made in 1936 and 1937, as well as a collection of earlier photographs. Two of the latter are reproduced in Gowans, Alan. *Architecture in New Jersey*. Princeton (1964) and Greiff, Constance M. *Lost America: From the Atlantic to the Mississippi*. Princeton (1971).

DOCUMENTATION:

In addition to Downing: Perpetual Policy #2553, Franklin Fire Insurance Company Records, HSP; Starr, S. *A Word of Self Defense*. Trenton (1850); AB; J; St A

BIBLIOGRAPHICAL REFERENCES:

D: 13; F: 27-30; M: 40-43; S-AA: 12; S-PULC: 118; Lancaster, Clay. "Italianism in American Architecture before 1860." *American Quarterly*, IV, 2 (Summer 1952): 127-48; Meeks, Carroll. "Henry Austin and the Italian Villa." *Art Bulletin* XXX, 2 (1949): 145-49

FOLLOWING THE LEAD of Meeks [146], a date of 1837 has usually been assigned to Riverside. Fairbanks [28], however, points out that "the building must have been finished sometime between 1838 and 1839, for Bishop Doane was issuing statements from St. Mary's parsonage as late as Jan. 1, 1838, whereas in 1839, his publications bore the address 'Riverside.'" This hypothesis can now be confirmed on the basis of the insurance survey, which is dated 8 May 1839.

The drawing owned by Winterthur is a tracing, on the basis of the uneven and tentative quality of the line probably not made by a trained draftsman. The angle of view and size of the drawing, however, are similar to perspective renderings made by Notman for preliminary presentation to owners of other residential projects. [see figs. 47.1 and 59.1] Certainly this drawing cannot have been made after the building was constructed, for it differs in small, but significant, details from what was built. The arched grouped chimney stack on the tower, for example, was replaced by polygonal pots in the actual construction; the pendant motif along the eaves was utilized on the drawing room block as well as that of the library; and the decorated corner blocks were omitted from the French windows. The Winterthur drawing was acquired along with a collection of drawings and other papers connected with A. J. Davis. Jane Davies has suggested that the tracing may have been sent to Davis, who drew the illustration of Riverside for Downing's *Treatise*, and that the initials "J. S." may stand for John [Jay] Smith, the known point of contact between Downing and Notman. [letter to author 2 Jan. 1978] If so, Downing and Davis must have been aware before publication of the changes noted above, since the published drawing of the house shows Riverside as built.

As is the case with Nathan Dunn's Cottage, the best documentation is Notman's own description, provided to Downing for publication:

Riverside Villa, the residence of Bishop Doane, at Burlington, New Jersey, is one of the finest examples of the Italian style in this country. For the drawings from which *figures* 29 and 30 are engraved, and for the following description, we are indebted to the able architect, John Notman, Esq., of Philadelphia from whose designs the whole was constructed.

The site of this villa is upon the east bank of the Delaware river, near the town of Burlington, and within a few rods of the margin of this lower stream. In designing it, the architect was desired to combine something of the character of the cottage and mansion, and to afford ample accommodation for the family and guests. In these he was eminently successful; and the enlightened proprietor pronounces the result, "a model of convenience, with every comfort and elegance desirable in a residence."

In the accompanying plan, *fig.* 30, *a,* is the hall; *b,* the vestibule; *c,* the dining-room; *d,* the library; *e,* the drawing-room; *f,* the parlour; *g,* Bishop D.'s room; *h,* dressing-room; *i,* water-closets; *j,* bath-room; *k,* store-room; *l,* principal stairs; *m,* back stairs; *o,* conservatory; *p,* veranda, etc.

The Delaware, at this part of its course, takes a direction nearly west; and while the river front, (comprising the drawing-room, hall, and library,) commanding the finest water views, which are enjoyed to the greatest advantage in summer, has a cool aspect: the opposite side of the house, including the dining-room, parlour, etc., is the favourite quarter in winter, being fully exposed to the genial influence of the sunbeams during the absence of foliage at that season. From this side of the house, a view is obtained of the pretty suburbs of Burlington, studded with neat cottages and gardens.

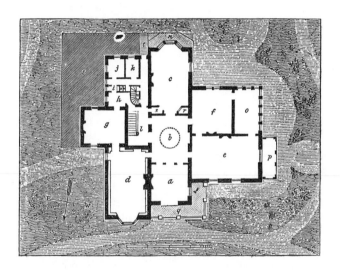

A small terrace with balustrade, which surrounds the hall door, gives importance to this leading feature of the entrance front. The hall, *a,* is 17 feet square: on the right of the arched entrance is a casement window, opening to the floor, occasionally used as a door in winter, when the wind is north. The vestibule *b,* opens from the hall, 17 by 21 feet. In the ceiling of this central apartment is a circular opening, with railing in the second story, forming a gallery above, which communicates with the different chambers, and affords ventilation to the whole house. Over this circular opening is a sky-light in the roof, which, mellowed and softened by a second coloured one below it, serves to light the vestibule. From the vestibule we enter the dining-room, *c,* 17 by 25 feet. The fine vista through the hall, vestibule, and dining-room, 70 feet in length, is here terminated by the bay-window at the extremity of the dining-room, which, through the balcony, opens on the lawn, varied by groups of shrubbery. On the left side of the vestibule, through a wide circular headed opening, we

enter upon the principal stairs, *l*. This opening is balanced by a recess on the opposite side of the vestibule. From the latter, a door also opens into the library, *d,* and another into the drawing-room, *e:* offering, by a window in the library, in a line with these doors, another fine vista in this direction. The library, 18 by 30 feet, and 16 feet high, is fitted up in the most superb and tasteful manner, and completely filled with choice books. The bay-window, seen on the left in the perspective view, *fig.* 29, is a prominent feature in this room, admitting through its coloured panes a pleasing, subdued light, in keeping with the character of the apartment. The drawing-room is 19 by 30 feet, with an enriched panneled ceiling 15 feet high. At the extremity of this apartment, the veranda, *p,* with a charming view, affords an agreeable lounge in summer evenings, cooled by the breeze from the river. From the drawing-room, a glazed door opens to the conservatory, *o,* and another door to the parlour, *f.* The latter is 18 by 20 feet, looking across the lawn and into the conservatory. Among the minor details are a china closet, *r,* and a butler's closet, *s,* in the dining-room; through the latter, the dishes are carried to and from the kitchen, larder, etc. The smaller passage leading from the main staircase, opens to the store-room, *k,* and other apartments already designated, and communicates, by the back stairs, *m,* with the servants' chambers, placed over this part of the house, apart from those in the main body of the edifice. The large kitchen area, *t,* is sunk one story, by which the noise and smells of the kitchen, situated under the dining-room, are entirely excluded from the principal story. In this sunk story, are also a wash-room, scullery, and ample room for cellarage, wine, coals, etc. A forcing-pump supplies the whole house with water from the river; and in the second story are eight principal chambers, averaging 360 square feet each, making in all 25 rooms in the house, of large size.

[Downing: 314-16]

Further detail is provided by the insurance survey. The plan appended to this survey indicates that one major change from the plan supplied to Downing was made on the interior. This was the lengthening of the vestibule at the expense of the hall, the division between the two continuing the line of the north wall of the drawing room.

Survey Made May 8th 1839 and reported to the
Franklin Fire Insurance Company of Philadelphia
For the Right Revd George W Doane
A Brick Dwelling part one story, part two story and a tower three story rough cast. Situate on the Banks of the Delaware in Burlington, Burlington County, New Jersey State. Basement story is divided into a Hall, Drawing room, Parlor, Dining Room, Vestibule, Library, Chamber,

Dressing room, Pantry, Bath House & a large and Small Entry. The Hall has double sliding Circular top panel Doors plain boards front next the River. One Window extending to the floor, Sash Doors and inside panel shutters 8 Lights 18 by 24 glass. Double folding doors leading to the vestibule with side lights 18 by 28 glass and lights over the top, plastered ceiling and block cornice. The Drawing Room has two french windows fronting the River and one South running to the floor each have 8 lights 18 by 24 glass with inside folding panel Shutters. A similar window also next the Conservatory: A fireplace with white marble Mantle, A Panel door communicating with the Vestibule and one also with the Parlor, height of the ceilings in the clear 14½ feet which are panel work with plaster mouldings, floors heart pine. Drawing Room, Vestibule, Dining room, Parlor & Library heated with heaters from the cellar.

The Parlor has one french window opening to the floor with 8 lights 20 by 24 with folding inside shutters & one also 8 lights 15 by 20 with outside Panel Door plain Ceiling and plaster Cornish [sic], one panel door into Vestibule, Door Casings plain Palasters and panel jambs, plain wash boards. A fireplace next the drawing Room, marble mantles and jambs: The Vestibule has a Circular Sky Light and Panel Ceilings with plain mouldings and cornice: Dining room has 3 french windows running to the floor forming 3 sides of an Octagon projecting from the building east, 5 lights high trimmings the same as those already described and one south same as the drawing room. A large closet on each side of the door leading to the vestibule with panel doors and 4 wooden Palasters at each end of the room, plain ceiling and block cornice. A fireplace with marble mantel and jambs, panel work over the octagon windows inside.

Bath House has a wooden bath tub lined with lead and circular lining to shower bath, 2 small diamond sash windows to open and shut, a panel door to a small entry 3 feet wide. Pantry room has shelves closeted with 5 sets of panel doors, one double sash diamond window and a panel door to the 3 feet entry; there is a Privy next to said Entry with two Panel doors; the dressing room between the Chamber and Privy with a double sash diamond window north and a Panel door communicating with a small entry which intersects the Main Entry. The Chamber which is the 1st Story of the Tower has a french window west similar to those of the Parlor and one east with 8 lights 18 by 24 otherwise similar. A panel door leading to dressing room and one leading to Library, plain ceiling and cornice, a fireplace north end with marble mantel and jambs. The Library has Gothic plaster ceiling. Book sash casing whole circuit of the room with small panel doors under, glass 11 by 18 and 14 by 18 generally, finished in the gothic order and oak painted, marble mantle fireplace same style, a double sash front door with single side sash doors projecting from the wall and forming 3 sides of an octagon, diamond glass and painted various colors at top,

having inside folding shutters, a panel door leading to the large Entry, the wall is lined with heart pine boards ploughed and grooved, there is one window north same as in the drawing room, the Library communicates with the Vestibule, Chamber and Entry by Panel doors. The Entry has an open continuous rail stairs to 2nd story, mahogany railing, scroll iron banisters and composition brackets.

2nd story has one room over the pantry and bath house and one over the dressing room. The one over the dressing room has one diamond window, the other 4 ditto. There is a cistern over the Privy and Entry by the bath holding 500 gallons filled from the River by a forcing pump. 2nd story to Tower one room, has one window fronting river and one back, 8 lights each 18 by 20 double frames and hung with weights, fireplace with marble mantle and jambs and iron grates, plain ceiling, one closet under stairs leading to 3rd story in the tower. 3rd story in the Tower (one room) has 3 windows fronting the River, 3 back and 2 north each 8 lights with circular heads, a fireplace with marble mantel and iron grate and one closet with panel door. All the doors are panel work, closed stairs to 3 story of Tower. The well hole over the Vestibule is circular with mahogany railing, iron banisters, sky light, circular glass painted, plain plastered ceiling and cornice. 2nd story over dining in two rooms, the one east has a double sash window south 8 lights glass 18 in sq hung with weights and a double sash, one east extending to the floor with Balustrades outside and inside folding shutters, a fireplace marble mantel and plain ceiling plastered as all the others 2nd story. The other Chamber over the dining room has one window north like the first described in the bathroom; the room over the hall like the first described over the dining room (with a side closet extra). There is a small dressing room between this and the circle round the well hole with one window 8 lights 18 in sq inside shutters, there are Balastrades to both windows to room over the hall supported by consoles. The room over the Parlor has one window east, one south and one west. Same description as the last, and a fireplace the same as the others. There is an entry running east and west through the center buildings and having panel doors communicating with the room plain finish, one closet by the side of the walk round the well hole. There is one window at the head of the stairs fronting the river double frame 8 lights 18 in sq inside shutters. Also one east, 8 lights 18 in sq no shutters. The roof to the Tower is 4 pitch cedar shingle and block cornish [sic], the other parts of the building which is two stories have double pitch cedar shingle roof and block cornice, the wings same kind of roofs with drop cornice.

There is a Conservatory south of the Parlor and east of the Drawing Room frame, glass front and roof and also an ornamental veranda south of drawing room.

Cellar and cellar kitchen under all the building except the Hall, Library and Drawing room finished plain. The building is new and finished in the most modern style and best manner. Earthern octagonal chimney to west.

Robt. Buckman Surveyor

An idea of how the house was furnished and equipped can be gained from an inventory made prior to an auction sale held in 1849, when Bishop Doane was in financial difficulties. Most of the items were bought in by his friends and remained at Riverside during his tenancy. It is interesting to note that the Bishop's room was by far the most lavishly furnished of the chambers.

Furniture, Household Goods, &c. at Riverside

Library
Desks, chairs, sofa, engravings, stands, etc.   70.00
Carpet, rugs, oil-cloth, blinds   18.00
Library, consisting of about 6500 volumes
   and pamphlets   7,000.00

In Hall
Chair, stove, stools, hat stands, oil-cloth,
   picture, rugs   30.00

Inner Hall
Ottomans, sofas, rugs, table, oil-cloths   50.00

Back Parlour
Cabinet, book shelf, sofa, mahogany chairs,
   table and cover, carpet and rug, work stand,
   pictures, looking glass, mantel and table
   ornaments, window curtains, stands, &c.   146.50

Drawing Room
Pictures, sofa, ottomans, chairs, tables,
   centre table and cover, work stand, figure
   and pedestal, clock and mantel ornaments,
   carpet and rug, vases   173.00

Dining Room
Sideboard, clock and mantel ornaments, case
   of drawers, looking glass, dining table,
   side table, chairs, shovel and tongs,
   screen &c., carpet and rug, pictures, dumb
   waiter ·   127.00

Entry and Stairs
Stair carpeting and oil-cloth, blinds   45.00
Oil-cloth and carpeting in entries on
   second floor   20.00

River Chamber
Bedstead and bedding, soft, arm-chair, wind-
   sor chairs, window curtains, bureau, chest
   of drawers, washstand and furniture, stool,
   table and cover, carpet, mantel ornaments,
   pictures, andirons, etc.   95.00

Garden Chamber
Bedstead and bedding, bureau and glass, chairs,
   carpet, table and stool, andirons, etc.,
   prints, window curtains   52.50

Jerusalem Chamber
Bedstead and bedding, bureau and glass, washstands and furniture, wardrobe, carpet,
   chairs, stand, prints   49.00

First Floor Chamber
Bedstead and bedding, looking glass, bureaus,
   steps, tables, chairs, carpet, wardrobe,
   curtains, andirons, etc. washstand, etc.   195.00

Third Floor Chambers
Stair carpet, bedsteads and bedding, carpet,
   wardrobes, blinds, pictures,   61.00
Furniture in servants' chamber,   25.00
Furniture in servants' chamber   15.00

Basement Room
Bookcase, bureau, table, washstands, etc.,
   chairs, carpet, stove   30.00

Nursery
Bedstead and bedding, carpet, washstand, etc.,
   bureaus, chairs   24.00
China $115, household linen $60,   175.00
Plate $300, contents of cellar $150   450.00
Kitchen furniture   30.00
Conservatory and green-house   150.00

[Starr: 26-27]

The library, Riverside, shortly before its demolition.
HABS photograph

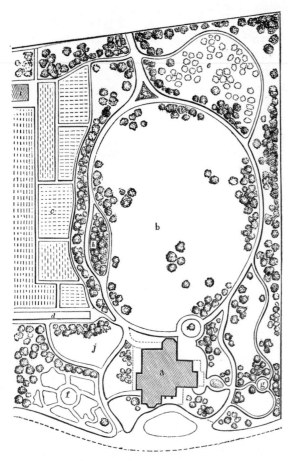

At Riverside Notman was responsible not only for the design of the house, but for "... the grounds, about six or eight acres in extent, laid out from the designs of John Notman, Esq. architect of Philadelphia...." [Downing: 73]

Again Downing published Notman's description of his work.

The house, *a*, stands quite near the bank of the [Delaware] river while one front commands fine water views, and the other looks into the lawn or pleasure grounds, *b*. On one side of the area is the kitchen garden, *c*, separated and concealed by thick evergreens and deciduous trees. At *e*, is a picturesque orchard, in which the fruit trees are planted in groups instead of straight lines, for the sake of effect. Directly under the windows of the drawingroom is the flower garden, *f*; and at *g*, is a seat. The walk around the lawn is also a carriage road, affording entrance and egress from the rear of the grounds, for garden purposes, as well as from the front of the house. At *h*, is situated the ice-house; *d*, hot-beds; *j*, bleaching green; *i*, gardener's house, etc. In the rear of the latter are the stables, which are not shown on the plan.

PRESENT STATUS:
Demolished

5.

ST. LUKE'S CHURCH
PHILADELPHIA
1839
Client: Vestry of St. Luke's Church
Project: design of new church

DRAWINGS: none
DOCUMENTATION:
Minute Book of the Vestry, St. Luke's and the Epiphany Church
BIBLIOGRAPHY:
D: 133; Shoemaker, Mary McCahon. "Thomas Somerville Stewart, Architect and Engineer." Unpublished M. A. thesis, University of Virginia, 1975

IN 1839 the vestry of St. Luke's offered a premium of $100 for the design of a new church. Seven architects replied, five submitting Greek Revival designs, while two, Strickland (presumably William) and Notman, offered Gothic plans. These two were also the most expensive, with estimates ranging from $40,-000 to $46,000. [Minutes: 13] T. S. Stewart's Corinthian offering was selected. Stewart's drawings and related manuscripts are now in the collections of The Athenaeum of Philadelphia.

PRESENT STATUS:
Unexecuted

6.

ASSEMBLY BUILDING

CHESTNUT AND 10TH STREETS, PHILADELPHIA
1839
Client: William Simpson [?]
Project: "Saloons" for assemblies, balls and
other entertainment

DRAWINGS: none
DOCUMENTATION:

> Letter, John Notman to Joseph Cowperthwait, 28 Mar. 1840, Henry F. duPont Winterthur Museum and Library; Philadelphia *Public Ledger*

LITTLE IS KNOWN about the original Assembly Building, but it must have been completed by late in 1839, when the following advertisement appeared.

> WINTER BALLS—attention clubs, etc. intending to give Balls during the ensuing winter are respectfully informed that the GRAND SECOND SALOONS of the ASSEMBLY BUILDING are now in readiness any evening for that purpose.
>
> The Second Saloon is peculiarly adapted for small select parties of 100 or 150 persons, as at a moderate price it combines all the privileges of the Dressing, Refreshment Rooms, etc. of the Grand Saloon. Application to be made at No. 7 Assembly Building to WILLIAM SIMPSON.
> [*Public Ledger*, 18 Nov. 1839: 3]

This building burned in 1852 and was rebuilt to the design of John McArthur, Jr. [*Public Ledger*, 2 Sept. 1852: 2; 26 Aug. 1852: 2; 17 Sept. 1852: 2] All known illustrations are of this second building.

Notman must have participated in construction of the first Assembly Building, although his precise role is unclear. In a letter to Joseph Cowperthwait, Cashier of the Bank of the United States, applying for an extension of a loan, he wrote:

> ... I am compelled to ask your consideration of the acceptance of the enclosed warrant of Attorney to confess judgment by the Proprietors, for $5200, on the Assembly Buildings, corner of Chestnut and Tenth Sts. as a Collateral security. The claim is founded on my Lien as entered, and certified by Thos. I. Wharton and Joseph A. Clay Esquires, as good for the claim, without suit, on 1st November next ... The cost of the building was $42,000. ...

So large a lien as $5200 suggests that Notman was employed in construction of the building as a contractor. Even at the height of his practice he never received more than five per cent of construction costs for architectural services alone.

PRESENT STATUS:
Demolished

7.

ACADEMY OF NATURAL SCIENCES

BROAD AND SANSOM STREETS, PHILADELPHIA
1839–1840
Client: Building Committee of the Academy
Project: design for new building to house library, museum, and meeting rooms

DRAWINGS: none
OTHER EARLY ILLUSTRATIONS:

> A woodcut appears in *The Stranger's Guide in Philadelphia*, Philadelphia (1862); a photograph, made after the addition of the third story, is in Looney, Robert F. *Old Philadelphia in Early Photographs 1839-1914*, New York (1976), 171.

DOCUMENTATION:

> Minutes of the Academy of Natural Sciences of Philadelphia, VI-VII; Report of Committee on Plans 28 Feb. 1837, and Correspondence of William Maclure, Coll. 182, Library of the Academy of Natural Sciences; J

BIBLIOGRAPHICAL REFERENCES:

> D:133; F: 36-37; Smith, Robert C. "John Notman and The Athenaeum Building." *Athenaeum Addresses.* Philadelphia (1951)

EARLY IN 1837, the Academy of Natural Sciences began to consider plans to construct a new hall on the site of their existing building at Twelfth and George [Sansom] Streets. A committee was appointed "to submit a plan for a new building for the Academy together with an estimate of costs...." [Minutes, 7 Feb. 1837]

Evidently several architects were consulted. The Academy owns four drawings signed by Thomas U. Walter, three floor plans and a flank elevation, dated 13 Feb. 1837; two signed by Frederick Graff, showing the plan of two floors, and a flank and facade elevation, dated 20 Feb. 1837; and two labeled S. Webb.

Also in the Academy's collections are ten unsigned drawings, seven plans, two flank elevations and one facade elevation. These were attributed to Notman by Dallett in 1959, an attribution accepted by Fairbanks. For a variety of reasons this seems to be an untenable conclusion. With the exception of some of the plans, notably that of the basement story, the drawings are crude. None has the finesse of Notman's drawings for the Library Company's offices. Nor does the style of the lettering or figures accord with his. Notman's name does not appear in connection with the 1837 competition for the Academy. Yet the drawings in this series are clearly for the site under consideration at that time. One elevation is labeled, in pencil, "yard" at the rear, and "12th St." at the front. The entire series appears to be a re-working of Walter's scheme for a four-story building. One of the flank elevations, in particular, is a sketch copy of Walter's design, with attached columns added and changes in the fenestration indicated. It is probable that these drawings, or at least some of them, were those submitted along with the Report of the Committee on Plans on 28 Feb. 1837. They coincide in dimension with the plans described, a building "92'6" on George Street and Forty three on Twelfth Street, ... to be four stories high (about 58 feet) with the entrance to the Academy in the centre of the front on George St."

William Maclure, president of the Academy, and prospective donor of the building, disapproved of the February plans for a four-story building. [Minutes, 25 July 1837] The committee reported on at least two other

schemes, but none was approved. [Minutes, 30 May and 13 June 1837] Perhaps the deteriorating financial conditions damped the Academy's enthusiasm for construction.

Almost two years to the day after the original committee had been appointed, it was deemed necessary that the Academy "adopt some settled conclusions regarding their new Hall." The directors resolved that the Academy

proceed as soon as practicable to construct a new Hall about 45 by 90 feet with end windows, sky-lights, basement story, galleries etc. according to a plan transmitted to Mr. Maclure & agreed to by him.

A new Building Committee was instructed to have a plan and estimates ready by the next meeting and was authorized to hire an architect or builder. [Minutes, 5 Feb. 1839] It seems evident that the major features of the design had already been determined and the role of the architect would be to flesh out the details and provide the building documents.

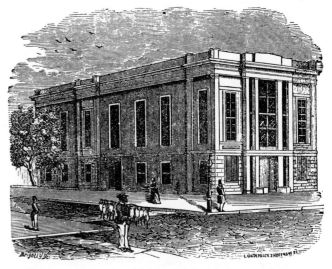

With agreement finally reached, the committee proceeded swiftly. They submitted a plan, which was accepted on 12 Mar. and, on 2 Apr., reported the purchase of a lot at Broad and George Streets. On 25 May the cornerstone was laid. A zinc box, carried by the janitor, followed by the members of the Academy in procession, was taken to the new site and inserted in the cornerstone. The box contained catalogues of the Academy's library and of its members and correspondents, as well as copies of other papers related to its activities, a map of Philadelphia, various newspapers and coins, and a document inscribed with the names of the members of the Building Committee and "Architect, John Notman Esqr." [Minutes, 25 May 1839] It is the first mention of Notman in the Academy's records, indeed the only one, except for a reference shortly before the building's completion to his proposal to construct bookcases. [Minutes, 28 Jan. 1840] The first meeting in the new hall was held on 18 Feb. 1840.

PRESENT STATUS:

Enlarged in 1851-1852 by the construction of an additional story, the building was subsequently demolished.

8.

JOHN NOTMAN HOUSE

1430 SPRUCE STREET, PHILADELPHIA
1839–1840
Client: self
Project: town residence

DRAWINGS: none
DOCUMENTATION:

Philadelphia Deed Book, GS-3: 105; John Notman to Joseph Cowerthwait, 28 Mar. 1840, Henry F. duPont Winterthur Museum and Library

BIBLIOGRAPHICAL REFERENCES:

D: 132

NOTMAN PURCHASED the Spruce Street lot in 1839. Despite the current depression he proceeded to build. In setting forth his temporary financial difficulties to Cowperthwait he wrote, ". . . within a month, I will have a house finished, I own in Spruce St. just West of Broad St. where the claims do not amount near to its value, at the fallen prices for property of this year."

The house became a life-long home for Notman and his wife. An inventory made after her death provides evidence of the building's internal arrangements during the Notman occupancy. [See p. 45]

PRESENT STATUS:

1430 Spruce Street, an undistinguished brick row house, still stands, with an added attic story.

9.

THE ATHENAEUM OF PHILADELPHIA COMPETITION

SIXTH AND WALNUT STREETS, PHILADELPHIA
1840
Client: The Athenaeum of Philadelphia
Project: Library, club rooms, and
rental offices

DRAWING 9.1:
Title: Athenaeum
Signature: John Notman Archt
Date: none
Scale: none indicated (probably scales 1/6": 1')
Other inscriptions: none
Description: rendered perspective
Medium: ink and wash, watercolor
Size: 13⅞ x 19¼ (35.2 x 49)
Owner: The Athenaeum of Philadelphia

DRAWING 9.2:
Title: none
Signature: John Notman Archt. et Delr.
Date: Philada Feb. 4 1840
Scale: none indicated (probably 1/6": 1')
Other inscriptions: North Front
Description: rendered elevation
Medium: ink and wash,
with pencil addition
Size: 16⅜ x 22-3/16 (41.5 x 56.3)
Owner: The Athenaeum of Philadelphia

ATHENÆUM

JOHN NOTMAN ARCH.T

Above: 9.1; *Below*: 9.2

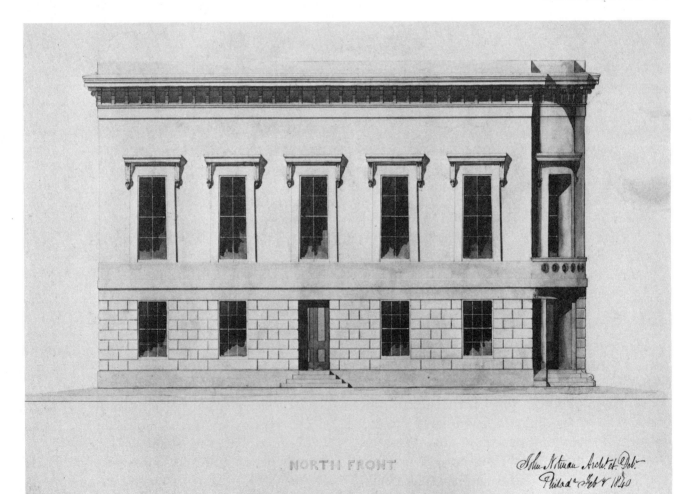

NORTH FRONT

John Notman Archt et Del.
Philada Feb 4 1840

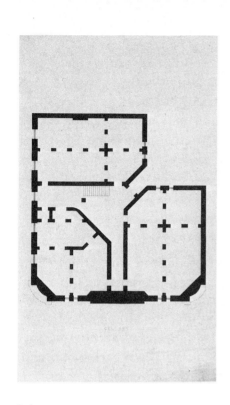

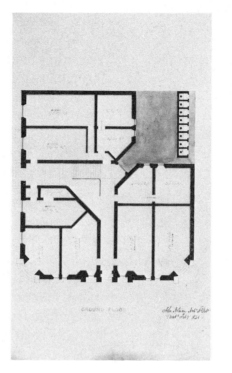

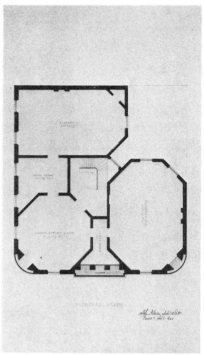

9.4

9.5

9.6

9.3

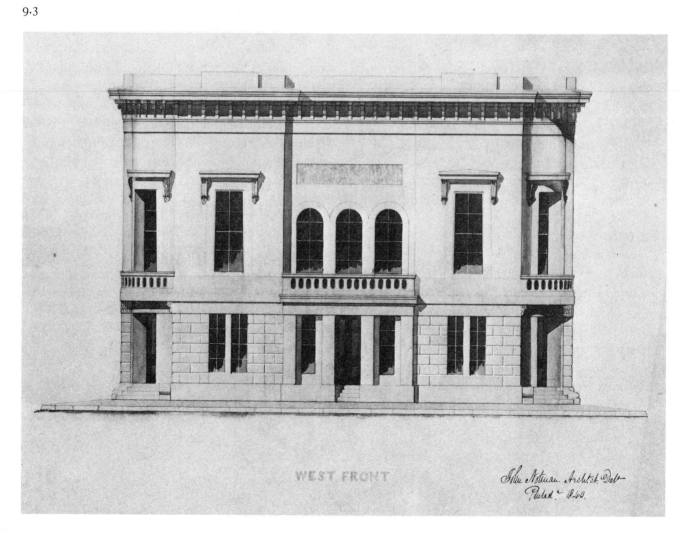

WEST FRONT

DRAWING 9.3:
  Title: none
  Signature: John Notman Archt. et. Delr
  Date: Philada 1840
  Scale: none indicated (probably 1/6": 1')
  Other inscriptions: West Front
  Description: rendered elevation
  Medium: ink and wash
  Size: 16⅜ x 22-7/16 (41.6 x 57)
  Owner: The Athenaeum of Philadelphia

DRAWING 9.4:
  Title: none
  Signature: none
  Date: none
  Scale: none indicated (probably 1/6": 1')
  Other inscriptions: Cellars
  Description: plan
  Medium: ink
  Size: 23⅞ x 18⅞ (60.7 x 47.9)
  Owner: The Athenaeum of Philadelphia

DRAWING 9.5:
  Title: none
  Signature: John Notman Archt et Delr
  Date: Philada Feby 1840
  Scale: none indicated (scales 1/6" : 1')
  Other inscriptions: Ground Floor
  Description: measured plan
  Medium: ink and wash
  Size: 23⅞ x 18-11/16 (60.7 x 47.5)
  Owner: The Athenaeum of Philadelphia

DRAWING 9.6:
  Title: none
  Signature: John Notman Archt. et. Delr
  Date: Philada Feby 1840
  Scale: none indicated (scales 1/6": 1')
  Other inscriptions: Principal Floor
  Description: measured plan
  Medium: ink and wash
  Size: 23⅞ x 18⅞ (60.7 x 47.9)
  Owner: The Athenaeum of Philadelphia

DOCUMENTATION:
  Minutes of the Board of Directors, The Athenaeum of Philadelphia

BIBLIOGRAPHICAL REFERENCES:
  A full discussion of The Athenaeum competition of 1839-40 is contained in Moss, Roger W. *Philadelphia Victorian: the Building of The Athenaeum* (scheduled for publication in 1980). Drawings 9.1-9.6 were unknown to Smith.

IN LATE 1839 the Directors of The Athenaeum, then housed in cramped headquarters in Philosophical Hall on Independence Square, proposed erecting their own building and solicited proposals from Philadelphia architects. Before the year was out William Strickland and Thomas U. Walter had submitted designs.

In February John Notman, newly proposed as a member of The Athenaeum, offered his plans for the Sixth Street site. In contrast to the classical building he was then finishing for the Academy of Natural Sciences, Notman's design for The Athenaeum contained several proto-Italianate features—a heavily rusticated ground floor, a dominating cornice, and triple arched windows behind a balustrade on the Sixth Street front. Within were rental offices on the ground floor and probably on the third floor as well, as had been called for by the building committee. The principal floor was devoted to a series of interlocking octagonal rooms, which were to serve the needs of The Athenaeum.

Probably because of the financial depression, The Athenaeum's board abandoned the idea of constructing a building on the Sixth Street site.

PRESENT STATUS:
  Unexecuted

10.

ATHENAEUM AND
LIBRARY COMPANY
FIFTH AND LIBRARY STREETS, PHILADELPHIA
1840

Client: The Athenaeum of Philadelphia and
the Library Company of Philadelphia

Project: combined facilities for the two institutions, with rental office space

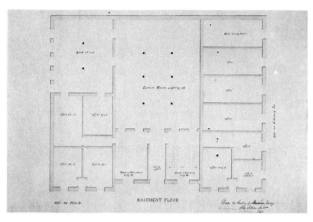

DRAWING 10.1:

Title: Design for Junction of Athenaem
& Library ("Athenaem" has been excised
and the words "Company & The Athenaeum
of Philada" added in another hand.)
Signature: John Notman Archt.
Date: 1840
Scale: none indicated (scales 1/6" : 1')
Other inscriptions: Basement Floor/116 ft
on Fifth St/90 ft on Library St.
Description: measured plan
Medium: ink and wash
Size: 19½ x 26¾ (49.5 x 68)
Owner: The Athenaeum of Philadelphia

DRAWING 10.2:

Title: Design for Junction of Athenaem
[sic] and Library
Signature: John Notman Archt.
Date: 1840
Scale: none indicated (scales 1/6" : 1')
Other inscriptions: Principal Floor
Description: measured floor and ceiling
plan
Medium: ink and wash
Size: 19¾ x 26⅞ (50.5 x 68.2)
Owner: The Athenaeum of Philadelphia

DRAWING 10.3:

Title: Design for Philadelphia Library
and Athenaeum
Signature: John Notman Architect
Date: Philadelphia July 1840
Scale: 1/6" : 1'
Other inscriptions: Plan of Ground Floor/
Fifth St./Library St.
Description: measured plan
Medium: ink and wash
Size: 17¾ x 23-7/16 (45 x 59.9)
Owner: Library Company of Philadelphia

DRAWING 10.4:

Title: Design for Library and Athenaeum
Signature: John Notman Architect
Date: Philadelphia July 1840
Scale: 1/6" : 1'
Other inscriptions: Principal Floor/Ref-
erences to Plan/Library Room The red
tint denotes the Bookcases/the stone tint
denotes the galleries/the blue lines show
the size of dome and of Lantern
Description: plan
Medium: ink and wash
Size: 17-9/16 x 26⅜ (45.3 x 67)
Owner: Library Company of Philadelphia

DOCUMENTATION:

Minutes of the Board of Directors, The
Athenaeum of Philadelphia

BIBLIOGRAPHICAL REFERENCES:

Moss, *Philadelphia Victorian*, discusses the
negotiations from which these drawings re-
sulted. Smith, Robert C. "John Notman
and the Athenaeum Building," *Athenaeum
Addresses*, Philadelphia (1951).

10.2

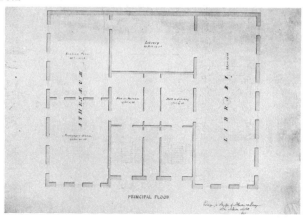

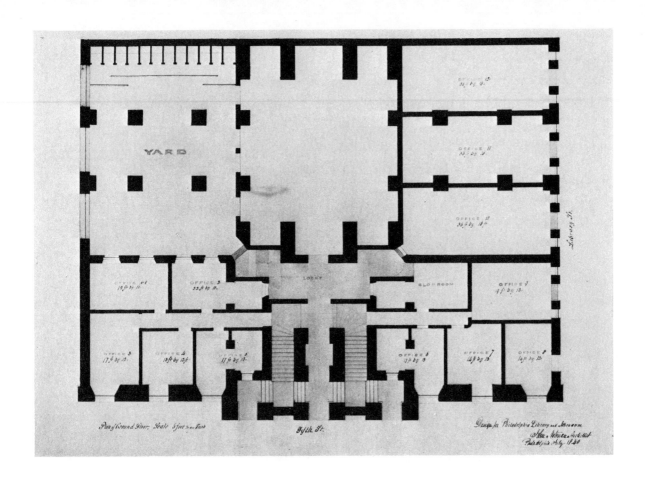

10.3

10.4

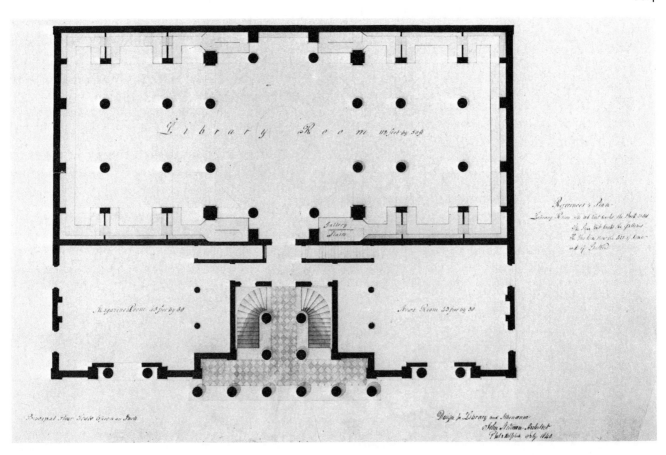

76

HAVING DECIDED not to build on the Sixth Street lot, The Athenaeum evidently entered into discussions with the Library Company of Philadelphia about a new building to house both institutions. The site chosen, as indicated by the drawings, was the one on Fifth and Library Streets already occupied by the Library Company and adjacent to which Notman's small office building had been erected. [see entry 1]

Two sets of drawings, one in possession of each institution, are the only surviving documentation for this project. The set belonging to The Athenaeum is less fully detailed and probably the earlier of the two. It shows eleven offices and a large lecture room, occupying what was evidently conceived as a high basement. Separate entrances and flights of stairs lead to the principal floor. This provides entirely separate spaces for the two institutions, with the exception of a library room at the rear that was presumably to be used by both.

In the Library Company plans the first floor has been raised. Among other considerations, this undoubtedly would have heightened the attractions of the offices for prospective tenants. Several of the offices have been reduced in size, allowing for the addition of a twelfth office and a more commodious lobby for the lecture room. Double, but not separate, flights of steps rise to the principal floor, where a single library and rooms for magazines and newspapers would serve the needs of members of both institutions.

PRESENT STATUS:

Unexecuted

11.

STEPHEN P. MORRIS HOUSE
SOUTHWARK, PHILADELPHIA
1840
Client: Stephen P. Morris
Project: residence

DRAWING 11.1:
Title: House for S. P. Morris
Signature: John Notman
Date: Philada 1840
Scale: 1/6" : 1'
Other inscriptions: Flank Elevation/Front Elevation
Description: measured elevations
Medium: ink
Size: 16⅛ x 23⅝ (41 x 60)
Owner: Historical Society of Pennsylvania (AIA)
Exhibition record: 200 Years of American Architectural Drawing, Cooper-Hewitt Museum, 1977
Publication record: Gebhard, David and Nevins, Deborah. *200 Years of American Architectural Drawings.* New York (1977)

DRAWING 11.2:
Title: No. 1 Front Elevation of S. P. Morris's House/Southwark/No. 2 Principal Floor of S. P. Morris's House
Signature: John Notman Archt.
Date: 1840
Scale: none indicated (scales ⅛" : 1')
Description: rendered elevation and plan
Medium: ink, wash and watercolor
Size: 23-3/16 x 17 (58.9 x 43.2)
Owner: Historical Society of Pennsylvania (AIA)
Exhibition record: 200 Years of American Architectural Drawing, Cooper-Hewitt Museum, 1977
Publication record: Gebhard, David and Nevins, Deborah. *200 Years of American Architectural Drawings.* New York (1977)

11.2

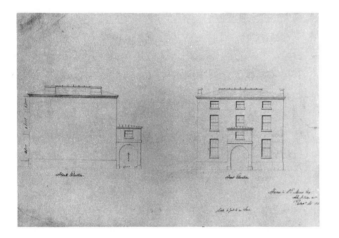

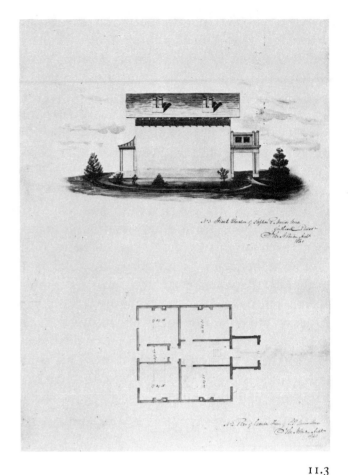

11.3

11.1

DRAWING 11.3:

>*Title:* No. 3 Flank Elevation of Stephen
>P. Morris house/Southwark Philada/No.
>4 Plan of Chamber Floor of S. P. Morris
>House
>*Signature:* John Notman Archt.
>*Date:* 1840
>*Scale:* none indicated (scales ⅛″ : 1′)
>*Other inscriptions:* none
>*Description:* rendered elevation and plan
>*Medium:* ink, wash and watercolor
>*Size:* 23⅜ x 16-7/16 (59.2 x 41.9)
>*Owner:* Historical Society of Pennsylvania
>(AIA)

BIBLIOGRAPHICAL REFERENCES:

>D: 133

STEPHEN P. MORRIS was a partner in the firm
of Morris, Tasker & Morris, which often supplied iron castings and plumbing equipment
for Notman's projects.

PRESENT STATUS:

>It is not known whether this project was
>ever executed.

12.

DESIGN IX, *Cottage Residences*
1841
Client: A. J. Downing
Project: design of small suburban residence

DRAWINGS: none
OTHER EARLY ILLUSTRATIONS:

A perspective and three plans appear in
Downing, A. J. *Cottage Residences.* New
York and London (1842).

DOCUMENTATION:

Letters from A. J. Downing to John Jay
Smith, John Jay Smith Collection, LCP

BIBLIOGRAPHICAL REFERENCES:

F: 32

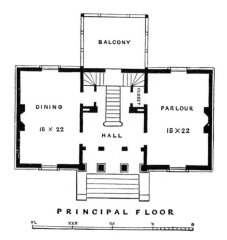

PRINCIPAL FLOOR

IN THE FALL OF 1841 A. J. Downing was in
correspondence with John Jay Smith about
Philadelphia projects that might be suitable
for inclusion in his forthcoming publications.
"I am preparing materials for my little vol.
on 'Model Cottages and Gardens,' to be published in the spring," he wrote on 3 Dec. 1841,
at which point, inserted in the margin, a check
mark and the name "Notman" appear. Certainly Downing and Notman must have been
in communication subsequently, for Downing
informed Smith on 21 Oct. 1842, "I am also
in debt (as a correspondent) to our friend
Mr. Notman who wrote me a very kind letter
which I will soon answer *in extendo.*"

The design Notman furnished was a relatively simple one. Probably he devoted comparatively little time to it. For, unlike his
other work, Design IX is derived with comparatively little change, except the omission
of decorative details, from the house illustrated
as Plates 17-19 in E. W. Trendall's *Original
Designs for Cottages and Villas*, published in
London in 1837.

Downing described the house in a straightforward way, stressing the heating system and
offering suggestions for materials. It also appeared in the four subsequent editions of *Cottage Residences.*

A Cottage in the Italian or Tuscan Style.

The design for this cottage, Fig. 72, has been kindly
sent us for this work by J. Notman, Esq., Architect, of
Philadelphia.

In the plan of the principal story, Fig. 73, there is an
entrance hall with a handsome staircase, and an apartment on either side; that on the right being a parlor, and
that on the left a dining-room. In the piers on either side
of the staircase are spaces which designate hot-air flues,
which proceed from the furnace in the basement, and by
means of registers, warm all the apartments in the house,
although the four principal ones have fire-places besides,
for occasional use if necessary.

The first flight of stairs ascends half the story, and on
a level with the landing here is the broad and airy balcony
in the rear, entered by a fair round-headed window, opening to the floor. Underneath, this balcony forms a kind of
partly enclosed apartment, serving as a wash-room or outer-
kitchen in summer.

There is also a balcony over the recessed porch in front,
which is a pleasant appendage to the chamber floor. This

floor, Fig. 74, affords three pleasant bed-rooms, and there is a fourth of more ample size in the third story of the central portion of the cottage, which is, both with regard to its proportions and the fine bird's-eye view it commands, a very pleasant apartment.

The plan of the basement, Fig. 75, sufficiently explains itself. In the middle of the hall below is the furnace for supplying heated air, and on either side are the kitchen, the store-room, and the fuel cellar.

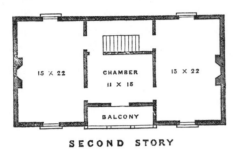

SECOND STORY

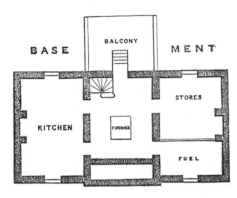

This design, Mr. Notman remarks, might be altered and improved, without any variation of the present form, by elongating the flanks, and adding a suite of rooms in the rear. It may be built of brick and cement, or of wood; and a very simple kind of interior finish would be in the best taste for a cottage of this class. The roof may be covered with tin, zinc, or shingles, and the joints between the roof of the wings and the wall of the central portion should be well protected by broad lead or copper flashings or strips, running up a foot or more on the roof and wall, and being built in the latter in the usual manner.

Estimate.—This cottage, well constructed of solid materials, and neatly finished, would cost $3,000. If built of wood, filled in with brick, the expense might be slightly reduced. The design has been executed in a more elegant and costly manner near Philadelphia.

Although the house built from this design near Philadelphia has not been identified, the Jacob Holt House in Warrenton, North Carolina, is a clapboard version of Design IX, as was the demolished house known as Dunleath in Greensboro, North Carolina.

13.

THE CHINESE COLLECTION
HYDE PARK CORNER, LONDON, ENGLAND
1841–1842
Client: Nathan Dunn
Project: design of museum to house Nathan Dunn's exhibit of sculpture, painting and objects brought back from China.

DRAWINGS: none
OTHER EARLY ILLUSTRATIONS:
The entrance pavilion appears as the frontispiece in [Dunn, Nathan]. *Ten Thousand Chinese Things: A Descriptive Catalogue of the Chinese Collection.* London (1842). It is also shown on a handbill in the Collection of the Haymarket and Other Theatres, Reference Department, Buckingham Palace Road Library, Westminster Public Library. An interior view was published in *The Illustrated London News*, I, 13 (6 Aug. 1842): 204.
DOCUMENTATION:
Notman, John. *Description and Estimate of Design Submitted by John Notman, Architect for the Smithsonian Institution.* Washington (1847); *Old Humphrey's Walks in London and its Neighborhood.* London (n.d.); reports of the opening of the museum appeared in the following London newspapers on 23 June 1842: *Times, Morning Chronicle, Morning Herald, Spectator, Morning Post.*

Entrance, Chinese Collection. *Courtesy PUL*

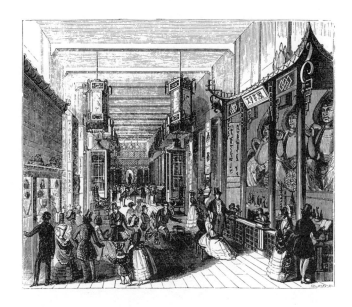

Fancy to yourself, standing by the wayside, within a bow shot of Apsley-house, a showy Chinese pagoda, of two stories, with green roofs, edged with vermilion, and supported by vermilion pillars, bearing on its front a hieroglyphic inscription, signifying "ten thousand Chinese things." [*Walks in London*: 328]

For a period of a few years this "showy" apparition stood in what must have been a rather startling contrast to the classical decorum of the Wellington Arch and Decimus Burton's screen, on a site now covered by the extension of St. George's Hospital. There is little doubt that Notman had a hand in its design, for, as he wrote,

... the lighting of museums properly was a subject of much examination by me some years ago, having to prepare a set of plans of a building for the exhibition of the Chinese Museum Collection, in London, England, when taken there from Philadelphia.
[Notman, *Design ... for the Smithsonian*: 6-7]

Nathan Dunn, the proprietor of the Chinese Collection, was one of Notman's earliest patrons, president of the Laurel Hill Cemetery Company and owner of The Cottage in Mount Holly, New Jersey.

Dunn was a China trade merchant, who had spent a dozen years in the Orient. He returned with materials for a display that must have resembled, in far more extensive form, the depictions of Chinese life still to be seen in the East India Marine Hall at the Peabody Institute in Salem, Massachusetts. The Chinese Collection was shown in Philadelphia from 1838 to 1841, sharing with Peale's Museum a building designed by Isaac Holden at Ninth and George Streets that was known as the Chinese Museum long after the collection had been removed. By 1841 the Chinese Collection was no longer economically successful in Philadelphia. The novelty had worn off and the city was still suffering from the financial depression that followed the panic of 1837.

Dunn offered motives more elevated than mercenary for removing the collection from Philadelphia, where it had been "visited by hundreds of thousands."

The proprietor has been induced to transport it to England at the suggestion of many of the most influential, scientific, and learned persons of the British metropolis and kingdom." [*Catalogue*: viii-ix]

The pagoda was not entirely the invention of either Dunn or Notman. "The exterior of the entrance to the building is in the style of Chinese Architecture, taken from a model of a summer house now in the collection." [*Catalogue*: 11]

Having observed what *The London Illustrated News* termed this "grotesque erection," the visitor could

enter the pagoda by a flight of steps to a vestibule, [which the *Illustrated News* described as "of extreme plainness"] and then ascend a larger flight, after which, pursuing your course along the lobby, you soon find yourself in a goodly apartment of a novel kind, more than two hundred feet long, broad enough and high enough to form a most agreeable promenade. [*Walks in London*: 328]

This apartment was, in fact "...225 feet in length, by 50 in width, with a lofty ceiling, supported by numerous columns; it is principally lit from above, through transparent blinds." [*Illustrated News*: 205]

Notman must have been pleased that the lighting to which he had given "much examination" had been noticed.

PRESENT STATUS:

Burned

14.

SPRING GROVE CEMETERY
CINCINNATI, OHIO
1845
Client: Spring Grove Cemetery Company
Project: overall design of rural cemetery

DRAWINGS: none
DOCUMENTATION:

Cist, Charles. *Sketches and Statistics of Cincinnati in 1851.* Cincinnati (1851); *The Cincinnati Cemetery of Spring Grove. Report for 1857.* Cincinnati (1857); *Spring Grove Cemetery: Its History and Improvements.* Cincinnati (1869)

BIBLIOGRAPHICAL REFERENCES:

M: 61-62; Marion, John Francis. *Famous and Curious Cemeteries.* New York (1977)

IN APRIL 1844 an organizational meeting was held to discuss formation of a rural cemetery in Cincinnati. [*Report for 1857:* 4] By August of 1845 the cemetery, named Spring Grove, was consecrated. [Cist: 147] All sources agree that the original plan was laid out by Notman. Probably Notman did not visit the site, but sent a design from Philadelphia, for his plan failed to suit the terrain. Even in the cemetery's early years

> It has . . . been materially improved; important alterations having been found necessary to adapt it to the surface of the ground. And it may be useful to others engaged in similar undertakings here to remark, that a large outlay might have been saved, with a manifest improvement of the plan, by a reduction of the roads and gravel walks to about one half the number proposed.
>
> [*Report for 1857* : 6-7]

In 1855 Adolph Strauch became superintendent and landscape designer. Within a quarter century after it was planned he had almost succeeded in further remodeling it "in conformity with the simplicity of the present style of improvement." [*Spring Grove*: 1869]

PRESENT STATUS:

So altered as to obliterate Notman's design

15.

NEW JERSEY STATE HOUSE
TRENTON, NEW JERSEY
1845–1846
Client: State House Commissioners
Project: Major addition and alterations to existing State House

DRAWING 15.1:

Title: none
Signature: Drawn by J. Notman (perhaps not in his hand)
Date: 1845
Scale: none indicated
Other inscriptions: (erased but decipherable) as it was in 1794
Description: perspective rendering
Medium: ink, wash and watercolor
Size: 9-7/16 x 13⅜ (23.4 x 33.5)
Owner: Ben Whitmire

DRAWING 15.2:

Title: Front - Elevation - State - House - Trenton/with - Additions
Signature: John Notman Architect/ Philada
Date: 14th April 1845
Scale: ⅛" : 1'
Other inscriptions: none
Description: rendering of elevation
Medium: ink, wash and watercolor
Size: 14¾ x 24-15/16 (37.5 x 63)
Owner: New Jersey Historical Society, 1927. 6.1

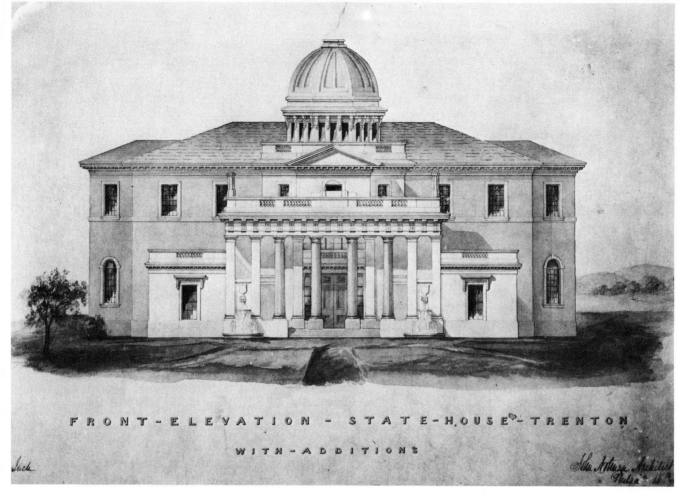

FRONT-ELEVATION - STATE-HOUSE-TRENTON

WITH-ADDITIONS

Above: 15.2; *Below:* 15.3

FLANK-ELEVATION - STATE-HOUSE-TRENTON

WITH-ADDITIONS

DRAWING 15.3:

Title: Flank - Elevation - State House - Trenton/with - Additions

Signature: John Notman Architect/ Philada

Date: 14th April 1845

Scale: ⅛″ : 1′

Other inscriptions: none

Description: rendering of flank elevation

Medium: ink, wash and watercolor

Size: 13-15/16 x 23¼ (37.9 x 59)

Owner: New Jersey Historical Society, 1927. 6.2

Publication record: Frazer, Alan D. "From the Collections." *New Jersey History,* XCIII, 1-2 (Spring-Summer 1975), 58

DRAWING 15.4:

Title: No 1 Additions and Alterations/on State House Trenton, N. J.

Signature: John Notman Architect/ Philada

Date: 28th April 1845

Scale: ⅛″ : 1′

Other inscriptions: Ground Plan

Description: Measured plan of ground floor

Medium: ink

Size: 17-15/16 x 19⅛ (45.6 x 48.6)

Owner: New Jersey Historical Society, 1927. 6.3

15.4

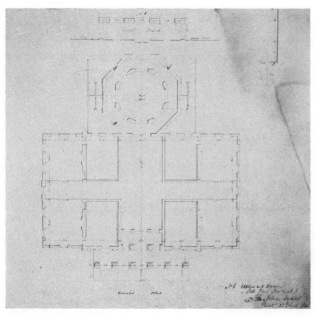

DRAWING 15.5:

Title: No 5 Additions and Alterations/on State House Trenton, N. J.

Signature: John Notman Architect/ Philada

Scale: There is a discrepancy between the scale illustrated on the drawing and the way it actually scales, which is ⅛″ : 1′

Other inscriptions: Elevation of North Front

Description: Facade elevation

Medium: ink

Size: 14¾ x 21-3/16 (37.4 x 53.8)

Owner: New Jersey Historical Society, 1927. 6.4

DRAWING 15.6:

Title: No 6 Additions and Alterations/on State House Trenton, N. J.

Signature: John Notman Architect

Date: 28th April 1845

Scale: none indicated (scales ⅛″ : 1′)

Other inscriptions: South (corrected from North) Elevation

Medium: ink with pencil emendations (some probably not in Notman's hand)

Size: 17 x 21-9/16 (43.2 x 54.8)

Owner: New Jersey Historical Society, 1927. 6.5

Publication record: Frazer, "Collections," 58.

DRAWING 15.7:

Title: No 7 Additions and Alterations/on State House Trenton, N. J.

Signature: John Notman Architect

Date: 28th April 1845

Scale: none indicated (scales ⅛″ : 1′)

Other inscriptions: Section

Description: longitudinal section

Medium: ink with pencil emendations

Size : 15⅞ x 22-15/16 (43.2 x 54.8)

Owner: New Jersey Historical Society, 1927. 6.6

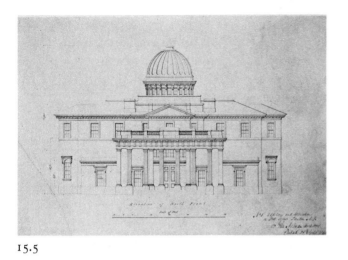

15.5

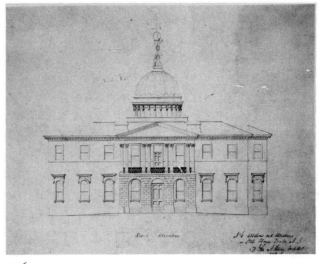

15.6

15.7

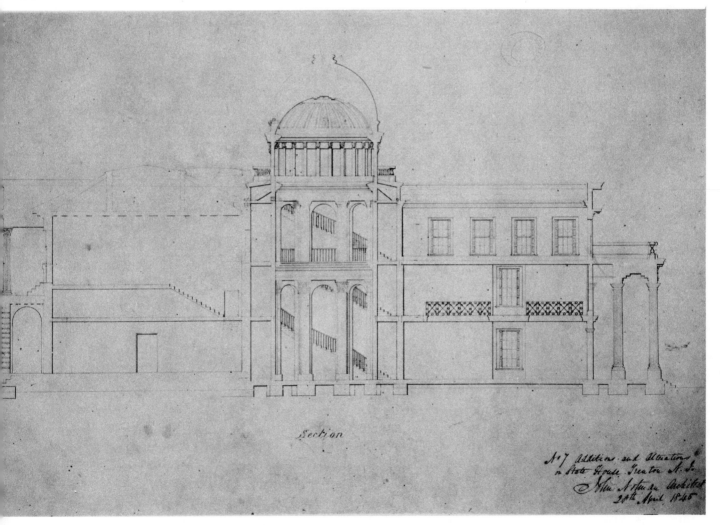

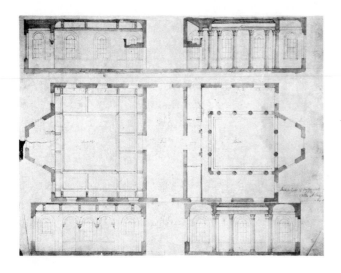

DRAWING 15.8:

Title: Sketch for Halls of Trenton State
H[ouse]
Signature: John Notman
Date: May 25 [th 1845]
Scale: 1″ : 6½–6¾′
Other inscriptions: Longt Section of Senate
Chamber/Transverse Section of Assembly
Room/Transverse Section of Senate/arith-
metic calculations
Description: sections and plans
Medium: ink and wash with pencil
emendations
Size: 17 x 21 (43.2 x 55.8)
Owner: New Jersey Historical Society,
1927. 6.7

OTHER EARLY ILLUSTRATIONS:

"State Capitol of New Jersey at Trenton/
Built 1794/Jonathan Doane Builder," A.
Frey del., T. Sinclair's lith, Phila., pub-
lished c. 1845; "State Capitol of New Jer-
sey at Trenton" (northeast view), and
"State Capitol of New Jersey at Trenton"
(southeast view), J. Notman, Phila. Arch't,
H. Whateley del., T. Sinclair's lith.,
Philada., c. 1845; "Southeast view of State
House/Trenton, N. J./Built 1794—Al-
tered and Enlarged 1845-6," A. Ibbotson,
del., T. Sinclair's lith.; vignettes on "Map
of Mercer County, 1849." Surveyed by J.
W. Otley and J. Keily, vignette signed by
C. Rein, published by Lloyd Vanderveer;
"Map of City of Trenton," lithograph by
Kollner, published by M. Dripps, 1849;

"Map of New Jersey," drawn by J. W.
Steel, published by Gordon and R. E. Hor-
nor, 1850; woodcut, drawing by J. R.
Chapin, engraved by Pierce, *Ballou's Pictorial*, 26 May 1855: 328

DOCUMENTATION:

This is the best documented of Notman's
non-residential commissions. Papers related to the 1845-1846 State House in the
Bureau of Archives and History, New Jersey State Library include: Report of Commissioners to sell State property, build
offices, etc., made to Legislature 16th February 1846; Notman's estimates and specifications; and bills from suppliers. Other
documentation is in *Votes and Proceeding
of the Sixty-Ninth General Assembly of
the State of New Jersey*. Camden (1845);
...*of the Seventieth General Assembly*.
Woodbury (1846). The commissioners' report appears in printed form in the latter.
Also, Trenton *State Gazette; Princeton
Whig*, J, StA.

BIBLIOGRAPHICAL REFERENCES:

F: 38-40; S-PULC: 120; Cohan, Zara. "A
Comprehensive History of the State House
of New Jersey and Recommendations for
its Continuation as a Historic Site." Unpublished M.A. thesis, Newark State College (1969); Hitchcock, Henry-Russell
and Seale, William. *Temples of Democracy*. New York (1976)

BY 1845 it had become apparent that New
Jersey's fifty-year old State House was both
in bad repair and inadequate for the government's needs. On 25 Feb. a committee appointed to study the situation reported that
the building needed a new roof, restuccoing
and other repairs, and that new offices should
be constructed in the yard in front. [*Votes and
Proceedings*, 1845: 481-82] On 2 Apr. a commission was appointed to oversee the necessary
repairs and construction of new facilities. Just
when the idea of separate buildings for offices
was abandoned is not certain, but it was probably after Notman had been retained.

Soon after the passage of the law, the commissioners procured the services of John Notman, Architect, of Philadelphia, to furnish them with plans and estimates for the buildings and repairs. . . . Those plans and estimates were prepared without delay, and the commissioners, after full examination, adopted the plans with some small modifications. [Commissioners' Report]

The commissioners, and Notman, had indeed proceeded with amazing speed. By 14 April Notman had produced a set of drawings, two of which [15.2 and 15.3] survive, showing north and east elevations. Rather than building separate offices, Notman proposed an office wing north of the original State House. The two were to be visually united by an octagonal link surmounted by a dome. The classical effect was to be heightened by a hexastyle Roman Doric portico on the new north front and a portico, also Roman Doric, attached to the old building on the south.

The architect made out complete drawings of the ground plan and upper stories of the new parts of the edifice, which is now erected, and also perspective views of the north and south fronts of the whole structure. [Commissioners' Report]

This must have been the set of drawings, dated 28 Apr., preserved in the New Jersey Historical Society. Numbers 2, 3, and 4 are missing. No. 3, described in section 18 of the specification, was a plan of the third story or of the roofs. Perhaps the other two were the missing perspectives. They were probably turned over to T. Sinclair and are represented by the two lithographs delineated by H. Whately. At the same time Notman may have provided Sinclair with an "existing condition" drawing [15.1], showing the old State House before alteration.

The new set of drawings incorporated the "modifications" discussed with the commissioners and gave Notman another two weeks in which to develop his design. Major differences included the elimination of the lion-spouted fountains on the north front and the substitution of windows for blind openings under the portico. On the south facade the rather weak one-story Doric portico was replaced by a one-story rusticated triple arcade

bearing paired Corinthian columns on the second level and surmounted by a pediment. On both fronts and on the flanks the arched windows of the old building were better integrated into the new design through the device of surmounting them with heavy lintels supported on consoles. The most significant change was to the dome. Raised higher on the roof and more richly paneled, it performed more effectively to unite visually the old and new construction.

The plans and elevations of the remodeled State House as proposed by the architect, Mr. Notman of Philadelphia, are now in the office of the Treasurer . . . We can add our testimony to that of all who have examined the drawings, as to the beauty of the design, and the admirable arrangement of the offices for public convenience. [*Trenton Sheet Anchor*, reprinted in *Whig*, 9 May 1845]

The dissenting note came from Princeton. "The Trentonians seem pleased with the plan adopted, but we cannot admire their taste. We think a better plan was handed in from Princeton." [*Whig*, 9 May 1845] (This plan was probably submitted by Charles Steadman, who had designed the Mercer County Court House, erected in 1839.)

Along with the revised plans, Notman presented full specifications. [Commissioners' Report] They are written in Notman's hand and, along with the contract, cover 22 pages of legal-size paper. As the excerpts below demonstrate, these amplify the information provided in the drawings, especially in regard to the appearance of the building's interior, and indicate what further drawings were to be provided to the contractors. The numbers indicate sections of the specification, which is unpaged.

. . . the part under the octagon to be dug out as a cellar to the clear depth of eight feet. [2]

The cellar walls are to be of stone, two feet thick under the octagon, two feet thick under each of the fire proofs and eighteen inches under the other walls. . . . [3]

The basement . . . shall be faced with hammer dressed stone, . . . the upper course to be tooled on the face and weather wash, set straight and where windows are in the elevation, this course will be as the sill, . . . a course of stone nine inches high of smooth tooled work will be set in the interior of the hall and octagon as the walls are built, at the highth [sic] of and to be as the washboard of the north hall and lateral passages, the octagon, rotunda and stairs.... [4]

The specifications continue by setting forth dimensions of the walls, to be of brick above the stone base, and calling for a slate roof over the main part of the north extension and tin roofs on the lower wings. Specifying wooden floors for most of the building, it provides that

The floors of the halls of entrance, the Portico, the South Porch and the lateral passages to the offices are to be laid with brown German square flags laid diamond ways.... The floors of the fireproofs to be laid with best paving brick.... [11]

Specifications follow for the flooring of the second floor and roof of the one-story offices.

The hall on the level of this [second] floor will be framed in the joisting, leaving two open spaces to the ground floor as shown in plan [— ?] These spaces will be finished by the thickness of the floor as shown in section, and surrounded by a cast iron balustrade with handrail of black walnut.... [14]

The framing for the roofs of the second story is then described. The joists are to form nailing faces for the cornice, in a manner "to be more fully shewn by working drawings in full sizes." [16] The flooring and roofing systems for the third floor are then described. "The third story which rises up on the side walls of the hall shall be one room devoted to the purposes of a Library, ..." [17]

The octagon is paved on the first floor; from this a stair of 30 risers, stone steps built into the wall and notched one to each preceding one, forming, except at the piers, what is called a hanging stair, leads to a landing over the present north door of State House at the hight [sic] of 15 feet from the first floor, from this landing a level galery [sic] leads around the rotunda, to the level of second floor offices, and from it, the landing, a flight of steps leads to the level of the second floor of the present State house; from the level of the above galery and over the first stair, a second stair of wood steps leads to the level of the library floor connected by a gallery between the rotunda and octagon as before, and a third stair over the others rises to the level of the raising floor of present roof, and by a flight of steps to the leads of the Balustrades surrounding the dome lights, from thence to the flats over the main roof as

seen on No 3 plan.... [18] The interior of the rotunda to be finished in antae or pilasters formed of brick plastered supporting a second order or entresol of pilasters which again is surmounted by the windows of the dome finished as shown in section with a pendentive ceiling under the dome.... [19] N.B. The piers of the rotunda will have arches turned between them at two stages in the lines of the interior octagon. [20]

Construction details for the dome are then described. Its exterior "will be covered with tin to be painted lead color." [20]

Descriptions of doors and windows follow. Of particular interest are the arrangements for the fireproof storage areas.

... inside of the wood door to the fireproofs, and to each of them, will be provided a complete set of double fireproof doors with proper iron frame and stone lintel and sill, ... the windows of all the fireproofs will also be provided with complete well fitted sets of Iron inside shutters, hung to an iron frame to be built inside of the wood frame with 4½ inch brick wall between the frames, each window to have a dressed stone sill of one stone and a dressed stone lintel, the thickness of the wall in width from the wood frame inwards, the fire proofs to be built with an air chamber completely around them opening to the external air. Full sized drawings of these detail [sic] will be provided in strict accordance with this specification. [23]

The eight rooms used as offices will each have a black marble mantle [sic] costing not exceeding thirty dollars, pattern to be chosen by the commissioners. The Library will have two such mantels. [25]

... The galleries and stairs (in the octagon) are to be provided with an Iron balustrade or bannisters with black walnut hand rail.... [26]

Following an added note on the joist framing of the second floor hall, another note appears:

N.B. It is also to be observed that there will be in addition to the stairs marked on the plans, a flight of steps from the second floor of main house to the level of the library or third floor of new house.... [29]

Further description of detailing and hardware of doors and windows follows, along with the requirement that interior woodwork is to be painted with three coats of white lead and linseed oil.

The portico on the north front will be arranged as drawn on plan No 1, the bases of the columns will be of cast iron placed on the stone plinths above mentioned, the shafts will be of brick so built as best to suit the plastering of the flutes, the capitals to be of cast Iron or Stone in one piece and the entablatures over the columns will be of brick arched between the columns on iron band strips, for which hoop Iron of size 2 inches wide 3/16 thick will be sufficient, the band of architrave will be of wood also the triglyphs, mutules and cornice, ... full size detail drawings will be furnished for all these cornices. ... [36]

The south porch having two stories in hight [sic] will have a basement of open arches, the piers to be of brown stone finished in rustic manner to the drawings; the superstructure will consist of eight columns set in pairs supporting a pediment the cornice of which will range with that of the main house ... the columns will be built of wood and the pediment of framing. ... [38]

Evidently, however, a change in plans was made while the specifications were in the course of preparation.

Instead of the south portico Basement being of stone it will be of brick built so as to be rough cast to imitate the rustic work as in the drawings, the steps, and base as high as the steps, to be of stone Fine tooled and the string course at the level of the second floor of the portico, this course to be ... worked around the plinths of the columns, which plinths are to be of stone. ... [51]

The upper floor of this portico, will be covered with asphaltum on boards. ... [52]

The plastering inside the rooms is to be 3 coat plastering finished white, the hall, passages and rotunda with octagon are to be of hard finished rough cast plastering, finished with the trowel after the float, and is to be lined out in imitation of stone courses, and afterwards tinted a stone colour; there will be 3 plaster cornices in the hight [sic] of the rotunda ornamented with dentils and castings, there will be a cornice of 15 inches girth in each of the offices, a cornice of 18 inches girth in the Library and each story of the hall and the upper ceiling of the hall will be divided into pannels with a moulding round each. [42]

Further information about interior details is interspersed with instructions for the exterior. For outside plastering existing work and new construction were to be handled "in the same style, the surface will be lined in imitation of stone courses and afterwards tinted a stone colour...." [43] The exterior of the octagon is described in some detail, along with the privies to be put up in the fenced yards adjacent to it. Embellishment of the octagon included "3 blank pannels shown in the walls of each side of the octagon with stone sills as seen in the flank elevation of first sketch for these improvements." [60]

Attention was also paid to alterations to the existing building. The stairs were to be removed, some windows altered, and openings made to communicate with the new construction. Of great importance were those changes that would integrate the old State House into the new design. The most significant alteration was to the roof, which was lowered in order to provide a proper pitch for a metal covering and also so that it would not challenge the dominance of the dome.

The roof of the old or main house to be stripped of the shingles & lath, and the principal rafters are to have an additional collar beam let in over the present one, taking the pressure off the upper main rafter when cut off over the Queen posts, an iron strap of size of those on other parts of the roof to be brought over the upper end of the rafter end and firmly keyed and bolted to and at each Queen post; these straps should also take hold of the collar beam introduced or another similar strap be put over the collar beam and fastened as the first; a stretching beam to be put in at the head of the Queen posts between each pair of rafters of size 6 by 10 inch and half rafters framed to the posts of each end main rafters so as to hip the roof at each end, the principal rafters will be cut off over at the top of the second collar beam, and the whole peak to that hight [sic] taken off the roof and a flat for metal covering will be made by framing joists (3 in. thick 10 in. deep 18 inches from centre to centre) into the upper collar beam, from the edge of the flat to the eaves the pitch will be altered by raising up the lower end of the small rafters about from 18 inches to 2 feet, then close board the whole roof over for slating, thus the whole cornice will be taken down and such parts of it as suits the remodelling will be used again; the roofs of the semi-hexagon projection will be reformed for slates. [39]

Additions of exterior trim also served to bring the old building into conformity with the new work.

The contractor will also furnish and put up a string course of plank to be fastened to and on a level with the window sills of the second story of the old house, and to be carried all around the old house from the pilasters of the portico south on one side, to the octagon on the other, each end to be the same, this will appear as a belt course of stone 12 inches two inches thick with a weather level on its upper edge and a deep groove on the lower, it must be well fastened to the wall between each of the windows and put up before rough casting and afterwards a moulding of wood will be put up under it, hiding the joint and after shrinking. [61]

The contractor will also provide and put up cornice heads supported on ornamental brackets over each of the windows in the lower story of old house, as shown in drawings, these heads will be put up before rough casting and will be covered completely on the top with tin, which will be as fast as possible. [62]

The specifications are followed by the contract, which requires approval of all work by the architect; a completion date of 20 Sept. for the exterior and of 15 Dec. for the entire project (with penalties); and a price of $23,250.

This contract had been let to the low bidders: Joseph Whitaker, William Phillips, James A. Howell and Edward Page. Acting again with incredible celerity, "The next day after the contract was made the Architect laid out, for the contractors the foundations of the new buildings, and the latter immediately broke ground." [Commissioners' Report] Furthermore, the contractors came close to meeting their deadlines. On 12 Nov., the Trenton *State Gazette* reported that, "Yesterday the finishing hand was put to the dome of the State House."

With the major part of the work completed, the commissioners resolved to go further.

If time had permitted they would have replaistered and refitted the Assembly room, the Senate Chamber and the Supreme Court room so as to make them uniform with the other parts of the building.   [Commissioners' Report]

On 25 May 1846 Notman submitted drawings for these alterations, of which one survives. [Fig. 5.8] Howell & Page bid $1250 on 27 July "to finish Supreme Court, Assembly & Senate Rooms in N. J. State House according to plans given by J. Notman Architect," but the bid of $1200 from James Allen & Son was accepted.

PRESENT STATUS:
The New Jersey State Capitol was enlarged subsequently several times after 1846 and was substantially rebuilt after a major fire damaged it severely in 1885. Virtually nothing remains of Notman's work except the cellar of the rotunda, and the roof alterations and some of the altered windows of the west wing of the 1794 building, which survived the fire.

16.

THE ATHENAEUM OF PHILADELPHIA

SIXTH AND ADELPHI STREETS, PHILADELPHIA
1845–1847
Client: The Athenaeum
Project: Library, reading rooms and rental offices

DRAWING 16.1:
Title: Plans & Elevations for Hall of Athenaeum
Signature: John Notman Architect
Date: Philadelphia—12th April 1845
Scale: none indicated (scales 1/10″ : 1′)
Other inscriptions: Flank-Elevation— No. 1/Adelphi-Street; Front-Elevation— No. 1/Washington-Square/Ground Floor; Principal Floor
Description: rendered elevations and measured plans; marginal sketch of beams with brick arch in section
Medium: ink, wash and watercolor
Size: 19½ x 28⅞ (49.6 x 73.3)
Owner: The Athenaeum of Philadelphia

DRAWING 16.2:
Title: Plans & Elevations for Hall of Athenaeum No. 2
Signature: John Notman Architect Philada
Date: 12th April 1845
Scale: none indicated (scales 1/10″ : 1′)
Other inscriptions: Flank-Elevation—No. II/Adelphi-Street; Front Elevation—No. II/Washington-Square/Ground-Floor; Principal-Floor
Description: rendered elevations and measured plans
Medium: ink, wash and watercolor
Size: 19⅜ x 28-5/16 (49.2 x 71.9)
Owner: The Athenaeum of Philadelphia

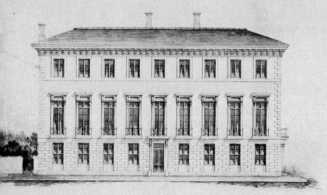

FLANK-ELEVATION-N°1

ADELPHI-STREET

FRONT-ELEVATION-N°1

WASHINGTON-SQUARE

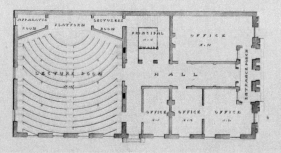

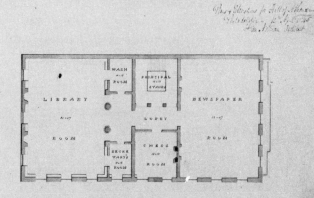

GROUND FLOOR

PRINCIPAL FLOOR

Above: 16.1; *Below*: 16.2

FLANK-ELEVATION-N°II

ADELPHI-STREET

FRONT-ELEVATION-N°II

WASHINGTON-SQUARE

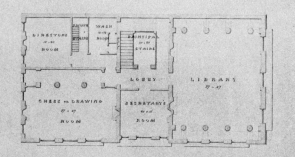

GROUND-FLOOR

PRINCIPAL-FLOOR

DRAWING 16.3:
> *Signature:* none
> *Date:* none
> *Scale:* none indicated
> *Other inscriptions:* none
> *Description:* perspective rendering
> *Medium:* ink, wash and watercolor
> *Size:* 11¾ x 20¾ (29.8 x 52.8)
> *Owner:* The Athenaeum of Philadelphia
> *Exhibition record:* Philadelphia: Three Centuries of American Art, Philadelphia Museum of Art, 1976
> *Publication Record: Philadelphia: Three Centuries of American Art,* Philadelphia (1976)

DRAWING 16.4:
> *Title:* No. 3 Plan of Athenaeum Philada
> *Signature:* John Notman Archt
> *Date:* 7th May 1845
> *Scale:* none indicated (scales ⅛″ : 1′)
> *Other inscriptions:* 1st story
> *Description:* measured plan
> *Medium:* ink and wash
> *Size:* 9¾ x 16-5/16 (24.8 x 41.4)
> *Owner:* The Athenaeum of Philadelphia

DRAWING 16.5:
> *Signature:* none
> *Date:* none
> *Scale:* ⅛″ : 1′
> *Other inscriptions:* none
> *Description:* plan of lecture hall
> *Medium:* ink and wash
> *Size:* 12⅞ x 16¼ (30.2 x 41.3)
> *Owner:* Historical Society of Pennsylvania (AIA), X-R-18

DRAWING 16.6:
> *Title:* Athenaeum, Philadelphia
> *Signature:* J. Notman Archt.
> *Date:* none
> *Scale:* none indicated
> *Other inscriptions:* none
> *Description:* perspective rendering
> *Medium:* ink and wash
> *Size:* 10⅜ x 14¾ (26.4 x 37.5)
> *Owner:* Historical Society of Pennsylvania

DRAWING 16.7:
> *Title:* Athenaeum, Philadelphia
> *Signature:* John Notman Architect
> *Date:* None
> *Scale:* 1/10″ : 1′
> *Other inscriptions:* Longitudinal Section No. IV/Flank Elevation
> *Description:* measured section and elevation
> *Medium:* ink
> *Size:* 24 x 18 (60.9 x 45.7)
> *Owner:* The Athenaeum of Philadelphia

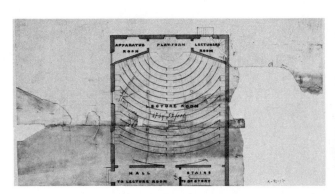

16.5

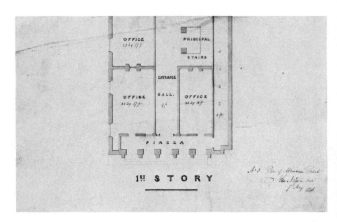

16.4

Above: 16.3; *Below*: 16.6

ATHENÆUM PHILADELPHIA   J. NOTMAN ARCHT

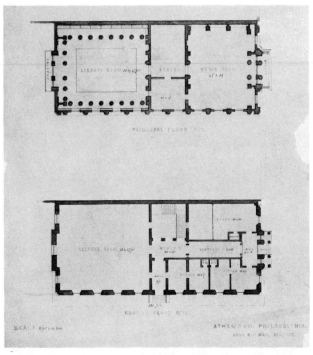

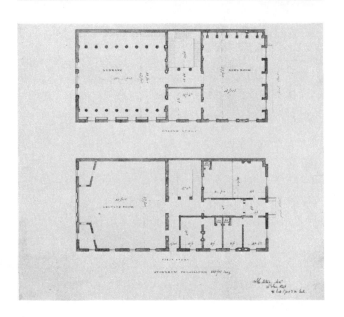

DRAWING 16.8:
  Title: Athenaeum, Philadelphia
  Signature: John Notman, Architect
  Date: none
  Scale: 1/10″ : 1′
  Other inscriptions: Principal Floor No.
  IV/Ground Floor No. IV
  Description: measured plans
  Medium: ink and wash
  Size: 24 x 17-15/16 (60.9 x 45.6)
  Owner: The Athenaeum of Philadelphia

DRAWING 16.9:
  Title: none
  Date: none
  Scale: none indicated
  Other inscriptions: none
  Description: perspective rendering
  Medium: ink, wash and watercolor
  Size: 7⅛ x 10-3/16 (18.1 x 25.9)
  Owner: The Athenaeum of Philadelphia
  Exhibition record: Philadelphia: Three
  Centuries of American Art, Philadelphia
  Museum of Art, 1976
  *Publication record: Philadelphia: Three
  Centuries of American Art,* Philadelphia
  (1976)

DRAWING 16.10:
  Title: Athenaeum Philadelphia 110
  feet long
  Signature: John Notman Archt
  Date: 26th June 1845
  Scale: ⅛″ : 1′
  Other inscriptions: Second Story/First
  Story/ Sixth Street/Sixth Street
  Description: measured plans
  Medium: ink and wash
  Size: 20⅞ x 21-15/16 (51.8 x 55.7)
  Owner: The Athenaeum of Philadelphia

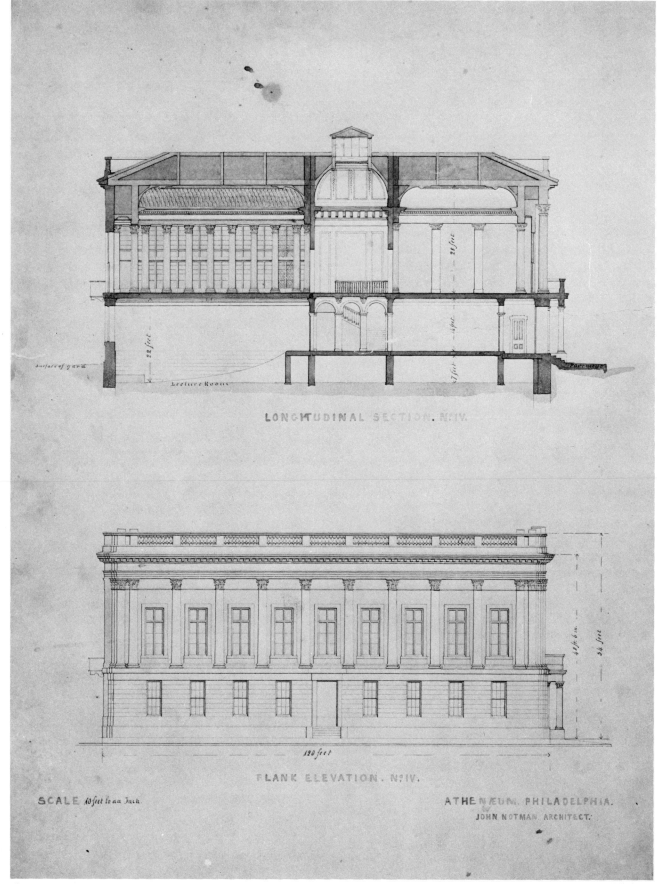

LONGITUDINAL SECTION. Nº IV.

FLANK ELEVATION. Nº IV.

SCALE 10 feet to an Inch.

ATHENÆUM, PHILADELPHIA.
JOHN NOTMAN ARCHITECT.

16.7

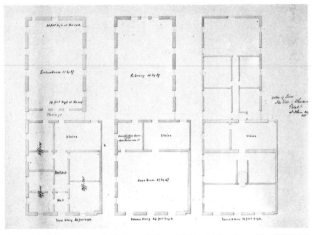

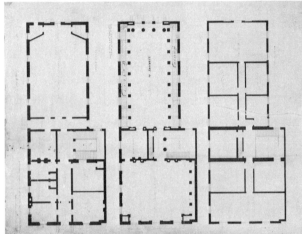

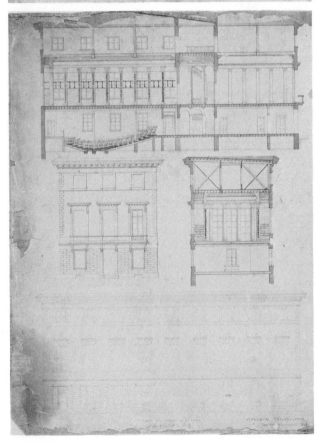

DRAWING 16.11:
  Title: Outline of Stories/New Hall of Athenaeum/Philada
  Signature: J Notman Archt
  Date: 1845
  Scale: none indicated (scales ⅛″ : 1′)
  Other inscriptions: First Story 14 feet high; Second Story 24 feet high; Third Story 14 feet high
  Description: rough plans
  Medium: ink on cardboard
  Size: 19½ x 25-15/16 (49.5 x 65.9)
  Owner: The Athenaeum of Philadelphia

DRAWING 16.12:
  Title: Outline Plans of Athenaeum, Philadelphia
  Signature: John Notman, Architect
  Date: 1845
  Scale: ⅛″ : 1′
  Other inscriptions: Third Story/Second Story/First Story/125 Feet on Adelphi Street/50 Feet on Sixth Street
  Description: measured plans
  Medium: ink and wash, with pencil emendations
  Size: 24⅞ x 18⅞ (63.2 x 47.9)
  Owner: The Athenaeum of Philadelphia

DRAWING 16.13:
  Title: Athenaeum Philadelphia
  Signature: John Notman, Architect
  Date: 1845
  Scale: ⅛″ : 1′
  Other inscriptions: Outline Longitudinal Section/Elevation of Front Outline/Transverse Section Outline/Flank Elevation in Outline
  Description: elevations and sections
  Medium: ink and wash
  Size: 24⅞ x 18-7/16 (63.2 x 47.2)
  Owner: The Athenaeum of Philadelphia
  Exhibition record: Two Centuries of Philadelphia Architectural Drawings, Philadelphia Museum of Art, 1964

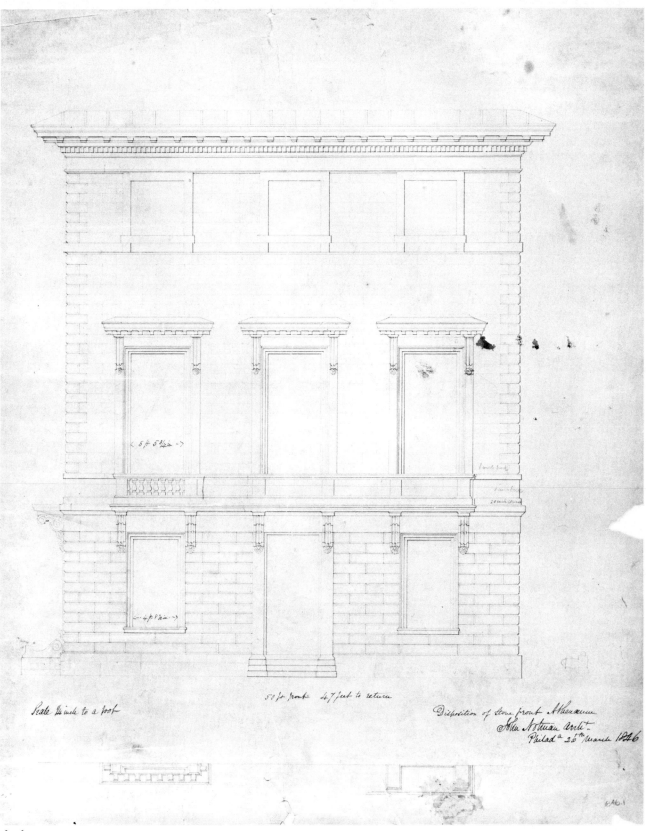

Scale ¼ inch to a foot

50 ft front   47 feet to return

Disposition of Stone front Athenæum
John Notman artt
Philada 26th March 1846

16.16

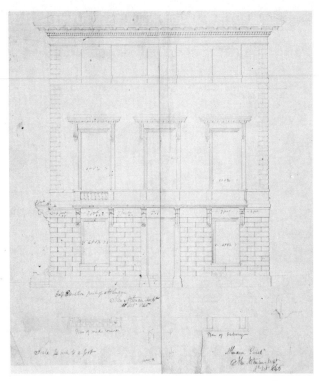

16.14-15

DRAWING 16.14:
> *Title:* Half Elevation front of Athenaeum
> *Signature:* John Notman Archt
> *Date:* 18th Oct 1845
> *Scale:* ¼" : 1'
> *Other inscriptions:* plan of wind. cornice; mathematical calculations on back of drawing
> *Description:* working elevation and partial plan; part of drawing 16.15, from which it has been cut
> *Medium:* ink
> *Size:* 18½ x 8¼ (47 x 29.9)
> *Owner:* The Athenaeum of Philadelphia

DRAWING 16.15:
> *Title:* Athenaeum Philada
> *Signature:* John Notman Archt
> *Date:* 18th Oct 1845
> *Scale:* none indicated (scales ⅛" : 1')
> *Other inscriptions:* plan of balcony
> *Description:* working elevation and partial plan; drawing 16.14 has been cut from this sheet
> *Medium:* ink with pencil emendations
> *Size:* 22 x 8-15/16 (55.9 x 22.7)
> *Owner:* The Athenaeum of Philadelphia

DRAWING 16.16:
> *Title:* Disposition of Stone Front Athenaeum
> *Signature:* John Notman Archt
> *Date:* Philada 25th March 1846
> *Scale:* ¼" : 1'
> *Other inscriptions:* 50 feet front 47 feet to return/Athenaeum; notes on measurements on back
> *Description:* working drawing of facade elevation and partial plans
> *Medium:* ink, with pencil emendations
> *Size:* 21⅞ x 17⅞ (55.5 x 45.4)
> *Owner:* The Athenaeum of Philadelphia

OTHER EARLY ILLUSTRATIONS:

A lithograph, drawn by P. A. Nicholson after drawing 16.9, was published by T. Sinclair in 1847. It appeared as the frontispiece of the *Thirty-Second Annual Report of The Athenaeum of Philadelphia*, Philadelphia (1847); *Address Delivered at the Opening of the New Hall of the Athenaeum of Philadelphia on Monday, October 18th, 1847, by Thomas I. Wharton*; and *Address Before the Historical Society of Pennsylvania 28th January, 1848, on the Occasion of Opening the Hall in the Athenaeum by William B. Reed*, Philadelphia (1848). A similar view is reproduced in Tuthill, L. C. *History of Architecture from the Earliest Times*, Philadelphia (1848). Variants of a view drawn by Nicholson B. Devereaux were published in Jones, A. D. *Illustrated American Biography*, New York (1853); *Gleason's Pictorial Drawing-Room Companion*, 5 Aug. 1854; and *The Stranger's Guide in Philadelphia*, Philadelphia (1862).

DOCUMENTATION:

Minutes of the Board of Directors and letters from John Notman to the Building Committee, The Athenaeum of Philadelphia; Philadelphia *Public Ledger*; J

BIBLIOGRAPHICAL REFERENCES:

D: 132; F: 38; S-PULC, 19; Dallett, Francis James. *An Architectural View of Washington Square*, Philadelphia (1968); Moss, Roger W. "The Athenaeum of Philadelphia." *Nineteenth Century*, I, 1 (Winter 1975: 16-17); *Antiques* (December, 1978), CXIV, 1264-1279; *Philadelphia Victorian: The Building of The Athenaeum* (scheduled for publication in 1980); Smith, Robert C. "John Notman and the Athenaeum Building." *Athenaeum Addresses*. Philadelphia (1951); Kennedy, Arthur M. "The Athenaeum: Some Account of Its History from 1814 to 1850." *Transactions of the American Philosophical Society*, XLIII (1953): 260-265; T; W

THE ATHENAEUM'S failure to construct a hall in 1840 did not signify that the desire for a new building had been abandoned. Rather it seems to have been a prudent postponement attributable to uncertain economic conditions. With financial recovery underway in the early 1840s, the board appointed a committee to choose a site. Although documentation for the earlier of The Athenaeum's efforts is sparse, the 1845-1847 building campaign is among the most fully documented of mid-nineteenth century building projects. It is recounted in full detail in Moss, *Philadelphia Victorian*.

In early 1845 purchase of a lot at the corner of Sixth and Adelphi [now St. James] Streets was authorized. [Minutes, 23 Feb. 1845] The committee evidently again solicited designs from several architects; from the surviving drawings and the committee's report it is known that at least four submissions were received: from Richard A. Gilpin, John Haviland, Napoleon LeBrun, and John Notman.

Notman was, of course, already familiar with The Athenaeum through his participation in the abortive 1839-1840 deliberations. [see entries 9 and 10.] On 12 Apr. 1845, he submitted two alternative drawings, both showing flank and front elevations as well as plans. The first [fig. 16.1], with its principal entrance on Sixth Street, proposes the use of half of the first floor as rental offices. The second [fig. 16.2] devotes all the interior space of both ground and principal floors to the institution's purposes. Both show a third story, presumably for rental, in elevation, although plans for this floor are not provided. The exteriors are similar, despite some differences in emphasis and detailing. Both were conceived in the style of an Italianate palazzo with heavily rusticated basement story and quoins, powerful cornices, and windows with projecting heads resting on consoles lighting the *piano nobile*. These designs were undoubtedly among "the several" submitted to the board without a recommendation. A new Special Building Committee was appointed to pursue the matter. The board requested that the committee seek plans for a building 50 feet on

Sixth Street by 120 on Adelphi. [Minutes, 21 Apr. 1845]

The original committee, although indecisive, had preferred the designs of Gilpin, Le-Brun, and Notman, and these architects continued to submit alternative schemes. On 7 May 1845, Notman provided a third design [figs. 16.3-16.5]. Only a perspective and the plan of the first floor survive, and, strangely, the latter has been split, with the front portion preserved at The Athenaeum and the rear among the drawings heretofore unidentified at the Historical Society. In general this project is a modification of his first offering, with a simplified main entrance on Sixth Street and fewer, but larger, offices on the ground floor. A separate hall has been provided along the south wall to give access to further rental space on the third floor without disturbing The Athenaeum's members ensconced on the *piano nobile*.

If this third scheme was calculated to satisfy the economy-minded on the Building Committee, Notman's fourth proposal [figs. 16.6-16.8] seems meant to appeal to those with an appetite for grandeur and a lingering taste for the forms of the Classical Revival. The building has been reduced to two stories. The main entrance, on Sixth Street, is fronted by a portico with paired Corinthian columns bearing a full entablature. The *piano nobile* is circled by attached Corinthian columns and pilasters and capped by an imposing balustraded parapet. The most elaborate effects, however, are reserved for the interior. The space allotted for a third floor in the earlier plans is now utilized for a dome over the stairhall, and deeply coffered ceilings crown the news room and library, the latter generously adorned with palmetto leaves.

This fourth design by Notman must have been among those presented to the board. The minutes clearly state that Notman's was a two-story building, while Gilpin proposed three stories, and LeBrun's design could be adapted to two stories or three. The board may have also reconsidered Notman's earlier proposals; for in selecting him they instructed him to

prepare plans and estimates for a three-story structure. On 23 June the committee reported to the board on plans for a building estimated to cost $27,000. This was not satisfactory. Architect and committee were, in effect, sent back to the drawing board to produce a proposal that could be executed for $24,000.

By 30 June the committee was able to present Notman's final proposal to the board. The architect had returned to his original conception of a building modelled on a Renaissance palazzo. It is not certain whether the small perspective [16.9] was presented at this time or prepared later as the basis for a lithograph published at the time of the dedication. In either event, it represents the facade behind which two alternative plans could be constructed. [16.10-16.11] Each provides a main entrance on Sixth Street, flanked on either side by a generous window, and a secondary entrance on Adelphi, with four openings on either side. One plan, dated 26 June 1845, shows a building fronting 110 feet on Adelphi Street, carried to a 47-foot interior throughout its entire lenth. The second, simply dated 1845, extends the Adelphi Street frontage to 125 feet. This elongation primarily affects the rear portion of the building, although some minor variations, creating larger offices at the expense of the stair hall, are also made to the front. The 15 additional feet in length enabled Notman to set the south flank of the rear portion of the building back ten feet from the party wall, thus providing natural light to the library and proposed lecture hall. The board promptly resolved "that the Building Committee be authorized to contract for the erection of a building on either of the above reported plans...."

The committee's choice was the second alternative. By 11 July specifications were issued in broadside form, and the builders of Philadelphia were invited to submit bids by 19 July. In the interim they would have "the opportunity of examining the plans and elevation by calling on Mr. McIlhenny, the Librarian, at any time between 8 and 12 o'clock daily,..." These were undoubtedly drawings

16.12 and 16.13. The specifications, which are quoted in full in Moss, *Philadelphia Victorian*, describe one major feature not revealed in the drawings.

> There will be an entresol or half height room over the Chess room, not shown on the plan; it will be lighted from the main stair, the partition enclosing the stair of access to it, to be the height of its floor, with bannisters similar to those on the principal stair placed on top of it.

Additionally the specifications make clear that the exterior finish was to be marble. The entire rusticated first story was to be of this material, as was all the trim of the Sixth Street front, except the cornice, which was to be of wood. Marble was also to be used for much of the trim on Adelphi Street. Sixth Street was to have

> ... marble equal in quality and color to Freedly's Eastern Marble, or to Hitner's second quality; to be sound, free of shale, or natural flaw, and of equal color throughout, clear of dark streaks or discoloration.

On Adelphi Street, inferior marble, or even a pale granite, was permissible. The upper floors on all the visible fronts were to be covered with mastic and that on the south flank with rough cast.

John McArthur, uncle of the architect of the same name, who would later compete with Notman for several commissions, was the low bidder. However, before the contract could be executed, several stockholders petitioned the board to put the entire question of building to a vote of the membership. This was not accomplished until 8 Sept., when the board's decision to proceed was upheld by a vote of 148 to 80. By this time McArthur felt that he could no longer adhere to his bid and asked for an additional $2,000. The committee, in consternation, conferred with Notman, who agreed to undertake the contract himself. The total cost was set at $24,782, and Notman agreed to a completion date of 1 Feb. 1847. [Minutes, 15 Sept. 1845]

A few weeks later work on the excavation was begun. [Philadelphia *Public Ledger*, 10 Oct. 1845, 2] Meanwhile, Notman had prepared a working drawing for the facade.

[16.14 and 16.15] It soon became apparent that compromises were necessary if The Athenaeum's financial requirements were to be met. On 10 Nov. 1845 the board agreed to the substitution of brownstone, actually a red sandstone, for the marble. Subsequently, the board voted to build the floor of the rear room on the first story level, rather than pitched, and to eliminate the fixed seating, so that the room could be rented as office space. [Minutes, 31 Mar. 1846] Nevertheless, at the annual meeting, John C. Montgomery, chairman of the Special Building Committee, could report with satisfaction that the new hall "will combine elegance of design with convenient accommodation" and be "a striking addition to the architectural ornaments of our city." [Minutes, 3 Feb. 1846]

Construction resumed in the spring after the usual winter building hiatus. Meanwhile, Notman had executed a new working drawing for the facade, dated 25 Mar. 1846. This was necessitated by a decision to execute the entire front in cut stone, rather than coating the upper two stories in mastic, as had been proposed in the specifications. The start was late, because of delay in obtaining what the *Public Ledger* erroneously described as "granite" from the "celebrated quarries at Newark, N. J. As the stone for this building has now commenced arriving, we may anticipate the resumption of work upon it." [Philadelphia *Public Ledger*, 7 May 1846; 2] Work progressed steadily thereafter and by the end of the year the building was under roof. By this time, however, it was apparent that the deadline of 1 Feb. 1847 could not be met. Notman wrote to the building committee on 25 Jan., explaining that the delays had been caused by weather and difficulty in procuring stone of the proper dimensions, and requesting a three-month extension. This was granted, but it was not until seven months later, on 25 Aug., that the *Public Ledger* could report that the scaffolding had been removed, and not until October that The Athenaeum's members moved to their new quarters.

Despite the delays, all concerned were well pleased with the results, including the architect. In an architectural description, accompanying the lithograph printed in The Athenaeum's annual report for 1847, Notman wrote, with no pretense of false modesty:

It is an excellent specimen of the Italian style of architecture, treated with spirit and taste. It has a bold and imposing appearance from the simplicity and unity of the design, and a perfect expression of its purpose; and though an astylar composition (without columns), the beautiful proportions of its parts, the fine details and massive crowning cornice, give it an air of stateliness and grandeur most impressive as a piece of street architecture.

PRESENT STATUS:

Handsomely restored in 1975, and declared a National Historic Landmark in 1977, The Athenaeum remains a proprietary library. It has also become a research center for studies in nineteenth-century social and cultural history.

17.

CHAPEL OF THE HOLY INNOCENTS

BURLINGTON, NEW JERSEY
1845–1847

Client: Bishop George Washington Doane for St. Mary's Hall

Project: chapel for Episcopal private school for girls

DRAWINGS: none

OTHER EARLY ILLUSTRATIONS:

A lithograph of the interior, c. 1869, is reproduced in Stanton, Phoebe B. *The Gothic Revival & American Church Architecture.* Baltimore (1968).

DOCUMENTATION:

Doane, George Washington. *Diocese of New Jersey: Episcopal Address to the Sixty-Third Annual Convention.* Burlington (1846); *... to the Sixty-Fourth Annual Convention.* Burlington (1847); *The Ecclesiologist,* VIII (October 1847): 67-68; Princeton *Whig*; J

BIBLIOGRAPHY:

D: 131; F: 65-69, 95-100; S-PULC: 118; Hills, George Morgan. *History of the Church in Burlington, New Jersey.* Trenton (1876)

"BISHOP DOANE, on Friday, laid the corner-stone of the Chapel of the Holy Innocents for the use of the pupils of St. Mary's Hall, Burlington." [*Whig*, 3 Oct. 1845] Doane himself remembered the date as a Thursday, 25 Sept., and described the purpose of building somewhat more poetically as the "religious uses of the Christian household of St. Mary's Hall." [Address, 1846: 5] In his address for 1847, Doane reported:

On Thursday 25 March (Annunciation of the Blessed Virgin Mary,) I consecrated the Chapel of the Holy Innocents, ... The building ... is well nigh perfect in its propriety and convenience; and does great credit to Mr. Notman, under whose direction it was erected.

[Address, 1847: 10-11]

The Ecclesiologist published a long and generally favorable review of the building, quoted below, evidently based on a description that had appeared in Doane's publication *The Missionary.* Unfortunately, no copy of the relevant issue of the latter periodical seems to have been preserved in a public collection.

Chapel of the Holy Innocents, St. Mary's Hall, Burlington, New Jersey.—This, the chapel of S. Mary's Hall (for the training of young ladies) in Burlington, was consecrated on the Feast of the Annunciation, in the present year, by the Bishop of New Jersey, in whose parish as well as diocese it is situated (for unhappily the American episcopate is as yet purely territorial). A wood-cut of the exterior, and a description, are given in the number for May of the "Missionary," a periodical on Church subjects, published at Burlington under the superintendence of the Bishop. The plan of the chapel, of which Mr. Notman is architect, is a parallelogram; broken, however, on the south side by an organ-chamber projecting transept-wise, but not extending beyond the line of the side walls. It is a great pity that this should have been allowed to interfere with the general design. The style is Middle-Pointed, except that the west window and that of the organ-chamber are triplets—a solecism of course. The chapel "is of sandstone, with buttresses, and a bell turret, and a cross" at the east end, unhappily a plain one, "and has an open timber roof" of a good pitch. "The length, which is 81 feet, by 27 in. width, is broken by a triplet window, inserted in a high peaked gablet; beneath which stands a fine organ, opposite the entrance from S. Mary's Hall. The chancel window is of most excellent proportion, and quite unique in this country, being from the ancient English church of Stanton S. John. The choir seats face each other, running lengthwise with the building, from the chancel," *i.e.* sacrarium, "to the organ." We trust from this description that they are reserved for the use of the inmates of the Hall; if so they will be the first instance, we should imagine, of an *exclusively* (several almshouses are partially so) female community sitting in choir to be found in the communion of Canterbury for the last three centuries. "The other half is filled with open seats crosswise, leaving an aisle," *i.e.* passage, "the whole length, from the door at the garden entrance; over which is another triplet window. The woodwork is painted to represent old oak, and is admirably done." The chapel has "stained glass windows. The chancel window is the gift of one noble heart. It is not quite complete; but the design, part of which is executed, is most beautiful and appropriate.... A beautiful communion set is coming out for the chapel, from a friend of the Bishop in England.... Matins are celebrated in the chapel at six A.M., and vespers at half-past seven every day; besides which there is "a short voluntary service at noon." We are not disposed to be critical upon so admirable a first beginning in the New World. We have pointed out some features which we could have wished otherwise. We are glad to see the idea of a college chapel grasped as it appears to be in this instance. One remark, in conclusion, must be made, which will be trust be taken in good part, that it is quite contrary to precedent for the chapel of a college to have different dedication from that of the college itself. It is a sort of violation of the unity of the institution.

PRESENT STATUS:

Still maintained in its original use, the chapel has been altered by a modification of the south wall, made when another building was conjoined to it in 1868, and by an enlargement of the organ chamber. Acoustical tile has been attached to the ceiling and much, although not all, of the original plain stained glass has been replaced with more elaborate windows.

Chapel of the Holy Innocents. *Author's photograph*

18.

NEW JERSEY STATE LUNATIC ASYLUM

(Trenton Psychiatric Hospital)
EWING TOWNSHIP, NEW JERSEY
1845–1848
Client: Commissioners to Build the Lunatic Asylum
Project: State hospital for the insane

DRAWINGS: none

OTHER EARLY ILLUSTRATIONS:

The plan was reproduced in "New Jersey State Asylum." The *Pennsylvania Journal of Prison Discipline and Philanthropy*, II, 1 (1846): 57-60; and in *Annual Report of the Officers of the New Jersey State Lunatic Asylum at Trenton*. Trenton (1849); the latter publication also contains a perspective view of the prison, drawn and engraved by J. I. Pease from a daguerreotype by J. X. Mason; vignette on "Map of Mercer County," 1849, surveyed by J. W. Otley and J. Keily, published by Lloyd Vanderveer; "View of the New Jersey Lunatic Asylum at Trenton," *Gleason's Pictorial*, 5 June 1862: 361; photographs in the collections of the New Jersey Historical Society.

DOCUMENTATION:

Kirkbride, Thomas S. *Notice of Some Experiments in Heating and Ventilating Hospitals*. Philadelphia (1850); ... *Remarks on the Construction and Arrangement of Hospitals for the Insane*. Philadelphia (1847); *Minutes of the Votes and Proceedings of the Sixty-Ninth General Assembly of the State of New Jersey*. Camden (1846), ... *of the Seventieth General Assembly*. Woodbury (1846), ... *of the Seventy-Second General Assembly*. Rahway (1848); New Jersey *State Gazette*; Princeton *Whig*

BIBLIOGRAPHICAL REFERENCES:

F: 40-41; S-PULC: 120; Cooledge, Harold Norman Jr. *Samuel Sloan (1815–1884), Architect*. Ph.D. dissertation, University of Pennsylvania, 1963. University Microfilms, Inc.; Hurd, Henry M. *The Institutional Care of the Insane in the United States and Canada.* Baltimore (1916)

IN 1844 Dorothea Dix prepared a report on the manner in which the insane of the State of New Jersey were cared for or, rather, for the most part abandoned. Early in 1845 she presented a memorial to the legislature, which aroused in that body "a strong perception of the need for a State Asylum for the Insane." [*Whig*, 28 Feb. 1845: 2] The perception culminated in rapid action. By the following month a bill authorizing construction of such a facility had passed. [*Whig*, 21 Mar. 1845: 2] Two commissions were appointed, one to purchase a site and one to build the facility. By July the former had selected a site, a 111-acre farm, situated about two-and-one-half miles west of Trenton along the Delaware River. [*State Gazette*, 7 July 1845: 2]

Meanwhile the commissioners were visiting other mental hospitals and conferring with Miss Dix and other experts on the care of the mentally ill preparatory to choosing a design. By the fall they "adopted" the plan of "Dr. Kirkbride of Philadelphia, as drafted by Mr. Nottman [sic]." [*State Gazette*, 26 Sept. 1845: 2] As the commissioners explained:

> And having examined *some* of the principal Asylums for the insane in this country, and several *plans* of Asylums, which were presented, they finally adopted the general form submitted by Dr. Thomas S. Kirkbride, superintendent of the Pennsylvania Hospital for the Insane, and drawn out, arranged and adapted to the exterior elevation as shown in the prospective view by John Notman, Architect, of Philadelphia, as embracing, in their judgment, most of what was desireable, in the institutions visited, and the plans inspected.
>
> [Report of the Commissioner to Build the Lunatic Asylum, in *Votes and Proceedings*, 1846: 36-27]

Thomas S. Kirkbride was one of the mid-nineteenth century's advanced thinkers and practitioners, not only about the treatment afforded the insane, but also about the importance of suitable physical facilities as a component of the medical approach to mental illness. His theories are summarized in his *Remarks on the Construction and Arrangements of Hospitals for the Insane*, first printed in the *American Journal of the Medical Sciences* for January, 1847, and issued in the same year as a separate pamphlet. Kirkbride believed that a pleasant site, with "agreeable scenery" was of importance. "A hospital for the insane should always be located in the country," but close to a sizeable town and good transportation. Fifty acres was the minimum size to permit farming and gardening as a form of therapy.

The building should be well sited on this property so that rooms utilized by the patients "should have the most extensive view and the most desirable scenery, and that every possible advantage may be derived from the prevailing winds of summer." Although expressing a lack of interest in the "details of external architecture" and believing that "all extravagance or excessive ornament is to be avoided," Kirkbride believed it important that the building

> should always be in good taste,—appropriate for the locality in which it was placed, and calculated to produce a pleasing impression on all who see it. Such a building... exercise[s] a most favorable influence on many of the insane.

He proceeds to spell out the facilities that should be provided.

> Let the size adopted be what it may, proper apartments are required for the resident officers of the institution, and for the family of its medical superintendent,—for all the domestic operations of the house, and those engaged in carrying them out, and for the comfortable accommodation of at least five, (preferably of seven), distinct classes of patients of each sex. Each class will occupy a ward, and in, or connected with each ward, should be a parlour, a dining-room, a clothes-room, a bath-room, a water closet, a corridor with chambers on one or both sides of it, an associated dormitory, rooms for two attendants, so that one may always be present with the patients, a stairway, a dumb waiter, and a funnel for soiled clothes, dust, &c., leading to the basement story. The only exception is perhaps, in the wards occupied by the lowest class of patients, where parlours may be dispensed with.
>
> Special provision should also be made for the worst class of patients, that is, for the very noisy, violent and filthy, and for those whose complete isolation on any other account, is particularly desirable.

Kirkbride felt that the best design for such a hospital was one with a central section with wings at right angles. If the hospital was of large size, additional sets of wings should be set back from the first. Proper heating and ventilation, and a supply of good water he considered of the utmost importance.

Most of the views contained in the present essay were given to the commissioners of New Jersey, when consulting me relative to the details of an institution for that state, which should combine economy in the cost of first construction and subsequent management—ease of supervision, perfect classification of its patients, and all the requirements for their efficient treatment. The general plan and the form of building which I suggested were subsequently adopted, and will be found embraced in the designs by John Notman, Esq., of Philadelphia, the accomplished architect of the hospital, and who is superintending its erection.

Kirkbride concluded his essay with a description of the building. Partly on the basis of this pamphlet, and also because Kirkbride went on to plan a number of other mental hospitals in collaboration with Samuel Sloan, scholars have tended to minimize Notman's contribution. Robert Smith says Notman "was engaged to interpret and execute the plans of Dr. Thomas S. Kirkbride." [PULC: 120] Fairbanks refers to the building as "adapted by Notman from plans furnished by Dr. Thomas S. Kirkbride." [40] Cooledge, although stating that the degree to which Kirkbride influenced Notman is indeterminable, infers that the 1847 pamphlet is about the Pennsylvania, rather than the New Jersey hospital. [135-36]

Contemporary sources, however, were well aware of the importance of Notman's role in the design. In a letter to one of the commissioners, written 23 Nov. 1845, Dr. Bell of Boston's McLean Asylum wrote,

I had much pleasure in my interview with your architect, Mr. Notman, who appeared to be so thoroughly informed on the subject of the construction as applied to the insane, as to lead [sic] nothing to be desired.
[Quoted in *Star Gazette*, 26 Nov. 1845: 2]

The article in the *Pennsylvania Journal* notes that the description of the plan was supplied by the architect of the building. In the course of his description Notman indicated the relative roles assumed by the architect and the physician.

The design is by J. Notman, Architect, who will superintend the erection. The plan is arranged by him from the observations of the commissioners, on their tour through the Eastern Hospitals for the Insane, and from the suggestions of Dr. Thomas S. Kirkbride, of the Pennsylvania Hospital for the Insane, who gave this general form of building as the best which his practical experience and scientific knowledge suggested for the comfort and cure of patients within the economy necessarily observed in a state institution. [*Pennsylvania Journal*: 60]

Although the "details of external architecture" did not interest Kirkbride, they were, of course, of great importance to Notman.

The exterior will be in the simplest style of architecture. A Tuscan portico of six columns marks the centre and entrance. A boldly projecting cornice of the same style will be continued around the whole, yet its architectural effect will be good, from its great size, the well-arranged advancing and receding disposition of the wings, the variety in height, and the fine proportions of the several masses of building. The whole length is four hundred and eighty feet. [*Pennsylvania Journal*: 60]

New Jersey State Lunatic Asylum, c. 1860.
From the collections of the New Jersey Historical Society

The commissioners' report provided additional information on the projected building:

The building consists of a central part, sixty feet in front, eighty four feet deep and four stories high. This department is designed for the use of the Superintendent and assistant, &c.

On each side of the central building, and at right angles with it, but a few feet back from the front, a wing extends 120 feet, thirty nine feet deep and three stories high. To each of these wings is added another wing of equal depth and height, and ninety feet in length, on a line parallel with the front of the other, but 25 feet back; thus presenting an entire front of four hundred and eighty feet.

This mode of construction is considered preferable to having return wings, on account of ventilating the building, and making suitable provision for noisy patients, &c.

The building fronts forty degrees east of south, affording a fine view of the City of Trenton, South Trenton and Morrisville, and a beautiful and extensive prospect of the country on both sides of the Delaware river. The position of the Asylum is such, as to admit the rays of the sun to every part of it, an object, considered of great importance in such an Institution. The accommodations are calculated for about two hundred patients.

The materials of the Building are *stone* for the foundation and entire external wall, from the quarries in Ewing, about two miles from the farm; and *Brick*, for the internal parallel and cross walls.

[*New Jersey State Gazette*, Jan 19, 1846: 2]

As to the plan published in the *Pennsylvania Journal*, Notman explained:

Properly speaking, we should call this the second story, as the basement story under it is elevated three steps from the general ground level; but this best shows the arrangements of the wards, which we hope to render intelligible in their various parts by the appended explanatory references. The plan shows the size and general form of the building on the ground. The height is generally three stories, except the centre and the projecting pavilions terminating the first lateral ranges or wards on both sides of the centre, which are of four stories. The cellars extend under the whole.

The basement story, in the centre building, contains a reception room for patients, officers' and domestics' dining rooms, store rooms, kitchen and scullery. In the first range of wings on either side respectively for male and female patients, are, work rooms, domestics chambers, bakehouse, washing, ironing and drying rooms. In the extreme range of wings are, respectively, the male and female violent patients' wards, and under the portico A is a carriage way to set down patients or others in severe weather.

In the first story, A is the portico, B the entrance hall, C the halls of centre and corridors of wards, D the house parlour, E general business room, F patients' visiters' room, G office of Physician, H the associated dormitories,* I stairs, K dining rooms, L day rooms, M bath rooms, N water closets, O clothes rooms, with foul clothes funnel beside them, P passages between the wards, R attendants' rooms, S spaces with windows from the floor to the ceiling for light and air. The others are single rooms for patients.

In the second story the wards are arranged similar to this. The front rooms of the centre building are for the physician's family; the back part will be in one room for a chapel, lecture, and general meeting room for patients.

In the third story of the centre building will be rooms for the matron and assistants, and steward and assistants. In the third story of the pavilions will be associated dormitories, or infirmary, as required.

Thus the whole is divided into ten distinct wards, five for each sex; each ward will accommodate from twenty to twenty-five patients, and the rooms common to them, as a dining room, bath room, water-closet, clothes room, day room or parlour and attendants' rooms. The stairways are private to each ward, from the hall of basement story. The single rooms are eight feet by ten feet, and eleven feet high, clear. The associated dormitories of each ward accommodate from one-third to one-half of its occupants, and the rooms for these dormitories vary in size to contain from two to eight patients. The corridors are twelve feet wide and eleven feet high; and are lighted at each end by windows the entire size of that space, except at their junction with the centre building, where are spaces marked S opened laterally with windows from floor to ceiling; thus giving the greatest facilities for common ventilation, with abundance of light.

---

* By mistake the front corner room at the extremity of the extended wing has been lettered H. It was designed for a day-room; but may be used if required as an associate dormitory.

[*Pennsylvania Journal:* 58-59]

The system for heating and ventilation was highly advanced.

For warming the building it is arranged that the space in the cellar enclosed by the walls of the corridors in the whole length of the building shall be a chamber, in which the air admitted at sundry points from the exterior, will be heated moderately from the surface of pipes containing hot water or steam circulated through them, and will be conducted in flues in the walls of the corridors to all the rooms in each ward, and to the corridors at many points. For this purpose and for ventilation, there will be built a series of flues in all the extent of the walls of the corridors. The arrangements for ventilation are as follows:—A large flue or air-trunk is constructed at each end of the corridors, with partitions, so that each corridor will have an ascending or descending current, as the season and state of atmosphere may demand. These air-trunks will terminate below in an air-drain, which will again terminate at the necessary fire-places of the establishment,—or, at points distant from those places, at fires provided for the purpose of burning the impure air. Above, the air-trunks will terminate in a shaft or chamber which forms an ornamental erection over the roofs of the pavilions, central and extreme; and the impure air will be burned off at those points, if forced action be necessary. Flues of ventilation from every room are connected with the main trunks; the regulators of the supply of fresh warm air and the valves for ventilation are so proportioned that currents of air will be entirely avoided. By these arrangements it will be in the

Plan of the New Jersey State Lunatic Asylum. *Pennsylvania Journal of Prison Discipline and Philanthropy* power of the managers to cool the air in the chamber and distribute it over the house in summer, as a perfect supply of water will be afforded from the reservoirs intended to be placed in the roof of the centre building.

[*Pennsylvania Journal*: 59-60]

Further detail was supplied when the building was complete.

The warming is effected by steam, generated by four large tubular boilers, placed in the ground story of the centre building, two on either side, the steam circulating through ranges of wrought iron pipes placed in air chambers beneath the corridors, or halls, of the wings. These chambers are seven feet high, twelve feet wide, and correspond in length to the two ranges of wings on either side of the centre building; the latter, being warmed from separate chambers under the central hall. The cold air is admitted to the chambers through openings in the side walls near the ground, and the warm air allowed to escape from the top of the chamber, through flues nine inches square, in the same walls, to the halls and rooms above; a separate flue being used for each story, and a valvular register placed at the outlet near the floor, for regulating the degree of heat or quantity of warm air.

The heat, thus furnished, is of a very mild bland character, having none of the dry suffocating quality of the ordinary furnace heat.

The arrangement of admitting it at many points, by about two hundred openings with registers, serves to equalize the temperature, much more perfectly than can be done by the common arrangement of furnaces in the extremities of the wings, with outlets only at those points.

The sitting rooms, dining rooms, and a portion of the bed rooms, are warmed by registers opening into them; the others are warmed from the halls, by the passage of air through an opening over the door of each room, in the usual way.

The ventilation is effected by means of openings from near the top of each room, into other flues of the same size as those for the transmission of heat.

These terminate in horizontal trunks in the attics that lead to the upright foul air shafts, situated beneath the campaniles, where the air is discharged. The upright shafts are heated by the passage of steam pipes through them; thus steam serving the double purpose of assisting the ventilation and heating water for bathing and other purposes in the wings.

[*Annual Report*: 32-33. See also Kirkbride, *Heating and Ventilating Hospitals*: 10-11.]

The building was lighted by gas, "and presents a very cheerful aspect at night." [*Annual Report*: 33] Fixtures for the heating, ventilating, plumbing and lighting systems were supplied by Morris, Tasker and Morris of Philadelphia. [*Annual Report*: 32]

Construction on the asylum did not, however, proceed as rapidly as on the State House. Although ground was broken in 1846, the first inmates were not admitted until May 1848. [*Whig*, 21 Apr. 1848: 2] At that time the work on the grounds was not complete, although plans were being made to "plant trees and shrubbery . . . according to the tasteful design by A. J. Downing. . . ." [*Annual Report*: 35]

PRESENT STATUS:

In 1972 the center pavilion was removed and a contemporary building substituted. The wings still stand, with extensions added in 1856 and 1866.

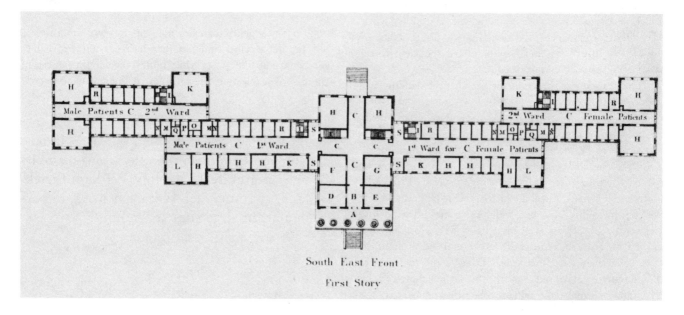

South East Front.

First Story

19.

IMMANUEL CHURCH
NEW CASTLE, DELAWARE
c. 1845[?]–1850
Client: Vestry of Immanuel Church
Project: alterations to chancel

DRAWINGS: none
DOCUMENTATION:

Minutes of the Vestry, Immanuel Church

BIBLIOGRAPHICAL REFERENCES:

F: 150-54

IMMANUEL CHURCH'S unsatisfactory transaction with Notman is recorded in the following report made to the vestry on 15 July 1851:

The Committee heretofore appointed to superintend the alterations, improvements and repairs of Immanuel Church, New Castle, Delaware, report to the Vestry of said Church.

That Messrs. Booth and Read on the 3rd of April, 1850 waited on Mr. John Notman, architect in Philadelphia, and conferred with him on the alteration of the chancel of Immanuel Church aforesaid, according to a plan furnished by him some years previous. That Mr. Notman undertook to execute this plan for five percent upon expenditures but his compensation not to exceed thirty to fifty dollars. That the committee invited proposals for the work contemplated, received several and submitted them to the Vestry of said Church and at a meeting and resolution thereof contracted with the following persons. . . .

That after considerable delay which in part he [the contractor] alleged was caused by Mr. Notman's not having sent him working drawings and for the residue of which he assigned in excuse his engagements in other work, Mr. Dixon commenced the execution of his contract on the 9th of July, 1850 and has completed the same to the satisfaction of your committee. . . .

That as soon as the frame of the chancel window was set up dissatisfaction was expressed with it for being too small. That the attention of your committee was immediately turned to this matter. That Mr. Dixon admitted the frame not to be according to Mr. Notman's plan but alleged that he could not make it as the working drawing required without its being disproportioned. That Mr. Notman had made a mistake in the height he had given to the chancel ceiling and had seen the frame when got out and approved it. That after some delay Mr. Notman came to the Church at the request of your committee, pronounced that it was a mistake, that it was Dixon's and said that he should correct it. That though the latter expressed his willingness to make the window the dimensions that Mr.

Notman should direct, your committee could not succeed in obtaining from him the necessary directions and feeling they had been neglected and trifled with and were not justified in further delay, caused the window to be enlarged by lengthening it 21 inches.

That on the 27th of September, 1850 Messrs. Booth and Read went to Philadelphia and after viewing the stained glass in several churches, contracted with John Gibson, of that City, for stained glass to fill the space left for it in the chancel for $100., together with a wire screen to protect it, not to cost more than $10 or $12., the whole to be completed in four or five weeks and to be at his risk until put up.

That in October last Mr. Notman expressed in a letter to Judge Booth great dissatisfaction with the committee for their alteration of the window, alleging that it marred his plan and would injure his reputation as an architect. That your committee though satisfied that Mr. Notman by his own neglect of duty had compelled this alteration, yet wishing to avoid further difficulty consented that he should alter the window as it then was so as to make in accord with his plan on condition that the Church should not thereby be put to additional expense and that it should be done at once.

That Mr. Notman acceded and Mr. Dixon at his request took the working drawing to Philadelphia but could never obtain his instructions or a plan for the alterations he had so earnestly, if not vehemently, pressed and nothing further has been done by Mr. Notman or heard from him in this matter.

That your committee at length directed Mr. Gibson (who had been instructed because of the difficulty raised by Mr. Notman to suspend his work) to proceed with the glass for the window lengthened 21 inches and he promised it by the middle of December last.

That your committee regret to state that Mr. Notman had been guilty of great neglect of duty and that he has disengenuously endeavored to cast upon them the blame of delay, which justly rests upon himself.

That this gentleman has not sent to your committee a bill for his services and whether he is or not entitled to compensation and if so what under the circumstances of the case is a question they feel to be their duty to submit to the Vestry.

PRESENT STATUS:

As Fairbanks has pointed out, it is impossible to distinguish the alterations made by several architects, notably William Strickland, at Immanuel. Notman's work, in particular, he describes as "minor."

20.

PENNSYLVANIA ACADEMY OF THE FINE ARTS COMPETITION

CHESTNUT STREET, PHILADELPHIA
1846
Client: Committee on Plans
Project: restoration and enlargement of art museum and school

DRAWING 20.1:
   Title: Sketch of Interior of the/North Gallery, Academy of Fine Arts, Philadelphia.
   Signature: J. Notman archt.
   Date: none
   Scale: none indicated
   Other inscriptions: none
   Description: rendering showing gallery with exhibition hung

Medium: ink and colored wash
Size: 10 x 12⅝ (23.3 x 32.1)
Owner: Pennsylvania Academy of the Fine Arts
Exhibition record: "History Gallery." Pennsylvania Academy of the Fine Arts, 1976-

DOCUMENTATION:
Minutes of the Board of the Pennsylvania Academy of the Fine Arts, 1805-1858; Correspondence of the Pennsylvania Academy of the Fine Arts, 1846; Philadelphia *Public Ledger*

BIBLIOGRAPHICAL REFERENCES:
Force, Debbie. "A Research Project on the Architectural History of the Pennsylvania

Academy of Fine Arts." Unpublished paper, University of Pennsylvania, 1977; Meyers, Melvin. "The Architectural History of the Pennsylvania Academy of the Fine Arts Before 1870." Unpublished paper. University of Pennsylvania, n.d.; T

IN JUNE 1845 a fire broke out at the Pennsylvania Academy. The result was "disastrous in the extreme.... The two galleries, east and north of the main building or rotunda being almost totally destroyed." [*Public Ledger*, 13 June 1845: 2] The rotunda, however, was little injured. Almost immediately the trustees called in John Haviland to undertake repairs to the rotunda. His plans were approved early in August and the work was completed by September. [Meyers: 22]

Meanwhile the Committee on the Academy was "authorized to advertise for plans and estimates for erecting fire proof galleries adjoining the Rotunda on the west, north and eastern sides of it." [Minutes, 22 Aug. 1845: 243 ½] The plans were to be submitted by 10 Oct., but evidently this deadline was extended. It was not until 13 Apr. 1846 that the board considered plans with accompanying estimates and specifications submitted by R. A. Gilpin and the firm of Carver & Hall. Carver and Gilpin attended this meeting to explain their plans, and Notman and Haviland were invited to attend the next meeting, presumably for the same purpose. The board voted to limit the cost of construction to $15,000. [Minutes, 253-54]

Haviland and Notman attended the meeting of 20 Apr. and explained their respective plans and estimates. [Minutes: 254] Notman subsequently submitted a written explanation of his drawings.

Academy of Fine Arts, Philadelphia

To the Committee on Plans
Gentlemen,

I submit to you herewith a series of drawings explanatory of my Design for rebuilding the Academy.

No 1 is the plan of Shops and the elevation I propose on Chestnut St. for the front of shops and entrance, and shews as much of the Portico to Academy as will be seen through the entrance from the opposite side of Chestnut St.

No 2 is a section through the entrance, the Portico and Rotunda, shewing in the latter, the present floor taken away, but a gallery of communication to the three—galleries and a stair to basement, the Centre group is placed on a pedastal [sic] built up from lower floor. This alteration would effectively ventilate the basement as well as light it in a great degree.

No 3 is the plan of basement story shewing access to it from each side of present portico steps; from the rotunda by stairs. The Lecture room I have made 75 feet by 38 and placed the forum on the south side as being easily accessible to Lecturers by private stairs. This room has ample entrances and opening, the rotunda to basement as I propose would make to it a magnificent vestibule.

No 4 is the plan of the principal floor shewing the Rotunda opened to basement and the gallery of communication to exhibition galleries. This gallery in the rotunda would be guarded with a balustrade forming a continued pedastal for busts as shown in No 2.

No 5 are sections of the building longitudinal and transverse shewing the heights of Lecture room, school rooms etc and the manner of support.

No 6 are sections before submitted to you. They may be useful to compare the additional parts.

No 7 The framed drawing is a sketch of the interior of principal gallery shewing the manner and style of roof; the crossing of the ornamental rafters, by the lantern light, will not interfere with the direct light, more than a sash bar.

The whole may be done for Fifteen Thousand dollars, conditioned the Contractor has the use of the old material in rebuilding. Should you still desire divisions in the long gallery, they can be introduced without increase of cost. All which Gentlemen is respectfully submitted for your approval and am

> Your Servt
> John Notman
> May 4th 1846
> [Correspondence, 1846]

On 4 May the board again reviewed the plans, by now down to three, Haviland having withdrawn. The board voted to award a premium of $100 to each of the architects for his plans "on condition that the same shall become the property of the Directors of the Academy to be used by them either wholly or in part." Carver & Hall and Notman were requested to furnish "detailed and complete specifications and estimates" before the next meeting on 7 May. [Minutes: 256-57] This Notman was unable to do, as he explained to the chairman, although he provided some additional information.

Philada May 7th 1846

Hyman Gratz, Esq.
Dear Sir,

Your note of 5th inst informing me of the vote of Manager of Academy of Fine Arts was duly received, but, being absent from the city, I did not see it til last night. I am therefore unprepared with the specifications and estimate requested for today, I can have them ready on Monday if agreeable.

My proposition embraces the introduction of Gas, Water, and two Water Closets. The floors of all the basement *rooms* to be of wood, as driest; the floors of the lobbies and rotunda in basement, to be paved with German flag polished. The most economical mode of heating so many rooms would be by the hot water system, the most expensive at first. The ventilation would be complete, vents provided for gas smoke which with pendant, bracket, or chandelier remanents are considered as furniture and not included in building estimates. The gallery of Rotunda to be fireproof as the other floors, to be six feet clear width, within the balustrade. This gallery may be placed two feet higher in the walls of rotunda without injury to proportion provided the rotunda is opened to the basement. It would be improved by the additional height, as the Hall of the Academy of Fine Arts, it might be open to the public always, and be the exhibition room of original pictures for sale. I am Sir

Most respectfully Your Servt
John Notman
[Correspondence, 1846]

At the meeting on 7 May the board voted. Gilpin received five votes and Notman two. [Minutes: 257] Advised of the decision of the board and of the offer of the premium, Notman sent a brief letter.

Philada May 11th 1846

Hyman Gratz Esq
Dear Sir

Will you do me the favor to present my respectful thanks to the Directors of the Academy of Fine Arts for their kind and considerate offer of remuneration for my design, but it is not customary to retain the drawings, unless with the services of the author. I therefore most respectfully decline the offer if on that condition, and respectfully remain Sir.

Your   Servt
John Notman
[Correspondence, 1846]

The drawings were probably returned, the one now in the Academy's possession being a recent gift. It is undoubtedly the drawing described as "No. 7" in Notman's submission letter.

Richard A. Gilpin produced for the Academy a *retarditaire* Greek Revival building. As Tatum [57] has pointed out, his "chief qualification may have been a brother on the building committee."
PRESENT STATUS:
Unexecuted

21.

FIELDWOOD
(Woodlawn, Guernsey Hall,
Marquand Park)
PRINCETON, NEW JERSEY
1846
Client: Richard Stockton Field
Project: landscape design for estate grounds

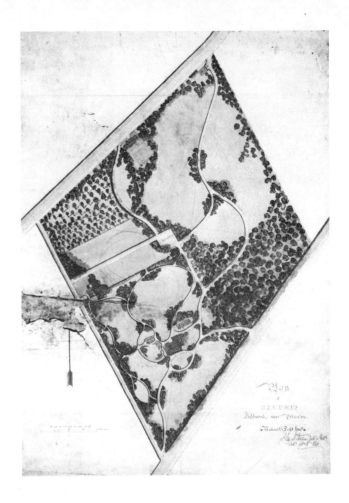

DRAWING 21.1:

Title: Plan/of/Grounds/Fieldwood, near Princeton/Richard S. Field Esqr.

Signature: John Notman, Archt. et Delr.

Date: Philadelphia October 19th, 1846

Other inscriptions: north arrow

Scale: 1″ : 1 chain

Medium: ink and water color

Description: plan of grounds, showing disposition of roadways, paths, plantings and buildings

Size: 32¼ x 22⅜ (81.9 x 56.4)

Owner: Princeton University Library, Marquand Papers

Publication record: Greiff, Constance M., Gibbons, Mary W., Menzies, Elizabeth G. C. *Princeton Architecture*, Princeton (1967)

OTHER EARLY ILLUSTRATIONS:

Early photographs of the grounds are owned by the Princeton University Library, the Historical Society of Princeton and descendants of the Marquand family. A selection was published in Delanoy, Eleanor Marquand. "Guernsey Hall." *Princeton History*, 2 (1977): 4-17.

DOCUMENTATION:

Letters from George Washington Doane to Richard S. Field and from Richard S. Field to Elias Boudinot, PUL; Downing, A. J. *Treatise on the Theory and Practice of Landscape Gardening*, 6th ed. New York (1859)

BIBLIOGRAPHICAL REFERENCES:

D: 133; M: 45-47; S-PULC: 119-20; Hageman, John F. *Princeton and its Institutions*. Philadelphia (1879); Marquand, Eleanor. "The Trees of Guernsey." T.s., 1937, PUL

RICHARD S. FIELD'S VOCATION was law. He served as Attorney General of New Jersey, United States Senator in 1862, and Judge of the U. S. District Court from 1863 to 1870. His avocations were the Episcopal Church and horticulture. He was a founder of Trinity Church, Princeton, and an early president of the New Jersey Horticultural Society.

Field purchased his estate in 1842, and is said to have spent ten years landscaping it. [Marquand, 1] In the spring of that year he was planting trees received from England. [Field to Boudinot, 25 Apr. 1842] By 1845 he was evidently thinking of its development, including a name. "Field of Fieldwood would be quite the thing," wrote his friend George Washington Doane. [Doane to Field, 15 Dec. 1845]

Full development, however, did not start in 1846 and the estate as completed differed in many respects from the plan of that year. The 1846 plan called for preservation and integration of three of four earlier buildings on the grounds, to be used as gardener's house, cottage and lodge. New structures to be erected included stables, located approximately in the center of the property, and a greenhouse and grapery flanking the rear of the main house. As the property was actually developed, the house marked for the gardener seems to have been removed. The stables were built at the rear of the cottage and the greenhouses and grapery at the back of the lodge. Nor did the main house conform to the outline on the plan, although its approximate location and orientation were followed. [See entry 59]

PRESENT STATUS:

Although building lots around its periphery have been developed, about 20 of the original 40 acres are preserved, including the woodland, as a municipal park.

22.

SMITHSONIAN INSTITUTION
WASHINGTON, D. C.
1846
Client: Chancellor and Board of Regents of the Smithsonian Institution
Project: building to house museum, library, lecture hall and rooms, and offices

DRAWING 22.1:
Title: No 1 Ground Plan/Smithsonian Institute
Signature: John Notman Architect
Date: Philada Decr 23rd 1846
Scale: 1/12″ : 1′
Other inscriptions: Whole length 395 feet/ Premium awarded by the Regents Jan. 20 1847 $250 (second line not in Notman's hand)
Description: measured plan
Medium: ink and wash
Size: 24½ x 37⅛ (62.2 x 94.3)
Owner: Smithsonian Institution Archives, DC-28-A12

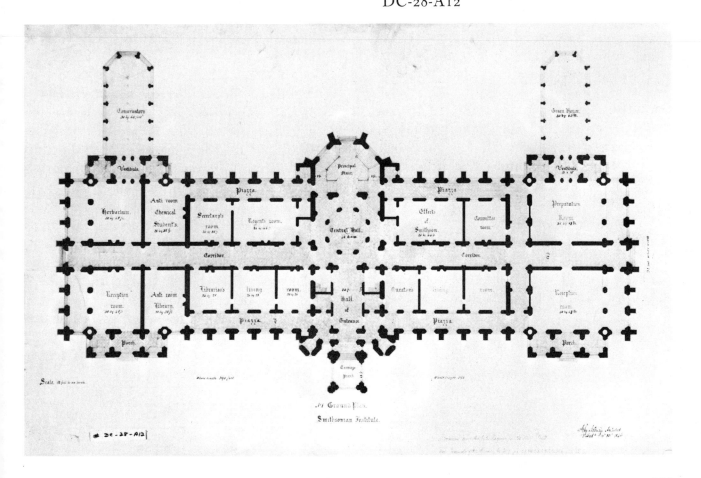

DRAWING 22.2:
 Title: No 2 Second Story/Smithsonian
 Institute
 Signature: John Notman Architect
 Date: Philada Decr 23rd 1846
 Scale: 1/12″ : 1′
 Other inscriptions: none
 Description: measured plan
 Medium: ink and wash
 Size: 24 x 37-15/16 (61 x 96.4)
 Owner: Smithsonian Institution Archives,
 DC-28-A13

DRAWING 22.3:
 Title: No 3 South Front/Elevation/
 Smithsonian Institute
 Signature: John Notman Architect
 Date: Philada Decr 23rd 1846
 Scale: 1/12″ : 1′
 Other inscriptions: none
 Description: rendered elevation
 Medium: ink, wash and watercolor
 Size: 23-5/16 x 37⅞ (59.3 x 96.2)
 Owner: Smithsonian Institution Archives,
 DC-28-A8
 Publication record: Loth, Calder and Sad-
 ler, Julius Trousdale Jr. *The Only Proper
 Style.* Boston (1975)

DRAWING 22.4:
 Title: No 4 Third Story/Smithsonian
 Institute
 Signature: John Notman Architect
 Date: Philada Decr 23rd 1846
 Scale: 1/12″ : 1′
 Other inscriptions: none
 Description: measured plan
 Medium: ink and wash
 Size: 24-11/16 x 37½ (62.7 x 95.3)
 Owner: Smithsonian Institution Archives,
 DC-28-A14

DRAWING 22.5:
 Title: No 5 North Front/Elevation/
 Smithsonian Institute
 Signature: John Notman Architect
 Date: Philada Decr 23rd 1846
 Scale: 1/12″ : 1′
 Other inscriptions: 395 feet/175 feet high
 Description: rendered elevation
 Medium: ink, wash and watercolor
 Size: 23¼ x 37-11/16 (59.2 x 95.7)
 Owner: Smithsonian Institution Archives,
 DC-28-A7

DRAWING 22.6:
 Title: No 6 End Elevation/Smithsonian
 Institute
 Signature: John Notman Architect
 Date: Philada Dec. 23rd 1846
 Scale: 1/12″ : 1′
 Other inscriptions: Transverse Section/
 Longitudinal Sections
 Description: sections and rendered
 elevation
 Medium: ink, wash and watercolor
 Size: 23-5/16 x 27½ (59.2 x 95.3)
 Owner: Smithsonian Institution Archives,
 DC-28-A15
DOCUMENTATION:
 Notman, John. *Description and Estimate
 of Design Submitted by John Notman,
 Architect for the Smithsonian Institution.*
 Washington (1847); Smithsonian Institu-
 tion, Record A; much of the same material
 is contained in "Smithsonian Institution.
 Report of the Board of Regents, submitted
 to Congress of the operations, expendi-
 tures, and condition of the Smithsonian In-
 stitution." U. S. Congress Documents, 29th
 Congress, S. Doc. 211, 3 Mar. 1847
BIBLIOGRAPHICAL REFERENCES:
 Loth, Calder and Sadler, Julius Trousdale.
 The Only Proper Style. Boston (1975);
 Reiff, Daniel D. *Washington Architecture
 1791-1861.* Washington (1971)

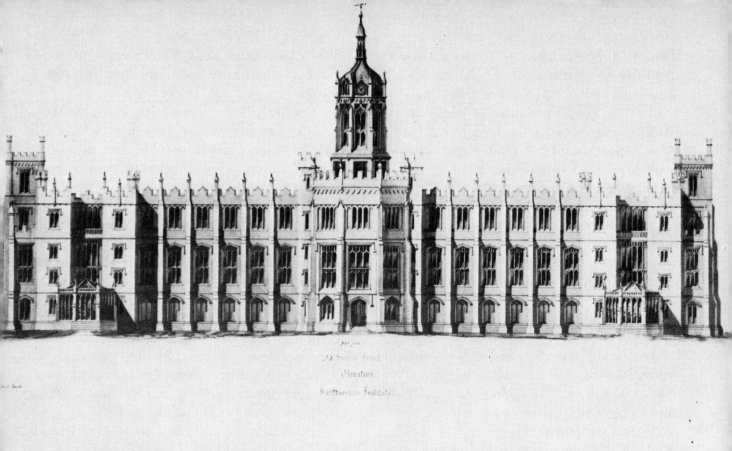

22.3

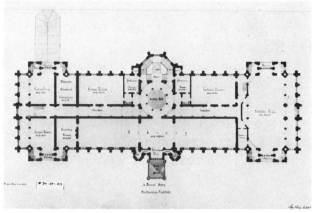

22.2

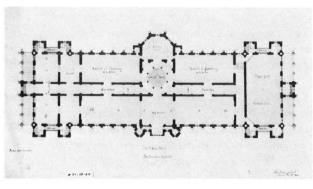

22.4

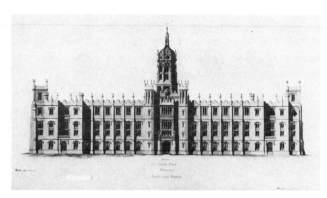

22.5

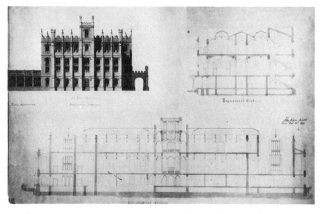

22.6

THE PUBLISHED RECORDS dealing with the choice of an architect for the Smithsonian Institution do not reveal much of what transpired within the committee. But it requires very little reading between the lines to realize that what appeared to be an open competition was probably, to put it bluntly, rigged.

On 9 Sept. 1846 Robert Dale Owen, son of the founder of New Harmony, presented to his fellow board members a plan for the Smithsonian prepared by his brother David Dale Owen and Robert Mills. One William Archer also submitted a plan. After some discussion, the Chancellor, Secretary and Executive Committee were authorized to obtain plans for erection of a suitable building.

In carrying out these instructions, the committee visited several cities, including New York, Boston and Cincinnati, to view public buildings. They also interviewed a number of architects, among them James Renwick, Jr., Richard Upjohn, Martin Thompson, Owen G. Warren, Isaiah Rogers, and Ammi B. Young. In Philadelphia

Mr. Strickland and Mr. Walter were called upon, but were unfortunately absent from the city. Mr. Haviland was also called upon; but not being seen, all necessary information was sent to him through the mail. Mr. Notman was seen and repeatedly conversed with.

[S. Doc. 211 : 6-7]

These conversations must have impressed the committee, for Notman accompanied them on a trip to Trenton to view the Lunatic Asylum and State House. "In examining these edifices, advantage was derived from the constant presence and intelligent remarks of Mr. Notman." [S. Doc. 211 :7]

A notice was also placed in the Washington newspapers inviting submissions. When Napoleon LeBrun, who had not been interviewed, wrote to inquire about the deadline he was informed that submissions would be accepted until 25 Dec. [Record A: 58] It is not known whether LeBrun sent drawings or, indeed, whether all of the architects interviewed did so. In addition to Mills and Archer, John Haviland, James Renwick, Jr., Isaiah Rogers, Owen G. Warren, the firm of

Wells and Arnot, and Notman submitted designs, the two latter accompanied by printed letters.

Notman's "intelligent remarks" were of no avail. Even before his drawings, which are dated 23 Dec. 1846, were submitted, the building committee voted unanimously on 30 Nov. for Renwick as the Smithsonian's architect. [S. Doc. 211 : 8] On 20 Jan. 1847, before listening to the other architects who had traveled to Washington to make presentations, the Regents ratified the building committee's choice. Premiums of $250 were awarded to Wells & Arnot, Notman, Haviland, and Warren, on condition that the drawings would become the property of the Smithsonian. Over the next several days, although the decision was already made, the board nevertheless heard presentations from Haviland, Notman, Arnot, Rogers, Archer, Renwick and Mills, evidently without informing the losers of the futility of their effort. [Record A: 69-70]

Notman seems to have broken his usual rule of asking for the return of his drawings and accepted the premium. Ironically, all but two of Renwick's drawings were destroyed in a fire, while full sets of the Notman, Warren and Rogers drawings survive.

At least one copy of Notman's submission letter also survives, at the Princeton University Library. Although he lost the competition, the letter elucidates, more completely than any other document, Notman's approach to questions of program and design.

TO THE CHANCELLOR AND BOARD OF
REGENTS, SMITHSONIAN INSTITUTION

GENTLEMEN: In compliance with the request of your Committee, I have the honor of submitting the accompanying design and drawings for your inspection, of the proposed building for the Institution.

I have to regret the late period at which I received the reports necessary to a clear knowledge of your wants, as having too little time for the preparation of interior views of the more important rooms; their effect may be judged from size and height, but illustration by drawing is required for a complete understanding of their finished appearance. In the following explanation of the drawings I will endeavor to make clear the whole design.

In arranging the Plan concentration is an object, as affording obvious and easy access from point to point of the interior, gives command of the whole building for a general system of heating and ventilation by interior wall flues, is a sounder construction with less material, and greatly cheaper, as the exterior walls are most expensive; and with a glance at the Plan it is seen that half the external wall only is necessary to a building of two rooms deep instead of one; for these reasons I doubled the Plan, with a corridor between the rooms; besides, the light is more agreeable from one side than from both, and better suited for display of objects either of nature or art; the rooms are narrower than proposed, as a room of 50 feet width ought not to be less than 35 feet high, if effect from proportion is desired; this would not allow a third story, or if made lower and a third story built, the floors would have to be encumbered with columns or supports of some kind, or a most expensive construction of floor to carry the museum must have been adopted; also, it is an axiom in proportion, that a mass of building is incapable of grandeur, if it is higher than its width of general base on the ground; these, and the material to be employed in the construction considered, I am enabled to offer you a richer finish of exterior design than the proposed expenditure apparently warrants, and these are reasons for my adopting the style of the exterior, as being best adapted for high architectural effect from a comparatively inferior material in small blocks.

It is known as the collegiate style, sometimes called the later Tudor; it prevails at Oxford and Cambridge Universities, the Inns of Law, Westminster Hall, the Palaces of Hampton Court, Eltham, Linlithgow, Falkland, St. James, and many halls and mansions in Great Britain, and in the town halls on the continent of Europe.

In appearance it is neither castellated nor ecclesiastical, but expresses large rooms and halls well lighted for public purposes; a proper expression of use and purpose in a building is one of the best points in a design, when gained without sacrifice of other advantages and at great cost; in this it is obtained with a gain in convenience, and best display of stone work from the many angles and projections of towers and buttresses; the corners or quoin stones of these and the window jambs I propose to be dressed or worked stone, the intermediate spaces of plain rubble work; this is one of the cheapest and soundest modes of building, and is most effective, with the features and details of this style of Gothic architecture.

The drawings I have numbered for reference.

No. 1, is the ground plan; (I have not made a cellar plan, as that is obvious, or may be as desired;) the floor is 3 feet (three) above the general level of the ground, on which the building is 395 feet in length over all; it is 170 feet deep or wide through the centre, including carriage porch and stairs; 132 feet deep through the extreme wings at the tower projections, and 110 feet through in the body of the building, measuring over the buttresses. This floor is appropriated to the private uses of the Institution; the division and sizes of rooms are not arbitrary on this floor, only by the walls of substruction; the rooms may be varied from this arrangement and differently appropriated; rooms are marked for the residence of a Librarian, and a Janitor or Curator; rooms for the Board of Regents and Secretary; a room for the effects of Smithson, and a Committee room. The rooms in each extreme wing are of large size, and are supposed necessary for the reception and preparation of specimens for the museum, galleries of art, &c., and for lectures, illustrations, and apparatus in science. On both sides or fronts of the building where strong direct light is neither desirable nor necessary, piazzas are made within the line of walls, forming four sheltered ambulatories or cloisters, each 90 feet long by 10 feet wide; they are also passages from one point to another. The corridors are direct from end to end of the building, connecting all the rooms, and are lighted from the central hall and lateral passages. The entrance hall is 20 feet wide, and extends from the carriage porch to the central hall, which is octagon in form, lighted from above the roof and from the stairs; it is circumscribed by galleries at the level of the several floors, and is the point of distribution to the several rooms from the stairs; in the centre of this hall on this floor I have marked a pedestal for the statue of Smithson, as the best situation for it. This hall is 90 feet high to the floor of the bell tower, lantern, (or observatory, as it may be appropriated,) under which are the eight windows which light it.

The principal stairs are placed in a projection of semioctagonal figure, forming the centre of the south front; they are spacious, double and single lights alternately, of easy rise and access.

There are eight doors of entrance—three on each front, one on each end; the public entrances are central, opening directly to the principal halls.

There are stairs in each tower on the south and north fronts, so that each lecture room has its stair. The height of ceiling is 15 feet clear.

The halls, corridors, piazza, and porches, to be paved.

No. 2, is the second story floor.

Visiters to the Institution necessarily pass through the central hall to reach this floor; in passing up the stairs its form will be seen to advantage; the combination of the central hall and stairs will have, in this plan, a picturesque and highly architectural effect, seen from the first floor, or from any of the landings or galleries. If grandeur of interior is to be indulged in any where, it ought to be in the hall and stairs of this Institution, leading as they do to spacious and lofty rooms; it is to be observed, too, that the richness of the whole is produced by form and proportion, not by costly labor. From the gallery of the hall opens the leading corridors, and immediately from its centre the library. This room occupies the whole north front of the main part of the building, exclusive of extreme wings, being in length 215 feet, in width it is 38 feet clear of all projections; but it is common to mark the width, as to the depth of the window and opposite recesses, in which case it is a room of 40 feet wide, 215 feet long. For reasons before stated, viz., the great weight that may be placed in the Museum over it, and for the better, indeed true proportion of this room, I have adopted this width. The height is 27 feet 6 inches clear in the centre; less it should not be for a room of this size. Its extreme length unbroken would be monotonous; this is avoided by the actual construction, in the centre, by the walls of the centre building, advanced into the room, and spanning it with an arch, giving an apparent centre and two lateral rooms, en suite; the centre room being nearly square, will be finished on the ceiling in groined arching, the lateral rooms by arched ribs boldly projected spanning the width. These lateral rooms will be perfect in proportion, being nearly half their length in width, and two-thirds that width in height; this slight break in the room and ceilings will produce variety and interest; to see a room at a glance, of such a size as this, is tiresome; there is no wish to look twice. The Librarian's desk I place in the recess, (made by the large bay window over the principal entrance of north front,) the space so made is about 14 feet by 18, being ample for this purpose, and he is in complete command of the whole room, opposite the only doors for public entrance to the Library. The Reading room is at the end of the Library, of size 28 by 38 feet, having access from the corridor, and from the lower stair if desired. Directly under this room, is one I have marked ante-room to Library; this I thought necessary to the Librarian, for the reception and deposit of books, boxes, pamphlets, &c., before being bound and regulated for the shelves, and all other work of his office improperly done in the Library. The walls of the Library alone, without having lateral cases encumbering the floor, by the windows being on one side only, will contain 75,000 volumes; and this having the cases 20 feet high. When the books increase beyond that, the cases may be carried to the ceiling, and will contain one-third more, or the whole numbered required, equal 100,000 volumes. Opposite the Library, separated by the corridors, lighted from the south front, are the two second size Lecture rooms, each to contain 500 persons seated; besides this, the lecturer's space on the floor will be 400 square feet, besides a large room for professor to each and a sub-lobby, with stairs to an entresol room over the professor's; these rooms will be each about 14 feet high, as the whole height of Lecture rooms is 29 feet from floor to floor. These Lecture rooms may be fitted up as desired, their purposes not being clearly defined in the report. Attached to that I have marked Chemistry as the student's working laboratory, 28 by 38 feet; it would be fitted up with the latest arrangements in practice, with supply of water, sinks, flues, &c., for thorough cleanliness and ventilation.

In the extreme west wings are two smaller Lecture rooms; one may be for Anatomy, the other as described in report. They are lighted partially from above, from the

roof of the aisled projections; they will each contain 350 persons seated, besides the necessary room for the professor and apparatus. They have each their private stair, besides a public stair for audience from the corridor.

In the extreme east wing is the large Lecture hall, of size 70 by 100 feet, containing seats on the floor for 1,500 persons, which may be increased by a gallery in the aisle to 2,000; this room is in height 45 feet, embracing the second and third story; it is accessible direct by five stairs, one in each tower, and one in the lateral corridor, besides from the principal stair; these will disperse a large audience in a few minutes. Its capability, as a room for speaking and hearing, is good; its proportion being acoustically correct; behind the rostrum the wall is formed to throw out the voice, and there is no space of wall opposite to return it in reverberation; the light is ample on the first line of windows; this will be increased by those of the clear story, as seen on the end elevation, No. 6; and in cases of illustrative demonstration, the light may be direct from the roof on the subject. This is not likely to be required, as the light will be agreeable to the audience, being on back, and will directly illuminate the lecturer and rostrum. A professor's room is provided, of 15 by 20 feet. One of the rooms under this hall may be a preparation room, for subjects illustrative of lectures here. This room, indeed the whole house, will be amply warmed and ventilated; for which purpose the octagon towers in the internal angles of the south and north towers, are carried up, as air shafts; besides, the four towers on the external angles of the central building, two of which are octagon on the north front, those on the south are square, will have shafts for air continued in them, as well as discharge pipes of water closets, &c. The interior walls will have flues for hot air, and smoke flues will be confined to them, as they are disagreeable to the sight on outside walls, and weaken them.

No. 3 is the third story.

The central hall and stairs is continued as on second story; on the right and left of the hall are the galleries for statuary and paintings; they are each 80 feet long by 40 feet wide, to the window recesses, and 25 feet high to the ceiling of lantern lights. I have shewn in the elevations Nos. 4 and 5, the third story as lighted by perforating the panels under the parapet, but it will not alter the appearance of the building should they not be perforated at all; the light of them is unnecessary for works of art, or the contents of museum; indeed it is disagreeable, but they are required for thoroughly airing the walls and floor, which contract mustiness in time, in rooms only lighted from the ceiling, however good the ventilation. I may here remark that the lighting of museums properly was a subject of much examination by me some years ago, having to prepare a set of plans of a building for the exhibition of the Chinese Museum Collection, in London, England, when taken there from Philadelphia. I found that, in a room lighted from both sides, the objects were seen most imperfectly; the spectator having the light in his eyes if examining objects at the side of the room, and he shades the light if the object is in the centre; it is especially disagreeable if seen through glass cases, as the conflicting lights dazzle on the glass, teazing the eye to get a right position.

The museum is 255 feet long, and may be continued 100 feet more by using the rooms over the extreme wings on the west; a room of 28 by 38, at the end of the statue gallery, may be a studio for painting or statuary. The centre of the museum will be higher at the entrance, where the walls of centre building cross it, and will suit the exhibition of high objects. The centre hall is lighted over the roof of this centre building; and if desired that the lantern should be used for a separate purpose, and not for bells, it can be so arranged. I judged it necessary for bells and clock, as well as being the centre and relieving point of the building.

I propose to roof the building with slate and copper, on cast iron rafters; the principal of these pending below the ceiling in the form, and with the decoration of the style of architecture I have given. The lantern lights being a continued light the length of each room, will have cast iron sash, glazed with plate glass, made to the form as in section No. 6.

The towers at the east and west extreme ends are used in the first story as entrance porches, in the second story partially as points of communication, on the third the same, and on the fourth may be places of observation in science, or bell towers; one angle of each will have discharge shafts for air.

No. 4 is the south front, and shews the elevation of the greenhouse and conservatory. I have not embodied those places in my design, but as applique, as they are unwholesome, their required surfaces of light does not agree with any style of architecture; but as adjunct, they require a great deal of dirty work and material in them, which is better done if they are out of direct observation. The size of them is 30 feet by 65 feet each, and 25 feet high in the centre; they are directly entered from the building, and will be highly ornamental thus placed and formed, as a parallel perspective view of this front would shew.

No. 5 is the north front; on this is seen the carriage porch elevation, a structure necessary to comfort in a building of so many purposes.

The general height of the building is 75 feet to the top of the parapet; the height of the extreme end towers is 100 feet, and of the central tower is 175 feet. No. 6 has on it the elevation of the ends, both being alike.

The perspective view (framed) shows the general appearance at the distance of 200 yards; on it is slightly tinted the kind of stone work of the exterior, having dressed stone on all the corners, jambs of windows, and doors; all the parapet copings, the cornices, and the bases, the pinnacles and turrets, will also be of dressed stone; the intermediate spaces of walls will be of good rubble work in courses, if the stone procured are favorable for it; but this

part of the walls, it is seen on the elevations, are a small part of the structure; the windows being lofty and wide, together with buttress and other projections, all displaying dressed stone in prominence, will make the work appear rich and elaborate; the sky line is broken by pinnacles and parapets, giving the whole a most ornate character from any point of sight, and the prominent features centralize and balance in any view; there is no straggling of parts, no aim at picturesqueness, beyond the actual purpose of the building. The drawings have necessarily been hastily executed, but the plans and constructive detail have been well considered. If I have departed from the suggestive plan accompanying the reports, it is for the gain of economy in material and work, sound construction, and better proportion of rooms, a sheltered and direct communication to every room within the building, and a more imposing building as a whole externally; strip it of every tower and pinnacle, it would still be a respectable pile. In making the design I have kept in view the proposed expenditure, closely calculating the expense of every feature added; no inducement of display in design and drawing has led me beyond that. I have also complied with the conditions of your committee in the number of rooms, and in the space required for each. To this I have added some small rooms, and an addition of several feet in height to each story; thus the cellar will be 8 feet clear height; the first story, or ground floor, 17 feet from the floor to the floor of the second story; from the floor of the second story to the floor of the third story, 29 feet; and from the floor of the third story to the ridge of roof, 25 feet. If the stone to be used are of good building shape and size, I propose to make, as required, the foundations of concrete, the cellar walls 3 feet 6 inches thick, the buttress foundations 4 feet thick, the walls of first story 3 feet thick, the walls of second story 2 feet 6 inches thick, and those of the third story 2 feet 3 inches, exclusive of brick lining; the tower walls, and parts which are built higher, would be proportionably thicker; the main interior walls to be two brick and a half in thickness.

I propose to make the building thoroughly fire-proof throughout, by using cast iron beams and joists, filled in between them with brick work, constituting in fact a wall in the floor—a mode of building I carried out at the Academy of Natural Sciences in Philadelphia. Over this to lay a board floor, as usual, being the most comfortable and clean; the walls, corridors, &c., to be paved in polished stone, laid as shown on No. 1. By using cast iron for beams, they can be made ornamental to the ceilings, as I have before mentioned for principal rafters; it is seen, too, that their strength is greatly increased by the form required in this style of architecture. Those over the library, for instance, I would make of proven strength, to carry 50 tons; this supports 600 feet of floor area of the museum. The greatest or severest trial of a floor is packing it with men as close as they can stand. On this space only 30 tons of human beings could stand—a load greater than the average contents of a museum; consequently, the floors would be of double strength. I also propose to make all the window frames of cast iron, the glass to be set in lead; the glass to be all plate glass, if the Government will drawback the duty for this building, as plate glass is now made in England at about 3 shillings sterling per square foot for windows, and facilities are gaining daily in that manufacture, that give hopes it will be much less by the time this building would be ready for glazing.

The doors would necessarily be of wood; iron doors are impracticable and annoying where much in use. Iron shutters would be provided to the doors, if needed, to prevent communication of fire. I propose to make the doors of oak, varnished; the other wood fittings of every description to be of oak, or of walnut wood.

The building to be amply supplied with water for every purpose desired, to be taken from the public water works, if any in Washington, or from a well to be made, and distributed over the building by force pump.

An apparatus for the manufacture of gas to light the rooms of the building, with pipes to distribute it to the necessary points of illumination.

To construct an apparatus for heating air, so as perfectly to warm and ventilate the whole building, of easy management.

Having had much experience in building, and knowing the work to be done, thoroughly and practically, with perfect confidence, I hereby make offer, and bind myself to erect, building, and finish the building for Smithsonian Institution, as designed by me, to specifications to be made based on my drawings, and this description, on condition that stone are supplied for ($1.25) one dollar twenty-five cents per perch, for the sum of two hundred and fifty thousand dollars, and to finish the building in three years from the time of commencement, and to give security for the due completion of contract.

I may add, that if a less expenditure on buildings is considered necessary by your honorable Board, I can point out such modification of this design, preserving the exterior appearance, as will reduce the expense from 20 to 30 per cent. on the above estimate.

I have the honor to be, gentlemen, your most obedient servant,

JOHN NOTMAN,
Architect, Philadelphia.
WASHINGTON, *Dec. 26th, 1846.*

23.
REFECTORY, PRINCETON THEOLOGICAL SEMINARY
PRINCETON, NEW JERSEY
1846–1847
Client: Building Committee for Refectory, Princeton Theological Seminary
Project: building to house refectory, steward's quarters and infirmary

DRAWINGS: none
DOCUMENTATION:
Accounts, bank vouchers and letters, Hodge Collection, PUL; Minutes of the Board of Trustees, 1824-1890 and Receipt Book for moneys expended in building of New Refectory 1847, Princeton Theological Seminary
BIBLIOGRAPHICAL REFERENCES: none

Refectory, Princeton Theological Seminary.
Author's photograph

To SUPPLY BOARD for their students at reasonable prices the trustees of the seminary

> Resolved, that it is expedient, to build a Refectory, & Steward's house, & that Mr. Cooley, Mr. L.W.R. Phillips, & Dr. Hodge, be a committee to proceed to erect such buildings; & they are hereby authorized to borrow, if necessary, a sum, not exceeding, $4,000.
>
> [Minutes, 29 Sept. 1846: 453]

The committee proceeded with celerity, although they soon determined that the budget was not adequate.

> The Building committee made the following report, which was accepted.
>
> The committee appointed to erect a new Refectory, for the use of the Theological Seminary, beg leave to report, that immediately after their appointment, they applied to Mr. John Nottman [sic], an experienced architect, for a plan of a suitable building. After some delay, Mr. Nottmann [sic] furnished the drawings for a building, 110 feet long, & one story & a half high, containing apartments for the steward, three hospital rooms, a dining room capable of accommodating from 125 to 150 persons, & other necessary accommodations. It was at first estimated that such a building could be erected for $5,500. But when the architect came to ascertain the cost of materials & labour at this time, in Princeton, he was of opinion that the building could not be properly finished under, at least, $6000.
>
> The committee at first proposed to reduce the size of the house; but as that would materially affect its convenience, they concluded to endeavor to put it up on the original plan, & by strict economy to bring it within the original estimate.... It was at first proposed to put a shingle roof on the building, & this was contemplated in the estimate furnished by the architect. But on consideration it was thought wisest to have a slate roof, with copper gutters & valleys, though at a considerable increase of expense.
>
> [Minutes, Nov. 1847: 471-72]

Notman eventually was paid $300 for his work.

The building, one and one-half stories high, consists of a central section with shallow projecting hip-roofed pavilions at either end. The sandstone walls are unadorned except for broad-banded brownstone window surrounds.
PRESENT STATUS:

> In use as the Administration Building of Princeton Theological Seminary

24.

IVY HALL
PRINCETON, NEW JERSEY
1846–1847
Client: Richard Stockton Field
Project: law school

DRAWINGS: none
OTHER EARLY ILLUSTRATIONS:
> Photographs, PUA

DOCUMENTATION:
> Minutes of the Board of Trustees of the College of New Jersey, III; Princeton *Whig*

BIBLIOGRAPHICAL REFERENCES:
> D: 133; F: 33; *The American Architect* CVIII, 2081 (10 Nov. 1915): 317; Collins, V[arnum] Lansing. *Princeton Past and Present.* Princeton (1931)

ON 23 JUNE 1846, the College of New Jersey appointed professors for its new law school. [Minutes] Construction of a building was under way in 1846 when a letter to the local newspaper "commend[ed] to the favourable notice of your readers the new law building now erecting in this place." [*Whig*, 18 Dec. 1846: 2] On 22 Dec. 1846 the trustees of the college ordered that the law books in the library were to be "deposited in the building now preparing for the law school." [Minutes] Notman's responsibility for the design is documented by an article on the slightly later Second Presbyterian Church, which refers to him as the architect of the law school. [*Whig*, 1 Dec. 1848; see entry 37]

Richard Stockton Field, Notman's patron at Fieldwood (see entries 21 and 59), is said to have borne the expense of erecting the law school, in which he served as professor until its demise in 1855. [Collins: 22-23] This seems likely since there are no reports on its construction in the trustees' minutes.

An article in The *American Architect* reports the gift of two drawings to Princeton University, one of which is described as a front and side elevation and ground plan of Ivy Hall, the other being of the chapel. No

Ivy Hall. *Courtesy PUA*

drawing of Ivy Hall can be found in the University's collections, although there are two of the chapel [See entry 27], so the article may have been in error.

PRESENT STATUS:

> After the law school closed, the building was used as offices for the Delaware and Raritan Canal Company, a private library (from which its name derives), and a college eating club. It now belong to Trinity Church, which uses it as choir offices and robing rooms.

25.

ST. THOMAS'S CHURCH
GLASSBORO, NEW JERSEY
1846–1847
Client: Vestry of St. Thomas's Church
Project: design of rural church

DRAWINGS: none
OTHER EARLY ILLUSTRATIONS:

> There are twenty measured drawings made in 1937 in the Historic American Buildings Survey.

St. Thomas's Church. *Author's photograph*

DOCUMENTATION:

> Doane, George Washington. *Diocese of New Jersey: Episcopal Address to the Sixty-Third Annual Convention.* Burlington (1846); *Sixty-Fourth Annual Convention.* Burlington (1847)

BIBLIOGRAPHICAL REFERENCES:

> F: 67-71, 101-105; *One Hundredth Anniversary, St. Thomas' Episcopal Church.* Glassboro (1946); Stanton, Phoebe. *The Gothic Revival and American Church Architecture.* Baltimore (1968)

THIS SMALL GOTHIC REVIVAL CHURCH is built of the deep red sandstone known locally as "ironstone." Stanton [46], following information in the Inventory of Church Archives of New Jersey, dates the building 1840, but as Fairbanks [69-70] has indicated, the documentation bespeaks a later date. That indefatigable supporter of rural churches and layer of cornerstones, Bishop George Washington Doane, reported:

> At six o'clock, in the evening of that day (April 18), I laid the corner stone of the new Church at Glassborough, ... The Church to be erected here will be of stone, after a plan by Mr. Notman, in what may perhaps be called the rural Gothic; and what deserves to be followed elsewhere, is undertaken on the responsibility of a single individual.
> [*Address*, 1846: 20]

A year later:

It is with pleasure we state that the new Church, the corner stone of which was laid about a year since, is now entirely up and can be made ready for consecration in a few weeks. It is a substantial and beautiful building....

[*Proceedings*, 1847:29]

The chancel is said to have been added during the Civil War [*Anniversary*: 1], a tradition that seems plausible, since both the stone and the masonry technique utilized differ from that of the nave. Fairbanks [105] records an oral tradition that the lich-gate is coeval with the church. Stylistically, however, it appears to be a product of the 1880s.

PRESENT STATUS:

Still maintained as active church

26.
CHURCH OF THE ASCENSION
LOMBARD STREET ABOVE ELEVENTH,
  PHILADELPHIA
1846–1850
Client: Vestry of the Church of the Ascension
Project: redesign of church facade

DRAWING 26.1:
  Title: Sketch for Church of
  "The Ascension" Epis.
  Signature: John Notman Architect
  Philada.
  Date: Feby 20th 1846
  Scale: 1/10" : 1'
  Other inscriptions: Elevation./Plan./
  Front line of Church/street line
  Description: elevation and plan of facade
  Medium: ink and wash
  Size: 20⅞ x 15¾ (53 x 40)
  Owner: Historical Society of Pennsylvania
  (AIA), Y

DRAWING 26.2:
  Title: none
  Signature: John Notman/Architect/
  Philad (stamp)
  Date: none
  Scale: ⅛" : 1'
  Other inscriptions: Front Elevation/Plan
  Description: elevation and plan of facade
  Medium: ink and wash
  Size: 21½ x 17¾ (54.5 x 45)
  Owner: The Athenaeum of Philadelphia
DOCUMENTATION:
  Philadelphia *Public Ledger*; J
BIBLIOGRAPHICAL REFERENCES:
  F: 72-74, 106-110; Smith, Robert C.
  "John Notman and the Athenaeum Building." *Athenaeum Addresses*. Philadelphia
  (1951): 26

BECAUSE THIS BUILDING, which no longer exists, appears not to have been recorded photographically, conclusions about its appearance as executed can only be speculative. Both Smith and Fairbanks infer that the Lombardic design in the Historical Society's collection was utilized. Neither seems to have been aware that the untitled drawing at The Athenaeum, on the basis of a coincidence of dimensions, is an alternative design for the same project and, in fact, was probably the one selected.

Fairbanks [106] quotes a late nineteenth century account of the church by a Rev. Mr. Hodge pasted into a scrapbook in the Church of the Ascension Papers in the Registrar's Office of the Diocese of Pennsylvania. According to this, the original church, consecrated in 1836, had "two rows of square windows on the sides, hung with venetian blinds; the staircases came directly up into the chancel." When this was considered inadequate in 1847 "Mr. Upjohn of New York, and Notman, of Philadelphia, both advised the sale of the edifice and the erection of a new building, rather than the attempt to improve it." The account indicates that this idea was abandoned and the church remodelled. Contemporary documentation, however, proves that the sequence of events was not so neat.

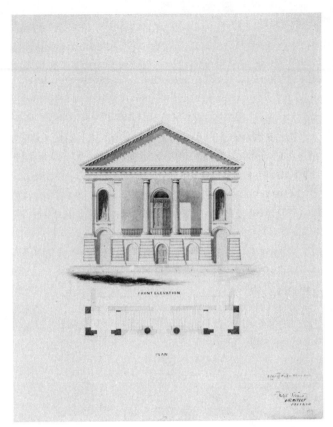

26.1

26.2

Church of the Ascension—The vestry of the Church has purchased the large lot of ground at the corner of Lombard and Broad sts, with the view of erecting a commodious edifice in the old English style of Gothic architecture. The designs have been executed by Richard Apjohn [sic], Esq., the Architect, and the building, if erected according to them, will be a beautiful addition to the public edifices of this city.   [*Public Ledger*, 17 Mar. 1847: 2]

It is possible that Notman, as early as 1846, was proposing, in the Historical Society drawing, remodelling of the existing facade rather than execution of a new building. In any event, after a few years, this was the course followed. On 19 Jan. 1850 the *Public Ledger* reported that the interior repairs, carried out by Notman's brother-in-law John Gibson, were complete. By late in the year the exterior of the church was also finished as indicated in the following notice (italics added):

The Church of the Ascension—This Church, in Lombard Street, above Eleventh, was re-opened for public worship on Sunday last, the whole exterior and interior having been greatly improved by the alterations that have been carried into effect since it was closed in August last. The building, which before was nothing but a plain brick edifice with square door-way and unsightly windows, have given place to a handsome arched entrance and long windows of a beautiful and appropriate form. The whole exterior is now being painted stone color. *The basement is now hidden from view by a wall with arched door-ways.* The changes in the front were made according to a design furnished by Mr. Notman, proving his great skill in making so much of the materials he had to work on.

[*Public Ledger*, 16 Nov. 1850: 1]

Although both Notman's designs were characterized by arched entrances and long windows, this description appears to indicate that The Athenaeum drawing was followed. Surely the tower and arcaded stairways in the Historical Society drawing would not have been ignored had they been erected.

PRESENT STATUS:

Demolished

27.

CHAPEL, COLLEGE OF
NEW JERSEY
PRINCETON, NEW JERSEY
1847

Client: Building Committee of Trustees of
College of New Jersey (Matthew New-
kirk, Chairman)
Project: non-denominational
Protestant chapel

DRAWING 27.1:
Title: Chapel Nassau College/
Princeton N.[J.]
Signature: John Notman Arch[t].
Date: April 13th 1847
Scale: none indicated (scales ⅛″ : 1′)
Other inscriptions: Front length 50 feet
Description: elevation and sections
Size: 19½ x 14⅜ (49.5 x 36)
Medium: ink and wash, with pencil
additions and figures
Owner: Princeton University Archives

DRAWING 27.2:
Title: none
Signature: none
Date: none
Scale: ⅛″ : 1′
Other inscription: Flank whole length
70 feet
Description: elevation and measured plan
Size: 19¼ x 14⅛ (48.9 x 35.9)
Medium: ink and wash
Owner: Princeton University Archives

OTHER EARLY ILLUSTRATIONS:
Numerous photographs, PUA
DOCUMENTATION:
Minutes of the Trustees of the College of
New Jersey
BIBLIOGRAPHICAL REFERENCES:
"Current News and Comment, Architec-
tural Drawings of Interest Acquired by
Princeton University." *The American Ar-
chitect.* CVIII, 2081 (10 Nov. 1915): 317;
Greiff, Constance M., Gibbons, Mary W.
and Menzies, Elizabeth G. C. *Princeton
Architecture.* Princeton (1967)

AT A MEETING of the college's board of trustees on 22 Dec. 1847 a committee was appointed
"to take Measures for the erection of a New
Chapel at a cost of $5,000 on such site, as they
may deem most expedient." [Minutes: 471]
Abruptly at the June meeting of the trustees
this committee was dissolved and a new committee appointed with "full powers to alter
the plan." [Minutes: 479]

At a special meeting of the board called for
13 July 1847, the reasons for the trustees' actions, and the subsequent behavior of the two
committees were revealed.

That the committee entered on the duties of their office immediately after their appointment.

At their first meeting they made arrangements, to ascertain the amount of money thus far expended upon the
present structure, and to secure the drawing by a com-
petant Artist of a plan, which should be free from the objections of the one previously adopted.

The final decision of the committee was postponed to
the 15th of the month, as the earliest practicable period
for them to assemble, with the hope of having the necessary information and preliminary plans prepared. About
a week ago, the Chairman of the committee received a letter from the Chairman of the old Committee on the
Chapel, in which, the latter stated, that if the present
committee determined to alter the plan of the Chapel, he
would feel it to be his duty to call a meeting of the
Trustees.

This declaration from so respectable a quarter at once
induced the Chairman of the present committee to take
measures to call a meeting of the Trustees without delay.

The object was partly to attempt to reconcile conflicting opinions in a fair and Honourable manner, and partly
to [?] the responsibility of a final decision, under the
peculiar circumstances of the case, where it properly belonged.

The point to be decided by the present meeting, is shall
the present building go up without alteration, or not?—
The committee would here remark, that in their judgement, the form of *a Cross*, is not *the* form for a Presbyterian Chapel.

Cruciform Architecture, is so identified with popery
that it becomes [?] us to beware of adopting its insignia.
We know that the Cross is a form dear to Christians
from all its original associations. Far be it from us to assume a position of irreverence towards this sacred object.
But the history of the Church proves, that when the Cross
has been imitated externally in buildings and crucifixes it
has tended to degrade religion, and introduce superstition.
For ages it has been the badge of the man of sin. More
recently in this country the Puseyites have exalted it in all

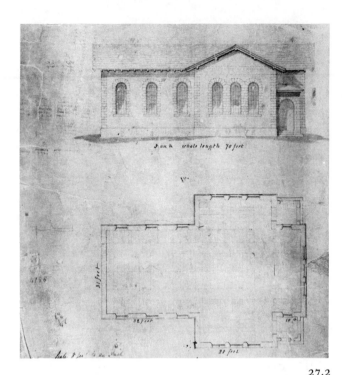

27.1

27.2

their semi-popistical ceremonies, have introduced into their architecture as symbolical of their sympathies with a religion, that neither we nor our fathers were able to endure. Your committee think that the Cross form ought not to have been selected for the Chapel of our College. It is nothing to the purpose to say that the former committee intended nothing by it. However innocent they were, the building completed, will remain an unanswerable argument against Presbyterian objections to popish symbolism.

Least of all ought such a building to be erected where the minds of the young can be easily familiarized with a form of architecture condemned by our church in general.

There are other objections, connected with economy, good taste and convenience, which have had weight with some members of the committee and of the board of Trustees.

Indeed your committee believe that if the Plan had been submitted originally to the Trustees, it would have commanded but a very few votes, if any at all.

But what can be done now? That, the Trustees have been called to-gether to decide. The committee state the fact that the walls are two-thirds up, that all the stone has been engaged—and that a verbal contract has been made with a carpenter. It is also undeniable that the present Cross form is a difficult one to alter, the length being too narrow for a rectangular building, and the arms, or transcript, being too wide. Still, after all the consideration which your committee have been able to give the matter, they believe, that a neat, plain, rectangular building, more convenient and tasteful can be erected, than the present, at the same estimated cost of $6,000.

With these explanations your committee submits the question to the Board of Trustees. They wish it to be un-

derstood that they wish to be discharged from all share in superintending the advancement of the present building.

When the committee was appointed, it was well known that a majority of them had expressed themselves in favor of some alteration. If the Trustees decide that no alteration shall be made, your committee suggest that the old committee be restored to the superintendance of the building. [Minutes: 493-95]

Parsimony, or at least prudence, won over piety and the trustees resolved "that the chapel be finished according to the plan of the architct, ..."

PRESENT STATUS:
Demolished

28.

HUGUENOT SPRINGS
NEAR MIDLOTHIAN, VIRGINIA
1847
Client: Huguenot Springs Company
Project: landscaping grounds of spa

DRAWINGS: none

OTHER EARLY ILLUSTRATIONS:

"Map of the Huguenot Springs Farm Situated in Powhatan County, Va." Novr. 30th 1870. Surveyed for Majr. Jas. B. Ferguson. J. B. Latrade, Civ. Eng.; lithograph in Moorman, John J[ennings]. *The Virginia Springs*. Richmond (1854). The same lithograph appears in the 1857 edition, but not in the 1859 edition.

DOCUMENTATION:

Records of the Hollywood Cemetery Company, Richmond, Virginia, I, 1847-68; D.s. A. S. Wooldridge to William B. Phillips, 26 July 1856, Phillips mss., Virginia Historical Society; *Historical Sketch of Hollywood Cemetery*. Richmond (1875); *Richmond Enquirer*

BIBLIOGRAPHICAL REFERENCES:

D: 137; M: 50-56; Weaver, Bettie W. "Powhatan County's Forgotten Spa: Huguenot Springs." *Virginia Cavalcade* (Winter, 1969): 13-16

AT A TIME when taking the waters seemed unceasingly popular, Virginia's springs were among the most favored. Huguenot Springs advertised its July opening in June 1847 [*Enquirer*, 22 June 1847: 3], at which time "shady promenading ground" was "under improvement." By the next year "important improvements have been made—smooth and shady walks, and level roads through the ample forest grounds attached to the Springs...." [*Enquirer*, 11 July 1848: 3]

The association of Notman's name with these improvements rests on his letter of 16 Aug. 1847 to Thomas T. Giles.

As to the Springs, I could visit them this fall. The plan of proceeding is, for the Company to have prepared, if they have not one already, a Surveyor's plot or map of the ground to be laid out, with position of the buildings at present on it marked. This ready I will come on and take a view of the place, noting on the map the general features. This may occupy there a couple of days or so. I return [to Philadelphia] and make the plan to a large scale, with directions to staking it out; or will return with it and stake out walks drives etc., with proper places for planting.

[The letter is quoted from Records of Hollywood Cemetery: 18, in Morgan: 52. Unfortunately, the record book is now lost.]

Notman did make such a visit [*Historical Sketch*: 6], but there is no evidence that the work planned by him was carried out. Certainly there is nothing particularly distinguished or unusual about the grounds.

The landscaping at Huguenot Springs consisted of a straight drive from the River Road through a wooded area, terminating in a long oval in front of the hotel. The oval ran through avenues of trees and bounded a lawn. On either side were "rows of cabins, placed a little irregularly and at varying distances, but which, partly seen and partly concealed among the scattered trees, contribute to a picturesque effect." [Moorman: 285]

PRESENT STATUS:

In 1856 the Springs were sold to William B. Phillips. (D.s. Wooldridge to Phillips.) During the Civil War the Springs was a Confederate Hospital. The hotel burned around the turn of the century. [Weaver: 15-16] Presently the site is occupied as a private residence. Five cottags, two moved and three much altered, remain, as do the oval drive, and picturesque groupings of trees.

29.

BANK OF NORTH AMERICA

CHESTNUT BETWEEN THIRD AND
    FOURTH STREETS, PHILADELPHIA
1847–1848
Client: Bank of North America
Project: design of new banking house

DRAWINGS: none

OTHER EARLY ILLUSTRATIONS:

Engravings of the building are reproduced in Rae, Julio H. *Philadelphia Pictorial Directory & Panoramic Advertiser, Chestnut Street from Second to Tenth Street.* Philadelphia (1851); Smith, R. A. *Philadelphia, as It Is, in 1852*; and Tuthill, Mrs. L. C. *History of Architecture.* Philadelphia (1848).

DOCUMENTATION:

Minutes of the Bank of North America, Book 16 and Bank of North America Ledger 13, Bank of North America Records, HSP; Philadelphia *Public Ledger*; J; St A

BIBLIOGRAPHICAL REFERENCES:

Smith, Robert C. "John Notman and the Athenaeum Building." *Athenaeum Addresses*. Philadelphia (1951)

ALTHOUGH THE ERECTION of the Bank of North America and its cost are well documented, Notman's name does not appear in the bank's financial records or minutes. As was generally the case in the nineteenth century, responsibility for construction was delegated to a building committee [Minutes: 10 May 1847], along with appropriation of a sum of money. It was this committee that dealt with the architect. In the case of the bank, the sum alloted was $20,000, quickly raised to $25,000. [Minutes: 24 May 1847] The actual cost of the building proved to be $26,612.66. [Ledger: 6]

Although the committee evidently made few reports to the board, the public was kept well informed.

The plan of the building about to be erected by them is, we think an admirable one, differing very essentially from anything now in the city. It will be one hundred feet deep and the banking room forty feet in height, from floor to ceiling, with a front the whole height of German freestone, similar to that with which Trinity Church in New York is built. From what we know of the plan, we admire their taste. [*Public Ledger*, 31 May 1847: 2]

The North American Bank Vault—The fireproof which is now being built in the new banking house of the North American Bank, in Chestnut street, above Third, attracts general attention, and the precautions which are taken to preserve its contents from the ravages of fire and to defy attempts of robbers, are worthy of being copied by similar institutions. It occupies a space of about fifteen feet square and will, in all, be two stories high. Solid walls of brick work, twelve inches thick, are building to enclose the fireproof, and in the centre of these walls are ranged bars of iron about four inches apart, placed in a perpendicular position, so that an attempt to break through any portion of the wall would be an almost impossible achievement; there are also to be plates of iron built in the wall, to render a breach still more difficult. In order to exclude the heat from the interior, in case of fire, the actual walls of the vault are to be constructed within those already de-

scribed, so as to allow a space of about three inches between them for the free circulation of air all around the enclosure intended to contain the valuables. [*Public Ledger*, 20 Aug. 1847: 2]

North American Bank Building—Quite a crowd assembled for the last two days opposite this building, gazing at the operations of the workmen, in placing upon the architrave above the doorway, the massive blocks which compose the pediment cornice, designed to surmount this showy entrance. The public appear to be quite curious to know the exact features which the building will present, and watch with much interest the progress that [it] is making towards its completion. The beams to support the roof of the edifice are now in their places, and will give some idea of the height and dimension of the banking room. It is to be lit from sky-lights in the roof, as well as by three ample windows on the Chestnut street front. The upper portion of the front will be even richer in ornament than that already up. [*Public Ledger*, 21 Oct. 1847: 2]

PRESENT STATUS:

Demolished.

In the late nineteenth century the building was altered according to plans made by John Windrim; a copy of one sheet of these plans is among the bank's records. The changes included addition of an attic, masked by raising the cornice, and substitution of a portico, with columns bearing a balustrade, for Notman's pedimented doorway.

Tuthill. *History of Architecture*

30.

MEDARY
NORTH PHILADELPHIA
1847–1848
Client: Harry Ingersoll
Project: residence

DRAWINGS: none
OTHER EARLY ILLUSTRATIONS:

A floor plan appears in Perpetual Policy #7926, Franklin Fire Insurance Co. Records, HSP; a photograph, showing the house after additions were made in the late nineteenth century, is in D.

DOCUMENTATION:

Downing, A. J. *A Treatise on the Theory and Practice of Landscape Gardening*, 6th ed. New York (1859); Fisher, Sidney George. Diary, HSP

BIBLIOGRAPHICAL REFERENCES:

D: 134

Plan of Medary. *HSP*

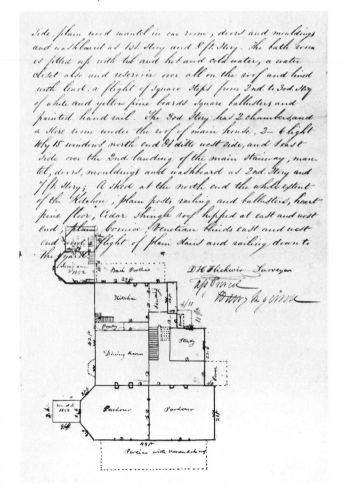

THIS WAS ONE OF THE SIMPLEST of Notman's villas, lacking the complexity and spatial interplay usually characteristic of his plans and somewhat awkward in its exterior massing. The attribution to Notman rests on a reference in the sixth edition of Downing [554-55]:

In the neighborhood of Philadelphia there are many fine places; among them is *Medary*, the residence of Harry Ingersoll, Esq. A tasteful and substantial house, built by Notman, we believe, with pleasure-grounds of very considerable extent, ...

The date of Medary's construction is well documented by Sidney George Fisher and the insurance survey. On 27 Aug. 1847 Fisher "Went to Harry Ingersoll's. He has bought 40 acres near Fox's—and is building a very good house." On 1 Nov. 1847 Fisher recorded a visit by A. J. Downing and noted that "Fisher [at Alverthorpe] had him two days—Harry Ingersoll one day." Fisher, although naming Downing, does not mention an architect's name, but this is of no particular significance, since he never refers to Notman in his many entries about Alverthorpe and The Athenaeum's new building.

The property was insured on 24 July 1847, with the survey made 23 Sept. 1848. On 23 Nov. Fisher visited the Ingersolls "First time since they got into their house . . . The handsomest country residence I ever saw in cottage style. It is replete with every convenience and luxury." As may have been the case with Prospect, it appears that Ingersoll insured his property before it was fully completed and ready for occupancy.

The house was of stone with cedar shingle roof. Interior embellishments included

a brochadilla and Sienna marble mantel in front rooms and a black and gold Italian marble mantel in dining room; Stucco cornice in 3 rooms, and Hall and ribbed ceiling west south room . . . cast Iron ballusters; mahogany newell post and hand rail. . . .

The exterior was enlivened by

a doorway east side with outside porch and roof supported by 3 shaped wooden bracketts shingle roof pointed shingles; a doorway also west side from dining room; outside half octagon porch, with glass door; a cover over it with shaped brackets; and a balcony over it with Iron railing.

The house had "a furnace in the cellar for heated air which appears to be safe," and, on the second floor, a bathroom "with tub and hot and cold water, a water closet also."

· Dallett found the most remarkable feature of the house as it appeared in later years the bracketed mansard roof, which, if original, "was one of the very first so conceived in the United States." [D: 134] The insurance survey, however, shows that this was not the case, describing the original roof as "hipped all around." An amendment to the survey of 6 Nov. 1867, describing "sundry alterations and additions," includes "An Attic Story... French roof, broken pitch...2 dormers...." A further addition to a service wing, surveyed 31 Oct. 1871 had a "mansard roof" with "4 light dormer window (pediment)...."

PRESENT STATUS:
Demolished

31.

WING 3, NEW JERSEY STATE PENITENTIARY
TRENTON, NEW JERSEY
1847–1848
Client: Commission for Building of State Prison
Project: building to house bakery, kitchen and laundry

DRAWINGS: none
DOCUMENTATION:
> *Acts of the 71st Legislature of the State of New Jersey.* Trenton (1847); ... *of the 78th Legislature* ... Mount Holly (1854); ... *of the 84th Legislature* ... Paterson (1860); *Minutes of the Votes and Proceedings of the Seventieth General Assembly of the State of New Jersey,* Woodbury (1846); ... *of the Seventy-First General Assembly,* Rahway (1847); *Report on the Condition of the New Jersey State Prison,* Trenton (1847); Trenton *State Gazette;* J

JACKSON [224] lists the New Jersey State Prison as one of Notman's works. This, in itself, would not constitute adequate documentation, but Notman is also given credit for the prison in an obituary in the Trenton newspaper. [*State Gazette,* 7 Mar. 1865: 2] Although it is certain that John Haviland was responsible for the original design of the prison, it is probable, given the two citations, that Notman provided plans for some subsequent work. Of the mid-nineteenth additions proposed or made to the prison, a wing planned, but not executed, in 1854, was designed by J. C. Hoxie [*Acts,* 1854: 376]; one authorized in 1860 was by Chauncey Graham. [*Acts,* 1860: 600]

The only construction for which Notman could have been responsible is what has become known as Wing 3, extending to the southeast of Haviland's administration building. In their reports for 1846 and 1847 the legislative committee and the prison doctor discussed the unhealthy conditions caused by cooking and washing within the confines of the prison structures. Heat and odor from these activities rendered some of the nearby cells uninhabitable. [*Votes and Proceedings,* 1846: 151; Report: 5]

The committee recommended that an additional wing be erected to the main building, of size sufficient to afford accommodation for the steam engine and machinery, with suitable apartments for washing, baking and cooking.

On 4 Mar. 1847 an act authorizing construction and appointing five commissioners to oversee the task was passed. [*Acts,* 1847: 173-74] The building was completed by early 1848. [*State Gazette:* 5 Feb. 1848]

PRESENT STATUS:
Access to the penitentiary is difficult to obtain and photography within the walls forbidden. Wing 3 has been all but swallowed up by subsequent construction, but appears to have been a simple, functional building. Like the rest of the construction within the walls, including Haviland's administration building and original wing, it is scheduled for demolition over the next several years.

32.

GREEN HILL PRESBYTERIAN CHURCH

GIRARD AVENUE ABOVE SIXTEENTH STREET,
PHILADELPHIA

1847–1849

Client: Trustees of the Green Hill
Presbyterian Church

Project: new church

DRAWINGS: none

OTHER EARLY ILLUSTRATIONS:

An engraving appears in *Manual of the
Green Hill Presbyterian Church*, Philadelphia (1859).

DOCUMENTATION:

Minutes of the Trustees of the Green Hill
Presbyterian Church, I, 1847-1880, Presbyterian Historical Society

BIBLIOGRAPHICAL REFERENCES:

F: 80-81; Waite, Diana S., ed. "Morris,
Tasker & Co's Illustrated Catalogue."
Architectural Elements. Princeton (n.d.);
White, William P. and Scott, William H.
The Presbyterian Church in Philadelphia.
Philadelphia (1895)

WITHOUT ATTRIBUTING the building to Notman, Fairbanks pointed out some similarities
to both the design for an unidentified transept
church [70.5] and St. Paul's, Trenton [38].
In fact, both these designs postdate Green
Hill.

However, there is no doubt that Notman
was the author of Green Hill. The Minutes
of the Trustees of Green Hill Presbyterian
Church, to which all dates cited below refer,
provide ample evidence that he served as
architect, and probably contractor, for the
church. On 28 Aug. 1847 the trustees "Resolved that Mr. Notman's plan for building
the Green Hill Presbyterian Church be
adopted." It is not certain whether this resolution passed, for at the next meeting one of
the members was requested to obtain an estimate of a plan by John Carver. Carver attended a meeting of the trustees on 11 Sept.,
and presented his plan for a church "after the

Green Hill Presbyterian Church. *Author's photograph*

normal architecture" to cost $10,000. This was
accepted, conditioned on approval of major
prospective donors, and Carver was asked to
prepare drawings and specifications.

Ten days later one of the trustees was asked
"to call on Mr. Notman relative to our not
carrying out his plan." Notman must have
protested. He had the support of one of the
donors, a Mr. McCallister. McCallister, "having stated the peculiar engagement we were
under to Mr. Notman," the trustees resolved
to consult again with the architect.

On 30 Sept. Notman submitted a design
for a $10,000 building, followed by specifica-
tions and additional drawings on 8 Nov. These
were finally approved on 22 Nov. On 11 Jan.
1848 the board voted to pay Carver's bill of
$100 for his drawings. At the same time a first
payment of $500 was made to Notman. The
church must have been completed by the end
of the following year; Notman's bill, showing
a balance due of $2,210.26, was dated 15 Dec.
1849.

The exterior facade gives little hint of the
extraordinary interior. A wide nave and narrow aisles are defined by slim cast-iron col-

umns bearing heavy hammer beams. These resemble pattern 415 on page 58 of Morris Tasker's 1860 catalogue. The sanctuary is flooded with light both from windows with perpendicular tracery in the aisles and large dormers in the roof of the nave.

PRESENT STATUS:

Later known as the Girard Avenue Presbyterian Church, the building is currently maintained in excellent condition as the Christ Temple Baptist Church.

33.

ST. MARK'S CHURCH
1625 LOCUST STREET, PHILADELPHIA
1847–1852
Client: Vestry of St. Mark's Church
Project: new church for Anglican congregation

DRAWING 33.1:
Title: Church of St. Marks Philada
Signature: John Notman Archt
Date: Sep 18th 1847
Scale: none indicated (scales approximately 1/10″ : 1′)
Description: rendered flank elevation
Medium: ink, wash and watercolor
Size: 18⅞ x 24 (47.9 x 61)
Owner: Historical Society of Pennsylvania (AIA), R-13
Exhibition record: "Two Centuries of Philadelphia Architectural Drawings." Philadelphia Museum of Art, 1964
Publication record: Stanton, Phoebe. *The Gothic Revival and American Church Architecture.* Baltimore (1968); Tatum, George. *Penn's Great Town.* Philadelphia (1961): Pl. 82

DRAWING 33.2:
Title: Church of St. Marks Philada
Signature: John Notman Archt
Date: Sep 18th 1847
Scale: none indicated (scales 1/10″ : 1′)
Other inscriptions: Outline Aisle/Piers/Section
Description: partial longitudinal section; transverse section
Medium: ink and wash
Size: 24-13/16 x 18 13/16 (63 x 47.7)
Owner: Historical Society of Pennsylvania (AIA), R-14

DRAWING 33.3:
Title: Church of St. Marks Philada
Signature: John Notman Archt.
Date: Sept. 18th 1847
Scale: 1/10″ : 1′
Other inscription: Plan.
Description: measured plan
Medium: pencil, ink, and wash
Size: 18¾ x 24⅝ (47.6 x 62.5)
Owner: Historical Society of Pennsylvania (AIA), R-15

DRAWING 33.4:
Title: none
Signature: none
Date: none
Scale: none indicated
Other inscriptions: none
Description: elevation, south flank
Medium: ink
Size: 14-7/16 x 22-3/16 (36.7 x 56.3)
Owner: Historical Society of Pennsylvania (AIA)

DRAWING 33.5:
Title: none
Signature: none
Date: none
Scale: none indicated
Other inscriptions: none
Description: elevation, north flank
Medium: ink
Size: 17⅛ x 24-7/16 (43.5 x 62.1)
Owner: Historical Society of Pennsylvania (AIA)

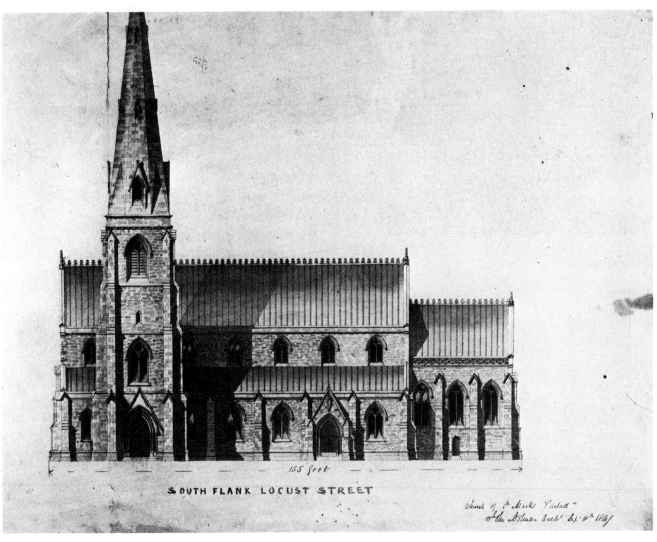

SOUTH FLANK LOCUST STREET

155 feet

Above: 33.1 ; *Below*: 33.2

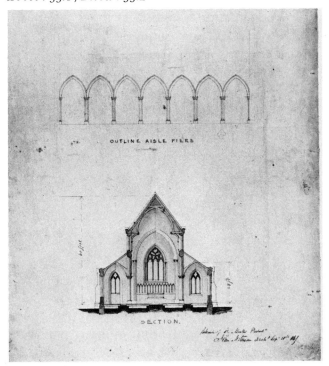

OUTLINE AISLE PIERS

SECTION.

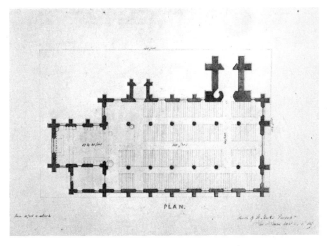

PLAN.

33.3

33.4

Above: 33.5; *Below*: 33.6

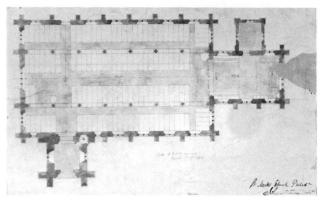

33.8

DRAWING 33.6:
    Title: none
    Signature: none
    Date: none
    Scale: none indicated
    Other inscriptions: none
    Description: elevation, west end
    Medium: ink
    Size: 16 x 17-11/16 (40.7 x 44.9)
    Owner: Historical Society of Pennsylvania (AIA)

DRAWING 33.7:
    Title: S. Marks Philadelphia (not in Notman's hand)
    Signature: none visible (may be present under attached plan of a casket)
    Date: none
    Scale: none indicated
    Other inscriptions: none
    Description: traced perspective
    Medium: ink
    Size: 20¼ x 16¼ (51.5 x 41.3)
    Owner: Henry F. duPont Winterthur Museum and Library, M 60.348.1

DRAWING 33.8:
    Title: St. Marks Church Philada
    Signature: John Notman Archt
    Date: none
    Scale: ⅛″ : 1′ (given in pencil)
    Other inscriptions: Tower 175 ft high
    Description: plan, probably traced
    Medium: ink and wash
    Size: 12-5/16 x 10-5/16 (31.3 x 53.2)
    Owner: Henry F. duPont Winterthur Museum and Library, M 60.348.2

S. Mark Philadelphia

33·7

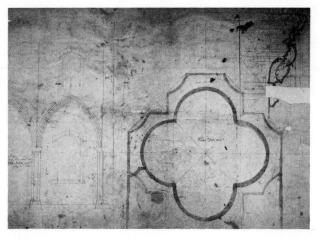

33.9

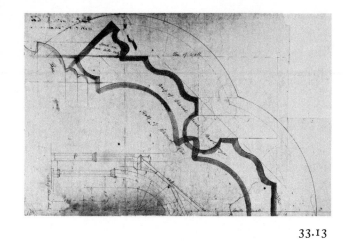

33.13

Above: 33.10; *Below*: 33.12

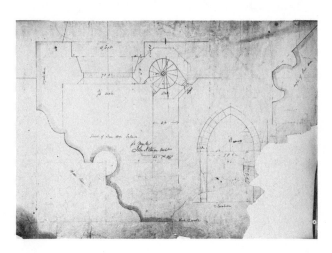

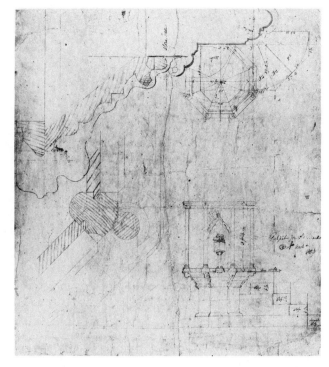

Above: 33.14; *Below*: 33.15

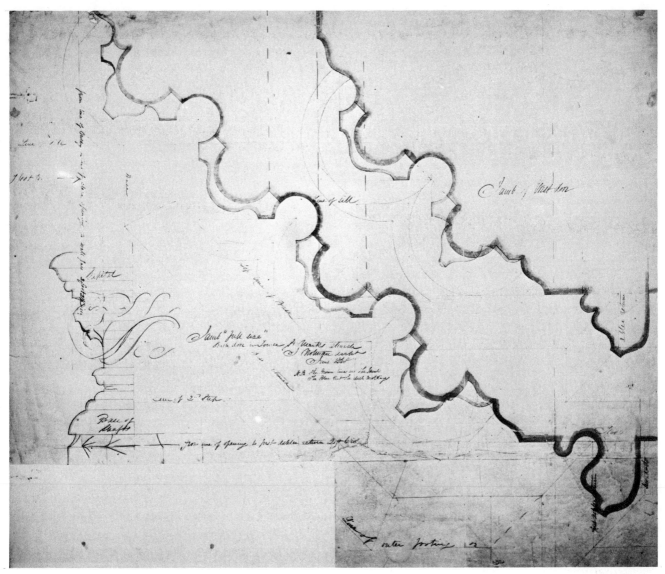

33.11

DRAWING 33.9:
   Title: Details of Nave Pillars "full size"/
   for St. Marks Church Philad
   Signature: John Notman Archt
   Date: May 30th 1848
   Scale: Full and ¾" : 1'
   Other inscriptions: none
   Description: plan of pillar; details of capitals; partial longitudinal section
   Medium: ink and wash
   Size: 34¾ x 54-5/16 (88.3 x 138)
   Owner: Historical Society of Pennsylvania (AIA)

DRAWING 33.10:
   Title: Elevation of/South Door in
   Tower/St. Mark's Church
   Signature: J. Notman Archt.
   Date: June 1848
   Scale: none indicated (scales ¾" : 1')
   Other inscriptions: none
   Description: elevation and plan
   Medium: ink and pencil
   Size: 26-1/16 x 24-3/16 (66.2 x 61.4)
   Owner: Historical Society of Pennsylvania (AIA), R-1

DRAWING 33.11:
Title: Jamb "full size"/South door in Tower of St. Marks Church
Signature: J. Notman Archt.
Date: June 1848
Scale: Full
Other inscriptions: N. B. The Brown lines are the Jambs/The Blue tint the Arch Moldings
Description: plans and elevations of details
Medium: ink and wash
Size: 33-1/16 x 38⅛ (84 x 96.8)
Owner: Historical Society of Pennsylvania (AIA)

DRAWING 33.12:
Title: St. Marks
Signature: John Notman Archt
Date: Sep 1st 1848
Scale: ¾" : 1'
Other inscriptions: Jamb of Tower door Interior/Elevation/Angle of Stair door
Description: plans and elevations of details
Medium: ink and wash, with pencil notations
Size: 24⅜ x 38⅛ (61.8 x 96.9)
Owner: Historical Society of Pennsylvania (AIA)

DRAWING 33.13:
Title: none
Signature: none
Date: none
Scale: none indicated (scales full and approximately ⅜" : 1')
Other inscription: Half of Chancel arch Moldings/Half of Chancel Pier/Half Chancel Arch
Description: plans and elevation of details
Medium: ink and wash
Size: 31⅞ x 19-11/16 (81 x 50)
Owner: Historical Society of Pennsylvania (AIA)

DRAWING 33.14:
Title: Spire light St. Mark's Tower
Signature: John Notman Archt.
Date: 1852
Scale: Full size and 1½" : 1'
Other inscriptions: Elevation/Jaumb [sic]
Description: elevation and plans of details
Medium: ink and wash
Size 26-11/16 x 31¼ (67.9 x 79.5)
Owner: Historical Society of Pennsylvania (AIA)

DRAWING 33.15:
Title: Pulpit for Ste Marks
Signature: N Archt
Date: 1859
Scale: none indicated (scales full and 1½" : 1')
Other inscriptions: none
Description: plan, elevation, and details
Medium: ink and wash
Size: 24-7/16 x 22-7/16 (61.2 x 57)
Owner: Historical Society of Pennsylvania (AIA)

OTHER EARLY ILLUSTRATIONS:
Two similar undated lithographs show the church in perspective. The first, which closely resembles the Winterthur tracing, is entitled "St. Mark's Church Philadelphia," John Notman Archt. Below the tower entrace is a coat of arms with the motto "Sigillum Ecclesiae S. Marci Philada. 1848." The second is entitled "St. Mark's Church/Philadelphia," John Notman, Architect, drawn on stone by Roy Mackintosh. An engraving, also similar to the Winterthur tracing, is illustrated in *Philadelphia as It Is, in 1852.*

DOCUMENTATION:

Minute Book of the vestry of St. Mark's Church in the City of Philadelphia, A.D. MDCCCLVIII to A.D. MDCCCLXIII; *The Ecclesiologist.* VIII (April 1848), IX (August 1848); Pearson, Charles L. Diaries., Coll. W. Houstoun Pearson; Philadelphia *Public Ledger*; Smith, R. A. *Philadelphia as It Is, in 1852.* Philadelphia (1852); AB; J; StA

BIBLIOGRAPHICAL REFERENCES:

D: 132-33, F: 74-79, 111-33; Massey, James C., ed. *Two Centuries of Philadelphia Architectural Drawings.* Philadelphia (1964); Mortimer, Rev. Alfred. *St. Mark's Church, Philadelphia and its Lady Chapel.* New York (1909); Stanton, Phoebe. *The Gothic Revival* and *American Church Architecture.* Baltimore (1968)

IN TERMS OF DRAWINGS the best documented of all Notman's works are the two Philadelphia Protestant Episcopal churches, St. Mark's and St. Clement's, and The Athenaeum. Because he served as contractor as well as architect for these buildings the surviving drawings include some of the working drawings, as well as presentation renderings and preliminaries. Together with the written documentation, the drawings for St. Mark's provide an unusually full account of the architect's role in a project carried out over a long period of time.

In June 1847 the vestry of St. Mark's Church appointed William Musgrove, George Zantzinger, John R. Wilmer, J. Wilmor Cannell, and George Helmuth members of a committee to oversee construction of a new church. [Minutes: 1] On 18 Sept. 1847 the committee met to consider "Plans and Specifications of a church Building" presented by Notman, but did not adopt them. [Minutes: 3] These must have included the first three of the drawings, which bear the same date as the meeting.

Perhaps unsure that Notman's plans were entirely suitable for high church ritual and

In order to secure a better choice of plans application was made by letter to the Ecclesiological Society of England, from whom was obtained a plan, which from certain peculiarities it was not considered desirable to adopt.

Mr. Notman since offered a plan including some improvements from the English drawings, which met with the approbation of the committee, ...

The ambiguity of this statement led Tatum [180] to describe St. Mark's as built from plans sent over from England, as modified by Notman. Fairbanks [75-76, 119], however, points out that the original design for St. Mark's is, in fact, quite similar to that ultimately employed. Notman's modifications to his first scheme, including the excision of a porch on the south flank and changes to the fenestration of the tower, are represented by the next three drawings in the Historical Society's series.

Confusion about the authorship of St. Mark's should have been settled by an apology from England.

A letter received from Mr. Notman, the architect of this church of St. Mark's, informs us the design which we criticized approvingly in our April number (vol. viii, 285) was altogether his own, and not indebted, as we had supposed—misled by an expression in the letter of a correspondent—to the tracings furnished by the kindness of Mr. [Richard Cromwell] Carpenter. We are sorry to have made this error, and are pleased to be able to express that its correction justifies us in thinking more highly than before of Mr. Notman's ability. We never compared the two designs, we should add. We received Mr. Notman's tracings from Philadelphia, and understood that they were an adaptation from the English design:—the latter had gone out some months before to America, and we had no copy by us for comparison. . . .

[*Ecclesiologist*, IX: 13-14]

Fairbanks [119] has concluded that the tracings mentioned are those now at Winterthur, which were sold at Sotheby's in London in 1960.

At any rate, there was no confusion in the minds of Philadelphians. When construction began it was reported:

The corner stone of a new Protestant Episcopal Church, to be named after the evangelist St. Mark, is to be laid on the 25th inst., ... The style it adopted is the Gothic, after plans designed by Mr. Notman, the experienced architect of our city. [*Public Ledger*, 7 Apr. 1848: 2]

Having seen his design accepted, Notman offered to contract to execute it for $30,000. On further reflection, however, he increased the estimate and offered the vestry three alternatives, which were considered at its meeting of 8 Feb. 1848.

1st To erect the church in exact conformity with his last plan and specifications for Forty two thousand Dollars. 2nd To build it on the same plan, to the top of the tower for Thirty five Thousand Dollars—3dly To Build it on the same plan with the Tower to the height of first story for Thirty Thousand Dolls. In either case he agreeing to take Five thousand Dollars of the amount in Scrip—

On motion it was Resolved that the Building Committee be authorized to see Mr. John Notman in regard to his third proposition offered by him to them, viz "That the church be erected in strict accordance with the design and specifications submitted by him, the Tower to be built to the height of first story, and ascertain his willingness to contract for the same, for the distinct sum of $27,000. subject however to certain conditions of payment to be agreed upon at the time." [Minutes: 4-5]

Notman rejected the lower figure, and at a vestry meeting on 12 Feb. 1848 it was announced that agreement had been reached on the "third proposition." [Minutes: 6-7]

Details of the design were evidently not complete when construction began. The next three drawings, of exterior detailing, are dated in May and June 1848. By fall the building was far enough advanced so that drawings for the interior were required, one for the tower stairs and door being dated 1 Sept. Shortly threafter, on 2 Oct., it was reported that differences between Notman and the supplier of stone for the interior might delay completion of the building. [Minutes: 14] By 18 Oct. the building committee could report that

... after Sundry interviews and conversations with Mr. Notman the most favorable proposition they were able to elicit from him, is, that for the consideration of the sum of $800 he will continue to line and furnish the aisle walls with the same stone, and in similar workmanship with that which is now done; finish the gables, and nave or clerestory walls with Trenton Stone, which is to correspond as nearly as possible with the stone at present in the gables, and in a style of workmanship to show as well as the three first courses of stone next above key-stone of arch of western doorway. [Minutes:23]

Thereafter progress appears to have been smooth. By spring the following notice, with its vivid description of the original appearance of the interior, appeared.

LOCAL AFFAIRS. The St. Mark's Episcopal Church.—This beautiful church edifice is now rapidly progressing towards completion; and it will be quite a feature among the many architectural structures that are plentifully scattered in the vicinity of the location which it occupies in the southwestern section of the city. The architect is John Notman, Esq., whose taste is evidenced in the many architectural beauties that have been constructed under his superintendence throughout our city. The following notice of St. Mark's is slightly compressed from a description accompanied by a plate, in the March number of Godey's Magazine:

This church edifice is composed of brown free stone of the most pleasing tone of color, in the decorated style of Gothic architecture that prevailed in the last quarter of the thirteenth and the beginning of the fourteenth centuries; a period in which it may be said to have attained the highest point of graceful proportion and luxuriant beauty. The churches of this period are distinguished for their fine proportions and beauty of interior effect, and the elegance of the windows, being richly foliated in the head or arch. The length of the church is east and west, and is 150 feet in all over the buttresses.

The tower is on the south side, near the west end, attached to the aisle wall, projecting all its size, and makes the breadth at the point 91 feet. The tower is nearly on the line of houses on Locust street. Standing in the middle of the square, advanced from the church, it becomes the most important feature in the street view. Its whole beautiful outline, from base to finial, seen at a glance—all of stone—will be not a common object in our streets. The plan is thus adapted to suit the site—the tower is in the position of the south porch, for which its first stage will be used, though it is the principal entrance by a deeply recessed and richly moulded doorway, ornamented with foliated shafts on the jamb.

It is square built with buttresses to the height of 80 feet from the base; it is then resolved into an octagon spire 90 feet high, broached on the angles with three tiers of spire lights alternating. The belfry has coupled windows on each face, and the spire is terminated with a finial and a cross.

The windows of the aisles and clerestory, on the flank, are of two lights, or parts divided by mullions of stone which is foliated in the arch, showing different patterns; the windows have moulded worked stone jambs.

The church comprises a chancel, a nave and aisles, an organ or choir aisle with a convenient vestry. The interior is 131 in length, 56 feet wide, and 54 feet high. The chancel is 88 feet deep, 23½ feet wide—the roof being of a different elevation with the main body of the building.

This portion is constructed of cut stone, so as to show the material on the interior. The floor is to be paved with encaustic tiles, and at the east end rises four steps to the altar. An open screen of oak will mark the division of church and chancel. The window over the altar is of five lights, and will be of painted glass of an appropriate design. The chancel will have a polygonal ceiling of oak divided into panels, and on the other part of the building, the roof will be open-timbered framed of oak, with hammer and collar beams moulded—the whole construction being visible. The nave is 28 feet wide and 100 feet long, and the north and south aisles are each 14 feet wide by the same length. The division between the main body of the church and the side aisles is in seven bays on each side, the piers and arches of cut stone, supporting the clerestory with bracket shafts between each window for the support of the roof timbers. The organ aisle is a continuation of the north aisle, with an arch open to the chancel. The seats will be of oak of a suitable design. The windows are to be glazed in quarries set in lead, having borders of colored glass, the great window at the west end is to be of four lights, and those of the aisles, of three lights each. A small arch entrance is under the large window, another door is on the north side opposite to that through the tower, and the vestry and chancel have each their entrance door. The gables of the roof are to be decorated with handsome ornamental cresses, and a neat crest tile is to be carved on the ridge. There will be room to seat 1000 persons, and many seats will be free.

[*Public Ledger*, 22 Mar. 1849: 2]

Work still continued. On 5 June 1849 Charles Pearson took the cars from Trenton to Philadelphia, "walked up to Mr. Notman's in Spruce street" and, in company with the architect, "went over the new church he is building in Locust street between Schuylkill 7th & 8th St Marks (I believe)...."

St. Mark's was dedicated on 21 May 1850 [*Public Ledger:* 21 and 22 May 1850], finished, as had been agreed, up to the first stage of the tower. The following year the vestry contracted with Charles Lacey of Jersey City, New Jersey, for completion of the tower for the sum of $12,063.92. Lacey agreed that

... said tower and spire shall be built and erected in all respects in accordance with the design and drawings made by John Notman, of the City of Philadelphia, architect, and exhibited to him, and according to the specifications hereto annexed; and that the materials as herein after mentioned shall be furnished, and the whole work done and erected to the entire satisfaction of said John Notman in every respect, and that the same shall be completed on or before [blank] And the said Charles Lacey further agrees and binds himself to supply all the stone exterior,

of sound quality brown stone from the Quarries of Little and Belville, New Jersey, and to supply all the stone necessary for walls, otherwise of best rubble building stone, from quarries in the neighborhood of Philadelphia, (say Lieper's) as well as, and together with all the mortar, lime and sand, and all the labor of every kind in stone cutting, building, and furnishing material and work for the proper and workmanship like completion of the stonework of the said tower and spire, and all the scaffolds and scaffolding necessary for the work throughout, as well as all power and means of raising the stone and material to its place, and all these the said Charles Lacey shall find and provide at his own proper cost and expense.

And the said Charles Lacey further agrees to find the stone of sizes and shapes so as to make good bond in the window jambs the broaches and the angles of the spire, to the satisfaction of the said John Notman, and will clean down and joint the spire as the scaffolds are taken down so as to be impervious to water-pointing the joints with best cement.... [Loose ms. in Minutes]

In this case again Notman provided at least one sheet of details after the contract was signed.

The tower and spire were completed by the summer of 1852.

Episcopal Church of St. Mark. The spire of this beautiful Gothic edifice has been crowned by a gilt cross, and the scaffolding used by the workmen in the construction of the spire, is being removed. This church edifice being now complete, is the most perfect specimen of the quaint old English Gothic style, and with the school-house adjacent, presents a most imposing and picturesque appearance. [*Public Ledger*, 26 July 1852: 2]

One drawing in the St. Mark's series appears to be misdated. This is a sketch, with molding details, for the pulpit. The year is indecipherable, but appears to read either 1839 or 1859. Probably the date should be 1849, at which time the pulpit and other interior arrangements of the church were under discussion. In a letter to the vestry dated 20 June 1849, and inserted in its minutes, Notman wrote:

As I have stated verbally to several of your number, that I would put up screens in the organ aisle arches instead of one in the chancel arch, I hereby propose to make that change without further charge or alteration of contract, please let me have your order for this if approved, and for the purposed alteration (from the proper position of the pulpit) all which is respectfully submitted by

Yr. obdt Servt
Mr. Notman

St. Mark's remains one of Philadelphia's most active and popular churches. It stands on the exterior much as Notman designed it, with the exception of the Lady Chapel, added to the design of Cope and Stewardson between 1898 and 1902. The interior, however, as Mortimer indicates, has been greatly enriched. An alabaster reredos and altar, imported from England, were installed in 1892. In 1898 a cloister was built along the north flank. Carved oak choirstalls, the organ gallery and grille, the roodbeam in the chancel arch and other ornamental woodwork were added by Henry Vaughan in 1905-1906. He also superintended the rebuilding of the foundations and the installation of steel beams to reenforce the floor.

34.

HOLLYWOOD CEMETERY
RICHMOND, VIRGINIA
1848

Client: Hollywood Cemetery Company
Project: design of grounds, including
   principal roads, and entrance lodge
DRAWINGS: none
OTHER EARLY ILLUSTRATIONS:
   "Plan of Hollywood Cemetery/Richmond Va." lithographed by P. S. Duval. This lithograph showing the plan of the grounds and a plan and elevation of a lodge appeared in Elliot & Nye's *Virginia Directory* for 1852. An early map of the grounds hangs in the offices of the Hollywood Cemetery Company.

BIBLIOGRAPHICAL REFERENCES:
   D: 136-37; M: 57-63; Catterall, Mrs. Ralph, letter to Francis James Dallett, Jr., 16 Jan. 1958; Mitchell, Mary, letter to author, 15 Apr. 1978

IN THE SPRING OF 1847 two Richmond residents, Joshua J. Fay and William H. Haxall, visited Boston and went to see Mount Auburn. Impressed with its "solemn grandeur," they determined to propose a similar establishment for their city. [*Historical Sketch*: 5] On their return to Richmond, joined by two others, they purchased a 42 acre plot and by 3 Aug. 1847 had formed a company. One plan was submitted, but in the fall, "the Board availed themselves of a visit which Mr. Notman, architect, of Philadelphia was making to Virginia, for the purpose of laying out the grounds at the Huguenot Springs, to engage him to prepare a more complete and precise plan...." Notman's plan arrived in February 1848, along with a suggestion that the cemetery be named Holly-wood, in honor of the beautiful trees adorning the grounds. [*Historical Sketch*: 6-7]

The plan was also accompanied by a report. Perhaps stung by the criticism that the plan for Spring Grove had encompassed too many roads [see entry 14], he explained at great length the purpose and arrangement of the roads at Hollywood.

REPORT
ACCOMPANYING PLAN OF HOLLY-WOOD CEMETERY,
RICHMOND VA.

*To the Board of Directors of
Holly-wood Cemetery, Richmond:*
   GENTLEMEN—In arranging the plan of the Cemetery I have adopted the position of the entrance, on the northeast corner, as most convenient to the city, and as very favorable to an extensive view of the grounds on entering; an impression of extent being highly desirable, where the surface comes to be so much subdivided as in a public cemetery.

That is also the most desirable point to get the first glance of the beautiful variety of hill and valley, which distinguishes Holly-Wood above any cemetery I have seen. No other one has, as this has, three or four valleys opening into a greater one—and that capable of great beauty by being properly planted and laid out.

But beauty must be secondary to use, if circumstances will not admit of their being united. This I have endeavored to do in laying out my plan. How far I have succeeded you will judge on comparing the plan with the grounds.

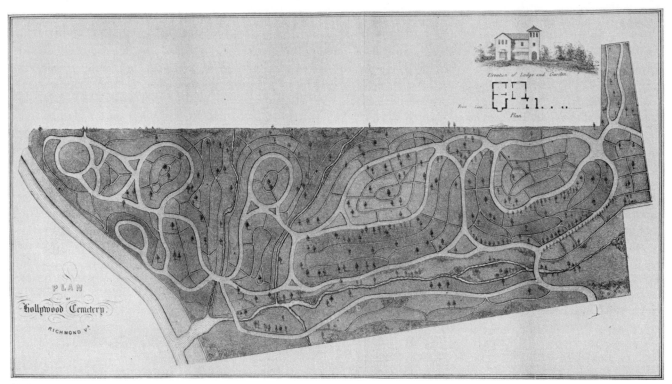

"Plan of Hollywood Cemetery," Elliot and Nye's *Virginia Directory, Courtesy The Virginia Historical Society*

You may be surprised, taking the first view of the plan, at the number of roads on it; but the absolute necessity of the carriages getting near the lot at a funeral is so apparent in practice, as to make it imperative, that the roads should not be farther apart than the length or breadth, as it may happen, of five or six lots, with foot-paths between parallels of double lots, and occasional grass-path crossings.

On this rule the roads are laid out, at the same time leading them by such routes as best to display and view all the beauty of the grounds, and that little or no cutting or grading will be required; on this plan deep excavation will be necessary only at two places, one rising the hill by section A., going towards where the first entrance was proposed, the other on the road under or east of Harvie's lot. Some trimming of the bank will be needful to a good road on the east side of the principal run of water in the main valley. The roads are made as direct as the shape of the ground will admit to every part of the Cemetery, leaving no point unvisited favorable for views, or useful for lots, or prominent as a site for monuments. Making roads will not be expensive in Holly-Wood, for there is plenty of gravel; in many places, say two-thirds of the route of road, by removing the surface soil, the road is made. The roads necessarily wind and turn to avoid acclivities; this is an advantage, as it produces many angles and corner lots, which are sought for, as you will find; they will be first bought up, being desirable for the display of a monument or tomb. The roads I have made twenty feet wide; it is unnecessary to cut them more than fourteen or fifteen feet wide, thus leaving a grass border on each side, of two and a half or three feet, in the power and control of the Cem-

etery Company, for the purpose of planting or other decorative occupation, and prevents the appearance of the railings and enclosures of lots crowding on the drives.

Five bridges are necessary on the whole route. These may be readily and simply constructed of the trunks of the white oaks that have been cut down, laid on abutments of dry stone walling on each side of the runs or brooks, built without mortar; the granite on the ground might be easily quarried to serve the purpose; a simple rustic railing made of the branches of the trees cut down (with the bark on) placed on each side, will be in better keeping with the place and purpose than the most expensive railing planed and painted. Surface gutters will be necessary in some parts of the road to carry across surface water from the declivities,—they can be provided at the points where necessary, when the work of making the roads is in progress.

I have not named on the plan the roads or avenues, as it is common to do, after trees and plants, such as Elm Avenue, Magnolia Avenue and so on; this has been done at Mount Auburn, and I think in Greenwood and also Greenmount Cemeteries; but would suggest that they be called after the name of the first person who shall erect a handsome monument or family tomb, or to whom such shall be erected; for instance, if you have the tomb or monument of Chief Justice Marshall on a section of road, what more appropriate name than Marshall Avenue? And should the Washington monument of Virginia be erected on the circular lot, shown on the south-west end of the grounds, the road leading to it would be Washington or Monument Ave. Again, the main road in the greater valley might be Valley Avenue, or East Avenue; that leading by

Harvie's lot, might be Harvie's Avenue. I suggest these, as I wish the Holly-Wood Cemetery to be "*sui generis*," original in every thing, as it has a distinctive and superior character of ground, which, with the splendid panoramic views from it of the city and river, makes it equal to the best in the country. My aim in the plan is to enhance these advantages and show the excellent taste which directed its choice and appropriation to this purpose. The naming of the roads, then, I will leave to your judgment, as it might seem presumption in me to do it on the permanent plan, without consulting your Board of Directors. Inserting the names is easily done on the map at any time as you may decide.

Objections may be made to the great number and length of roads. In reference to these, I would say, they combine the uses shown above, together with the perfect opening up or exposing the whole of the grounds to the casual visitor. The pleasure of a drive over a variety of surface with such charming views, will induce visitors. Of easy access, a drive through them will indeed be delightful. Many are interested by the novelty and beauty and become purchasers of lots—thus one class of the public are with you.

Again; the thinking part of the community, the grave and the sad, seeing the last resting-place of their friends and family so well cared for, so decorated by your efforts, will readily join you. Their best feelings are with you; they will feel that their own ashes are never to be disturbed in Holly-Wood,—that it is sacred forever.

The foot-paths are six feet wide and are generally parallel to the main lines of roads and avenues. These footpaths it is not requisite to cut out and prepare at this time; they may be done, as is rendered necessary by the lots being taken up; they are made for the easy access to the lots, as each lot should have one open front at least. On the declivities the paths are of course carried athwart, to render them easy to the pedestrian. Like the roads, the naming of them follows their purpose and occupation; but with these may be used the names of plants and trees, as it better suits a path to be so named than an avenue. What more pleasing in a cemetery, for instance, than the "Willow-path," or the "Cypress-path?" Many other names of trees assimilate as euphoniously with path. As these roads and paths may appear, and indeed prove to many, a labyrinth, they should be designated on direction boards, occasionally.

The sections of the grounds made by the roads, and paths I have marked on the plan as A, B, C, and so on alphabetically. These embrace large parts of the grounds and are circumscribed by the roads—hence, when the nominal letter is found, it includes all the part within the broad road; this makes the sections of easy reference, as each section commences and ends its own numbers. The lots are marked on the plan in faint black lines, varying in size from two hundred feet to eight hundred feet,—thus suitable to all demands and requisitions as to space, and of

varied surface. The smaller of the lots in size, from 200 to 350 feet, are invariably on level ground or nearly. The larger sizes are on the hillsides, declivitous ground, as best suited for vaults or mausoleums, built with vertical, finished front instead of monument. Lots of this character are of great variety in position and aspect and suitable for every taste. The divisions of the lots on the plan are not arbitrary, nor need they be binding, as they are very faintly drawn,—that a line may not be a barrier to any purchaser having two lots, if so desired; and as the lots are sold the lines on this plan can be made stronger and deeper, thus marking the lots sold, showing at a glance which are to be sold and where choice may be made by intending purchasers; as the superintendent will mark off each lot as sold. I have not numbered the lots either, for the same reason, that two or three may be taken by one person. These two or three thus incorporated, should carry one number only, which will prevent confusion in the books and map. Again, it may be desired to divide some of the lots. I have spaced into three or four, lots for poorer persons, or those having small families; this is easily regulated on books of the Cemetery and on the record, if not numbered on the map, and there the division may be numbered as done without disturbing the chronicling of sales.

The fences being already completed, the next useful things are the buildings required. In these I have confined the design to the lodge, or superintendent's house at the gate, merely adding to and altering the brick house now near the proposed entrance, which is the best, as being nearest the city, and may be rendered otherwise unobjectionable by the proper cutting down of the street laid out on the east side of the Cemetery, making an easy access, but which appears dangerous at present, as the descent is quick and steep from the street to the grounds of the Cemetery north of the south house (brick house.) After the grounds are entered the road will be easy if well done, and to this plan. To the brick house, I have added a room with bow window on the line of the street, so as to command the approach to the gate from it by the porter or gate keeper, thus preventing delay of entrance. I have also added a bell tower, of simple form; in the upper part, a bell should be placed accessible by visitors, to notice a desire of entrance, and also of size sufficient to be tolled on funeral occasions. The lower part of this tower would be a covered porch with a verandah to the road front, and another at right angles to the entrance; the house would have three rooms on each floor, thus making it a comfortable residence for the superintendent of the Cemetery. Another house of frame is on the property, which may be moved to the other side of the entrance gate, easily making it a residence for the assistant sexton. Beyond this, on the north, I have marked stables and sheds for the vehicles and horses of lot-holders and visitors. This is a temporary gateway till farther improvement is desirable. It is not, therefore, such an entrance or gateway as I would design, had it to be made anew, but the easiest and most economical use of the house now there.

Having gone over the useful and necessary work of the Cemetery, I will now describe what may be called the artistical, which pertains to the planting of trees and other ornamental work necessary by the Company. The whole of the valley or main run of water being from north to south is unavailable for the purposes of burial, but may be rendered highly ornamental to the main design by judicious planting. I have, therefore, marked it as decorative ground; the run of water I have marked as it may be carried, and has been naturally, so as to form an island. This may be planted in magnolias and other flowering shrubs of damp and watery natures and growth, so as to be a beautiful feature in the landscape, and indeed the entire of the main valley may be so used, as it is entirely unavailable for burial purposes. In some parts it is well grown in poplars, elm, &c., but is wanting in trees and bushes of lower growth, In order to form groups of these, I have desired the gardener employed (Mr. Graeme,) to procure all he could from the natural woods, the trees that are indigenous being invariably the best to thrive, and be ornamental in the place desired. By this means and the proper guidance of the water, the main valley of Holly-Wood may be of the most beautiful description, varied and pleasing. The east hill should be planted densely, the plants may be of any kinds—better it should be overgrown with the common pine than remain in its present state; anything growing on that side would make the Cemetery seem more private, which is very desirable, as all who feel must know —and indeed it may be laid down as a rule, that all the exterior fences of a rural cemetery ought to be enveloped in shade of trees or young plantings of trees, else why do we fence our lots, or shut out the world's otherwise, if not in grief—therefore, all along the east and west fences should be thickly planted, occasionally spreading out wide as I have marked upon the plan on these two lines. Beyond these the planting of the grounds by the Cemetery Company is confined to the borders of principal roads and angles thereof, as it will be found that planting of ornamental trees and shrubs will be done extensively by lotholders; still a row or rows of tall tapering evergreens should be planted by the Company on the leading thoroughfares after entering the gate, as it renders solemn the whole grounds afterwards seen. There are many points and angles formed by the roads that should be also planted by the Company, but all these "time will show." The only piece of water I have considered desirable, is at the debouch of the water into the culvert at the canal; this would be easily dammed by a retaining wall (some twenty or thirty feet from the canal as the line may be) built of sufficient height to dam the water to the desired breadth of pond—this is to be recommended also as a regulator to the emission of the waters of the main run, rendering it placid in its bed, which once cut to the desired size and shape, will be without the trouble and expense of alteration.

Thus, gentlemen, I have endeavored to explain my plan for Holly-Wood Cemetery; should my services be further desired, please inform me at your earliest decision that I may regulate my time so as to visit and stake out the roads, &c. The plan on yellow paper is the key to the principal plan. In trust, gentlemen, that the design may please, I have the honor to be

Your most obd't serv't,
JOHN NOTMAN.
[*Historical Sketch*: 19-25]

Construction began in July 1848. [*Historical Sketch*: 8] By June 1849, when the cemetery was dedicated, the results were now "visible on every hand...standing upon the summit of Holly Wood Hill, how beautiful and teeming with interest is the view on every side." [*Address*: 13-14]

PRESENT STATUS:

The major features of Notman's plan survive, although the construction of a lake and the passage of city sewers through the cemetery have altered or obliterated the water courses. The entrance lodge suggested by Notman was never constructed and he appears to have had no hand in the design of the present lodge.

Ellarslie. *Courtesy Trenton Free Public Library*

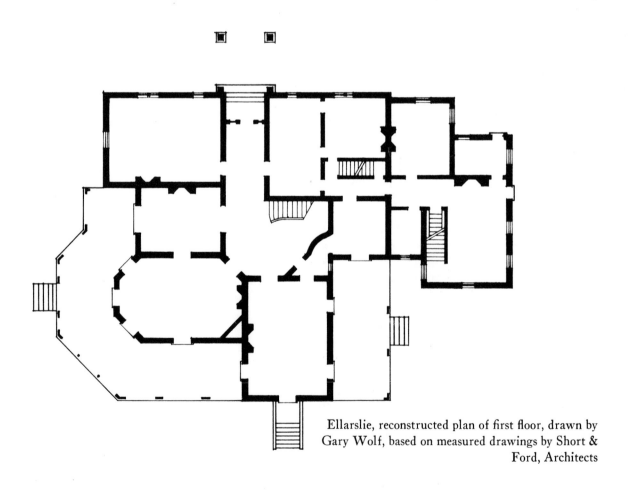

Ellarslie, reconstructed plan of first floor, drawn by
Gary Wolf, based on measured drawings by Short &
Ford, Architects

35.

ELLARSLIE
TRENTON, NEW JERSEY
C. 1848
Client: Henry McCall
Project: residence

DRAWINGS: none
OTHER EARLY ILLUSTRATIONS:
  Photographs in Trentoniana Collection, Trenton Free Public Library
DOCUMENTATION:
  Mercer County Mortgages, Mercer County Court House; Stockton, Sarah Marks. Diary. PUL; Pearson, Charles L. Diary. Coll. W. Houstoun Pearson; Trenton *Daily True American*
BIBLIOGRAPHICAL REFERENCES:
  Danser, Willard S. "Trenton in Retrospect." *Trentonian,* 14 June 1961; Greiff, Constance M. "A Preliminary Report on Ellarslie." Unpublished manuscript, Trenton Museum Commission, 1974; Podmore, Harry J. *Trenton—Old and New.* Edited and revised by Mary J. Messler. Trenton (1964); "Old Landmarks Around Town." *Trenton Sunday Times,* 12 June 1910; other clippings in Trentoniana Collection, Trenton Free Public Library

THIS ITALIANATE VILLA was originally sited on an estate of approximately 135 acres in Ewing Township northwest of Trenton. The McCalls were a Philadelphia family, who also had business interests in the New Jersey city. The house can be dated on the basis of mortgages, one for $10,000, dated 28 Nov. 1849 and another for $4,583.34 on 15 June 1850, sums which would roughly equal the value of a substantial house with outbuildings.

Further confirmation comes from the diaries of two other Notman clients. On 2 Feb. 1848 Sarah Marks Stockton noted in her diary: "Notman came, saw and spoke of house, Gave John Plan of McCall's house (Trenton) liked very much—." The next day the Stocktons "Prepared for Trenton quite early—saw McC's house—pleased." It is not possible, however, to tell whether this was Ellarslie or the house of Henry McCall's uncle, Robert McCall. [see entry 85] The other diary provides more positive documentation. On 17 Mar. 1849 Charles I. Pearson and members of his family, contemplating retaining Notman to design a house, went "to Henry McCall's house up the river road above General Cadwalader's place, we met Mr. Notman there and went over the whole house."

When the McCalls attempted to sell Ellarslie in 1860 it was advertised as:

COUNTRY SEAT
For Sale
A MOST ELIGIBLE AND ELEgant country seat, with ten acres of land situated a quarter of a mile from the city of Trenton, New Jersey, up the Delaware river road.

The dwelling house is a handsome, modern, substantially built stone edifice, rough cast, with broad piazzas, and in perfect condition. There are two parlors, dining room, wide hall, and furnace in the cellar; six chambers, besides the servants' apartments, two kitchens, and a room supplying the water for the house from a ram. There are two pumps, an ice house, stabling for four horses and four carriages, a gardener's house, extensive garden grapery and greenhouse, all in order, with numerous plants, pear trees, and other fruit trees, besides evergreen and ornamental trees around the premises, in perfect and flourishing condition.

Immediate possession will be given, with the option under separate agreement, of the purchaser's availing himself of a quantity of excellent modern furniture, now in the house, such as tables, bedsteads, bureaus, chairs, &c.

HARRY McCALL
1101 Chestnut street
[*Daily True American*, 23 March 1860]

PRESENT STATUS:
  Ellarslie is currently being partially restored and rehabilitated for adaptive use as a museum for the City of Trenton.

36.

JOHN P. STOCKTON HOUSE
(Allison House; now known as
  Walter Lowrie House)
PRINCETON, NEW JERSEY
1848–1849
Client: John P. Stockton
Project: residence and grounds

DRAWINGS: none
DOCUMENTATION:
  Stockton, Sara Marks. Diary,
  1848-1854. PUL
BIBLIOGRAPHICAL REFERENCES:
  D: 133; M: 47-48, S-PULC: 133; Bill,
  Alfred Hoyt. *A House Called Morven.*
  2nd ed., Princeton (1978); Greiff, Con-
  stance M., Gibbons, Mary W. and Menzies,
  Elizabeth, G. C. *Princeton Architecture.*
  Princeton (1967)

John P. Stockton House. *Courtesy Mrs. Walter Lowrie*

THE FIRST of Notman's Princeton villas was
erected for a son of Commodore Robert F.
Stockton and his delightful, if spoiled, southern wife. Fortunately Sara Stockton kept a
diary of the progress of her new house, to
which all entries below refer.

Plans for the house were under discussion
during the month of January 1848. [26 Jan.
1848] Probably it was her father-in-law who
conducted the preliminary discussions with
Notman, for it was the "Com [who] arrived
with *N.* brought house plans etc." [1 Feb.
1848] These were evidently "stock" plans, not
specific plans for their house, which would ar-

rive three weeks later. The following day
"Notman came, saw and spoke of house. Gave
John Plan of McCall's house (Trenton) liked
very much—" This was probably the plan of
Robert McCall's house which very much resembled what was eventually built for the
young Stocktons, although it may have been
Harry McCall's Ellarslie. [see entries 35 and
85] The next morning the Stocktons "Prepared
for Trenton quite early—Saw McC's house—
pleased." There was then a hiatus, with Notman presumably busy at his drawing board.
On 21 Feb. "Notmans plans arrived, very
much pleased."

Work must have begun as soon as the ground
was sufficiently thawed. On 28 May "The
house is improving fast—the walls were put
up yesterday—" By midsummer the building
was going under cover. "The Roof of the
house is at last commenced. I am delighted as
it looks so fine . . . it must be so very comfortable to think all this is mine." [10 Aug. 1848]

Soon afterwards the Stocktons "received
Notman's plans for the grounds of our place,
I do not think it is very good as it breaks the
lawn—however he cannot determine at present." [26 Aug. 1848] A month later Sara again

Went up to the 'house', it begins really to be very
elegant, I am delighted with everything, those rooms are
so fine and large, it will take so much money to furnish it
frightens me, all the upstairs floors are down. I hope the
staircase will be so[on] fixed that we may be able to walk
all over it, I shall be so happy when we get there—
[7 Sept. 1848]

Sara's fright was not sufficient to keep her
from spending several days in Philadelphia
buying furniture. "Went to Moores & Cam-
pions, ordered our furniture . . . garnet velvet
& Rosewood[?] for one Parlour Green and
Rose for the other. . . ." [5-9 Oct. 1848] Later
she would equip the house with Cornelius
chandeliers. [10 July 1850]

In the spring of 1849 she reported that
"The house is *at length* finished to my great
joy." [12 May 1849] Preparing to move in she
could not help speculate, obviously with pleasure, "I wonder how I shall behave under
my new honours as mistress of the finest house
in P____ and one of the finest in N. J."

Second Presbyterian Church and Manse, c. 1865.
Collection Edmund Cook

PRESENT STATUS:

Now known as Walter Lowrie House, the building serves as the official residence of the president of Princeton University. Owners subsequent to the Stocktons effected numerous changes, notably the removal of the service wing, substitution of masonry verandahs for the original cast iron, extension of the dining room, and addition of a Gothic library, designed by McKim, Mead and White, across the west front. Nevertheless, the core of the house survives much as Notman designed it.

37.

SECOND PRESBYTERIAN CHURCH
PRINCETON, NEW JERSEY
1848–1849
Client: Building Committee of the
Second Presbyterian Church
Project: church and manse

DRAWINGS: none
OTHER EARLY ILLUSTRATIONS:
Photograph in the collection of PUA
DOCUMENTATION:
Princeton *Whig*
BIBLIOGRAPHICAL REFERENCES:
Greiff, Constance M., Gibbons, Mary W. and Menzies, Elizabeth, G. C. *Princeton Architecture.* Princeton (1967)

NO EARLY RECORDS for this congregation exist. However, Notman's responsibility for the design is documented by the following item from the local newspaper:

The Building Committee of the Second Presbyterian Church has contracted for a church edifice 70 by 32 feet with tower, somewhat after the old English style of building—steep roof, pointed window, diamond sash, &c. The plan was drawn by Mr. Notman, the architect of the new State House and Lunatic Asylum at Trenton and the Law School and the splendid mansion of John P. Stockton, Esq. now in progress of erection in Princeton.

[*Whig*, 1 Dec. 1848: 2]

The church was dedicated on 29 Sept. 1849. [*Whig*, 21 Sept. 1849: 2]

It seems likely that Notman was also responsible for the design of the adjacent manse in Gothic cottage style.

PRESENT STATUS:

The church, stripped of its tower, and with totally altered fenestration, including dormer windows, has been turned sideways on the lot and is part of an office complex. The manse survives, although its bargeboards have been removed, and is also used as offices.

38.

ST. PAUL'S CHURCH (P. E.)
TRENTON, NEW JERSEY
1848–1851
Client: Vestry of St. Paul's Church
Project: small church or "chapel of ease"

DRAWING 38.1:

Title: St. Paul's/South Trenton, N. J.
Signature: none
Date: none
Scale: none indicated (probably 1/9″ : 1′)
Other inscriptions: Trenton, N. J.
Description: flank elevation
Medium: ink and wash
Size:
Owner: Historical Society of Pennsylvania, 2-2

DRAWING 38.2:

Title(s): St. Paul's/South Trenton, N. J.; St. Paul's Church/Trenton, N. J.
Signature: John Notman, Archt.
Date: 1851
Scale(s): 1/9″ : 1′; 3/8″ : 1′
Other inscriptions: Sectional elevation of tower/Addition to tower
Description: facade elevation, section and details of tower
Medium: ink and wash
Size:
Owner: Historical Society of Pennsylvania (AIA), Z-1

DOCUMENTATION:

Doane, George Washington. *Diocese of New Jersey: Episcopal Address to the Sixty-Third Annual Convention.* Burlington (1846); ...*Address to the Sixty-Sixth Annual Convention.* Burlington (1849); Pearson, Charles L. Diaries. Coll. W. Houstoun Pearson; Trenton *State Gazette*; J

BIBLIOGRAPHICAL REFERENCES:

F: 80, 134-40; S-PULC: 124

AS EARLY AS 1846 the idea of an Episcopal church to serve rapidly industrializing and developing South Trenton was proposed. Bishop Doane supported the project, considering "most desirable, and, I think, entirely feasible, a chapel of ease in South Trenton." [*Addresses*, 1846: 16] On 25 Feb. 1848 the following entry was made in the church records:

Resolved, that Rev'd Samuel Starr and Rev'd Enoch Reid be requested to procure from Mr. Nottman [sic] an estimate of the probable expense necessary to enclose a suitable Church Ediface [sic]. [Quoted in F: 134]

By early August the foundations were being dug [*State Gazette*, 4 Aug. 1848: 3] and at the end of the month the cornerstone was laid. [*State Gazette*, 23 Aug. 1848: 3] By fall it was announced that

The new Episcopal Church now in process of erection in South Trenton, will soon be ready for public worship. It will be, when completed, a very neat edifice.

In March the building was sufficiently completed so that members of the Pearson family attended services. [Diary: 18 Mar. 1849] Soon afterwards

On Thursday, in Easter week, 12 April, I consecrated St. Paul's Church, South Trenton.... The building is from a plan by Mr. Notman, and does him credit. It is of early English, with a tower, designed to bear a spire. The Nave and Chancel are both open roofed.

[Addresses, 1849: 15]

Charles Pearson accompanied his mother to services in June and commented that "It is a neat little edifice at present, although it is entirely unfinished. It is to be in the form of a cross." [Diary: 17 June 1849]

In this Pearson was mistaken. Even without a plan, the two drawings make it clear that the church was never intended to have a transept. It was, in fact, built very much as shown in the drawing, except that the blind bay, shown directly behind the tower in the flank elevation, was omitted.

The upper stages of the tower and the spire were evidently not constructed until 1851, when Notman added a more detailed drawing of these features to an existing sheet. According to Fairbanks [137], the spire may have been erected in a slightly simplified version. It has been taken down.

The drawing in the Historical Society of Pennsylvania's collection, numbered X-R-15, which Fairbanks [140] suggests may represent another design for St. Paul's, is in fact identical with the plan for St. Bartholomew's. [see entry 70]

PRESENT STATUS:

Extant, but abandoned

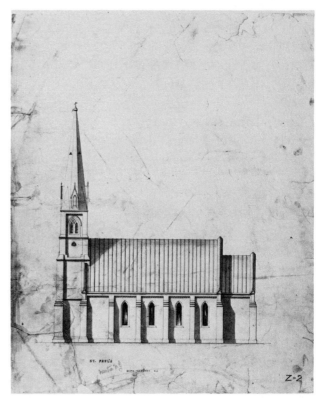

Above: 38.1; *Below*: 38.2

39.

ROWHOUSES
WALNUT STREET BETWEEN FIFTH AND
  SIXTH STREETS, PHILADELPHIA
1849
Client: John R. Wilmer,
  Messrs. Cornell and Jones
Project: town residences

DRAWINGS: none
OTHER EARLY ILLUSTRATIONS:
  A photograph of one of the buildings, 524
  Walnut, appears in J.
DOCUMENTATION:
  Philadelphia *Public Ledger;* J

ASIDE FROM HIS OWN RESIDENCE, this represents Notman's only known essay in this ubiq-
uitous Philadelphia form. Jackson [224], in
attributing one of these houses, 524 Walnut
Street, to Notman, says that it "was the first
brownstone residence erected in Philadelphia." Even if this was the case it was not
alone, for according to a contemporary account it was one of three.

  On the north side of Walnut street, between Fifth
and Sixth, there is now in progress ... a block of these
dwellings which may be particularly mentioned, the fronts
of which are composed of brown stone. They are building
for Messrs. John R. Wilmer, Cornell and Jones, from designs furnished by Mr. Notman, the architect. The basement is of the Connecticut brown stone, and the other portions of the same description of material from the Jersey
quarries. The door ways and windows are in the Roman
style, with heavy ornamented cornice lintels and carved
trussels [?], which are unique in design. The contractor is
Mr. John D. Jones, and the stone work is by T. C. Simpson, who has beautifully carried out the effect intended by
the architect. These dwellings have each a front of 22
feet, extending a depth of about 70 feet. They are each
furnished with fire proofs built in the walls, which are
found to be requisite, for the safety of valuables in these
times when despite our system of night police burglaries
are so frequent.   [*Public Ledger,* 29 Jan. 1849: 2]

Obviously urban living in the nineteenth
century, as in the twentieth, had its perils.
PRESENT STATUS:
  Demolished

40.

GLENCAIRN
TRENTON, NEW JERSEY
1849–1850
Client: Isaac Pearson
Project: residence

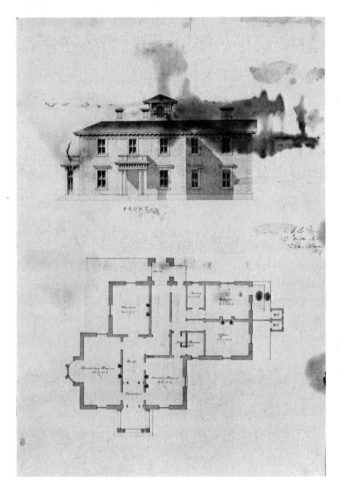

DRAWING 40.1:
  Title: Residence for I. [corrected from C.]
  L. Pearson, Esq./Trenton, N. J.
  Signature: John Notman
  Date: 1849
  Scale: none indicated (scales ⅛″ : 1′)
  Other inscriptions: Front
  Description: rendered elevation and
  and plan of first floor
  Medium: ink and colored wash with
  pencil emendations
  Size: 25⅛ x 17⅝ (63.8 x 44.8)
  Owner: W. Houstoun Pearson

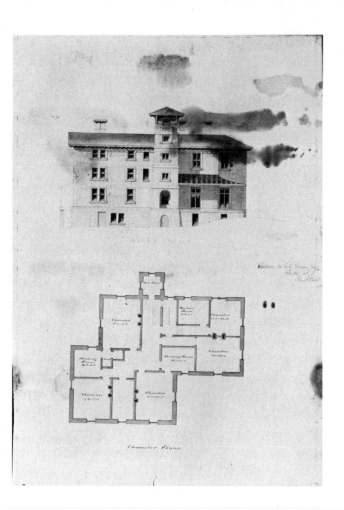

DRAWING 40.2:
Title: Residence for C. L. Pearson, Esqr./ Trenton, N. J.
Signature: John Notman
Date: 1849
Scale: none indicated (scales ⅛″ : 1′)
Other inscriptions: River front/ Chamber Floor
Description: rendered elevation and plan of second floor
Medium: ink and colored wash with pencil emendations
Size: 25 x 17⅝ (63.4 x 44.8)
Owner: W. Houstoun Pearson

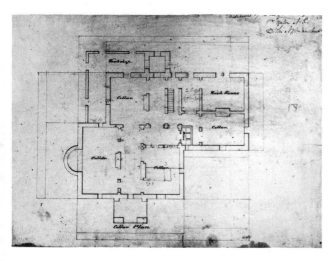

DRAWING 40.3:
Title: Residence of [   ]/Trenton, N. J.
Signature: John Notman, Archt.
Date: none
Scale: none indicated (scales ⅛″ : 1′)
Other inscriptions: cellar plan
Description: plan
Medium: ink with pencil emendations
Size: 12-2/4 x 18-1/6 (32.3 x 45.9)
Owner: Historical Society of Pennsylvania (AIA)

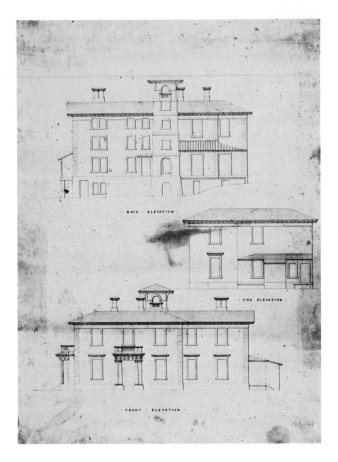

DRAWING 40.4:
Title: Mr. Pearson's House/Trenton, N. J.
(probably not in Notman's hand)
Signature: John Notman, Archt.
(probably not in Notman's hand)
Date: Apr. 1849 (probably not in
Notman's hand)
Scale: none indicated (scales
approximately ⅛″ : 1′)
Other inscriptions: Back Elevation/End
Elevation/Front Elevation
Description: outline elevations
Medium: ink
Size: 23-15/16 x 17-7/16 (59.6 x 44.4)
Owner: Historical Society of Pennsylvania
(AIA)
OTHER EARLY ILLUSTRATIONS:
A photograph is reproduced in Podmore,
Harry J. *Trenton Old and New.* n.p.
(1927).

DOCUMENTATION:
Specifications for Residence of Charles L.
Pearson, Esqr., contract, and Diary of
Charles L. Pearson, Coll. W. Houstoun
Pearson
BIBLIOGRAPHICAL REFERENCES:
D: 133; S-PULC: 120

NO OTHER NOTMAN RESIDENCE is so well documented as Glencairn. Not only do the plans
and specifications survive, but Charles L.
Pearson's diaries provide a day-to-day account
of the progress of its construction. Although
Charles's father Isaac actually owned the
property and paid the bills, Notman can be for-
given for naming Charles as the client on the
specifications and some of the drawings. For
it was Charles who met with Notman to discuss the plans and their modifications, and
Charles who visited the building site daily,
often, one feels, slowing rather than hastening
the progress of the work. All quotations below, unless otherwise credited, are from his
diary.

On 6 Jan. 1849 Charles Pearson made preliminary inquiries about a building lot on the
corner of State and Calhoun Streets, in what
was then the outskirts of Trenton. By 19 Jan.
negotiations for its purchase were almost
complete, and Pearson "met John Notman
architect, & walked with him over our anticipated purchase of lots to enable him to draw
out a sketch of the building." On 29 Jan. Pearson wrote to Notman, presumably to inform
him about the progress of negotiations for the
lot.

Notman was evidently spending time in
Trenton in connection with other commissions,
for on 8 Feb. Pearson wrote, "I had a chase
after Mr. Notman in the street & overtook
him nearly by the lots we talk of purchasing.
I had some talk with him. . . ." A week later a
purchase price for the property was finally
agreed to. The following week, on 21 Feb.,
Pearson "put a letter in the Post-Office for
John Notman, architect telling him that we
had purchased a lot at last." Notman must already have made preliminary sketches; the

next day "after dinner we were all busy looking over a plan for a house, which I received while we were at dinner, ... & talked about it & all the internal arrangements."

On 26 Feb. Notman came to Trenton. "Father & Mother came to town also ... where we had a general consultation about the plan of our house and settled it. Mr. Notman to draw out the finished sketch & working plans." Notman was back in Trenton on 13 Mar. "with a partial sketch of our proposed new house, but he found the cost would exceed his limit, & thought best to consult, he went away about 6½ o'clock." The family spent the morning of 16 Mar. trying "to ascertain in what way we can contract the dimensions of it so as to bring it within a reasonable price." In the afternoon "Mr. Notman called to see us. We remained chatting with him & explaining our proposed alterations of his plan of the house...."

On 30 Mar. the Pearsons received "a roll containing the plan & specifications for our new house." These specifications, major portions of which appear below, provide a good deal of information about the appearance of Glencairn and about mid-nineteenth century building technology.

The house to be erected and finished according to the plans and drawings as made by John Notman Architect of Philada being the same as approved by Mr. Pearson.

The size of the house on the ground to be as on the plans—and the heights to be in basement or cellar seven feet 6 inches, (7 ft 6) clear height, the first story fourteen feet (14 ft) clear height and the second story twelve feet (12 ft) clear height, the height of these two stories will be in three stories over the kitchen, in height 9 ft, 8 ft 6 and 7 ft 6 in....

The exterior walls of the house to be built of stone with corners, hammered header and stretcher, window jambs the same, the windows to have stone sills, and stone lintels tooled or skew back arch hammered, the water table to be a hammered course with bevel set off. The stone must be laid on their natural beds as random coursed work on the east and north fronts, or as near the quality of work as the stone will allow without hammer dressing, as it is desired not to skew the tool mark on the walls but at angles.

The mortar to be made of bar sand, and fresh Lime well mixed, and the external faces of walls to be neatly pointed with mortar coloured to the tint of the stone. The walls fronting to the river and the kitchen side will be good ruble [sic] work well laid and pointed, the walls to

be laid up solid, strong, and of good masonry no edging of stone or unbonded work will be allowed....

The two main partition walls from front to back and one partition wall from end to end shall be of (9 in) nine inch brick work with the Chimneys built to them, they will be on piers and arches in cellar and continue to the roof. There will be flues for hot air built to each principal chamber, and the fire places will be open.... The roof to be covered with slate on boards laid in best manner with tin eave gutters well painted flat covered with tin do, and conducters at proper places for the water to be led to the ground at which will be spout stones.

The eaves to be finished with a neat block cornice of 2 feet 6 inches projection worked to drawing.

The tower will have the upper story of wood framed or of nine inch brick work neatly flush boarded exterior painted as stone the eaves will be 3 feet in projection finished as main house, access from it to the roof and continued access by back stairs. The Verandah will have good floor laid tight with supports to roof of iron, the roof to be curved pattern covered with tin painted, the cieling of plaster.... The Bath and Water Closet will be in the Second story of Tower entering from the half pace of stairs, which will be on level of back stair first landing, a reservoir will be placed over this room, of the capacity of (1000) one thousand gallons, at least, to be strongly framed of wood lined with lead, this reservoir will be supplied by a ram worked by the springs on the ground from this reservoir supply pipes will (be) taken to the kitchen boiler and sink to the bath and water closet and to all the chambers if desired, sinks will be placed in the kitchen, in the wash room below it and in the store room—The Porch will be of wood having Columns & Pilasters with cornice and balustrade around balcony formed by the roof. The bow window will have also a balustrade and balcony, both of them on stone bases.

The whole of the wood work as usually painted will have 3 coats of white lead and oil of best quality. The last coat on the shutters to be green that on the doors of principal rooms to be of shades of colour as may be desired conditioned they are plain colours.... the sash and frames will be painted stone colour outside, the porch and bow window to be sanded, the roof of the balcony to be painted in stripes bronze and pale yellow, the iron work of bronze. The wire frames to have 3 coats of paint, the eaves cornice sanded.... the drawing room will have a cornice to girth 20 inches the dining room and Library or parlour a cornice to girth 18 inches—the hall to have a cornice to girth 15 inches all these girths to count on moldings only free of the plain surfaces of facias connected with them, a centre flower to be placed in the hall in the dining drawing and library rooms where the gas pipes come through the cieling. ... The Plumbing to consist of connection with leading pipe from ram to supply the reservoir from thence to every point mentioned, the bath having a shower and douche, the kitchen & wash house, and to the several chambers as desired—the reservoir to be lined with 5 lbs lead the Bath tub with 6 lb lead, the sinks with 7 lb lead the pipes of conduction to be ¾ bore of strongest quality with cocks as wanted of lever handled pattern.

A patent Water closet with China bason lift trap and water trap and weight cock of supply of the most improved construction to be fixed in good working order in the bath room. . . .

A privy of size 10 feet by 6 ft. on the ground, will be placed at the end of the above shed, ...

A competent furnace to be built in the cellar (central) so as to give air flue to drawing room Library Dining room and halls with main staircase and the principal chambers on second story, neat bronze valves to be set at points of emission—fresh air to be conducted to it in a wood box.

It is to be observed, that the upper story of Tower will be of nine inch brick work finished in cement colour of the house instead of frame as before mentioned.

The Attic will be in 2 rooms both lighted by lanterns, the sash in them to open for ventilation, and to be on the four sides, a third room will be dark—. . . .

There is to be a bell with pull from the Front door—the drawing room the Library & dining room, the four best chambers and one for servants being in all nine bells.

The Chimney tops to be of brick neatly finished, with cement coloured to the stone of the house.

On 31 Mar. Notman

called here in the morning . . . & staid a couple of hours, talking about the house, the plan of it, etc. His estimate is higher than we wished to give for a house, but still Father is unwilling to diminish the size of it & I expect it will be built according to the plan drawn out, which is to cost $10,000.

On 5 Apr. Notman returned to Trenton and spent the morning "settling upon the plan of our new house, making the whole of the internal arrangements, finishing the specifications, etc. & the house, or digging for the cellar is to be commenced next Monday." The estimate had by now risen to $11,000. On Monday 9 Apr. the family went

to meet Mr. Notman there to lay out the ground for house. . . . Mr. Notman was not there. . . . He came at length, but his men disappointed him & went home to dinner, he to his at Snowden's. . . . After dinner I drove Father to town again & the ground was staked & the contract with Mr. Notman signed.

The following Saturday "We met Mr. Notman in town & he purposes to commence digging the cellar on Monday." The Pearsons

drove to the house on Monday, but Notman was not there. On Tuesday 17 Apr. digging of the cellar commenced. Notman visited the site on Friday, and on Saturday Pearson went to Philadelphia, where he looked at furnaces and ranges at [Dennis?] Murphy's, mantels at [Michel] Bouvier's, and plumbing supplies at Forsyth & Brothers.

By 1 May the cellar was almost complete and on 4 May Notman again visited the site. Foundation work commenced on 7 May. Notman was there on 9 May, but a storm had halted the work. On 11 May there was a major snag.

I discovered that there was an error in the size of the building, cutting off a great deal from each of the rooms, which of course is entirely inadmissible. I trust the error is accidental, but I very much feel it is the result of design.

The next day Pearson went to town to wait for Notman, who did not appear, and to whom he then sent a telegram. The problem must have been resolved, for it is not mentioned again. Ten days later Pearson

authorized Mr. [John] Grant [the mason] to finish the corners of the building in a different style, the stones projecting & chamferred (bevelled off at the edges) at an additional expense of 200 dollars. . . .

On 27 May he authorized other payments including "ornamental stones over the lintels of 4 lower front windows, at 12 to 15 dollars each" and "Panneling the frieze" for $100.

Work went on through the spring and summer, but not with sufficient rapidity to satisfy Pearson.

Mr. Notman promised to send the Gas fitter up this morning, but I waited until after 11 o'clock & he came not. . . . I am in hopes the whole building will be ready for the slaters this week, it appears to me to have gone up quite slowly, there were not masons enough.

By 20 Aug. the roof was almost complete and the painters had begun work. During August and early September Pearson met with the gas fitters, plumbers and the supplier of the furnace and range. Notman was often present at these meetings, and was obviously supervising the work closely. On 10 Oct.

Pearson and his mother met Notman in Philadelphia to choose the mantels, three in grey-veined Italian marble from John Struthers & Son and six others from John Baird. Three days later Notman was in Trenton where he and Grant were "busy measuring the walls," possibly an indication that the work was still to be calculated by measure as construction had been in the eighteenth century.

At the end of November the house was close to completion, but there were some difficulties.

The base of the front portico was commenced this morning [28 Nov.], but Mr. Notman having committed an error in the number of the steps, having too few, it was discontinued.

Details and extras were being attended to. On 8 Dec. Pearson went to Philadelphia "to Mr. [John] Gibson's, a stainer of glass, to inquire about the price of a stained glass door for the reservoir room...." Meanwhile the difficulty about the portico must have been resolved, for it was finished on 12 Dec. "as far as it can be done this winter."

With the house enclosed, work on the plumbing went forward, and carpets were chosen, a "Tapestry Brussels" at $1.70 a yard. Carpenters, plasterers and painters were still busy in the house at the end of February. By March the work was virtually complete. On the eleventh Notman called on the Pearsons to discuss his bills. He was paid $1,000, with $1,358 still due. On 15 Mar. Pearson noted "The house begins to look like living in it now, were it not for the smell of the paint." Twelve days later the family moved in.

Still there were finishing touches to be added. The roof leaked, as did the side doors of the bay window. In late May the painting was patched and in June the cellar was whitewashed. Lightning rods were installed in August, and in October green shutters were fitted to the tower windows. In November Pearson installed weather stripping of canton flannel around the doors and windows.

Glencairn was a residence at which Notman appears to have played no part in the landscape design. Charles Pearson was a dedicated amateur horticulturist. As soon as the lot was purchased he undertook elaborate drainage procedures and the installation of such features as a grotto and pond. For several years he busied himself with improving it with fine specimens of trees and shrubs. His diaries are as valuable a document of mid-nineteenth horticultural tastes as they are of the history of a construction project.

Pearson also took upon himself responsibility for the improvement of the hydraulic ram that provided the water supply, as well as other aspects of the plumbing. Nineteenth-century plumbing could have its perils. On 28 Sept. 1850, he and George, one of the servants, "undertook to clean out the reservoire [in the tower] but failed & I fell into it head first, by George['s] carelessness."

On the whole the Pearsons were pleased with their house, with the furnace that kept it at an even 70 degrees in the winter and with the luxury of daily baths. Still, had they had it to do over again, they might never have started.

When building this house Mr. Grant put in many expensive flag stones where others of a common kind would have answered a better purpose & cost very materially less, it was done to swell the bill I believe. The experience I have gained by the building of this house would lead me to avoid building in future, or if I did, to employ honest men, & not give contracts to architects, but keep the whole under my own control.

PRESENT STATUS:
Demolished

The Episcopal Academy. *Courtesy Trustees of the Academy of the Protestant Episcopal Church in the City of Philadelphia*

41.

THE EPISCOPAL ACADEMY
LOCUST AND JUNIPER STREETS, PHILADELPHIA
1849–1850
Client: Building Committee of the Board of Trustees (Horace Binney, Chairman)
Project: private school for boys

DRAWINGS: none
OTHER EARLY ILLUSTRATIONS:
A woodcut, showing the building before the upper stories were added to the wings, appears in Smith, R. A. *Philadelphia As It Is, in 1852.* Philadelphia (1852)
DOCUMENTATION:
Minutes of the Trustees of the Academy of the Protestant Episcopal Church in the City of Philadelphia, III; Philadelphia *Public Ledger*; J; StA
BIBLIOGRAPHICAL REFERENCES:
D: 136

THE EPISCOPAL ACADEMY, a revived eighteenth-century institution, reopened in 1846. By 1849 it was well enough established to purchase property on Locust Street and appoint a committee to obtain plans for a building. [Minutes: 1 Mar. 1849] The progress of their work was consistently reported to the trustees. That Notman must have served as contractor for the building, as well as architect, is attested by the total sum paid to him, $12,000.

A good description of the internal arrangements appeared soon after it opened.

The Academy of the Protestant Episcopal Church.
—The elegant and spacious brown stone edifice, intended for a school house and erected in Locust St, at the corner of Juniper, was opened yesterday. It has been erected under the supervision of the Episcopal Church, and the schools will be under the superintendence of the Rev. Mr. Hare. The building is in the Elizabethan style, a handsome structure, five stories in height. As a specimen of school architecture, it is one of the most complete buildings which has ever been put up. The pupils enter the grounds by the rear gate. They then go into the basement of the edifice and visit the "cap room." Each pupil in commencing his tuition is given a number which designates him whilst in the establishment. Upon entering the cap room, therefore, he goes to the rack bearing his number, hangs up his cap, overcoat, (if stormy weather.) and deposits his India rubber shoes and umbrella in a receptacle and stand especially appropriated to him, so that every thing is systematic and there is no confusion on dismissing the school.

In the first story there is a neat chapel fitted up, with oak benches. Religious services are solemnized here every day, as a part of the exercises of the school. The second, third and fourth stories are appropriated to the use of the school, being divided into recitation and class rooms and apartments for the tuition of the various branches of education. They are all fitted up with handsome desks, chairs, blackboards, etc., and every modern appliance for teaching. Gas pipes run through the centre building, to which burners may be applied, in case it is deemed advisable to open night schools. Each recitation room has a set of pigeon holes, in which the scholars deposit their books, according to their numbers.

The entire upper story is fitted up for a gymnasium, with all the modern apparatus; so that the scholars are insured bodily exercise as well as mental application. Ventilation is particularly attended to; air flues connect with every room, and have openings near the floor and ceiling of each room. The cupola which surmounts the edifice is so arranged as to cause a constant draught of air throughout the building. The arrangements for ventilation are the most complete which we have ever seen in any public edifice. Each room is warmed by heated air. The number of scholars which can be conveniently accommodated is over two hundred. In case it is necessary, wings may be added to the building, which will double its capacity.
[*Public Ledger*, 3 Sept. 1850: 2]

PRESENT STATUS:
Demolished

42.

ST. MARK'S PARISH SCHOOL
LOCUST STREET BETWEEN SIXTEENTH AND
   SEVENTEENTH STREETS, PHILADELPHIA
1849–1850
Client: Vestry of St. Mark's Church
Project: parish school, to be erected adjacent
   to church then under construction

DRAWINGS: none
OTHER EARLY ILLUSTRATIONS:
   A portion of the building is visible in a
   lithograph entitled "St. Mark's Church/
   Philadelphia," drawn by Roy Mackintosh.
DOCUMENTATION:
   Minute Book of (proceedings) of the Ves-
   try of St. Mark's Church in the City of
   Philadelphia—A.D. *CDCCCXLIII* to A.D.
   MDCCCLXIII
BIBLIOGRAPHICAL REFERENCES:
   F: 114-17; Mortimer, Rev. Alfred. *St.
   Mark's Church, Philadelphia and its Lady
   Chapel.* New York (1909)

IN THE SPRING OF 1849, while St. Mark's
Church was still under construction, Notman
approached the vestry's building committee
with a proposal to build a parish school to the
west of the church. On 10 Apr. 1849 the vestry
considered this proposal,

... offering to erect a School building in accordance with
the accompanying plan, including furnace, paving, and a
wall ten feet high between school house and the west line
of the church for the sum of $3,000.

Evidently no decision was made until the
building committee and the architect examined
the site. On 14 Apr. it was reported that

A closer examination of the ground upon which it was
contemplated erecting the proposed School building, has
satisfied the Committee, as also Mr. Notman the architect,
that the church has sufficient ground upon which said
building might be erected without marring the appearance
of the church, they therefore offer the following resolution
—Resolved. That the western end of the church lot, be
used as a site for the School house, and that immediate
arrangements be entered into for its erection—.

[Minutes: 35-37]

The building must have been erected very
quickly. The school opened in January 1850.
By 1852 an enlargement was required. [Mor-
timer: 6] Because the financial accounts for
the school are commingled with those for the
church, it is impossible to determine precisely
what either building cost.
PRESENT STATUS:
   The original lines of the school are somewhat obscured by later alterations and
   additions.

43.

ST. LUKE'S CHURCH
CAREY STREET, BALTIMORE, MARYLAND
1849–1850
Client: Vestry of St. Luke's Church
Project: new church

DRAWINGS: none
DOCUMENTATION:
   Minutes of the Vestry of St. Luke's Church
BIBLIOGRAPHICAL REFERENCES:
   Stanton, Phoebe. *The Gothic Revival and
   American Church Architecture,* Baltimore
   (1968)

AS RECOUNTED BY STANTON [298-300], Notman's abortive dealings with the vestry of St.
Luke's are revealing both of architectural
practice in the mid-nineteenth century and of
his temperament.
   St. Luke's began discussing erection of a
church in 1847, considering plans by Richard
Long and at least one other architect. In Mar.
1849 Notman wrote to the vestry, offering to
prepare a plan or plans

... but I will expect the plan to be carried out and I to be
employed to do so by contract or otherwise and to be paid
for it, as I cannot afford to give my time on a risk or
chance of adoption. If I contract for the church no charge
will be made for the drawings.

He suggested stopping to meet with the vestry on his return journey from Washington, where he was attending the inauguration of President Zachary Taylor.

It was not until the following September that the vestry began to negotiate with Notman in earnest. Evidently they had found his preliminary designs to their liking and requested working drawings. Notman informed them that the charge for providing them would be one half of one per cent, to be included in the five per cent generally charged for supervision. "I will with pleasure carry out the plan if adopted, for which the established charge by good and bad architects is 5 per cent on the cost, with all expenses of travel, etc. paid." In contrast to his actions at St. Mark's and St. Clement's, he refused to act as contractor because he was unfamiliar with Baltimore prices for material and construction. He added that if the designs were not to be utilized, he would like them returned. He wished to send them to a church in Savannah, Georgia, for consideration.

The vestry, evidently unwilling to pay so high a fee as five per cent, requested a price for providing drawings and detailed specifications to be carried out by a local contractor. Notman found this proposal objectionable, not wanting his design to be "carried out by mere builders who seldom preserve the spirit of the style." He offered the drawings for $225. The vestry countered with an offer of $150, but wanted specifications as well. These were sent in Feb. 1850, by which time the Savannah commission had been lost. No payment was ever made to Notman.

PRESENT STATUS:
Notman's drawings were not utilized. The church was begun on designs drawn by Niernsee and Nelson of Baltimore and completed according to those of John W. Priest.

44.

WASHINGTON MONUMENT
RICHMOND, VIRGINIA
1850
Client: Unknown
Project: design for a monument, probably intended for Capitol Square

DRAWING 44.1:
Title: Washington Monument/ Richmond, Vaginia (sic)
Signature: John Notman Architect
Date: Philada Aug 4th 1850
Scale: none indicated (scales 1/13″ : 1′)
Otehr inscriptions: Elevation
Description: rendered elevation
Medium: ink and wash
Size: 21 x 13-13/16 (53.3 x 35.1)
Owner: Historical Society of Pennsylvania (AIA), C-C1
DOCUMENTATION:
Capitol Square, Washington Monument Funds, Boxes 16 and 17, Virginia State Library
BIBLIOGRAPHICAL REFERENCES:
Brumbaugh, Thomas B. "The Evolution of Crawford's 'Washington.'" *The Virginia Magazine of History and Biography*, 70, 1 (Jan. 1962) : 3-29

THE IDEA OF ERECTING a monument honoring George Washington in the capitol of his native state was proposed as early as the second decade of the nineteenth century. Funds were raised, but it was not until the anniversary of his death in 1849 that the Virginia legislature authorized a premium of $500 for a plan and cost estimate, and not until the following October that the competition was advertised. [Brumbaugh: 6] Somewhere between 40 and 70 designers, amateur and professional, responded, among them G. Parker Cummings, Dietlef Lienau, John McArthur, Jr., Robert Mills and Napoleon LeBrun, who wrote to request the return of his drawings when Thomas Crawford's design was selected in February 1850. [4 Mar. 1850: Monument Fund]

44.1

Notman was not among those submitting drawings, and his drawing for the monument was made some six months after the competition was decided. It can only be surmised that during discussions of the landscaping of Capitol Square [see entry 45], he at least considered the idea of attempting to arrange a substitution of his design for Crawford's.

PRESENT STATUS:

Unexecuted

45

CAPITOL SQUARE

RICHMOND, VIRGINIA

1850–c. 1860

Client: Committee on the Capitol Square, Richmond City Council

Project: redesign of twelve-acre plot surrounding Virginia State Capitol

DRAWINGS: none

OTHER EARLY ILLUSTRATIONS:

"Map of the City of Richmond, Virginia," from a survey by I. H. Adams, Assist. U. S. Coast Survey 1858, published 1864; photographs in the collection of the Valentine Museum; stereopticon photographs, LCP

DOCUMENTATION:

Clippings from *Richmond Daily Times* and transcripts of *Senate Journal and Documents 1852-1853*, in "Capitol Square Data for Mr. W. W. Savedge," Sept. 1831, Virginia State Library; City Council Records, Richmond City, 12, 1848-1852; Mordecai, Samuel. *Richmond in By-Gone Days*, Richmond (1860)

BIBLIOGRAPHICAL REFERENCES:

D: 137; M: 63-64; 68-74; Scott, Mary Wingfield and Catterall, Louise F. *Virginia's Capitol Square*. Richmond (1957); Scott, W. W. and Stanard, W. G. *The Capitol of Virginia and of the Confederate States*, Richmond (1894)

Capitol Square, c. 1865. *Courtesy Valentine Museum*

FOR SOME 28 years after Jefferson's Capitol was completed the area around it was a wasteland of chinquapin bushes and jimson-weed, relieved only by two dells surrounding natural springs. In 1816 the legislature hired Maximilien Godefroy to prepare a landscape plan. Godefroy's solution was a symmetrical system of terraces, drives, and cascades, which was probably never totally executed. By the time Richmond was ready to erect its monument to George Washington [see entry 44], which would require changes in the arrangement of Capitol Square, Godefroy's plan was old-fashioned.

The City of Richmond had assumed responsibility for the square in 1824. Accordingly it was the city that on 16 Jan. 1851 passed an ordinance calling for the square's improvement. On 3 Feb. a committee was appointed to pursue the matter. [Council Records: 434-36]

This committee consisted of three men with whom Notman had had previous dealings: Thomas T. Giles, who had first contacted him about Huguenot Springs; William H. Haxall, a founder of Hollywood Cemetery; and Gustavus A. Myers, also a member of the cemetery's board, for whom Notman had probably designed a house. [see entry 73] It is probable that members of the city council had already been in touch with Notman as early as the summer of 1850, when he prepared a design for the Washington Monument. In a report published in the *Richmond Daily Times* on 24 July 1851 the committee strongly implied that they had approached Notman prior to their official appointment (italics added).

The committee very soon after its appointment communicated with his excellency, John B. Floyd, Governor of Virginia, in regard to the extent to which the committee would be allowed to make alterations in the existing plan of the grounds. . . . The plan for altering and improving the capitol square, prepared by John Notman, Esq. Architect and Landscape gardener, *which had previously* [been] *procured by the Council and a copy of which had been delivered to Governor Floyd,* . . . was approved by him. . . .

Floyd offered the committee *carte blanche*, convict labor and $300 to $400. This was to be added to the $500 available annually from the city. Work began in the spring with the planting of native forest trees, maples along Capitol Street, willow oaks along Bank Street, tulip trees along Ninth Street, and ash along Governor Street.

The report continued:

It was deemed advisable to commence the improvements of the Square itself on the western side thereof, . . . the ground on that side [has been] formed into gentle natural undulations, rising gradually to the base of the capitol and to the monument, . . . giving great apparent extent to the grounds and producing an agreeable variety and at the same time affording space for much greater extent of walks, leading in every direction where they may be useful or agreeable without the necessity of climbing steps and dividing the grounds into irregular and picturesque lawns.

The basin for the fountain on that side has been completed. . . .

Some of the walks have been laid out and partially gravelled. . . .

The committee went on to describe other contemplated changes, but a more succinct and accurate description appeared two days later in the newspaper.

. . . a dozen stout state convicts are engaged in the valley below [the monument site] leveling the hill north of the barracks. This task has been rendered necessary according to the plan of Mr. Notman to present in bold relief the Washington Monument and Capitol building. . . . walks will be made in every direction and as some compensation for filling up the beautiful vale south of the Monument a capacious fountain will be placed in the centre of the walk leading into Bank street, from which fountain a jet d'eau will rise, fully thirty feet in height. The eastern portion of the square will likewise undergo considerable change—the rugged features will be materially softened down, a fountain and jet d'eau to correspond with those on the western side will be placed in the valley near the state courthouse. . . .

The most beautiful feature of the contemplated alterations of the Square, however, will be found in the arrangement of the trees and shrubbery. Instead of planting these in parallel rows, like an ordinary orchard some attention will be paid to landscape gardening—groves, arbours, parterres, and fountains will combine to render the Square a place of delightful resort. . . .

We are satisfied, from an examination of the drawings of Mr. Notman, as well as from a knowledge of the refined and cultivated taste of the gentlemen composing the committee, that the Capitol Square will be one of the handsomest public parks in the Union, when finished.

[*Richmond Daily Times*, 26 July 1851: 2]

This consummation was not, however arrived at speedily. In 1853 Thomas T. Giles reported:

I had intended to restrict this radical change of the surface to that portion of the Square lying west of the Capitol, but during my absence from this city in September last . . . a beginning [was] made . . . , which if carried out, would have radically changed the grounds south, and to complete the plan of the "Committee," it would have been necessary to partially fill up the beautiful vale, east of the Capitol, and thus change the whole face of the public grounds. Though I regarded the alterations made upon the western portion necessary and proper, I did not think that those for the eastern portions would be an improvement, certainly not such as would be commensurate with the expense incurred thereby. For this reason, and the further one, that I doubted my authority either to cause such radical changes to be made, or to appropriate the contingent fund to the payment therefor, I caused the work to be suspended, till I should submit the question for your consideration and direction.

[Senate Journal, Doc. 26: 3]

The suspension must have continued for some time. A map of Richmond made in 1858, although sketchy, shows the basin on the west side of the square and the walk linking this feature with the monument, but not the corresponding basin and walk on the east. Photographs made in the early 1860s, however, show the project as complete.

PRESENT STATUS:

There have been many alterations to the square, notably the addition of the State Office Building in the southeast corner and of driveways in the northern sector. Most of the walks have been paved, and within recent years the straight walks running north from the basins have been replaced by shallow steps. Plantings have also been rearranged. Nevertheless, the major constituents of Notman's picturesque design survive, and Capitol Square remains an intensely used and enjoyed urban park.

46.

EMMANUEL PROTESTANT EPISCOPAL CHURCH
CUMBERLAND, MARYLAND
1849–1851
Client: Vestry of Emmanuel Church
Project: new church for existing congregation

DRAWINGS: none
DOCUMENTATION:
> Letters of Rev. D. Hillhouse Buel to Bishop William Rollinson Whittingham, Duke University Collections; Vestry Records, Emmanuel Church

BIBLIOGRAPHICAL REFERENCES:
> Stanton, Phoebe B. *The Gothic Revival and American Church Architecture*. Baltimore (1968)

EMMANUEL CHURCH had already received a design from Frank Wills of New York before determining to retain Notman in 1849. [Stanton: 280] By May he had provided a design for a large church with a nave 130 feet long and ample transepts, 60 feet wide, to allow for the separate seating of slaves. [Buel to Whittingham: 22 May 1849] Notman played an active role during construction, being present at the laying of the cornerstone, interviewing local workmen in March 1850, and spending considerable time in Cumberland during July of the same year. The church was under roof by Jan. 1851. [Stanton: 281]

Emmanuel Church cost $18,000, less than half the cost of St. Mark's, a saving made possible by the avoidance of elaborate detailing. Notman's fee was $1350. [Report of Mr. Semmes, Treasurer, 7 May 1851, Vestry Records]

PRESENT STATUS:
> Remains in original use

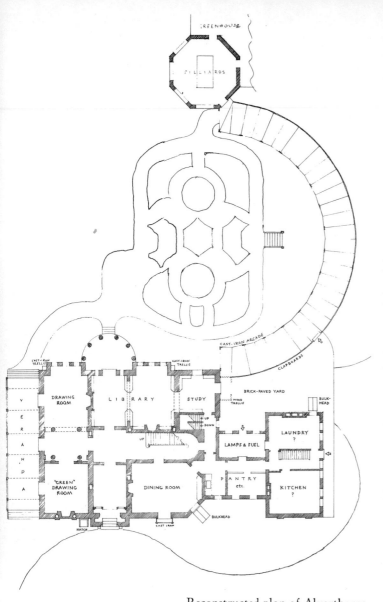

Reconstructed plan of Alverthorpe.
Drawn by Winslow Ames

47.1

47.

ALVERTHORPE
JENKINTOWN, PENNSYLVANIA
1850–1851
Client: Joshua Francis Fisher
Project: residence

DRAWING 47.1:
  Title: Alverthorpe
  Signature: J. Notman Archt
  Date: none
  Scale: none indicated
  Other inscriptions: Seat of J. Francis Fish [er] JFF/1851 (initials and date appear in stone inset in gable)
  Description: rendered perspective
  Medium: ink, wash, and watercolor
  Size: 12⅜ x 26¾ (31.5 x 67.9)
  Owner: Arthur Gerhard

ALVERTHORPE.

OTHER EARLY ILLUSTRATIONS:

Several early photographs are in the Historical American Buildings Survey; others are owned by members of the Fisher family. A selection of these, along with a reconstructed plan and section, were published in Ames, Winslow, "Alverthorpe *ex Tenebris." Nineteenth Century,* III, 3 (Autumn 1977): 66-73.

DOCUMENTATION:

Downing, A. J. *The Theory and Practice of Landscape Gardening,* 6th ed. New York (1859); Fisher, Sidney George. Diaries. HSP; J

BIBLIOGRAPHICAL REFERENCES:

D:133, 135

THANKS TO Joshua Francis Fisher's cousin, Sidney George Fisher, the diarist, the development of the Alverthorpe property is well documented. The dated quotations below are from this source. In early 1844 the cousins were exploring the environs of Philadelphia, looking for a farm suitable for conversion to a country estate. On the last day of February they visited a farm in Jenkintown that seemed suitable. It had an existing house "built of stone and very substantial and comfortable. It is badly situated, however—being on the road. —This is of no importance to him—as his plan is to build an English cottage for himself & keep the house on any farm he may purchase for a tenant." [3 Mar. 1844] This was the property Fisher settled on, paying $10,500 for it. Like Richard Stockton Field, he intended to take his time about developing his estate. "He does not propose to build this year, but to plant trees and get the ground in order on the spot chosen for his house.—When all his plans are accomplished, the place will cost at least $20,000." [11 Mar. 1844]

Three years later Fisher began to think in earnest about building. By this time he had probably abandoned thoughts of a "cottage" in favor of what would have been termed a "villa," for Sidney George Fisher thought the house would be "very large and elegant." He may already have had Notman prepare some preliminary drawings, since he had "determined on a site for his new house and on a plan for the house. . . ." The grounds still were of primary importance, however and he "had Downing—the author of books on landscape gardening and cottage architecture, to look at the place and advise him about the house and grounds." [1 Nov .1847]

Still Fisher did not act. The following summer his cousin reported that "He does not intend to build his new house for two years—but meanwhile is preparing the ground by planting &c." [13 Aug. 1848] The following year he again consulted "Downing—the landscape gardener—who was there for a few days to help him lay out the grounds of his place." [5 Nov. 1849]

Construction probably began in 1850. By the end of the year the house was nearing completion.

Joshua Fisher's new house is nearly finished and he will go into it next spring. It is also a very elegant affair—more architectural and more expensive than Henry's * [Sidney George Fisher's brother] but not I think so well contrived and convenient and the situation is far inferior. It is too near the road. . . . Nevertheless Alverthorpe will be a beautiful residence.

———
* which cost 45,000.

[31 Dec. 1850]

Contemporaries, as well as later viewers were impressed by the "effective architectural appearance . . . produced in connecting the mansion and greenhouses by a sort of cloister, or gallery." [Downing: 555] This remarkable semi-circular arcade was constructed not of stuccoed masonry, as shown in the rendering, but of iron and wood. The inner perimeter was formed of cast iron uprights and arches, the outer, much lower, wall of wood. Curved iron rafters supported on slender iron posts spanned the two, covered by a clapboard roof curved like half a ship's hull.

PRESENT STATUS:
    Demolished

48.

HENRY PRATT McKEAN HOUSE
(Fern Hill)
GERMANTOWN, PENNSYLVANIA
1851–1852
Client: Henry Pratt McKean
Project: residence

DRAWING 48.1:
    Title: Villa Residence/
    Hy Pratt McKean Esq.
    Signature: John Notman/Architect/
    Philada (stamp)
    Date: March 12th 1851
    Scale: 1/8" : 1'
    Other inscriptions: South/Front Elevation
    Description: rendered elevation
    Medium: ink and wash
    Size: 11¾ x 19 (29.8 x 48.3)
    Owner: Historical Society of Pennsylvania, BC 16-14 846
    Exhibition record: Philadelphia Museum of Art, 1964
    Publication record: Massey, James C., ed. *Two Centuries of Philadelphia Architectural Drawings.* Philadelphia (1964)
DOCUMENTATION:
    Downing, A. J. *Treatise . . . on Landscape Gardening,* 6th ed., New York (1859)
BIBLIOGRAPHICAL REFERENCES:
    D: 134-35

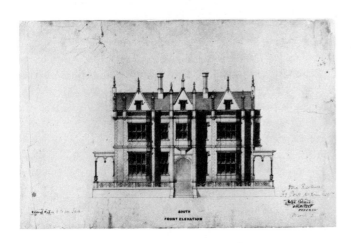

A Two Story Stone Mansion House situate at his Country seat known as Fern Hill between the Township Line Road and the Germantown Rail Road, in Germantown Township Philadelphia County $8000. Also a Two Story Stone Cottage Building on the same premises $2000 Insured.

The Mansion house is of dressed stone, Hemlock joist, Carolina floor boards and building all lathed and plastered. Reveal window frames with inside panel shutters to them, shutters sliding into the wall.

THIS DRAWING is Notman's only known essay in a major residence in Gothic style. Although the design might have pleased one of A. J. Davis's Hudson River clients, it seems not to have been acceptable in the Philadelphia environs, where castellated houses did not become popular until the waning years of the nineteenth century.

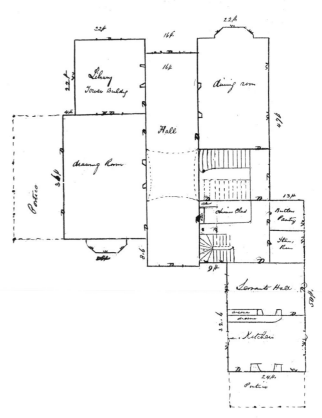

Fern Hill. *Reproduced from a photograph in D-PULC*

Fern Hill, as erected, was one of the most elaborate of mid-nineteenth century Italianate villas. The exterior was dominated by a massive four-story tower, 22 feet square. The interior, to judge by the description in the insurance survey, was almost as lavish as that of Prospect.

The first story of the main house is divided into a hall, dining room, stairway, Library & drawing Room; the Hall has a doorway front with folding panel doors side lights with circular top and a doorway back with folding sash doors having 6 lights glass & paneled ones sliding into the walls, a doorway with sash doors in stairway and the Hall is paved with encaustic tiles, 4 elliptic arches with carved brackets and pilasters, circular heads to all the doorways and finished with large bead mouldings with carved leaf caps to them, paneled wainscoting on the walls, 2 closets in Hall; the Main Stairway has walnut steps and rizers oak newell post with carved mouldings first Story and Square newells above. Open ballusters, and carved string and heavy moulded hand rail from the first to second story; the wood work in the Hall and Stairway is oak, ceiling laid off in sunk panels and bracketted cornice. The dining room has 2 doorways with folding sash doors having 8 lights 22 by 27 glass on the side and a Bay window

167

in 3 parts front, having 4 lights 25 by 19½ glass in the middle and 4 lights 17 by 19½ in each side division, paneld wainscoting on the walls, circular heads with large bead architraves with carved leaf Cap to doors and windows, an Egyptian marble mantel and sculptured frieze and pilasters, ceiling laid off in panel and stucco cornice and mouldings, the wood work in this room is of black walnut. The Library has a doorway front with folding sash doors with 4 lights 28 by 25 glass and 3 lights in the transom. Circular top. A window on the side, all finished with bead architraves with carved leaf mouldings, paneld wainscoting & French mantel of oak with carved moldings, stucco cornice & moldings on ceiling: The drawing Room has 2 doorways on the side with folding sash doors having 6 lights 22 by 27 glass and 2 lights in the top part, circular top to them, a Bay window in the End in 3 parts with 3 lights 23½ by 29 glass in each, inside folding panel shutters to them, paneld wainscoting, architrave & caps the same as described, a sett of plank double worked folding doors into Library, and plank double worked passage doors, a white statuary marble mantel richly sculptured in Basso Relievo; enriched stucco cornice & mouldings on ceiling, story 14 ft high in the clear: a window over the half-place of main Stairway with Circular top 3 lights glass in the top part and 10 lights 28 by 17 glass in the square.

The Second Story is divided into a Hall and Stairway, Six Chambers and dressing room and private stairway to the attic and Tower; an opening in the floor under the skylight with fan sash and enclosed with neat Iron railing, elliptic arches with carved bracketts & pilasters and large bead architraves with carved leaf Caps to the doorways the same as first story, walls lined with planed boarding; the rooms over the dining room is a chamber & dressing room, the dressing room has a window with 12 lights 20 by 14 glass sash in 2 parts hung with hinges, bath tub lined with planished copper, hot & cold water, 6 in. double faced architraves mouldings, surbase washboard 6, the chamber has one window the same on the side and 2-ditto front with 28 by 14 glass in them all recessed to floor & paneld below, Marble Mantel, paneld jamb casings to doorways and all the doors hung with hinges, a small entry off the dressing room, the room over the Hall is a study a twin window front with circular top 4 lights 24 by 15 glass in the square and 1 light in the circular part to sash, marble mantel, architraves mouldings, washboard, etc. the same. The room over the Library has a turn window front with 6 lights 14½ by 24 glass and 1 light in circular part in each, and 2 windows with 12 lights 18 by 16½ glass in the side all recessed to floor paneld below, inside folding panel shutters to all. Circular tops to all the doorways, marble mantel with sculptured bracketts; a flight of continued rail stairs with walnut hand rail, moulded ballusters open string, and newell post all of walnut up to the attic and to third story of the Tower and lighted by a skylight in the roof. A small

Chamber or Nursery and a large room over the drawing room, 1 window in the Nursery with 10 lights 13 by 20 glass and 2 lights in the circular part, marble mantel; the Chamber has 1 window in the East end and 2 ditto in the north end 13 by 18 glass with Circular tops to all and all recessed to floor & paneld below, marble mantel; the Chamber over the Hall has 1 window opening on to a Stone balcony with 12 lights 24 by 14½ glass with inside shutters, 2 closets a stairway off to first story and a water closet off stairway with a 2 light window in it, stucco cornice in all the rooms, 13 H 6 story; the Hall is lighted by a circular dome in the attic story; The Attic is divided into 6 rooms, walls 5 ft high at the eaves, 2-3 light windows front and west side, and closets in the rooms, rooms all plastered and finished as Chambers and store rooms; a circular skylight in the room over the Hall enclosed with 6 lights bent glass 4 ft 6 by 23 in. wide ground glass, and a skylight on the roof pitching 4 ways: the roof is hipped, Tin roof a pediment East side and north end with a ◯ window in each, heavy eaves, cornice & bracketts, raking & level cornice, gutters formed on eaves; The Third story of the Tower has a window in 3 parts with 5 lights 14 by 14 glass in each side and 6 ditto in the centre part with circular tops and 1 light glass in it, inside panel shutters, a window the same east side, white marble mantel and bracketts, panel doors, 13 ft. 6 in story, a flight of spiral stairs to the fourth story, open string fancy bracketts walnut rail and ballusters and walnut steps:

The Fourth Story of the Tower has 2-twin windows with 6 lights 12 by 21½ glass and inside panel shutters, to each, circular top, walls lined with planed boarding 3 ft. high, 12 ft. story, the roof pitches 4 ways, and eaves cornice & bracketts, Tin roof.

The Back Building first story is divided into a Kitchen, Servants Hall, Store room, Butlers Pantry, China Closet, Stairway and Water Closet room, The Butlers Pantry and store room have each an 8 light 12 by 16 window, a transom over doorways into entry and fitted up with doors & drawers, wash sink lined with copper hot & cold water; the China Closet is fitted up with shelves, and a Fire Proof Chest or Safe in it, a 2 light window in the Water Closet which has a Walnut seat & rizer, walls lined with planed boarding, a flight of continued rail stairs with walnut rail, walnut steps and moulded walnut ballusters and a 2 light window to light them from the first to second story; a flight of stairs to the cellar.

The Servants Hall has a doorway with folding sash door having 16 lights 13 by 17 glass on the west side and a 16 light trim window back 12 by 16 glass, dresser with doors and drawers, mantel shelf with Iron bracketts, single faced architraves & mouldings, washboard, panel doors; the Kitchen had a doorway with panel door transom & a 12 light 12 by 16 window in the end, and a 16 light twin window front & back, marble sink, kitchen range, dresser with doors and drawers and closets, architraves & mouldings, walls lined with planed boarding 3 ft. high. Story 10 ft. 6 in high.

The Second Story is divided into Stairway, entry, 2 bath rooms and 2 chambers and water closet room; the bath rooms have each a window with 8 lights 12 by 16 glass and transoms over the doors, bath tubs lined with planished copper, hot & cold water, shower bath and water closet in one room and bath tub hot & cold water in the other room, 1 window in the Entry and 2 closets also in entry. 2 windows in the Chamber and 1 Closet, the back room has 4 windows and 2 large closets, and all finished with surbase, washboard, 4½ single faced architraves mouldings double worked passage doors and [?] closet doors, 10 ft story. Double pitch roof wood eave cornice & bracketts, Tin roof; the attic is occupied with the Cistern or Reservoir for supplying the baths water closets etc with water; a flight of steps up to the attic of the main building with a frame bulk head over them and 3 small windows in it & closets underneath them.

A Porch on the East side of the Building supported by 6 fluted columns with carved capitals level, cornice, Tin roof and 16 ft wide.

A Porch also at North End of Kitchen with shaped posts level cornice and Tin roof, the sides enclosed with lattice work.

Outside sash and sash doors have been put to the lower story doors and windows and venetian shutters to second story frames East side. The Building has 3 furnaces in the cellar for warming the house; gas pipes introduced throughout; the first story floor is counter ceiled; and the whole Building finished in a good and substantial manner; American mortice latches or locks on all the doors.

D H Flickwin   Surveyor

PRESENT STATUS:
Drawing, unexecuted; building demolished.

49.

SPRINGDALE
MERCER STREET, PRINCETON, NEW JERSEY
c. 1851–1852
Client: Richard Stockton
Project: residence

DRAWINGS: none
DOCUMENTATION:
Letters of Charles Hodge, Hodge Collection, PUL
BIBLIOGRAPHICAL REFERENCES:
Greiff, Constance M. Gibbons, Mary W. and Menzies, Elizabeth G. C. *Princeton Architecture.* Princeton (1967)

Springdale. *Author's photograph*

THIS LEAST ELABORATE of the several villas designed for Commodore Robert F. Stockton's relations was the "gothic cottage" built for his son Richard. In early December 1850 Dr. Charles Hodge, professor at Princeton Theological Seminary, wrote to his brother, Dr. Hugh L. Hodge of Philadelphia, that he had heard that Richard Stockton planned to erect a new house on the Springdale farm, then on the periphery of Princeton. There were familial objections to the site, however, as being too far out of town. A few days later Hodge reported to his brother that Stockton had visited him to discuss purchasing eight acres across the street from the seminary's library. [Charles Hodge to Hugh L. Hodge: 6 Dec. 1850] The agreement was consummated the following month. [Charles Hodge to Hugh L. Hodge: 10 Jan. 1851]

Nothing further is known of the progress of constructing the house, but a few years later, Hodge wrote of it to a close friend, then Bishop of Virginia.

I simpathize [sic] with you in your building troubles. Get a good book (as I am told it is) written by a very foolish man, *Prof.* Fowler the phrenologist, on octagon houses. I have seen some plans of his which were striking not only from their effect, but for the wonderful facilities and roominess which that form allows of, at a moderate expense. Nutman [sic] of Phila., furnished, Richard Stockton, my next door neighbor, a plan of a gothic cottage, which cost some $14,000 & has literally two parlors & two chambers, & no more except a square room of eight or ten feet over the entry. This house where I live has four rooms on the first floor, five on the second & three finished rooms in the attic, besides three finished rooms in the basement, & cost less than $5,000. Build either an octagon or a square house—& eschew any thing pointed, unless you mean to build a palace.

[Charles Hodge to John Jones, 17 Jan. 1854]

PRESENT STATUS:

Extended to the west in the third quarter of the nineteenth century and to the east early in the twentieth, the house now serves as the official residence of the president of Princeton Theological Seminary.

50.

PROSPECT
PRINCETON, NEW JERSEY
1851–1852
Client: Thomas F. Potter
Project: residence

DRAWING 50.1:

Title: Sketch for New Hall/at Prospect, Princeton/Thos. F. Potter, Esqr.
Signature: John Notman/
Architect/Philada.
Date: none
Scale: none indicated
(scales approx. 1/10″ : 1′)
Other inscriptions: none
Description: rendered elevation of the south facade and ground floor plan
Medium: ink, pencil and watercolor
Size: 24 x 17¼ (61 x 43.8)
Owner: Princeton University Library
Publication record: Greiff, Constance M., Gibbons, Mary W. and Menzies, Elizabeth G. C. *Princeton Architecture.* Princeton (1967)

DRAWING 50.2:

Title: none
Signature: John Notman/
Architect/Philada (stamp)
Date: none
Scale: none indicated
Other inscriptions: Plan/Second Story;
North Elevation
Description: elevation and plan
Medium: ink and wash
Size: 24½ x 17-11/16 (62.2 x 45)
Owner: Historical Society of Philadelphia (AIA)
Publication record: S-PULC

DRAWING 50.3:

Title: none
Signature: John Notman/
Architect,/Philadelphia
Date: none
Scale: 1/10″ : 1′
Other inscriptions: Foundation Walls;
First Story
Description: measured drawings of cellar and first floor, including ceiling plan for latter.
Medium: pen, with penciled emendations and calculations
Size: 17¼ x 22¾ (43.8 x 60.3)
Owner: Princeton University Library

OTHER EARLY ILLUSTRATIONS:

Princeton University Archives holds a large number of early photographs.

DOCUMENTATION:

Perpetual Policy #13806, Franklin Fire Insurance Co. Records, HSP; Princeton *Whig*

BIBLIOGRAPHICAL REFERENCES:

D: 133; M: 44; S-PULC: 120; Bill, Alfred Hoyt. *A House Called Morven.* 2nd ed., Princeton (1978); Collins, V[arnum] Lansing. *Princeton Past and Present.* Princeton (1931), 2nd ed. Princeton (1945); Greiff, Constance M., Gibbons, Mary W. and Menzies, Elizabeth G. C. *Princeton Architecture.* Princeton (1967); Hageman, John F. *Princeton and its Institutions.* Philadelphia (1879); Meeks, Car-

50.1

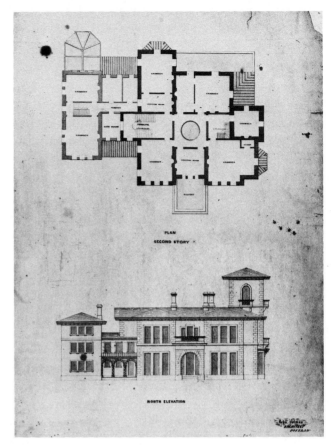

50.2

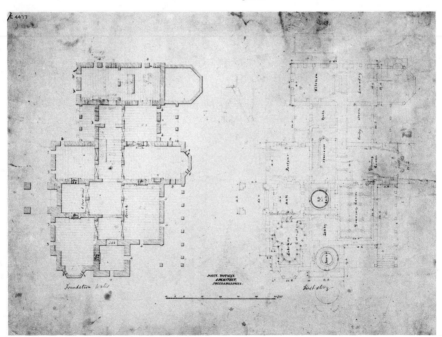

50.3

roll. "Henry Austin and the Italian Villa." *Art Bulletin*, XXX, 2 (1949): 145-49; Smith, Robert A. *Athenaeum Address*. Philadelphia (1951)

No firm documentation for the date of the design of Prospect can be found. Dallett, Meeks and Smith, presumably following Collins [1931: 175; 1945: 77], date the house 1849, but so early a date is precluded by the circumstances of the Potter family. Thomas F. Potter, for whom the house was designed, acquired the property by inheritance from his father, who died on 24 Oct. 1849. [Hageman, I: 314] Unless the son acted with unseemly haste, it is unlikely that the house was designed before 1850. The insurance survey for the house is dated June 1851. However, there are some discrepancies between the plans attached to the survey and the second and third of the Notman drawings, which show the house as built. These suggest that Potter may have been insuring a partially erected structure, to which changes were subsequently made. In any event a completion date late in 1851 or early 1852 is intimated by the following advertisement from the local newspaper: "For Rent—The House lately occupied by Thomas Potter Esq. on Canal St. Possession given on the first of April." [*Whig:* 9 Jan. 1852] Work on the property continued through the spring when the local newspaper reported that the old Academy building, which stood on Washington Road, had been taken down, since the ground was now part of the Potter estate. [*Whig:* 28 May 1852]

Thomas F. Potter was a brother-in-law, rather than, as Smith states, a cousin of Commodore Robert F. Stockton. (For explication of the familial relationships of Notman's Princeton patrons, see Bill, *Morven*.)

Of the three surviving drawings for Prospect, the first is obviously a preliminary sketch. The castellated tower with its offset cupola and multitude of windows gave way to a tower with hip roof and simple fenestration. The gables over the projecting bays were also replaced by hip roofs and the triple round-

Prospect, drawing room, c. 1870. *Courtesy PUA*

Prospect, dining room, c. 1870. *Courtesy PUA*

Prospect, library, c. 1870. *Courtesy PUA*

arched windows by squareheaded ones, while the number of windows across the drawing room front was reduced from three to two. The result is a composition of strongly integrated boxy masses in contrast to the rather diffuse conglomeration of forms in the preliminary sketch. Some changes were also made in the plan of the first floor as can be seen by comparison of the first and third drawings. The second drawing shows the north facade as built.

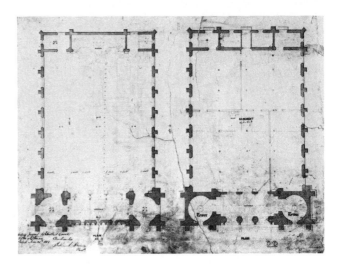

Prospect, chamber, c. 1870. *Courtesy PUA*

PRESENT STATUS:

Prospect remained in the ownership of the Potter family until 1877. It was then purchased for donation to the College of New Jersey and served from 1879 until 1968 as the residence of its presidents. It is now Princeton University's Faculty Club. Most of the house is well preserved, with the exception of the southeast corner, where a large addition for dining space has been made. In contemporary vein, but sensitive to the building and the site, the design is by Warren Plattner.

51.
CALVARY PRESBYTERIAN CHURCH

LOCUST STREET WEST OF
  FIFTEENTH STREET, PHILADELPHIA
1851–1853
Client: Trustees of Philadelphia Calvary
  Presbyterian Church
Project: new church

DRAWING 51.1:
  Title: Presbyterian Church/Locust Street
  Signature: John Notman
  Date: Philad May 20th 1851
  Other inscriptions: Witness present/Robert A. Govett/Contractor/John A. Bis [?]/ Past [or] Plan/Plan
  Description: measured plans of basement and principal floor.
  Medium: ink and wash
  Size: 18⅜ x 24½ (46.7 x 62.2)
  Owner: Historical Society of Pennsylvania, B-B

OTHER EARLY ILLUSTRATIONS:

Two copies of a lithograph, entitled "The Calvary Presbyterian Church/Locust Street,—Philadelphia/ J. Notman Archt." drawn by Steinegger and printed by A. Kollner, are in the collection of the Presbyterian Historical Society, Philadelphia.

DOCUMENTATION:

Correspondence, invoices, receipts and the Trustees Minutes for 1851-1855 are in the Calvary Presbyterian Church Papers, Presbyterian Historical Society; *North American and United States Gazette;* Philadelphia *Public Ledger;* AB; J; St A

BIBLIOGRAPHICAL REFERENCES:
  F: 83-85, 154-65

NOTMAN'S only major church for a dissenting congregation was commissioned in the spring of 1851. On 3 May the contract with the builder, Robert A. Govett, was signed, providing that he was to perform "to the entire satis-

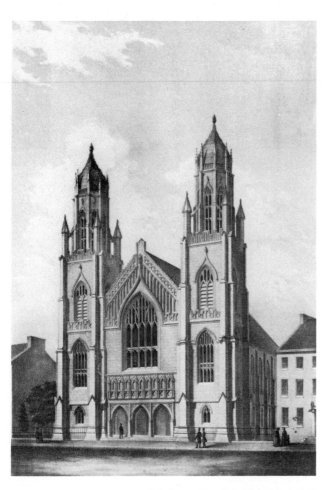

"Calvary Presbyterian Church."
Courtesy Presbyterian Historical Society

faction of John Notman Architect who will superintend and inspect the whole of the work in its progress." A marginal note spelled out that this was to be "according to plans &c. by John Notman." [Minutes: 14]

Construction began the following month.

The foundations have been commenced for a new and splendid Presbyterian Church, for a New School congregation, on the south side of Locust street, between Schuylkill Sixth and Seventh. The plan selected, in the early Gothic style, was furnished by Mr. Notman. It is to occupy a front of 80 feet, extending back to Rittenhouse street, a depth of 125 feet. On either corner of the front there will be a tower surmounted by a spire, the whole height being 120 feet.

The main entrance will be in the basement, and access to the floor and galleries of the church being attained by circular flights of stairs in the towers. The material used in the construction of the building, will be the Connecticut brown stone. Mr. Govet has the contract for building the edifice, which will be called Calvary Church.

[*Public Ledger*, 6 June 1851: 2]

Notman received a total of $2,290 for his services probably representing two and one-half per cent of the construction costs, which were reported to exceed $100,000. [Building Committee Receipts 1851-1855, I: items 3, 8, 18, 31, 91]

The church was dedicated in the fall of 1853, when it was described as a "magnificent Gothic structure" with a front "of the most imposing character." [*Public Ledger*, 4 Nov. 1853: 1] According to another newspaper account:

The Church is built in the perpendicular style of Gothic architecture, as it prevailed in the fifteenth century, and is a very fine and correct specimen of the admired period, so well adapted in form and association with the early days of the Reformation, for a Christian temple. It is one of the largest of our city churches, the size externally being 120 feet by 80 feet, excepting buttress projections. The front on Locust street is a regular composition, having a tower on each side of the centre, in which is the principal entrance, by three wide doors, arched, deeply recessed and moulded on the jambs. Decorative buttresses between and on each side support the hood moulds, set square, forming spandrels in the angles richly foliated. Over the doors is an arcade of vine, with angular buttresses, set on finely floriated corbels. The arcade is pierced for lights in three of the compartments. Over this is the great north window. The projection of its sill forms the cornice of the arcade. The window is 20 feet wide and 32 feet high, in five lights, divided in height by a transom. The centre is terminated in a high pitched gable to the roof outline, lightened in effect by the window arch rising high in the triangle, and further ornamented by an embrasured parapet on the line of the spring, continued across the towers, and the surface above this, panelled to the cornice. Under it the panels terminate in trefoiled heads, and over it is a parapet, in quatrefoils, with moulded coping, crocketted, to the rake of the gable, and terminating at the apex of an ornamental open niche, at the height of 85 feet.

The towers project beyond the centre, and are built square to the height of 85 feet; from thence they are octagon in form, their whole height being 135 feet. The buttresses are rectangular diminishing as they rise, by gablet set-offs, and terminating in octagon turrets with spires, crocketted above the lantern parapets. The octagonal parts of the towers have flying buttresses to the angle turrets, and have ogive canopied roofs, crocketed over, on the angles, to the carved finials; over all are the lightning rod terminations. The flanks of the Church are each in eight bays, with deep massive buttresses between the windows. This Church has the great advantage of each end fronting on wide streets, for ingress and egress. The front on Ritner [sic] street is broken in its outline by a lofty centre for the organ recess interior, with lower aisles, for stairs and floor. The first apartment, entering from Locust street, is a wide vestibule, paved with stone, and having a groined arch ceiling. Arched doors open at each end to the stairs in the towers, ascending to the church floor. These stairs are spacious, and are of stone with ample landings, on which arched doorways open to the church on either hand, the one to a lobby similar to the vestibule below, but open to the church through the gallery arches, the other to the side passage. The interior is at once simple and impressive; its simplicity not arising from want of decoration, for it has more than most churches; but the decoration it has is constructive, and therefore harmonious and pleasing. The coloring has been managed artistically. The interior dimensions are 114 feet in length, by 70 feet in width; of this the seats occupy by 90 by 70 feet, giving ample room for 1000 persons; the gallery will seat about 120 more—it is between the towers, in front. There are no side galleries, which leaves the side windows in full unbroken effect, giving, with the ceiling, an originality of form and finish.

The ceiling is 40 feet high in the centre, and 25 feet at the sides. Between the windows, spring (on corbels) massive curved braces, forming open spandrils continued in moulded beams to the ridge. An intermediate beam over each window with the purlins and braces, moulded, divide the ceiling into series of panels, the ground of which is plastered. Carved bosses entwine the intersections with pendants from the ridge beam; to these the gassiteers are suspended. The wood work is in oak color; the flat of ceiling a cream tint, and the walls of a warm stone tint. The windows are filled with enamelled glass with stained borders and heads. The north window is a very rich design, in lace pattern church glass. The organ is set over the pulpit, facing the congregation.

The basement contains a lecture room, two large school rooms, and a vestry room, all of which are amply lighted and well ventilated. A very fine bell, of upwards of a ton weight, is hung in the north-east tower.

The Church is substantially built of stone of brown color, finely cut at all mouldings and openings. It is all of the same material, cornices, copings, parapets, &c., giving the expression of a fine work. We congratulate the gentlemen engaged on the completion of their work, and the public on the spirit and taste which has added this beautiful monument to the architectural gems of Philadelphia. John Notman, Esq'r, was the architect.

[*United States Gazette*, 4 Nov 1853: 1]

PRESENT STATUS:
Demolished

52.

ST. PETER'S CHURCH
FORBES STREET AND CRAFT AVENUE,
PITTSBURGH, PENNSYLVANIA
1851–1852
Client: Vestry of Trinity Church
Project: new church or chapel of ease

DRAWINGS: none
OTHER EARLY ILLUSTRATIONS:
Copies of a set of measured drawings made by the Pittsburgh firm of Vrydaugh and Wolfe in 1900, preparatory to moving the church to a new site, are in the Historic American Buildings Survey.
DOCUMENTATION:
Vestry Minute Books of Trinity Cathedral; *The Ecclesiologist*, XII (Dec. 1851); *Pittsburgh Evening Chronicle*; J
BIBLIOGRAPHICAL REFERENCES:
D: 137; F: 166-70; Van Trump, James D. "St. Peter's Pittsburgh, by John Notman." *Journal of the Society of Architectural Historians*, XV, 2: 19-23.

SOON AFTER DECIDING, in Sept. 1850, that their expanding congregation required construction of another church, the vestry of Trinity Church, having acquired a lot, determined that "three of their number were to confer with Mr. Nottman [sic] concerning the new building." [Van Trump: 19] Three plans were presented to the vestry on 14 Mar. They selected the second, although requesting one bay less in the nave and a chancel of not more than eighteen feet in length.

According to Van Trump [19-20]

On April 15 the cornerstone was laid and on June 26 a committee reported to the Vestry that Notman had been employed to superintend the construction of the church. ... The building was finished late in 1852 and the first service was held in it on December 19 of that year.

An article published in *The Ecclesiologist*, while the church was under construction, provides an excellent description.

The parish of Trinity church, under the rectorship of the Rev. T. B. Lyman, is building a beautiful Gothic church on Grant and Diamond Streets, [its former loca-

St. Peter's Church. *Photograph by Jim Judkis*

tion] of very fine grained and kindly-working sandstone, brought from the Yoghiogheny river, which is a tributary of the Monongahela. It is in the early Middle-Pointed style, with nave, aisles, and chancel. The nave is 86 feet in length and the chancel 22 feet in depth, by 24 feet in width. The nave is separated from the aisles by beautiful clustered columns of a light blue sandstone, obtained at Deer Creek. There are no galleries, the organ being placed in an arched recess on the north side of the chancel. The tower, which is at the southwestern angle is 18 feet square at the base, and rises to the height of 150 feet. The church will seat 800. Every thing, window, roof, chancel, floor, &c., will be the most perfect of its kind. When completed St. Peter's Chapel will be one of the most beautiful specimens of ecclesiastical architecture in the country. The plan of the architect (Notman, of Philadelphia) was necessarily somewhat modified by the shape of the ground, but this will not, we think, mar the effect of the complete structure. The site is a remarkably fine one, overlooking a great part of the city. S. Peter's will at first be opened as a chapel to Trinity church, though we believe it is not the design of the mother church to make this relation permanent. It is to us a cheering sign of life, where the Church has hitherto made so little progress, to see this old parish coming forward at the call of its zealous rector, and con-

tributing an edifice which is to cost 40,000 dollars, to the cause of church extension....

[*Ecclesiologist*, XII: 432-33]

PRESENT STATUS:

Moved in 1901, St. Peter's has been altered in several respects. The chancel has been extended and at the opposite end, a porch or vestibule has been added. Three pointed-arched entrances in this have replaced the original portal, which was in the tower. The interior, however, in contrast to that of St. Mark's, has been little altered.

53.

RECTORY OF ST. ANNE'S CHURCH
MOVED TO 12 GREEN STREET,
    MIDDLETOWN, DELAWARE
1851–1853
Client: Vestry of St. Anne's Church
Project: modest rectory

DRAWINGS: none
DOCUMENTATION:

Journal of the Proceedings of the Sixty-Third Annual Convention of the Protestant Episcopal Church of the Diocese of Delaware. (Wilmington, 1853); St. Anne's Church, Vestry Records, St. Ann's Appoquinimy, 1808-1883
F: 34

FAIRBANKS, in noting this project, points to the documentation as conclusive, particularly a reference in the vestry records [93] to the Rev. Mr. J. Harrold as "authorized to make a contract on the *Plan* made by Mr. John Notman of Philadelphia...." Otherwise it is doubtful that the building would be ascribed to Notman, for it is, as Fairbanks indicates, "a clapboard house of no architectural distinction."

PRESENT STATUS:

Private residence, heavily altered in Colonial Revival style

54.

CATHEDRAL OF ST. PETER AND ST. PAUL

LOGAN SQUARE, PHILADELPHIA
C. 1851–1857
Client: Roman Catholic Diocese
Project: design of facade

DRAWINGS: none
OTHER EARLY ILLUSTRATIONS:

"Cathedral of St. Peter and St. Paul/ Philadelphia, The above building is two hundred and sixteen feet in length, and one hundred and thirty feet in width, the corner stone of which was laid in September 1846," drawn by John Notman, Esq., on stone by Schnabel, P. S. Duval's steam lith. Press, Phila.

DOCUMENTATION:

Philadelphia *Public Ledger*; Smith, R. A. *Philadelphia as It Is, in 1852*, Philadelphia (1852); AB; J; StA

BIBLIOGRAPHICAL REFERENCES:

F: 223-25; Griffin, Martin I. J., ed. *The American Catholic Historical Researches*, VII (July 1900): 132-33; Wainwright, Nicholas B. *Philadelphia in the Romantic Age of Lithography*. Philadelphia (1958); T; W

ALTHOUGH CONSTRUCTION of Philadelphia's Roman Catholic Cathedral occupied almost two decades, there is surprisingly little contemporary evidence about the process. The most complete account of the activities of several hands in its design is in an interview given by M. A. Frenaye in 1867 at the age of 85.

Mr. Frenaye said that the statement published at the time of the opening of the Cathedral, that Napoleon Le Brun was the architect of the Cathedral, was not correct —that the plan was the design of Fathers Maller and Tornatori, Professors in the Seminary, who, in early life, had studied architecture. Their plan was given to Napoleon Le Brun, who arranged it in architectural proportion and superintended the construction according to this plan. After a time, Mr. Le Brun, for reasons (not mentioned to me by Mr. Frenaye), was removed, and Mr. John Notman engaged to carry on the work. He was to receive five per cent. upon all expenditures. When his first bill was presented this error was observed, for it really was a pre-mium on rascality. Stone which would have been worked in the quarries at one-third less cost, were brought to this city for that purpose. By this means the freight was much greater. Mr. Notman was asked to alter the contract which had thus unwittingly been made with him. He declined, and was removed. It was he who designed the front and dome of the Cathedral. Notman was succeeded by Le Bruu [sic] who was again employed.

On Bishop Wood taking charge of the affairs of the diocese, he altered the dome which it was proposed to construct. Columns, which it was intended to construct at the base of the dome, were stricken out of the plan by Bishop Wood. The original plan of the interior was preserved.

[Griffin: 132-33]

Substantiation that the initial design of the exterior differed from that executed appears in a report published in early 1847. Citing "N. Le Brun" as the architect, it reviews the progress of the building, on which excavation began 18 Aug. 1846, with the cornerstone laid on 6 Sept. By the time work was suspended on 5 Dec. the foundations were mostly completed to ground level. A description of the projected facade follows:

The front will be simple, yet majestic in appearance. In the centre is a projecting screen of four Ionic coupled columns, projecting two thirds of their diameter, and crowned by a pediment with the name of Jehovah in the centre, surrounded by a glory, occupying the interior of the tympanum. At the extreme ends are four coupled pilasters. There will be three doors of entrance, ornamented with architraves and cornices—above each door there will be niches surrounded with impost mouldings....

The building is designed in the pure Roman style.

It is intended to erect the *campanile* or bell tower on the northeast corners of the lot. It will be about 90 feet high when completed, and designed in the Italian style.

[*Public Ledger*, 11 Jan. 1847: 2]

Just when LeBrun was replaced by Notman is uncertain. But by 1852 the present facade had been planned.

The front, on Schuykill Fifth Street, is a beautiful design, by John Notman, Esq., of a highly decorative character, very creditable to that gentleman's taste and skill. The plan consists of a portico of four gigantic columns, sixty feet high, and six feet in diameter, finished with richly sculptured bases and capitals; over these will be an entablature and pediment, in corresponding architectural taste. On the frieze will be engraved the words AD MAJOREM DEI GLORIA M. The apex of the pediment will be surmounted by a colossal figure of the Saviour, and on the opposite angles will be statues of two

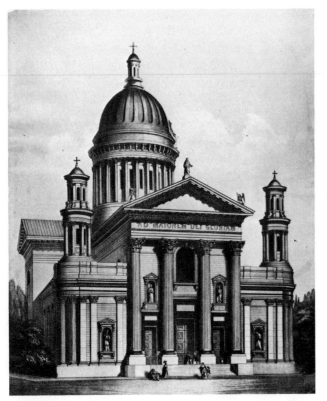

"Cathedral of St. Peter and St. Paul." *Courtesy HSP*

angels, in a kneeling position. The main entrance will be approached by a flight of nine steps, forty-eight feet long. Over the central doorway will be the large west window, and over the side doors will be niches to receive the figures of the patron saints of the church, St. Peter and St. Paul. These niches, together with the doorways and the large window, will be relieved with a bold and richly-executed architrave.... [Smith: 303]

No drawings for the exterior of the cathedral survive, but the lithograph published by Duval probably represents a perspective rendering prepared as a presentation drawing. Since Notman only prepared or turned over drawings for lithography related to his own work, the existence of the lithograph is, itself, a form of supplementary documentation.

When Le Brun was reinstated, replacing Notman, is unknown. The front was nearing completion in 1857 [*Public Ledger*, 10 July 1857: 1], but the building was not dedicated until 20 Nov. 1864. [T: 186]

PRESENT STATUS:

Notman's design for the exterior was modified, probably for reasons of economy. Neither the columns around the drum of the dome nor the corner towers were executed.

55.

PENNSYLVANIA RAILROAD FREIGHT DEPOT AND RAILROAD OFFICES

1852[?]

Client: Pennsylvania Railroad
Project: depot and offices with rental space

DRAWING 55.1:

   Title: Freight Depot Pennsa. R. Road
   Signature: John Notman,/
   Architect,/Philadelphia (stamp)
   Date: none
   Scale: none indicated (probably ⅛″ : 1′)
   Other inscriptions: none
   Description: rendered facade elevation
   Medium: ink and colored wash
   Size: 21⅞ x 36-11/16 (55.5 x 93.2)
   Owner: Historical Society of Pennsylvania (AIA)

DRAWING 55.2:

   Title: Pennsylvania Railroad Offices
   Signature: none
   Date: none
   Scale: ⅛″ : 1′
   Other inscriptions: Entresol/Plan/First story; Plan/Second story; Elevation; Elevation
   Description: measured plans and two versions of rendered facade elevation
   Medium: ink and wash
   Size: 25-11/15 x 34⅜ (65.3 x 86.8)
   Owner: Historical Society of Pennsylvania (AIA), T-2

DRAWING 55.3:

   Title: none
   Signature: none
   Date: none
   Scale: none indicated (probably ¼″ : 1′)
   Other inscriptions: none
   Description: rendered elevations, repeating with more detail, elevations in 54.2
   Medium: ink and wash
   Size: 22½ x 29-3/16 (57.2 x 74.2)
   Owner: Historical Society of Pennsylvania (AIA), T-3

FREIGHT DEPOT PENNS? R. ROAD.

55.1

55.3

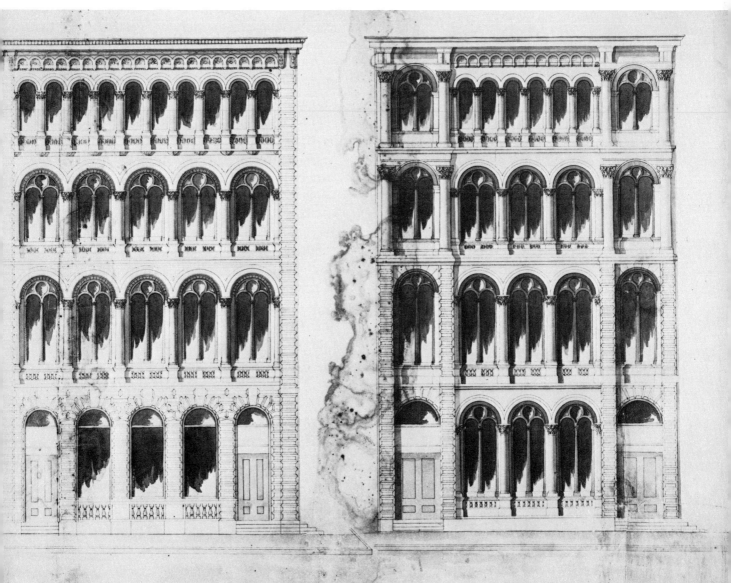

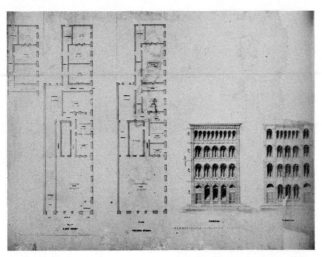

Above: 55.2; *Below:* 55.4

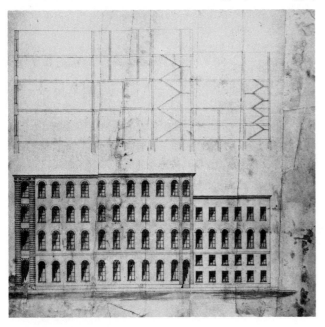

DRAWING 55.4:
>   *Title:* none
>   *Signature:* none
>   *Date:* none
>   *Scale:* none indicated
>   *Other inscriptions:* none
>   *Medium:* ink and wash
>   *Description:* longitudinal section and flank elevation
>   *Size:* 27¾ x 25-5/16 (70.5 x 64.3)
>   *Owner:* Historical Society of Pennsylvania (AIA)

DOCUMENTATION:
>   Philadelphia *Public Ledger*; J
BIBLIOGRAPHICAL REFERENCES:
>   D: 138; S-PULC: 132; Smith, Robert C. "John Notman and the Athenaeum Building." *Athenaeum Addresses.* Philadelphia (1951): 18

ALTHOUGH THE FIRST AND FOURTH of these have been filed in folders separate from the other two drawings, it is clear that all four are related. In particular, the fourth drawing, on the basis of its pattern of openings and levels, as well as the corner rustication, is demonstrably the flank of the building shown in plan and elevation in the second drawing. The freight depot is, of course, linked to the office by patronage. There is also apparent in the drawings physical damage that indicates that for a period of time they were stored together, the first three being heavily stained with a purple ink or dye. Furthermore, the handling of the rustication and arcading in both projects suggests that they were conceived as related.

The date of the drawing for the depot can be established. Announcement of the proposed construction of the building at Market and "Schuylkill Fifth" streets was made on 15 June 1852. The commission, however, went not to Notman, but to S. D. Button. [*Public Ledger*, 15 June 1852: 2]

There is no evidence as to when the office was designed. Jackson attributes the building to Notman [224], an attribution which Smith and Dallett accept, although Dallett points out that the building, as erected, did not follow the drawings. This is not surprising, since the commission, not executed until 1857, once again went to Button. [*Public Ledger*, 25 Aug. 1856: 2]

PRESENT STATUS:
>   Unexecuted

56.

MASONIC HALL
Chestnut Street, Philadelphia
1852–1853
Client: Grand Lodge of Pennsylvania
Project: new hall to replace William Strickland's Gothic edifice of 1808-1811.

Drawings: none
Documentation:
  Minutes of the Grand Lodge, III, 1849 to 1854. Philadelphia (1903); Philadelphia *Public Ledger*
Bibliographical references:
  T; W

In the fall of 1852, the Committee on Plans of the Grand Lodge of Pennsylvania solicited from the architects of Philadelphia designs for a new Masonic Hall. A sum of $25, later raised to $50 was to be paid for each plan submitted, with $150 being awarded for the winning design. [Minutes, 18 Apr. 1853: 321] Six architects submitted plans: John Carver, Edward Collins, John McArthur, Jr., John Riddell, Samuel Sloan, and Notman. [Minutes, 29 Nov. 1852: 269]

Notman, who by this time seems to have been reluctant to engage in competitions, sent the following letter with his drawings, in effect refusing to honor the committee's terms.

Dear Sir:—I send you herewith designs for the New Masonic Hall and regret that the short time I have had for their preparation prevents their being completed. I beg you to notice that in submitting them to the Committee I do so and have made them in performance of a promise to many friends amongst the Brethern [sic] and not in competition. I therefore do not adhere to the terms of the competition as to payment and as retaining the plans as in your letter of October 5th, but prefer the immediate return of the drawings, without remuneration should they not be adopted for construction by the Committee which is respectfully submitted.

I am Sir,
Your obedient servant
John Notman.
Nov. 1, 1852.

[Minutes, 18 Apr. 1853: 322]

In the light of subsequent events it seems unlikely that the committee understood that Notman had rejected their terms and was submitting his designs under an arrangement different from that proposed.

The committee selected the designs of Notman, Sloan, and Collins, and asked these three architects to redraw their plans to conform to certain interior requirements and at larger scale. [Minutes, 18 Apr. 1853: 322]

These plans were then sent out for estimates, which the committee presented in a report to the Grand Lodge.

Mr. Notman's plan, though grand and sublime, had the objection of having but one door and one window to the stores which it was thought would diminish the revenue to be derived therefrom and it was estimated that a hall agreeably to that plan would cost

With an iron front $70,000 00
" a stone " 77,000 00
Mr. Sloan's truly beautiful plan by his own
  estimate would cost
With an iron front $70,315 00
" a stone " 77,315 00

And in his estimates he only allows $300 each as the price of the sculptured figures in front, while the Committee are of opinion that such figures, as would not be derogatory to the craft of a Masonic Order, could not be obtained for less than $1,000 to $1,500 each.

The estimate for a hall built agreeably to
  Mr. Collins' plan were
With an iron front $61,887 00
" a stone " 69,387 00

While for architectural beauty and a pure specimen of the Gothic order the Committee considered it quite equal to the other two.

With regard to whether the front shall be of iron or of stone the Committee did not wish to assume the responsibility of deciding but ask for an expression of opinion in the Grand Lodge on that point.

The foregoing estimates shew that the amount of loan required to cover the cost of the new hall and the $9000 as before mentioned would be

With Notman's plan having a stone front
                              $86,000 00
              an iron do. 89,315 00
With Sloan's plan having a stone front .. 86,315 00
              an iron do. 70,837 00
With Collins' plan having a stone front .. 78,387 00
              an iron do. 70,837 00

The Committee have also had estimates made of the above plans for granite and marble fronts, either of which will add 10 or $12,000 over and above the cost of a stone front.

Under all these circumstances and after a critical examination into the detail and *minutia* and taking into consideration the splendour and beauty of Mr. Collins' plan, combined with its economy, it coming almost within the desired limits on expense, the Committee came to the unanimous conclusion to recommend for the approval of the Grand Lodge, the erection of a New Masonic Hall agreeably to the plan proposed and presented by said Mr. Collins.   [Minutes, 29 Noc. 1852: 268]

Despite the recommendation of the committee, the Grand Lodge voted to give the commission to "Brother" Notman. [Minutes, 29 Nov. 1852: 281]

The Committee on Plans was then dissolved and a Building Committee appointed. The new committee proceeded to "have prepared the specifications ... and the plans and elevations...." Several changes were called for at this time, including subcellars, strengthening of the interior walls, and rearrangement of the Grand Lodge room. Proposals were then invited from contractors and builders, including Notman, who declined being a competitor in the then state of affairs. Bids were received from six contractors, ranging from a low of $138,000 net to a high of $155,224, all well above the $85,000 the Grand Lodge had originally allocated for the project, although they were aware that the addition of cellars and added interior work would increase the cost. The committee thereupon

Resolved, that Bro. Notman be requested to furnish this Committee with his estimate of putting up the Masonic Hall, according to the plans and specifications submitted by him and embracing the changes suggested by the Building Committee, including therein the material of the old building and that said estimate be furnished the Building Committee by to-morrow morning at 12 o'clock.

To this after a day or two's necessary delay the following answer was received.

To the Building Committee of the new Masonic Hall.

GENTLEMEN,—To meet your request in note received of 14th inst. I have carefully estimated the work and materials required for the new Masonic Hall and find that the amount besides the old building is $126,350
My estimate of the front and tower and the decorations of rooms is as before, viz.: the difference between $51,000 and $85,00 and the old material .... ‎24,000

The basement increases the cost .... $ 16,000
Shewing the building without a front to be .... $ 76,350
The Committee on Plans estimate was 51,000
A mistake of about 50 per cent. or .... $ 25,350
for which I am in no way responsible.

I decline making any offer as before, the builders' offers being still undecided, but will cheerfully give you any information you may desire further, in the details of the above estimate which is respectfully submitted, Gentlemen, by

Your obedient servant,
JOHN NOTMAN.

PHIL., Mar. 18th, 1853.

As it is certain that the proposed new hall cannot be put up for the sum of $85,000 with or without the changes, which subsequent examination has shewn to be indispensable, it follows that the labors of the Committee must cease, until some other action is had in the premises by the Grand Lodge, what that action shall be is not for them to suggest, they merely state the facts and leave the decision to the wisdom of the Grand Lodge.

Signed (in behalf of the Committee), JAMES PAGE, *Chairman.*

PHIL., Mar. 18th, 1853.

[Minutes, 22 Mar. 1853: 310-12]

Notman was implying that the bids had far exceeded the budget, not because of his design, but because the committee had underestimated considerably the costs of the interior arrangements it had required. In effect he claimed that he could have built his building for $100,000 had it not been for the added interior costs.

Resolved, that the sum of one hundred thousand dollars *and no more be* and the same is hereby appropriated ... [for] the erection of a new Masonic Hall ... and that said Committee be and are hereby authorized and instructed to receive and decide upon plans and proposals for the building of said hall, ...

[Minutes, 4 Apr. 1853: 315-16]

By this time it was clear to outsiders that there were problems and that the competition was being reopened.

The Masonic Hall.—The design furnished by Mr. Nottman [sic] for the building to be erected upon the site of the old Masonic Hall, has been abandoned by the Grand Lodge on account of the estimates nearly doubling the limit originally fixed upon for the cost. The architects of our city are again engaged in making designs for the proposed structure to be submitted to a general meeting of the Grand Lodge on the 2d of May. The limit of cost now is $100,000, including a cellar beneath the basement, which was not originally designed. It has been determined not to have the building surmounted with a steeple.

[*Public Ledger*, 12 Apr. 1853:2]

The stage was set for a $6,000 misunderstanding. The Masons believed that the results of the bidding had released them from any arrangements with Notman; Notman did not. The documents setting forth the controversy are lengthy, but they reveal a good deal about Notman's personality and about conflicting attitudes towards the practice of architecture in the mid-nineteenth century.

Following the resolution of 4 Apr., the Building Committee once again solicited proposals from the city's architects for designs for a building not to exceed $90,000 in cost, $10,000 being reserved for contingencies. [Minutes, 18 Apr. 1853:318] Notman was among those receiving this request, to which he replied with the following letter:

GENTLEMEN,—I have received from your Secretary a note inviting from me that which I have already furnished, viz.: a design and drawing of front for the New Hall, this I have delivered which has been approved by the Grand Lodge, at the same time I am appointed as Architect, for the New Masonic Hall with the Building Committee and commissioned with you to adopt and complete a plan suited to the (my) design selected.

This I have done with your entire approbation and, by your orders, I have made all the drawings necessary to illustrate and explain in all its parts, the design and plan, and further, by your orders, I have drawn and written out specifications of the whole work and materials for contractors, and again at your request, and in my professional duty, I have estimated the whole building, all of which I have submitted to you. I declined to make an offer as you requested (as it would have been tampering with the rights of the builders who have made offers) while your decision was pending.

Having thus far matured the proceedings and perfected the drawings for contract, I am prepared to proceed with the building, or will cheerfully and without delay simplify or modify my design for you, or make a new one suited to the plan in any style of architecture, so as to meet the proposed expenditure as your appointed Architect and professional adviser. If you depend solely upon me, as is usual with Building Committees at this stage of the business, I feel bound to do this without charge. The usual courtesy being extended to me without competition, as my design in every way made current by you, shews all you want to others, and it is at once suggestive in every shape of the

desired building, such competition would now be unfair and Masonically dishonorable.

The compensation of an architect, capable of building his designs, is 5 per cent. on the whole cost of the building, should the Grand Lodge by you decide not to build. My charge as far as I have proceeded would be (3) three per cent. upon the whole estimate, should you decide to build, with or without my plan and drawings, or my further services, my charge would be five (5) per cent. on the last lowest estimate of the whole building.

I suppose these cases to make clear my answer to your question of what is my charge and, as the Grand Lodge is not incorporated, that I may depend upon the responsibility of you gentlemen, as the Building Committee, for the value of my services, rendered or to be rendered, for if you now invite me to further competition I must charge in addition to the above. If you ask me to modify or make new designs employed alone, as the architect, I repeat I will make them in every style and form and immediately on your answer and orders (which I wait) depend my proceedings and I am, Gentlemen,

Fraternally and respectfully
Your most obedient servant,
JOHN NOTMAN,
Archt.

APRIL 7th, 1853.

[Minutes, 18 Apr. 1853:319]

The committee met immediately to consider this communication and received a report from its chairman, denying that Notman had ever been retained as supervising architect.

I have carefully examined the extraordinary letter of Mr. Notman. I have also gone over the proceedings of the Committee on Plans, the action of the Grand Lodge and the proceedings of the Building Committee and no where do I find that Mr. John Notman was ever engaged, or contracted with as the architect for the erection of the New Hall, or as superintendent of the proposed building. He was originally applied to, by the Committee on Plans, to submit a design for the front, under a notice addressed in common to all the architects, that for the one approved and adopted the price allowed would be $150, with the expectation that the successful architect might be employed as the superintendent of the building, provided the contracting parties could agree upon the terms. A contract rendered impossible by the fact that the proposed New Hall could not be put up for the sum limited by the Grand Lodge, within which limit Mr. Notman with full knowledge of the amount, was bound in making his design for the front strictly to bring the cost. He has been simply employed as an architect to furnish a plan for front and to assist in the details of the interior plan and arrangements, a plan and arrangement in no way originating with, or designed by him, and in the preparation of the specifications and for former is entitled to $150.00 and for the latter to such fair compensation as his labors may be worth; but inasmuch as Mr. Notman has assumed in his communication that at the "Same time his plan was approved and adopted by the Grand Lodge he was appointed as architect for the New Hall with the Building Committee and commissioned with them to adopt and complete a plan suitable to the design (his) selected" and regards himself as "the appointed architect and "professional adviser of this Committee," a position which they do not now and never did consider him as occupying.

I conceive that it is not the duty, nor province, of this Committee to assume the responsibility and decide the question, but they should in my opinion refer the whole matter to the Grand Lodge for its action.

I am further of opinion that a communication should be addressed to Mr. Notman expressing the surprise of this Committee, at the extraordinary and unjust position he has assumed, and to utterly deny that he ever was engaged as the architect or superintendent for the erection of the building by this Grand Lodge, or any one authorized in its behalf. His right to compensation being limited to what may be fairly due him for the plan of the front and for such drawings and services as he subsequently and occasionally rendered the Grand Lodge, through the Committee, and further that the recent invitation to him to present a design for the front, should be withdrawn and he informed that his letter together with a report from the Committee will be submitted to a Special Communication of the Grand Lodge. [Minutes, 18 Apr. 1853: 320]

James Page, chairman of the committee, sent Notman a letter on 8 Apr., embodying the substance of the last paragraph of his report. [Minutes, 18 Apr. 1853: 321]

For the benefit of the Grand Lodge at a special meeting on 18 Apr., Page recapitulated the sequence of events that had led to Notman's selection on 29 Nov. 1852. One new fact was added about the preliminary deliberations. During the period when the final votes were being taken

... Mr. Notman's plan had been surreptitiously removed from the back room of the Hall, without the knowledge of the Committee for the purpose of being altered and improved thereby taking an unfair and undue advantage over the other architects. [Minutes, 18 Apr. 1853: 322]

Once Notman had been chosen, a series of further meetings was held to refine the plans and settle details.

Front to be of brown stone, December 7th, 1852. Notman's plan of front approved Dec. 20th, 1852. Mode of Building Committee's appointment fixed upon. Architect

to give ample security and the cost not to exceed $85,000 without the approval of the Grand Lodge. The plans of the interior arrangement referred to the Building Committee together with the architect. Committee on Plans discharged. From a number of names submitted to the R. W. G. Master by the several Lodges he selected a Building Committee. Which Committee was organized on the 28th of January, 1853.

They met on the 29th and resolved that the proposed new hall should be built under contract with one person; he giving ample security for the faithful fulfilment of such thereof. They directed the Secretary to invite Mr. Notman to attend the next meeting.

January 23d, 1853, Mr. Notman attended and considerable discussion ensued as to the detail in carrying out the plan adopted by the Grand Lodge, when he took the plans away for the purpose of meeting the wishes of the Committee preserving the architectural arrangement wherever practicable.

February 2d, 1853, Mr. Notman attended and had consultations with the Committee.

February 4th, 1853, a communication was received from Mr. Notman estimating the cost of subcellars.

February 7th, 1853, a discussion as to the interior plans or arrangement. Mr. Notman present and the amended and modified plans as to certain portions of the building as presented and proposed by him were adopted.

Meetings took place on the 10th, 14th and 22d when nothing material took place but on the 24th February, 1853, Mr. Notman being present the specifications prepared by him were read and referred to a sub-committee.

February 26th, 1853, Sub-Committee reported a number of alterations and additions to specifications, which were agreed to and they were ordered to be revised and printed.

March 2d, 1853, Report of Sub-committee as to delay in getting the specifications from Mr. Notman.

March 2d, 1853, The specifications were under discussion, with some alterations and additions prepared by Mr. Notman partly adopted and partly rejected and the specifications as finally decided were ordered to be printed.

March 5th and 7th, nothing material but the time for receiving proposals (the circulars having been previously sent to numerous builders) was extended to the 14th of March.

March 8th, Mr. Notman was directed to send the plans and elevation to Grand Secretary's Room before Thursday at 10 o'clock.

Mar. 11th The Committee directed that Mr. Notman be requested to attend at the Hall South 3d street, or send some qualified person to answer all questions that may be desired, by the different persons making estimates for putting up the Hall.

March 14th, Committee met, proposals received and all largely exceeding the limit. Mr. Notman was requested to furnish the Committee with his estimate for putting up the Hall according to the plans and specifications submitted by him and embracing the changes suggested by the Building Committee, including therein the material of the old building. [Minutes, 18 Apr. 1853: 322-23]

It was this request that produced Notman's communication of 18 Mar. 1853 maintaining that the excessive costs were the fault of the committee. No doubt his contention played some role in the committee's decision to reopen the competition.

Calling attention once again to Notman's letter the committee's report concluded:

With this statement of the course of the transaction between the Grand Lodge and its several committees and Mr. Notman, the Committee might conclude its report. It may not be considered out of place however for them, before doing so, to call the attention of the Grand Lodge particularly to the last communication received from Mr. Notman and some of the positions therein assumed, the more surprising as Mr. Notman was notified in the beginning that he was only to design a plan for the front and as to the contract for superintending the erection of the building, that was to be the subject of after and express arrangement between the parties, provided they could agree upon terms. No such contract has ever been made or entered into. The effort on the part of Mr. Notman seems to be to convert all that passed between him and the Grand Lodge as the architect of the front, necessarily and unavoidably employed in adopting that front to the interior plan (originally with the first committee) into a contract with him as the architect for the erection of the building, by which the Grand Lodge is irrevocably fixed and to which this Committee in every future step is bound to conform, not having the right to invite plans from any others. Whether this effort is to be regarded as a "fair business transaction," or to use his own language as "Masonically dishonourable," is not for the Committee to say, but for the sake of the Order, a purely charitable one in its design and tendencies, and whose funds should be carefully guarded and economically managed, in whatever light it may be considered, they sincerely hope the attempt may prove a complete failure. That he is entitled to the $150.00 for his front plan and to a liberal compensation for his time, skill and services as an architect, in assisting the Committee in arranging and modifying the details and for his drawings and specifications is not denied. When it was found to be imposisble to put up the building within the limits fixed, Mr. Notman's plan as well as all others fell through. No doubt it was the leaning of the Grand Lodge, as it was the intention of the Committee, to contract with him as the superintendent for the Building, had the contracts been perfected and Mr. Notman they believe had the same view of the subject himself, until he saw fit to change it through the operation of an afterthought.

In the letter referred to Mr. Notman does not say that he was employed by either Committee as the superintendent for the erection of the building. That engagement he puts upon the Grand Lodge asserting that what the Building Committee subsequently did, was in compliance with the resolution of the Grand Lodge. It is proper therefore to look at the action of the Grand Lodge to see how far Mr. Notman's position is sustained by its proceedings, in the Minutes there is nothing more to be found than the adoption of his design for the front and a reference of the plan of the interior to the Committee, in conjunction with the architect, on this slender basis he presents a claim which if successful is to deprive the Treasury of a sum exceeding $6000. Such an attempt in the mere business world, as between man and man, would be considered, even if technically available, wanting in fairness and oppressive, as between Brother and Brother, in a Masonic fraternity where the principles of Love and Charity are supposed to be *not* things of form, but matters of substance. It strikes the Committee as being reprehensible and without a precedent in the history of the Order and as tending to the destruction of all confidence among the members of the craft....

Unless otherwise instructed by the Grand Lodge they can have no further communication with Mr. Notman, but are now proceeding and will continue to proceed in the discharge of their duties as if he had never submitted a design. [Minutes, 18 Apr. 1853: 324-26]

Having heard the report the Grand Lodge entertained a written resolution prepared by William English.

Resolved, that the report of the Building Committee, together with the course they have adopted and as set forth in said report, design to pursue, be and the same is hereby sanctioned and approved, and that this Grand Lodge will assume all responsibilities for the plan of building, adopted at the Communication of the Grand Lodge held on the 7th of December last and all liabilities growing out of an abandonment of said plan. Considerable discussion took place. When Brother Joseph S. Riley moved to postpone to enable the parties to more fully explain, &c., which was duly seconded; but upon the question being put it was lost by a large majority.

Brother William English's resolution was then taken up and carried by a large majority.

[Minutes, 18 Apr. 1853: 326]

The commission for the Masonic Hall was given to Samuel Sloan. At its opening in 1855 memories of the original competition were still newsworthy, for the events were reported, in garbled fashion, on that occasion. [*Public Ledger*, 20 Sept. 1855: 1]

PRESENT STATUS:

Unexecuted

57.

CHURCH OF THE NATIVITY

ELEVENTH AND WASHINGTON STREETS,
PHILADELPHIA
1853–1854
Client: Vestry of the Church of the Nativity
Project: alterations and additions to existing
building

DRAWINGS: none
DOCUMENTATION:
Philadelphia *Public Ledger*
BIBLIOGRAPHICAL REFERENCES:
Smith, R. A. *Philadelphia as It Is, in 1852.*
Philadelphia (1852)

LITTLE FURTHER IS KNOWN about this church,
which stood in what is now a commercial and
industrial area in South Philadelphia, except
what was reported at the time of its reopening.

The Church of the Nativity.—The Protestant Episcopal Church at the corner of Eleventh and Washington
streets, Fourteenth Ward, under the charge of the Rev.
Mr. Wylie, has received extensive alterations and additions, demanded by its increasing congregation. The additions have been made upon plans prepared by Mr. Nottman, the architect, giving seventy additional pews. The
ceiling is finished in Gothic style, the ribs being painted in
imitation of oak, and the walls of stone color. In the new
portion of the building there are four circular and two
large Gothic windows, all of which are filled with stained
glass, manufactured for the purpose, by John Gibson, who
likewise executed the painting of the interior. The exterior
is ornamented by a porch, in keeping with the original design, affording an additional entrance to the church from
Washington street.   [*Public Ledger*, 22 Mar. 1854: 1]

Smith [177] attributes the design of the
original church to Napoleon Le Brun.
PRESENT STATUS:
Demolished

58.

ALL SAINTS CHURCH

745 SOUTH TWELFTH STREET, PHILADELPHIA
1853–1854
Client: Vestry of All Saints Church
Project: enlargement of existing building

DRAWING 58.1:
Title: Tower of All Saints Church
Signature: John Notman/Architect/
Philada (stamp)
Date: August 18th 1853
Scale: ⅛″ : 1′
Other inscriptions: Elevation/Plan
Description: elevation and plan of tower
to be added to existing building
Medium: ink
Size: 16½ x 9⅞ (42.5 x 25.1)
Owner: Historical Society of Pennsylvania
(AIA)
DOCUMENTATION:
Montgomery, Rev. Henry Eglinton. *A Pas-
toral Letter to the Congregation of All
Saints' Church, Philadelphia.* Philadelphia
(1855); Philadelphia *Public Ledger*; J

ALL SAINTS CHURCH, with J. and A. Ferguson as builders and architects, measuring
45 by 80 feet, was constructed in 1846. [*Public Ledger*, 16 Apr. 1846: 2]
Within a few years,

As the congregation and Sunday Schools continued to
increase, an enlargement of the church edifice was suggested, and a plan proposed by Mr. John Notman architect, was adopted.... The church was reopened...the
28th of May, 1854, although the alterations had been
completed early in the same year.... All Saints' Church is
cruciform, without the chancel recess. The nave and chancel together are 100 feet deep by 42 in width; the transepts are 26 feet wide by 23 feet 6 inches in depth.... The
parapet walls, which in the first plan of the church disfigured its exterior, have been taken down, and the eaves of
the roof brought over twelve inches.

[Montgomery: 7-10]

Further explanation of the additions was
published during the course of the alterations.

All Saints Episcopal Church. This Church edifice in
Twelfth street, below Fitzwater, is now undergoing alterations that will give additional accommodations to meet
the increase in its congregation, arising from the popular-
ity of the pastor, the Rev. Mr. Montgomery, and the
building up of the vicinity in which it is located. The eastern end of the edifice has been taken down, and an addition is to be put up, increasing the length 90 feet. The
addition will extend 24 feet north of the present northern
wall and the same distance south of the opposite wall, giving the edifice the shape of the letter T, and adding greatly
to the number of seats it now contains. A neat porch is to

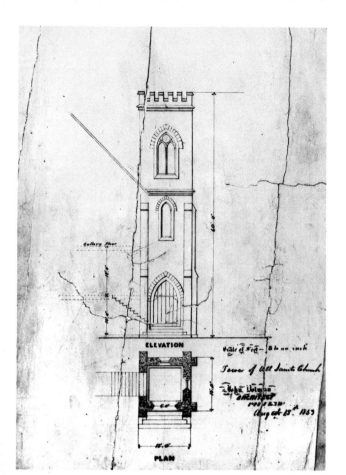

58.1

be added to the southwestern corner fronting on Twelfth street to contain the main entrance, and a stairway to the body of the building. When completed the church will have four doors of exit, there being one in each of the wings. The alterations have not caused any suspension of religious services, the end of the building being temporarily boarded up. [*Public Ledger*, 2 June 1853: 2]

Notman, then, was responsible for the transformation of the church to a cruciform plan, adding transepts and the chancel. If work was underway in June, the August design for a tower must have been an afterthought. In any event, it was not executed. Fairbanks [146-47] concludes that the geometric decorated east window and the arched chancel screen are Notman's work.

PRESENT STATUS:

Now known as Rising Sun Baptist Church (formerly Evangelismos Greek Orthodox church)

59.

FIELDWOOD
(Woodlawn, Guernsey Hall)
PRINCETON, NEW JERSEY
C. 1853–1855
Client: Richard Stockton Field
Project: design of residence and outbuildings

DRAWING 59.1:
Title: none
Signature: none
Date: none
Other inscriptions: none
Scale: none indicated
(approximately ⅛" : 1')
Medium: ink and watercolor
Description: Perspective rendering from southeast
Size: 13⅞ x 20⅛ (35.3 x 51.2)
Owner: Princeton University Library

OTHER EARLY ILLUSTRATIONS:

Numerous early photographs of the house are owned by Princeton University Library, the Historical Society of Princeton and descendants of the Marquand family. A photograph of the house, taken in the 1860s from the same angle as in the drawing above, is reproduced in Greiff, Constance M., Gibbons, Mary W. and Menzies, Elizabeth G. C. *Princeton Architecture.* Princeton (1967). A selection of other early photographs is in Delanoy, Eleanor Marquand. "Guernsey Hall." *Princeton History*, 2 (1977): 4-17.

DOCUMENTATION:

The Princeton Press; no documentation associating the project with Notman exists, except for the signed plan of the grounds. [see entry 21]

BIBLIOGRAPHICAL REFERENCES:

D: 127, 133; M: 45-47; S-PULC: 119-20; "An American Prize-Conversion of a Classic." *House Beautiful*, 118, 5 (May 1976): 136-41; Diamonstein, Barbaralee. *The Reborn Building: New Uses, Old Places.* New York (1978); "From Villa to Luxury Condominiums." *House and Home*, 47, 10 (Oct. 1975): 74-75; "Guernsey Hall,

Princeton." *Architectural Record*, 156, 8 (Dec. 1974): 116-17; "Guernsey Hall." *The Urban Land Institute, Project Referenec File: Attached Residential*, 6, 11 (July-Sept. 1976): Hageman, John F. *Princeton and its Institutions*. Philadelphia (1879). Thompson, Elizabeth K., ed. *Recycling Buildings: Renovations, Remodeling, Restorations, and Reuses*, an Architectural Recordbook. New York (1977)

FIRM EVIDENCE for the date of Fieldwood is lacking, but an article in the Princeton newspaper suggests that the house was under construction or finished by the summer of 1855. In July it was noted that "The residence of Richard S. Field has the most extensive arrangement of plants and shrubbery, and also of greenhouses, of the country." [*Press*, 13 July 1855: 3] Touting Gold's Patent Hydrostatic Steam Furnace, the paper added, "We understand that this apparatus will probably be put into Mr. Field's new house." [*Press*, 31 Aug. 1855: 3]

Although the perspective rendering of the house does not bear Notman's name, there is little doubt from the style of the drawing that it is from his hand. As built the house differed in some respects from the drawing, most notably in the substitution of a cast iron arched entranceway for one of masonry. The main entrance was from the southeast, not, as Morgan [47] infers, from the north. A small vestibule with Doric entablature gave access to the great domed octagonal stair hall with its Minton-tiled floor. An octagonal drawing room and parlor were to the left of the octagon; the dining room with its bay window, kitchen and service areas to the right. A separate entrance opened into the tower, which is said to have housed Judge Field's law library.

Eighteenth-century farmhouse at Fieldwood, converted to gardener's cottage by Notman.
Photograph courtesy William H. Short

PRESENT STATUS:

In 1912 the house was modernized and enlarged by the New York firm of Cross and Cross, brothers-in-law of its owner, Professor Allan Marquand. Cross and Cross transferred the main entrance to the north, adding, in sympathetic style, a range of rooms and porte-cochere on that front. In 1974 Guernsey Hall was converted to five condominium apartments by William H. Short, AIA, in a manner that preserved all its significant architectural features.

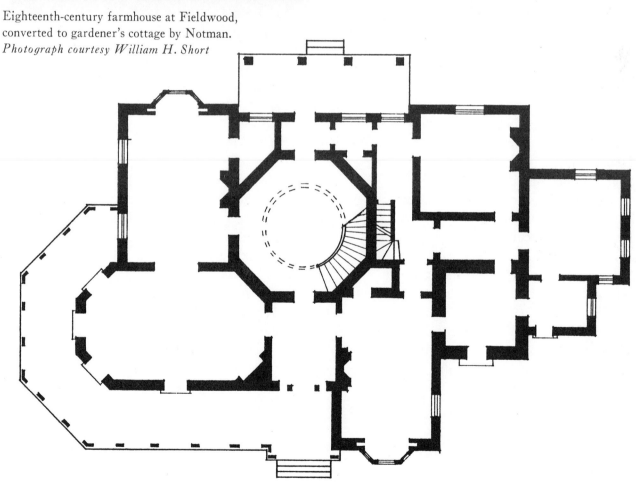

Fieldwood, reconstructed plan of first floor, drawn by Gary Wolf, based on measured drawings by William H. Short

60.

ACADEMY OF MUSIC
Broad and Locusts Streets, Philadelphia
1854
Client: Building Committee of the
   Academy of Music
Project: opera house

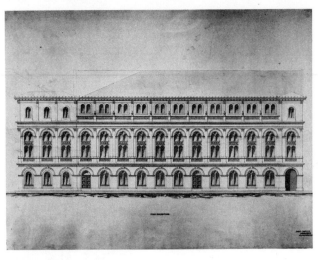

DRAWING 60.1:
   Title: none
   Signature: John Notman/Architect/
   Philadelphia (stamp)
   Date: none
   Scale: none indicated
   Other inscriptions: Front elevation
   Description: rendering of
   Broad Street facade
   Medium: ink and wash
   Size: 22-3/16 x 33¾ (56.3 x 85.7)
   Owner: Historical Society of Pennsylvania
   (AIA), P-8
   Exhibition record: Two Centuries of Phil-
   adelphia Architectural Drawings, Phila-
   delphia Museum of Art, 1964

DRAWING 60.2
   Title: none
   Signature: John Notman/Architect/
   Philadelphia (stamp)
   Date: none
   Scale: none indicated
   Other inscriptions: Side Elevation
   Description: rendering of
   Locust Street faced
   Size: 24¾ x 36⅛ (62.9 x 91.8)
   Owner: Historical Society of Pennsylvania
   (AIA), P-9

DRAWING 60.3:
   Title: none
   Signature: John Notman/Architect/
   Philadelphia (stamp)
   Architect/Philadelphia (stamp)
   Date: none
   Scale: none indicated (scales ⅛″ : 1′)
   Other inscriptions: First story
   Description: plan
   Medium: ink and wash
   Size: 37 x 25¼ (94 x 64.2)
   Owner: Historical Society of Pennsylvania
   (AIA), P-1

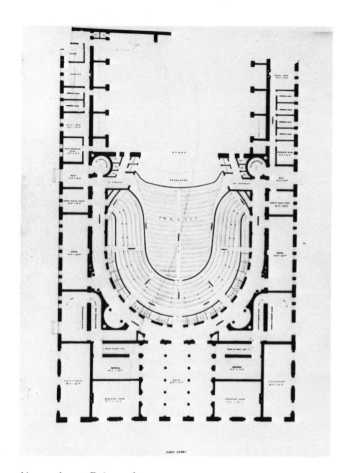

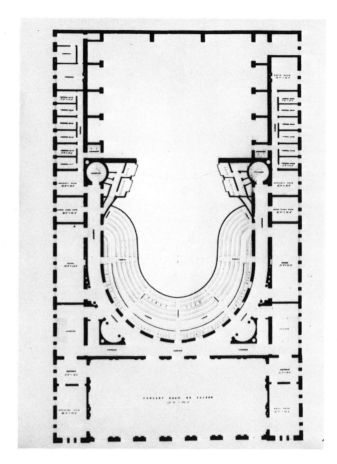

Above: 60.3 ; *Below*: 60.5

Above: 60.4 ; *Below*: 60.6

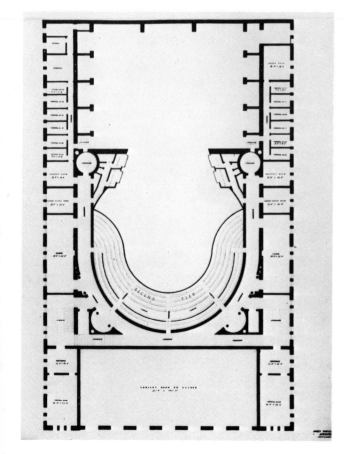

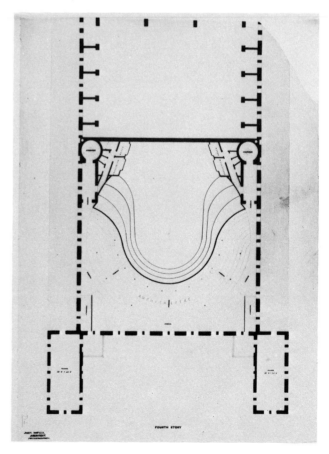

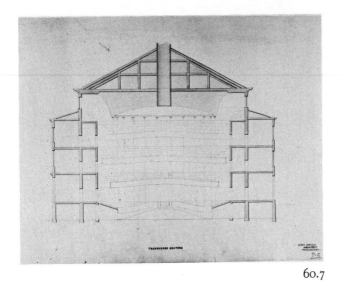

60.7

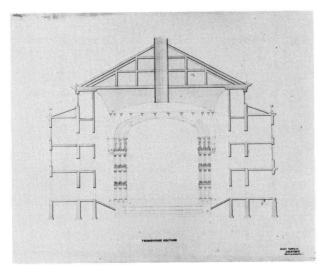

60.8

60.9

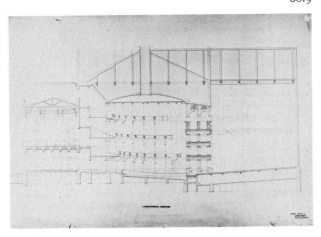

DRAWING 60.4:
Title: none
Signature: John Notman/Architect/
Philadelphia (stamp)
Date: none
Scale: none indicated (scales ⅛″ : 1′)
Other inscriptions: Second Story
Description: plan
Medium: ink and wash
Size: 33⅛ x 26⅛ (84.2 x 66.4)
Owner: Historical Society of Pennsylvania
(AIA), P-2

DRAWING 60.5:
Title: none
Signature: John Notman/Architect/
Philadelphia (stamp)
Date: none
Scale: none indicated (scales ⅛″ : 1′)
Other inscriptions: Third Story
Description: plan
Medium: ink and wash
Size: 33 x 26⅜ (83.8 x 67)
Owner: Historical Society of Pennsylvania
(AIA), P-3

DRAWING 60.6:
Title: none
Signature: John Notman/Architect/
Philadelphia (stamp)
Date: none
Scale: none indicated (scales ⅛″ : 1′)
Other inscriptions: Fourth Story
Description: plan
Medium: ink and wash
Size: 31⅝ x 23⅜ (80.3 x 58.9)
Owner: Historical Society of Pennsylvania
(AIA), P-4

DRAWING 60.7:
Title: none
Signature: John Notman/Architect/
Philadelphia (stamp)
Date: none
Scale: none indicated
Other inscriptions: Transverse Section
Description: section, showing arrangement
of seating tiers
Medium: ink and wash
Size: 19-11/ x 27-9/16 (50 x 70.1)
Owner: Historical Society of Pennsylvania
(AIA), P-5

DRAWING 60.8:

Title: none

Signature: John Notman/Architect/
Philadelphia (stamp)

Date: none

Scale: none indicated

Other inscriptions: Transverse Sections

Description: section, showing arrangement
of boxes

Medium: ink and wash

Size: 19-15/16 x 27-10/16 (50.7 x 70.4)

Owner: Historical Society of Pennsylvania
(AIA), P-6

DRAWING 60.9:

Title: none

Signature: John Notman/Architect/
Philadelphia (stamp)

Date: none

Scale: none indicated

Other inscriptions: Longitudinal Section

Description: section through entire
building

Medium: ink and wash

Size: 22-3/16 x 33¾ (56.3 x 85.7)

Owner: Historical Society of Pennsylvania
(AIA), P-7

DOCUMENTATION:

Philadelphia *Public Ledger*; the winning
set of drawings plus those of other entrants
have also been deposited at HSP.

BIBLIOGRAPHICAL REFERENCES:

Massey, James, ed. *Two Centuries of Philadelphia Architectural Drawings.* Philadelphia (1964); T; W

ON 22 Sept. 1854 the Building Committee advertised a competition for a new opera house.
[T: 186] The competition attracted wide
attention.

The plans for the new opera house were sent in on Friday
last by the architects of this and other cities, who have
been competing for the several amounts to be awarded to
the best plans. There were seventeen plans in all, including eleven by the architects of this city. There were also
three from New York, two from Baltimore and one from
Boston.   [*Public Ledger*, 19 Dec. 1854: 2]

PRESENT STATUS:

Unexecuted. The competition was won by
the firm of LeBrun and Runge.

61.

JACKSON BUILDING

ARCH STREET, PHILADELPHIA

1855

Client: Dr. C. M. Jackson

Project: Commercial building with
store and offices.

DRAWINGS: none

OTHER EARLY ILLUSTRATIONS:

"Dr. Hoofland's Celebrated/German Bit-
ters/and Balsamic Cordial./Prepared by
Dr. C. M. Jackson/No 418 Arch St./Phil-
adelphia." Printed by L. N. Rosenthal

DOCUMENTATION:

Philadelphia *Public Ledger*

BIBLIOGRAPHICAL REFERENCES:

Hitchcock, Henry-Russell. *Architecture
Nineteenth and Twentieth Centuries.* Bal-
timore (1958); Weisman, Winston, "Phil-
adelphia Functionalism and Sullivan."
*Journal of the Society of Architectural
Historians,* XX, 1 (March 1961): 3-19

THIS BUILDING, for one of Philadelphia's many patent medicine moguls, is, except for the Bank of North America, Notman's only known commercial commission. It appears to have resembled the unexecuted design for the offices of the Pennsylvania Railroad. Its chief impression at the time it was built seems to have been made by the introduction of a material new to Philadelphia.

Handsome Improvement.—Among all the improvements which have lately been made upon Arch street, none attracts more attention than the new store of Dr. C. M. Jackson, below Fifth st, and overlooking the burying ground of Christ Church. The front is an exquisite piece of workmanship, so different in effect from any work ever erected in the city that some who consider themselves connoisseurs have expressed the opinion that it must have been done in Paris and imported piecemeal. It is true the stone was imported, but not from Paris. It was brought from Caen, in Normandy (hence the name Caen stone.) and is the first which has ever been used in this city. The designs for the front were made by John Notman, architect, and the work was all done and the front erected by A. H. Ransom. The stone, when first cut, is very soft and can be easily worked. On this account it can be ornamented to a much greater extent than marble, granite, or brown stone. When exposed to the atmosphere it becomes very hard, and is capable of enduring the extremes of heat and cold without injury. During all the severe weather of the present winter the front of Dr. Jackson's store has not been the least affected. The stone is much used in France and to some extent in New York. When its qualities are known it will find general favor in our city. Its cost is about the same as brown stone. Mr. Ransom is now cutting for Dr. Jackson an elaborately carved counter from the same material. When finished it will show the adaptation of the Caen stone for inside as well as outside work. This kind of stone answers well to give variety to the character of our large buildings and, to a great extent, adds to the beauty of our streets; but, at the same time, while Pennsylvania is so rich in all kinds of stone for building, such as marble, granite, etc., there seems to be but little advantage in importing building material from such a distance for general purposes. And since iron has become so useful a material for building, there is still, it seems, less necessity for seeking abroad for material to beautify our streets, for Pennsylvania can afford an inexhaustible supply of this material, which, when placed in the hands of our skillful mechanics, is made to assume the richest forms ever cut by the artist's chisel. [*Public Ledger*, 27 Feb. 1856: 1]

PRESENT STATUS:
Demolished

62.

ST. CLEMENT'S CHURCH
CHERRY AND TWENTIETH STREETS,
   PHILADELPHIA
1855–1859
Client: Vestry of St. Clement's Church
Project: new church for Low Church
congregation

DRAWING 62.1:
   Title: St. Clement's
   Signature: none—initialed E.A.P.
   Date: none
   Scale: none indicated
   Other inscriptions: North Elevation
   Description: rendered flank elevation
   Medium: ink and wash
   Size: 26 x 23⅞ (66.1 x 59.5)
   Owner: Historical Society of Pennsylvania
   (AIA), S-14

DRAWING 62.2:
   Title: none
   Signature: none
   Date: none
   Scale: none indicated
   Other inscriptions: 20th St/Same plan
   suits/both Elevations/Cherry [Street], in
   pencil
   Description: plan and east elevation
   Medium: ink and wash,
   with pencil emendations
   Size: 24¾ x 26-7/16 (62.9 x 67.2)
   Owner: Historical Society of Pennsylvania
   (AIA), X-R-16

DRAWING 62.3:
   Title: Circular Window/St. Clements
   Signature: N. Archt/E.A.P.
   Date: none
   Scale: ½" : 1'
   Other inscriptions: none
   Description: elevations
   Medium: ink
   Size: 16⅝ x 25⅝ (42.3 x 65.1)
   Owner: Historical Society of Pennsylvania
   (AIA)

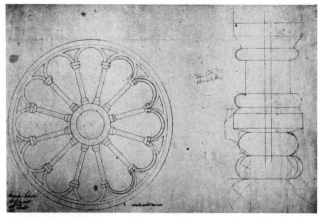

62.3

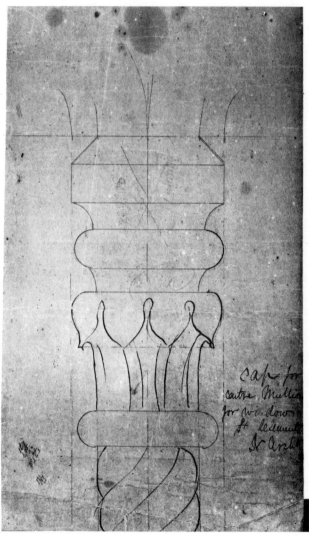

62.4

DRAWING 62.4:
   Title: Cap for/centre Mullion/for window/St. Clements/Windows/St Clements
   Signature: N Archt/N
   Date: none
   Scale: none indicated
   Other inscriptions: none
   Description: elevation
   Medium: ink
   Size: 33⅞ x 12 (86.1 x 30.4)
   Owner: Historical Society of Pennsylvania (AIA)

DRAWING 62.5:
   Title: Face or side of/Ring Pieces full size for centre of Rafters/Roof of St. Clements Church
   Signature: N. archt
   Date: none
   Scale: full
   Other inscriptions: none
   Description: working plan, elevations and sections
   Medium: ink touched with wash
   Size: 28-7/16 x 25¾ (72.4 x 65.5)
   Owner: Historical Society of Pennsylvania (AIA)

DRAWING 62.6:
   Title: Porch to Tower St. Clements Ch.
   Signature: John Notman Archt
   Date: none
   Scale: none indicated
   Other inscriptions: none
   Description: plan, elevation, and section
   Medium: ink
   Size: 25-13/16 x 17-5/16 (65.2 x 44)
   Owner: Historical Society of Pennsylvania (AIA)

DRAWING 62.7:
   Title: St. Clements Tower
   Signature: N. Archt
   Date: none
   Scale: none indicated
   Other inscriptions: none
   Descriptions: elevation upper two stages
   Medium: ink
   Size: 33½ x 19 (85.1 x 48.3)
   Owner: Historical Society of Pennsylvania (AIA)

NORTH ELEVATION

St Clements.

62.1

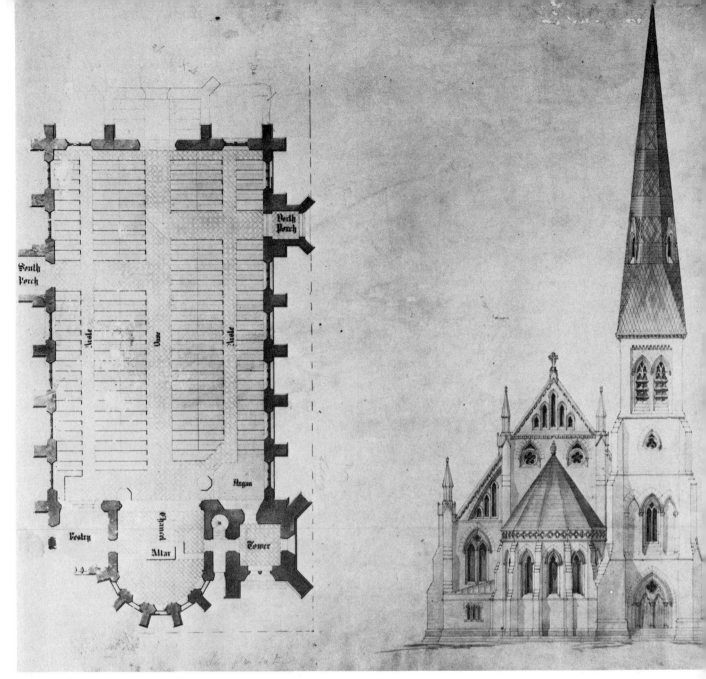

62.2

DRAWING 62.8:
    Title: Cap for Tower Buttresses/
    St Clement's Ch
    Signature: N. Archt
    Date: none
    Scale: none indicated
    Other inscriptions: Octagon shaft
    Description: working plan and elevation
    Medium: ink
    Size: 39⅝ x 26¾ (100.1 x 68)
    Owner: Historical Society of Pennsylvania
    (AIA)

DRAWING 62.9:
    Title: Plan of Belfry Stage—East Front of
    Tower/St. Clements Church
    Signature: N Archt/E.A.P.
    Date: none
    Scale: ¾" : 1'
    Other inscriptions: none
    Description: plan
    Medium: ink and wash
    Size: 27⅞ x 24½ (70.8 x 62.2)
    Owner: Historical Society of Pennsylvania
    (AIA)

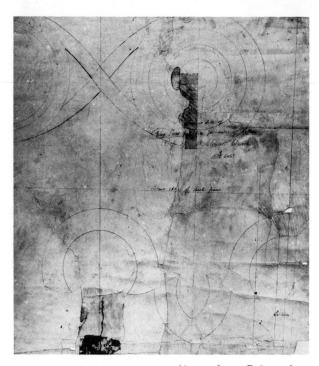

Above: 62.5; *Below*: 62.7

Above: 62.6; *Below*: 62.8

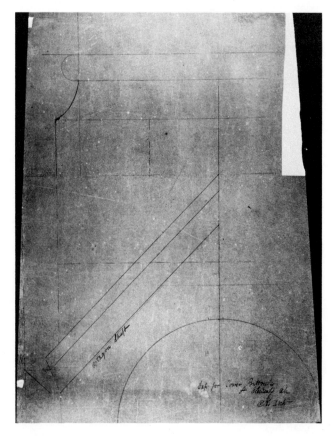

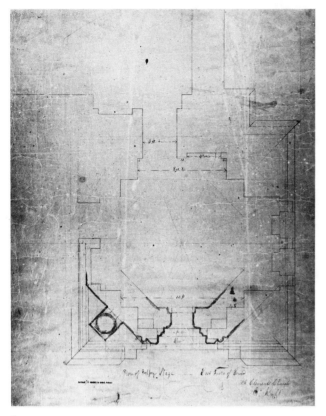

62.9

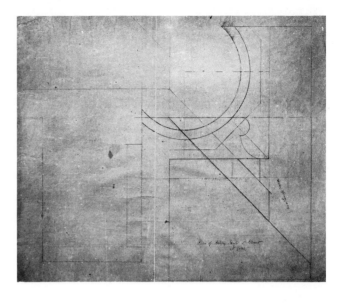

Above: 62.10; *Below*: 62.11

62.12

DRAWING 62.10:
   Title: Plan of Belfry Jambs St. Clements
   Signature: N Archt.
   Date: none
   Scale: none indicated
   Other inscriptions: none
   Description: working plan
   Medium: ink
   Size: 28-5/16 x 33⅝ (71.9 x 85.4)
   Owner: Historical Society of Pennsylvania
   (AIA)

DRAWING 62.11:
   Title: Gablets Tower/St. Clements Ch
   Signature: N. Archt
   Date: none
   Scale: 3″ : 1′
   Other inscriptions: Cornice/Coping/
   Leaf on Angles
   Description: working elevations
   Medium: ink, touched with wash
   Size: 32½ x 29-11/16 (82.5 x 75.4)
   Owner: Historical Society of Pennsylvania
   (AIA)

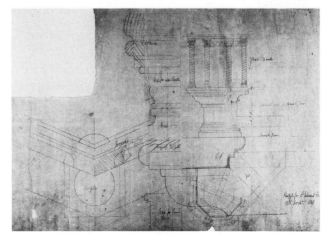

DRAWING 62.12:

Title: Pulpit for St. Clements Ch
Signature: N. Archt.
Date: 1858
Scale: 1½″ : 1′ and full
Other inscriptions: none
Description: working plans, elevations
and sections
Medium: ink, touched with wash
Size: 10-1/16 x 30-9/16 (56 x 77.6)
Owner: Historical Society of Pennsylvania
(AIA)

OTHER EARLY ILLUSTRATIONS:

A lithograph, entitled "St. Clement's
Church/Philadelphia.," J. Notman Archt.,
T. Sinclair's lith. Philada, shows the church
in perspective.

DOCUMENTATION:

Minutes of the Vestry of St. Clement's
Church, 1855-1878; *North American and
United States Gazette*, Philadelphia *Public Ledger*; AB; J; StA

BIBLIOGRAPHICAL REFERENCES:

D: 139; F: 88-89; 171-90

BECAUSE NOTMAN SERVED as contractor as
well as architect for St. Clement's, a significant number of the working drawings have
been preserved, as was the case at St. Mark's
and The Athenaeum, where he also acted in
a dual capacity. At St. Clement's few of the
presentation and preliminary drawings remain, only two to be precise, but they are of
extraordinary interest.

One of the drawings shows the north flank
of St. Clement's essentially as built, in a Romanesque or Norman, or, as one contemporary
source styled it, Byzantine vein. The other,
hitherto numbered X-R-16 and filed in a
folder of unidentified churches at the Historical Society of Pennsylvania, is clearly an alternative scheme for St. Clement's in English
Gothic guise. Even if the north side of the
plan were not faintly labeled "Cherry [St.]"
and the words "Same plan suits/both Elevations" were not penciled under the plan, the
plan itself is clearly that of St. Clement's. Such
prominent features as the semi-circular apse

and the tower at the northeast corner occur in
no other Notman church. The dimensions coincide as does the distribution of openings. At
the west end the plan of the vestibule that was
eventually built is penciled in. This feature
may not have been encompassed in the Gothic
version, although it appears in the flank elevation of the Lombard church as a projection
with a roof lower than that of the nave.

In any event both drawings probably date
from 1855, the year in which the congregation
of St. Clement's was formed. At the first meeting of the vestry it became clear that discussions with Notman were already well advanced
and that the alternative design represented by
the flank elevation had been accepted.

On motion, Resolved that the consideration of Mr.
Notman's specification be resumed.

The Committee on Plans &c. reported favorably of the
plan submitted by Mr. Notman, and that it with the accompanying specification be referred to a Building Committee of Four, which Report was accepted and the Committee discharged.

On motion, Resolved that a Building Committee of
Four be appointed, when the chair appointed Messrs
Lambert, Kirkham, Cook and Cooper.

On motion, the plans were referred to the Building
Committee, to report the lowest price for which the Building could be erected.   [Minutes, 20 Sept. 1855: 1]

Notman was evidently not the only architect consulted. The vestry decided to return to
"Mr. Potter, Architect" a set of plans he had
prepared [Minutes: 6] Presumably this was
the same Mr. Potter who later submitted proposals for completing the tower of Holy Trinity. [See entry 65] The identity of "Mr. Potter" is not further established. It may have
been the young Edward Tuckerman Potter.
Although he was at the time living in New
York, he was the son of Pennsylvania's Episcopal bishop, Rev. Alonzo Potter, from whom
he undoubtedly learned of proposed new
churches in Philadelphia. Potter later lived
in Philadelphia for a few years, signing the
charter of the Pennsylvania Institute of Architects in 1861 (see page 43) and being listed
in the city directory of 1863 as living on
Spruce Street.

One other possibility must be considered for the identity of Mr. Potter. Among the St. Clement's drawings are several initialed "E.A.P.," including the flank elevation. These are unique among Notman's drawings. No others carry any name or initials but his, nor has the work of any draftsman in his office been otherwise identified. There is no architect with those initials listed in the Philadelphia city directories for the 1850s and 1860s, or in the standard biographical dictionaries of architects. The identity of "E.A.P." remains a mystery.

Having chosen Notman as their architect, the vestry proceeded to negotiate with him as builder. As had been the case at St. Mark's, completion of the work in phases was contemplated. Proposals were solicited

... to furnish the walls of the church and roof the same, and to complete the walls of the Tower to the top of the first story, also in addition to this, to floor and complete the interior of the Church, including the glazing and painting, and in addition to this, to complete the Tower to the top of the Lantern.   [Minutes, 16 Apr. 1856: 7]

The vestry decided not to complete the tower, but

Resolved that the Chairman of the Building Committee be instructed to contract on behalf of the Vestry with Mr. John Notman for the erection of the Walls of the Church, the Walls of the Tower to the height of the eaves of the Church, and the Walls of the Chancel without column shafts on either side, together with the roof, and slating for the sum of Twenty four Thousand five hundred Dollars ($24,500) and if the column shafts on the exterior of the chancel can be erected for Five hundred dollars ($500) additional, to contract for the same.
                                [Minutes, 30 Apr. 1856: 7]

When the contract negotiations were complete, however, it appears that the tower was excluded. Notman was to receive a total of $20,500 in seven installments, the last one due when the roof was on, with a final payment of $3,000 to be made three months after completion of the contract. [Minutes, 2 May 1856: 7-8] With these terms agreed on, work began promptly, the cornerstone being laid on 10 May. Work progressed relatively smoothly, although change orders and upward revisions of the estimates were required. The most im-

portant of these was the discovery that the site had been excavated before, which necessitated a deeper foundation than had been anticipated. [Minutes, 19 June 1856: 9-10] By the summer of 1857 the sanctuary was being roofed.

The Church of St. Clement is situated on the southwest corner of Twentieth and Cherry streets. The corner stone of this was laid on the 10th of May, 1856, and it is now being roofed. It is built of Connecticut brown stone, and the style of architecture is the Byzantium, rarely adopted here. There is a novelty about it that cannot fail to strike the spectator. The width is from 70 to 80 feet, and the depth about 160 feet. The estimated cost is $26,000, though it will cost more to complete it. Like the Church of the Holy Trinity, it is designed to be surmounted by a tower and spire.   [Public Ledger, 30 July 1857: 1]

The drawings numbered 62.3 to 62.5 must therefore date from 1856-1857 when work on the exterior walls, roof, and probably the first two stages of the tower was undertaken.

Work was then suspended, not only because the first phase had been completed, but because of economic conditions. The financial panic of 1857, although not as severe as that of 1837, created a virtual cessation of building activity in Philadelphia. Early in 1858 the vestry was prepared to move forward to complete the church and sought estimates from Notman. He replied that the remaining work, including building the tower and spire, would cost approximately $18,500. Without the spire the price would be $12,472. After a series of negotiations, the vestry accepted Notman's letter proposal of March 1858, offering to complete the church for $17,233.50. [Minutes: 16-21] The drawings for the tower, 62.8 to 62.11, probably date from 1858. St. Clement's was opened on 2 Jan. 1859. [United States Gazette, 1 Jan. 1859: 1]

PRESENT STATUS:
Still in active use, St. Clement's has been altered many times, without, however, affecting the basic power of its exterior. The first alteration was carried out by Notman himself, with the addition of parish buildings to the west in 1864. [See entry 68] Other major alterations, largely designed by Horace Wells Sellers in the early twen-

tieth century, include the addition of a second story to the apse and the creation of a choir by the erection of chambers against the north and south walls between the apse and nave. The timbered vaulting has also been changed.

63.

NASSAU HALL
PRINCETON, NEW JERSEY
1855–1859
Client: Trustees of the College of New Jersey
Project: rebuilding and fireproofing of
   historic main building of college

DRAWINGS: none
OTHER EARLY ILLUSTRATIONS:
   "View of Nassau Hall, Princeton, N. J."
   Drawn by F. Childs, lithographed by Robertson, Seibert and Shearman, published by McGinness and Smith, 1860; another version was published by George Thompson; numerous photographs in PUA. There are 25 drawings of Nassau Hall in the Historic American Buildings Survey.
DOCUMENTATION:
   Cooper and Hewitt, Letterpress Books, New-York Historical Society; the following in PUA: Minutes of the Board of Trustees of the College of New Jersey; bills, contract with Bottom and Tiffany, and letters from Cooper and Hewitt to John Maclean, John Notman, and Charles S. Olden in General College Accounts 1855-1859; letters from John Notman to John Maclean and rough drafts and final copies of Building Committee Reports 1855 Maclean Papers; Building Committee Reports 1856-1859 in Trustees' Rough Minutes; *Princeton Press*
BIBLIOGRAPHICAL REFERENCES:
   S-PULC; reprinted with slight changes in Savage, Henry Lyttleton, ed. *Nassau Hall.* Princeton (1956); Greiff, Constance M., Gibbons, Mary W. and Menzies, Elizabeth G. C. *Princeton Architecture.* Princeton (1967)

"NASSAU HALL BURNT DOWN!" read a headline, a rare typographical form, in the *Princeton Press.* [16 Mar 1855: 3] The word "Again" might have been added, for it was the second major conflagration in the building's first century. Originally built to the designs of Robert Smith in 1754-1756, and rebuilt after the first fire to those of Benjamin Henry Latrobe in 1802-1804, the building had not been destroyed as completely as the headline implied. Impelled both by patriotic and institutional sentiment, those responsible thought of only one solution; to rebuild once again. Twice burned, and thus doubly shy, their most important stipulation was that the renewed Nassau Hall be fireproof.

The college seems to have saved every scrap of paper connected with the rebuilding of Nassau Hall, with the notable exception of the drawings. Although an elevation and plan, a design for a cupola, and working drawings are referred to in the documents, frequent searches for these, and indeed for any early drawings of Nassau Hall, have been unavailing.

Almost immediately after the fire, John Maclean, president of the college, must have requested Notman to visit Princeton and then wrote to him setting forth his requirements. From Notman's reply it can be inferred that Maclean stressed fireproofing and probably suggested central heating and an enlargement of the building to accommodate a library and picture gallery. Notman's response suggested additional changes, notably a more imposing central tower, and shifting the stairs from midpoint in the wings to the center of the building.

Philada March 22nd 1855
To The Rev John Maclean D.D. President
   College of New Jersey
My Dear Sir,
   I had your despatch to day, and have prepared a plan & elevation, which I hope you will receive with this, it is not a drawing of the roof, as you ask for but simply a restoration of the building as it was, with a loftier belfry or campanile, built up above the roof of brick. I have suggested on the plan a change in the position of the stairs, which distributes the students to the rooms as conveniently as before, keeps them central by lighting them from the top, they can be placed so, using a dark space, and by add-

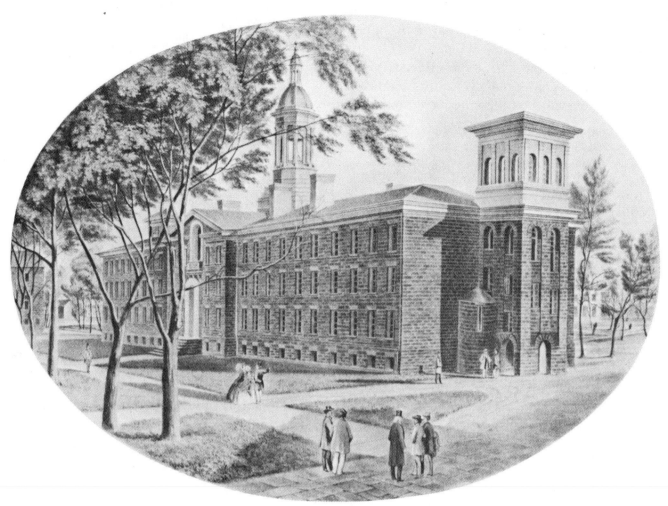

"Nassau Hall." *Courtesy PUA*

ing about 20 feet southward a Library is obtained of 36 feet square, 18 feet high and the Hall or Picture Gallery can be over it, lighted from the roof. There would be single rooms in the spaces of the stairs, as formerly, heating by furnaces will be easily done by the present flues.

I have estimated the roof of iron framing covered with slate. There is 11,400 feet of roof at 50 cents = $5700.00, a roof of timber and slate or shingles would cost about 40 cents = 11,400 @ 40— $4560.00

Extra cost of iron & slate roof $1140.

To make the floors throughout fireproof with wrought iron joists and brick arches will cost the iron additional only, the saving of timber being equal to the cost of brick it takes 110 tons which I suppose Cooper & Hewitt of Trenton would furnish rolled ready for use at $50 per ton making $5500.00

The stairs to be entirely of iron. The drawing I send to you and this is hastily done as I had but two days, yet the estimate is correct as I have done such work before which is respectfully submitted.

Yours truly,
John Notman

At a special meeting of the trustees, on 23 Mar. 1855, Maclean, after informing the board that the American Insurance Company of Philadelphia held a $12,000 policy on the building, reviewed his actions.

To enable the Trustees to know the condition of the walls, and to furnish some suggestions with regard to the best mode of rebuilding Nassau Hall, I requested Mr. John Notman of Philadelphia, to visit Princeton to examine the walls, and to furnish some estimates, in regard to the comparative expense of making the building fireproof and of rebuilding it as it was before. Mr. Notman came to Princeton, and he has given the requested estimates and also a drawing for the Front of the Edifice, which I submit to the Board for examination. I gave Mr. Notman to understand that I was not authorized by the Trustees to write to him on the subject, but wished to have his views that I might present them to the Board.

[Minutes: 78-79]

The Board responded by appointing as a building committee Maclean, chairman, James Carnahan, Eli F. Cooley, Henry W. Green, Charles Hodge, and Charles S. Olden. [Minutes: 79] This committee promptly met on 27 Mar. and passed the following resolutions:

1. That for the front, the Committee will adopt the plan presented by Mr. Notman: ...
2. That the division in the interior of the building be so arranged, if practicable, as to form single rooms, with two windows to a room—
3. That the roof be made of iron and slate.
4. That the rooms be made fireproof.
5. That Mr. Notman be requested to furnish working drawings and estimates. ...

[Report, June 1855]

On 5 Apr. the committee met again to consider Notman's estimates.

1. For an iron frame for the roof and slate— $ 5,000
2. For a frame of timber with slate— 3,650
3. To make the entries fireproof with iron beams and brick floors— 1,900
4. To build entirely fire-proof 31,500
5. To build as before with cornice & stairs of iron 23,000
6. Cost of Furnaces & flues, with valves for ventilation & stoves flues 2,750

This 6th estimate is included in those marked nos. 4 & 5.

Altering 24 of the existing rooms to make 36 single rooms would cost $2,000 more, bringing the total cost to $33,500. [Report, June 1855]

This was the proposal accepted by the committee.

Meanwhile, a suggestion for fireproofing had been put forth by Cooper and Hewitt. Although their office was in New York, the firm had established the country's first beam mill at Trenton in 1845. Their initial product was railroad rail, but by 1855 they were forming I-shaped structural members and actively promoting their use. Copies of correspondence in their letterpress book were probably originally far from perfect and age has not improved their legibility. Nevertheless, they provide important information about the state of mid-century building technology.

New York March 23rd 1855

Revd John McLean
    Prest. College of N. Jersey
        Princeton, N. J.
Dear Sir,

At the suggestion of Judge Dickinson, we enclose a circular showing the plan of our wrought iron beams and girders, by which you will be enabled to erect a fire proof building, at a small expense, and which, when it has stood long enough to get the name of "Old Nassau," will be in the infancy of its existence. ...

We may add that we have orders on hand for over fifty buildings, although we have been able to make the beams only about 6 mos.

Truly yours,
Cooper & Hewitt
[Letterpress Book XVIII: 73]

Notman was evidently aware of Cooper and Hewitt's work, for he had already mentioned them as a potential source of iron. As soon as he received the committee's decision to proceed with a fireproof building he must have been in touch with them. Their reply contains several indecipherable words, but the import is clear.

New York April 9th 1855

John Notman Esq.
    South side of Spruce St.
        below 15th St.
            Phila.
Dear Sir,

Your favor of [?] instant is just received here. Our Mr. Cooper will meet you in Trenton on Wednesday next, and give you [?] information. We think it better for you to come there, only because you can see the beams [?]. If you come up either in the [?] or 10 o'clock train from Phila, you will find Mr. C at the mill.

We enclose a circular and the official Treas. report, which will be [?] for reference. We will deduct 25% from the price of the beams in consideration of the use to which they are to be put.

Thanking you for your interest in the matter we are
faithfully yours,
Cooper & Hewitt
[Letterpress Book XVIII: 255]

The committee met again on 18 Apr. and took Notman's advice that structurally it would be inadvisable to remove some of the chimneys and cross walls to provide additional space for rooms. The committee also accepted his recommendation that "towers, each ten feet square in the interior be made at each end of the building for staircases." In the rough draft the words "with water closets at each landing" are crossed out. Considerations of economy evidently overcame those of convenience, and it was expected that future students would resort, as their predecessors had done, to the communal facility behind Nassau Hall known as the *cloaca maxima*. Later, however, water closets were incorporated. It was further decided that light wells would be constructed in the center of the building to provide both light and ventilation.

At a subsequent meeting on 23 Apr., the committee approved an extension to the south to form a library room 70 by 36 feet. It was also announced that an "agreement was made with Messrs. Cooper and Hewitt to furnish the college with iron beams of the size and weight of the best iron rails for rail roads. . . ." [Report: June 1855]

This decision appears to have been a major disappointment to Cooper and Hewitt, who had been trying to persuade Notman to utilize their new beams. The price differential was considerable, $55 per ton for the rails, versus $100 for the beams. Nevertheless, Cooper and Hewitt maintained that the greater load-bearing capacity of the beams would permit the use of wider spans and fewer joists, actually reducing the total cost. Even after the committee had reached its decision, Cooper and Hewitt tried to persuade Notman and Maclean to reconsider.

New York
April 25, 1855

John Notman Esq.
Phila
D Sir

Your esteemed favor of 24th inst is received. We can make the rails at 2½ cts per lb ($56 per ton) delivered at our business at Trenton thence to Princeton basin, the freight will be from 75 cts to $1 per ton. We annex two Patterns which are higher in proportion to their weight than our other patterns.

You will allow us to remark however that the beams at $1.25 per ft (at which price we will furnish them to *you*) are much cheaper than rails after making the allowance for the difference in price. The increased strength of the deep bar over the shallow one being in a greater ratio than the increase in price. This is the case when the *ul-*

timate strength of the bars alone is considered. But the application of wrought iron beams to resist transverse strains is determined in cases like the present by the resistance of the beams to *deflection*. The deflection increases in a much higher ratio than the decrease in ultimate strength as the depth is diminished. Again as a greatly increased quantity of material must be used with the shallow bars, the weight of the beams themselves and the arches between them will in our opinion produce a greater *deflection* with the spans you will require than can be allowed without making any allowance for any additional load. We will therefore most earnestly advise if the above shall not be satisfactory that a rail of the pattern proposed to be used be tested at Trenton as we are confident you will thus be satisfied of the correctness of our opinion that the deep beams only can be economically used. We shall be happy to make these experiments at our own expense. We have investigated the question of the strength of *wrought iron* beams and girders very fully and are entirely satisfied that the result of the experiment will satisfy you *beyond a doubt* of the greatly increased economy of using the deep beams if it does not show as we think it probably will that the *rails* cannot be used at all without an amount of deflection and sagging that you will deem entirely inadmissable. So decided have our experiments been that we are proposing to make beams 12 inches in depth expecting to effect a great saving thereby in the construction of fire proof floors even when the spans are not as great as you have, placing the beams farther apart and consequently increasing the span of the segmental arches. We have no hesitation in recommending the entire safety of arches of six feet span laid in cement and 4 inches thick at the crown. They are used by the government of this span and thickness and from experiments they have made are deemed perfectly reliable.

We are Very truly yours,
Cooper & Hewitt

New York May 12, 1855

Rev. John Maclean
Pres College of New Jersey
Princeton, N. J.
Dear Sir

Your esteemed favor of 10th inst is received. We are somewhat surprized at Mr. Notman's preference for rails over the beams. We can only explain it upon the supposition that he is unwilling to rely upon the brick arches when the beams are put sufficiently far apart to bring their full strength into effect. We have no doubt ourselves of the *entire safety* for your purposes of a four inch arch with a span of six or *eight* feet. And the writer would like to see Mr. Notman before this final decision to use rails. As regards the price of the rails, we are unable to name a lower price than that named to Mr. Notman as there will be no profit at that price when the proper care is taken to give you a sufficiently good article for your purpose. The price named was a cash price but we shall be happy to give any reasonable time that will make the payments more convenient to the college.

> We remain,
> Very truly yours,
> Cooper & Hewitt

Work on the building began in the spring, but in June the committee reported that

. . . in consequence of not receiving the iron beams as soon as we expected the work has not advanced with the rapidity which they hoped it would. They did expect that the beams for the 1st floor would have been inserted into the walls; and that the arches to rest against the beams would have been completed before this time.

The committee then set forth the premises on which they had based their decisions.

1st   to give full effect to the resolution of trustees to make the building fire-proof.
2.   to render it better fitted to the preservation of order, and for furnishing the occupants with rooms better suited to the purposes of a student: and this was one great inducement to adopt the plan of erecting towers, at the two ends of the building, in which the stairs should be erected: as they will contribute very greatly to the quiet of the rooms and of the entries, as well as add to the appearance of the edifice when it comes to be finished.
3.   The Committee have been desirous also to make all possible provision to secure perfect ventilation and proper attention to cleanliness.
4.   The estimate for the whole building is $37,000, which sum the architect considered abundantly sufficient.
To present at one view the plan finally adopted by the Committee, they would state
1st   That they have followed the instructions of the Board: and have retained both the outer and the inner walls: and have adhered to a general plan of the building as at first constructed.
2.   They have resolved to make the entire building fire-proof.
3.   They have decided to divide the building into *three* distinct apartments: two of them to contain lodging rooms, for the students; and the third to consist largely of the Old Chapel, enlarged and made fire-proof, that the College may have a room in all respects suitable for its Library, and for its collection of portraits.
4.   The entrances to the lodging rooms will be through the towers, at the ends of the building. The entrance in the room designed for the Library will be through the front door of the College.   [Report, June 1855]

Having conveyed the estimate to the trustees, Maclean may have had some doubts. Notman hastened to reassure him, although he suggested care to achieve economy.

> Philada July 2nd 1855

To The Revd John Maclean D.D.
My Dear Sir
    I have yours of 29 inst. I am so confident in the matter of expense that I would contract if desired, that it will not exceed 37,000 dolls. for the buildings but it is well to save judiciously, amongst other things. The window sills will be obtained of the quarry at Princeton for 30 to 35 cents a piece instead of 1½ to 2 dolls. I had asked Hy Laird to write to Trenton for the exact price of north river flags for them. He stated without authority that if at $1.50 they might be accepted. The person at Trenton (I. Grant, I believe) ever ready for a catch, answered he would order them. I requested that order to be stopped when I was last there and beg you will enforce the stoppage by your order. As besides the lesser cost we ought to have pride in building the College as originally done of stone from about Princeton. I would rather do so, than to have the finest cut stone. I trust the new quarries endeavouring to be opened will turn out well. I suppose I may leave my next visit till after the 4th, when I will be up unless you telegraph before.

> Most Respectfully yours,
> John Notman

The quarries referred to were on land belonging to the college and the grounds of the Potter estate, Prospect [Report: Dec. 1855], and did, indeed, supply the stone for the rebuilding.

By fall the ironwork was completed. Evidently some of the "I," or as Cooper and Hewitt termed them, "heavy," beams had been used in the roof. A controversy arose about the charges, Cooper and Hewitt claiming that they had not offered them at $1.25 per foot. [Cooper and Hewitt to Maclean, Accounts: 8 Oct. 1855] Eventually admitting that they had named the price, Cooper and Hewitt, agreeing to accept their loss, expressed themselves in language redolent of 19th century business morality.

. . . Allow us to add a word of explanation. We made our original offer entirely out of kind motives. We like to see colleges flourish and we do not want to make money out of them—neither can we afford to give away money beyond the use of our machinery and efforts—because we have obligations to discharge which must first be attended to. In this particular instance, there have occurred more little differences than in any transaction of this year. In the first place, an error was made by a clerk in copying an invoice which [?] beams into angle bars. In the second place, Mr. Notman understood the price of the angle bars to be $90 and we have no doubt that in a general conversation $90 may have been mentioned although we have no recollection of it. But we frankly admit that we ought to stand by our price, even if inadvertently named except upon the general principle that where the intention is to work for nothing, and the parties are men of honor, a general "statement" should not be pressed too hard against a conscientious discharge of the obligation.

Lastly in regard to the price of the beams, it seems that Mr. E. Cooper wrote a letter to Mr. Notman on the 25th April, of which by some oversight no copy was taken in our letter book or elsewhere, and we could not tell what language he used. In naming $1.25 per foot, he either made some error in a hasty deduction of 25%, or wrote from an impression that $1.25 was the result of such a deduction. Be that as it may, you now get the beams for less than cost. And please to be assured, that as it is not the first, and we suppose it will not be the last, time, when we have lost money in a transaction, so are we extremely glad that it has fallen to the lot of your useful and venerable institution to be the gainer by it. And we really hope that Dr. McLean & yourself, will not withdraw from us one grain of the kind feeling which we expected to establish between the college & ourselves by our offer. If you do, we shall be afraid to attempt to give away our profits any more.

[Cooper and Hewitt to Charles S. Olden]

Obviously problems were being encountered with the unfamiliar structural uses of iron. Notman was not convinced of the bearing capacities claimed by Cooper and Hewitt for their new structural shapes; conversely the latter appear to have had problems in calculating their costs and meeting delivery dates. Bottom and Tiffany, the Trenton firm that had contracted to fabricate the iron structure of the roof, also experienced difficulties in performing on time. Maclean explained to the trustees at their meeting on 18 Dec. that the building was behind schedule (italics added)

... chiefly from want of promptness on the part of those, who engaged to furnish the iron to be used, in constructing the floors and the roof.... The best apology perhaps that could be made by those who contracted to make the iron-frame for the roof is that *the work was different from any thing they had before done: and that they miscalculated as*

to the time it would take to finish it.... It is but fair to add, that the work has been done in the most substantial manner: ....

Maclean went on to report that most of the building was under roof. For the most part the roof was slate, but portions were of galvanized iron, as was the cornice. The entries were to be paved with brick and the stairs, for which iron had originally been specified, were to be made of stone. The top stages of the towers were to be of brick, painted and sanded to simulate stone. [Report: Dec. 1855]

Bottom and Tiffany's work had given sufficient satisfaction for them to be retained to fabricate and erect Nassau Hall's most striking new feature, the cupola, made of cast iron, except for the columns.

To the Revd John McLean D.D.
Dear Sir

Bottom & Tiffany have called on me to say in relation to the dome termination for the centre tower of the College. That they estimate to put it on complete including capitals and bases for the brick columns, at the sum of $1200 dollars (twelve hundred dolls) and if they are to do it they wish to begin now as it is particular work and will take some time to prepare patterns, etc. If deferred they think it will be more costly later in the season. Please write to me what you wish to be done in this matter.

Most respectfully yours
John Notman
Jany 25th 1856
Philada Mar 25th 1856

To The Rev John Maclean D.D.
Dear Sir

Bottom & Tiffany have written to me for the drawings of the dome. I left them with you. Will you oblige me by sending them to me immediately as B & T will call on me for them this week. Write to me also of how the account, between them and the College now stands as I can shew them the error of their acct as you sent it to me. Have you closed with them to make the dome & belfry?

Very respectfully yours,
John Notman

Even while the contract for this new work was under discussion, controversy arose with Bottom and Tiffany about the charges for their work on the roof. Notman's letters to Maclean on this subject seem to express lightly veiled annoyance that Bottom and Tiffany and the building committee were conferring directly. As architect he believed that he should be the client's representative, approving both the work and payment for it. The letters also reveal that some types of construction work were still priced on the basis of measure, not time.

Philada April 3rd 1856

My Dear Sir

I have your note of yesterday and would have liked to have been present with your Committee and Bottom & Tiffany. How they can make such demands on you is to presume that you will pay anything they choose to charge. Besides, they know very well that the architect's signature should be to every bill. It is not easy to shew you the absurd nature of their charges—but every mechanic understands it. Hy Leard will. You have the bill before you. The first item is measurement, of which 12966 feet is sloping roof, 1568 feet is the flat. The second is based on an error of theirs arising from their making a few of the *rafter pieces* too long. When the drawing was put in their hands they were told that the drawing shewed the construction of the roof and the number of the rafters, but that the building was there and they must measure it and fit it in every respect, as it was not a building to be erected but it *was there* for them to see and measure which Tiffany did do, but he was so long afterwards of making the roof that I suppose he forgot the sizes he had taken. They were also told and particularly directed to make the part of the rafter projecting over the walls of a length to suit the iron cornice and gutter, which I could not then decide as Mr. Adams would tell them exactly the length wanted. Tiffany said he knew Adams and he would see him and ascertain the length. Now this was merely the end of the sloping piece over the roof which might be 2 feet or 1 foot as desired thus.

It involved no work or change of the frame. It was as if a Carpenter had to cut a piece off the ends of his rafters. It had not

any lathe in it, nor was it constructively a part of the roof. When you made contract with Adams I asked if Tiffany had seen him about the projection for his cornice. He said no, but he would go to Trenton at once about it. He returned and told me the foot projected 14 inches too far. I went up next morning and found only one rafter up of the first section, with some others ready. I told Tiffany of his error in making them too long, to cut the end off, which was easily done, and to make the others of the proper length, all this he knew he was to do if he had attended to the matter properly. The second item therefore they have no ground to charge. The third is the same. The fourth is

another error. They had too great projection. The fifth, sixth, seventh & eighth I have no knowledge of any extra tension rods or rafters, spouds [?] or braces. On the contrary, I *know some omitted* where walls occurred to dispense with them. The ninth is for lathe on the flat of roof, which they overlook is measured to them as see before at 1568 feet at 35 cents = $548.80. Their charge is $457.60 thus a difference against them of $81.20. As for the days work, they have no charge, when a job is measured it includes everything and they have yet to overhaul and screw up the roof, so that I beg you will pay no more to them nor concede any charges as they ought by right to make deductions. I write to them by this post for a meeting so that we may settle the matter. I am always inclined to favour the mechanic when he shews a straight front and has exerted himself in the work but when such a trumped up acct comes in after the delay they made, I must go strictly by bargain.

Very respectfully yours
John Notman

Philada April 10th 1856

To The Rev. John Maclean D.D.
My Dear Sir

I received your note of yesterday this morning. Since I wrote to you Mr. Tiffany has called here. I told him you had ordered me to settle the bill with them and asked him (for which I had before written) to bring the drawings and other memoranda for a settlement. He hadn't them with him but promised to bring them. I also pointed out the unreasonable, unfounded charges in the bill as you sent it to me. He could not defend it, and from Bottom's again calling upon you before they meet me, I suppose they think as you have no data to defend yourself they will work on your fears to consent to pay the bill now. I ordered the work, and directed it, and know the whole matter and am the only one to settle it on your part, unless they are obstinate therefor I think your answer to them should be to go and settle with me if they can. If they cannot, and after you hear us, it will be time enough to think of a reference, but not now as they have never brought their bill to me for settlement. I could not get away to day indeed I expected Tiffany here for the other drawings and may not get up this week. I expect him tomorrow,

Very respectfully yours
John Notman

At the trustees' meeting of 24 June 1856 Maclean could report

. . . the building will be ready for the reception of students at the beginning of the next session. The work has been well done. It is we presume a firmer building than it was ever before. . . . There are to be nine furnaces in all. One for the Library room, and eight for the lodging rooms. . . . A contract was made with Messrs Bottom & Tiffany to furnish an iron-dome for the central tower of the building, and they engaged to have the work done on the 10th instant, and the Committee expected to have this part of the work completed before now. The excuse of Messrs B. & T. for not complying with their engagement is that the workman upon [whom] they relied to do this work was sick and unable to attend to it in time to have it finished as they promised to do, if it could be done [? . . . .] if not all the castings are ready; and they propose to begin the work this week.

The architect was requested to order the requisite dressed stone for the front door of the building as long ago as last autumn, or at least was told he might do so, upon the terms offered by Messrs Baldwin & Patterson of Newark. For some reason or other, probably from forgetting the matter, he didn't give the order. The door is to be much larger than the present one, & to be suited to the massive character of the building.

Nothing further has been done to the Library room; except to complete the roof. . . . the room [will be] shut up until funds are provided for its completion in whole or in part. . . .   [Report, June 1856]

Later in the summer, with the cupola nearing completion, Notman prepared final working drawings for his new heavily rusticated Tuscan doorway and the window over it. He would have preferred the latter to be a statuary niche, but seems to have been overruled by the client.

Philada Augt 9th 1856

To The Revd John Maclean D.D.
My Dear Sir

Having seen you after you had sent yours of 16th, I deferred answering it till I should receive the drawing of the Door from Newark which I got a day or two ago and in drawing it over, I would suggest to you that as ample light is afforded that entry or hall by the door that the window should be closed and finished as a niche for a statue. Even without a statue, a niche would be the finer feature and may induce the presentation of a statue. Let me have your opinion ere I finish the drawing, as soon as convenient to you.

As to my remuneration, I told when I commenced the College that 5 per cent on the estimate would be my charge. I have drawn on this as slowly as possible having received only 750 dolls. as yet being anxious to see the work done. I feel the want of money now at this bill settling time of year and if the College is in funds I would feel much obliged if you will send me 250 or 300 dolls by your answer or let me know that you cannot that I may otherwise provide.

I have not seen or heard from Bottom and Tiffany since I wrote of them before to you. When they are ready I will be so too.

Have [they] brought up or set up any of the Centre Tower yet? Above the cornice, which was on when I was there.

Most respectfully yours,
John Notman

To the Revd John Maclean D.D.
My Dear Sir

As you requested in yours of 23rd inst, I sent you the drawings yesterday by Adam's Express. The window drawings I had made a niche, it is therefor slightly rubbed, to bring it back to a window. Baldwin of Newark understands both. They have the light gray stone to do it. I will be up soon to see the dome on centre tower. In the mean time Mr. Olden has not sent the cheque. Will I draw on him?

Most respectfully yours
John Notman

Philad Augt 27th 1856

Again the project encountered delays and the shortage of funds must have been frustrating.

Since the date of the last Report [December 1856], but little has been [done] towards the completion of Nassau Hall. It was expected by the Committee that the stone work of the front door and of the window above would have been finished by the 1st of May. The contracts with the persons, who were to furnish the stone, & with with [sic] the stone cutter were made last autumn. They charge the fault of the delay on each other. The Committee would perhaps have been more urgent with them, had they had funds at command to pay for the work when done. . . . The moneys expended in the rebuilding the edifice, and for furnaces, water closets, & draining & leveling the grounds around the building amounts to $45,557.88. . . .
                    [Report, June 1857]

Notman received a total of $1050 for his services. [Accounts] This was considerably less than five per cent of the total project cost, but may have been based on the value of the new work for which he was actually responsible.

Probably the panic of 1857 hindered the college's fund-raising. In any event the library was not completed until 1859.

PRESENT STATUS:

Still in use as the main administration building of Princeton University, Nassau Hall has maintained most of the exterior wrought by Notman into its third century. The end towers, however, have been truncated in an early twentieth-century attempt to "recolonialize" the structure. On the interior the changes to adapt the building to varying uses have been more extensive, although on the ground floor the west corridor and flanking rooms retain their original configuration. The most prominent alteration has been the redesign of the library, now the Faculty Room, carried out by McKim, Mead and White in 1906.

64.

CHRIST CHURCH HOSPITAL
99TH STREET ABOVE WYNNEFIELD ROAD, PHILADELPHIA
1856
Client: Board of Managers, Christ Church Hospital
Project: health care facility for gentlewomen of limited means

DRAWINGS: none
DOCUMENTATION:

Minutes of the Board of Managers of Christ Church Archives; Letters concerning drawings for Christ Church Hospital, Henry F. duPont Winterthur Museum and Library

BIBLIOGRAPHICAL REFERENCES:

Massey, James C., ed. *Two Centuries of Philadelphia Architectural Drawings.* Philadelphia (1964)

AT A MEETING on 5 June 1854 the Managers of Christ Church Hospital

Resolved, that a committee of three be appointed to obtain the [?] preliminary information, and plans, for the erection of a Hospital Building for the accommodation of not less than one hundred Inmates on the ground purchased of Mr. G [?], west of Schuylkill, and to report to a future meeting of the Board.

The chair appointed Drs. Cooper and Willing, and Newbold the Committee.   [Minutes]

The committee appears to have been remarkably dilatory. It was over a year later that

The plans of Mr. Gries were submitted for the New Hospital building and on motion

It was resolved

That this board approve of the plan submitted and that the same be referred to com[mitte] on accts & Estates to prepare & lay it before the Vestries of Christ Church & St. Peters.   [Minutes, 12 Nov. 1855]

There is no mention of this resolution in the minutes of Christ Church's vestry, so what transpired thereafter is not clear. Perhaps the vestry suggested that other architects be consulted. In any event, Notman submitted a set of drawings the following spring.

Binney Esq. Jr.
Mr. Dear Sir

Will you be pleased to present the enclosed as explanation of my design for the new Christ's Church Hospital and oblige Sir.

Most respectfully yours,
John Notman
Apl. 17, 1856

Binney transmitted the plans to Prof. Joseph C. Booth.

It is unclear whether Notman submitted these drawings in a competition or for use by Gries. Six years later he attempted to gain access to them, but did not claim ownership, and had a claim for compensation against the trustees, as shown by the following correspondence.

Philada: Feb 8, 1862

Dear Sir

Will you oblige me by letting me have Mr. Notmans drawings, made for Christ Church Hospital.

Very truly yours,
Joseph A. Clay

Prof. Jos. C. Booth
U. S. Mint

Phil—Apr 4th 1862

To Profr Booth
Dear Sir

Will you be pleased to lend to Mr. Clay the drawings I made for Christ's Ch. Hosl. I saw them some time ago in Mr. Gries's office. All in one roll, excepting the perspective view, which was framed and glazed.

Mr. Clay will return them if desired in a few days, and oblige Sir

Yours truly
John Notman

My dear Sir

Mr. Notman thinks that the additional drawings were at Mr. Gries' office & that they have come into Dr. Cooper's possession. If you will send me the order he asks, I will be much obliged to you. I will see you to-morrow or on Monday. This application is totally independent of his claim for compensation from the Trustees. This I am sure we can easily arrange.

Very truly yours,
S/ J. A. Clay
April 4/62

Prof. Booth

It is not known whether the drawings still exist. Gries' drawings are in possession of Christ Church Hospital. [Massey, 64-65]

PRESENT STATUS:
Unexecuted

65.

HOLY TRINITY CHURCH
NINETEENTH AND WALNUT STREETS
(RITTENHOUSE SQUARE), PHILADELPHIA
1856–1859
Client: Vestry of the Church of the
Holy Trinity
Project: new church and parish building

65.1

65.2

DRAWING 65.1:
 Title: none
 Signature: none
 Date: none
 Scale: none indicated
 Other inscriptions: none
 Description: facade and flank elevations
 Medium: ink
 Size: 26 x 24 (66 x 61)
 Owner: Historical Society of Pennsylvania
 (AIA)

DRAWING 65.2:
 Title: Longitudinal Section of
 Holy Trinity
 Signature: none
 Date: none
 Scale: 1/8" : 1'
 Other inscriptions: Transverse Section;
 Transverse Section
 Description: longitudinal and
 transverse sections
 Medium: ink and wash, with pencil
 emendations and calculations
 Size: 23¾ x 26⅜ (60.4 x 67.1)
 Owner: Historical Society of Pennsylvania
 (AIA)

DRAWING 65.3:
 Title: none
 Signature: none
 Date: none
 Scale: ¼" : 1'
 Other inscriptions: none
 Description: transverse section, probably
 working drawing for vaulting
 Medium: ink and colored wash,
 with pencil measurements
 Size: 26½ x 23½ (67.5 x 59.2)
 Owner: Historical Society of Pennsylvania
 (AIA)

OTHER EARLY ILLUSTRATIONS:
 "Plan./Church of the Holy Trinity,/Rittenhouse Square, Philadelphia." John Notman, Archt., lithographed by T. Sinclair; photographs of the building under construction are in LCP.

65.3

"Plan, Church of the Holy Trinity." *Courtesy HSP*

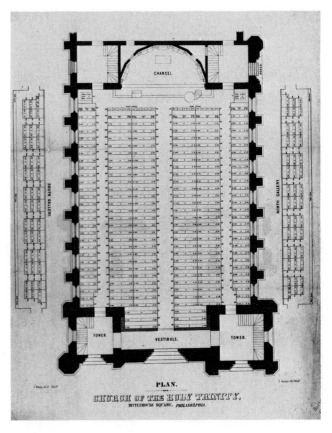

DOCUMENTATION:

Church of the Holy Trinity, Minutes of the Vestry, 6 June 1855-22 Dec. 1869; *Daily Evening Bulletin;* Philadelphia *Public Ledger;* AB; J: StA

BIBLIOGRAPHICAL REFERENCES:

F: 88-89, 191-204; Aspinwall, Marguerite, *A Hundred Years in His House, the Story of Holy Trinity on Rittenhouse Square.* Philadelphia (1956)

AS FASHIONABLE PHILADELPHIANS moved westward, new congregations were formed and new churches were built to minister to their needs. Only five years after St. Mark's was consecrated, a newly-organized group decided to erect another major Episcopal church three squares to the west and one north. Meeting for the first time in June 1855, the group appointed a building committee which, by the beginning of the new year had "conferred with four Architects, & examined their plans and sketches," but had "not yet found one in all respects suitable." [Minutes, 31 Jan. 1856: 8] Evidently the committee continued to confer with architects and the choice narrowed to two

The Committee on plans presented three designs by Mr. Notman for a Church in the Norman style, with estimates of the Cost of the building.

Mr. Bond also presented a design by Mr. Frazer for a Church in the Gothic style, accompanied with estimates of the cost.

On motion of Mr. Whitney it was resolved that Mr. Notman be requested to furnish detailed estimates, accompanied with such drawings of plan No 3, as will enable a competent builder to make understandingly a proposition to erect the Church.   [Minutes, 26 May 1856]

Notman proceeded to satisfy the committee's request. Two weeks later he submitted a design for the church in perspective, accompanied by plans and specifications. This was accepted in principle, except that one of the members wished to "flatten" the ceiling, and it was determined that details of the interior would be left to the discretion of the committee. Notman was to be asked to produce "such working drawings and full specifications as will enable a competent builder to estimate

understandingly the cost of the church." [Minutes, 10 June 1856: 21-22]

The bids were discouragingly high, $104,-500 and $115,300. Rather than modify his designs, Notman suggested that he serve as contractor. At the same time he was asked to provide additional drawings of the front, flanks and interior of the church. [Minutes, 30 July 1856: 24-25] Drawing 65.1 and 65.2 are probably part of this set. During the remainder of the summer and into the fall additional drawings and more detailed specifications were requested. By this time parish buildings had certainly been added to the program, if they had not been included from the first.

On motion the committee on plan were authorized to sanction the suggestion of Mr. Notman that the Sunday School building recede from the North line of the Church a few feet, also that the ceiling of the 1st and 3rd stories be made about 12 feet high, and that the 2nd story be made of such height as to make the whole elevation of the Sunday School Building correspond with the Church.

[Minutes, 6 Aug. 1856: 30]

In the spring the contract was finally signed and work began.

... a contract had been made with John Notman, which was duly executed on the 14th inst, by which Mr. Notman agrees to erect and build the Church and School Building and a Tower to the Church to the height of eighty four feet, for the sum of $67,473.00 (of which $5,000 are to be paid in the scrip of the Church)....

The Committee also reported that the excavation of the Cellar was commenced on the 19th inst.

[Minutes, 20 Mar. 1857: 40]

Construction progress was duly reported in the newspapers.

New Church Edifice-Corner Stone Laid.—The west end of the city is about to be improved by the erection of another elegant church edifice, the corner stone of which was laid yesterday afternoon, on Walnut street west of Rittenhouse Square. It is to be called the Church of the Holy Trinity, to be built in the Norman style, of brown stone, having a front of [?] feet, including the tower and steeple, and a depth of 161 feet. The principal front is on Rittenhouse street, and will be highly ornamental.

The steeple is designed to be 225 feet high, and the tower 84 feet to the base of the spire. The ceiling will be formed of three arches, the main one being semi-circular. In the rear of the church edifice will be the school house of 32 feet depth, which will obviate the necessity for a basement. The architect is Mr. John Notman.

[*Public Ledger*, 26 May 1857: 1]

The Church of the Holy Trinity, P.E., situated on Walnut street, west of Rittenhouse Square, the corner stone of which was laid on the 25th of May last is finely progressing. The base is completed and the first floor of joist laid. This will be a noble edifice in the Notman style of architecture, Connecticut brown stone being the material used. It is 64 feet front and 161 feet deep, including the school house which is already one story in height, and built of the same material as the church edifice. The estimated cost is $30,000.

[*Public Ledger*, 30 July 1857: 1]

Unfinished Churches.—The work upon the Church of the Holy Trinity (P.E.) west of Rittenhouse Square, is progressing, and the front, as far as finished, presents a noble appearance. The door way and windows are highly ornamented, the material used being Caen stone, which strangely contrasts with the Connecticut brown stone in the front. The Parochial School House in the rear of the church, fronting on Walnut street, is nearly ready for roofing.   [*Public Ledger*, 22 Apr. 1858: 1]

The first service at Holy Trinity was held on 27 Mar. 1859. [Minutes, 74] The appearance of the new church was duly described the following day.

The building was constructed of stone throughout, under the supervision of Mr. John Notman, Architect, and the style of its architecture is what is generally known as the Notman, although it is sometimes called the Venetian, Romanesque, or Lombardic Style, according to the country and period in which it was developed.

* * *

At the north-east corner of the building is a massive tower which has a base of thirty-two feet. It is designed to surmount it with a beautiful spire, having a height from the ground of 230 feet. At present the tower will be carried up to a height of only 84 feet; but the vestry feel confident of being able to add the other portion of the steeple in the course of a year or two. In addition to this tower, there are octagonal turrets which terminate the north-western and south-eastern corners of the building. The flanks exhibit buttresses and windows alternately; the buttress projections, after set offs, join and are combined by a parapet cornice on corbels, coped with the cable ornament.

The principal material used in the construction of the walls, is Connecticut brown stone. The door and window jambs and arches on the Walnut street front, are of Newark stone, and the sills, arches &c., on the Nineteenth street front, are of stone from the Albert quarries in New Brunswick, displaying a marked contrast with the other stone work, while harmonizing with the general appearance of the exterior, relieve it of monotony.

There are doors of entrance and exit at each end of the ground floor and the galleries, and a very large congregation can be dismissed from the building in a very few minutes. All the principal doors open into vestibules which are laid in stone; while the stairs leading to the galleries, from each of the four corners, are built of the same durable material. The interior of the church is no less imposing than the outside, and the mediaeval style of the arrangement of the building, with its immense rafters, and galleries supported on massive brackets of grained wood is not violated by the appliances which modern taste and luxury demand. The auditorium occupies the entire main building which we have described. The chancel is at the western end of the church, and the organ gallery is at the other extremity. This affords a clear interior space—including the recesses—of 118 feet in length, by 68 feet wide.... [the] massive stone corbels in each bay, and its form is what is technically called a "semi-quatre-foil cusped arch." In other words, it is vaulted in the centre, having lateral inclined vaults intersecting it over each window between the main rafters. The latter slanted boldly out, and being of dark grained wood that afford a fine contrast with the pure white with which the ceiling is finished. This effect is heightened by the rich cathedral tinted enameled glass of a beautiful and appropriate floriated pattern, with which the windows are glazed. It is designed to tint the ceiling; but even in its present condition it has a fine effect. The walls are painted in a color to harmonize with the rest of the interior.

The galleries upon the Northern and Southern sides of the church are supported on powerful truss brackets, which rest on stone corbels at each buttress. These supports are firmly anchored into the walls.

* * *

The organ gallery is at the east end; it is elevated six feet higher than the side galleries, and corresponds in depth and width with the chancel.

Additional light reaches the organ gallery through the large circular window in front. The organ at present in the church will soon be replaced by a large and magnificient instrument in process of building by the Messrs. Hook, of Boston. The church will be lighted at night by means of gas fixtures which will spring from the grained wood fronts of the galleries. These fixtures are in the hands of Messrs. Cornelius, Baker & Co. who are making them according to a special pattern, so as to be in keeping with the style of the church and its furniture.

The pews are of stained pine with walnut copings, and are upholstered and cushioned with crimson damask. There are 176 pews on the lower floor, and 84 in the galleries, making 260 in all, besides open seats along the entire length of the gallery walls, affording sittings for about 1100 persons, the middle aisle or passage is 6½ feet wide and the side passages 4½ feet wide. The aisles have been covered with crimson and black Brussels carpet, while the carpet in the chancel is very rich velvet of the same colors.

The chancel is a marked feature of the church. It is semi-circular in form, having a width of 34 feet and a depth of 17 feet. It is ornamented with an arcade on columns, supporting a semi-domed ceiling radiated to the chancel arch. It is lighted through stained glass at the apex. The ceiling of the chancel is beautifully gilt and colored, and it has a rich and elegant appearance. It is designed to place tablets containing the Lord's Prayer, Creed, Decalogue, &c., in the recesses between the columns joining the arcade of the chancel. Under the columns, in the latter, is the following inscription painted in antique letters:

"Glory be to the Father, and to the Son, and to the Holy Ghost. Amen."

The pulpit is outside of the chancel, at the north side. The reading desk is at the opposite side. The furniture of the chancel consists of a table, fixed stalls, and communion rail, all harmonizing with the general design of the interior.

At the western end of the main building and connected with it is a substantial stone structure, built to correspond with the church proper, which is designed for the accomodation of the schools, vestry, library, &c&c. of the church. The first floor of the school building is divided into four rooms, each 16 x 32 feet in dimensions, which are set apart and handsomely furnished as a vestry room, parish library room, infant school room, and ladies sewing rom. The second floor is in one room of 32 by 64 feet, which is fitted up in very neat and handsome style for a chapel. The room on the third floor is of the same size, and is devoted to the Sunday School.

[*Daily Evening Bulletin*, 28 Mar. 1859: 1]

Completion of the spire of Holy Trinity was not undertaken until two years after Notman's death. "Several plans" were presented. [Minutes, 6 May 1867: 273-74) The choice was finally narrowed to the "plan for a spire by either Mr. Frazer or Mr. Potter...." Frazer's plan was selected by a vote of seven to one. [Minutes, 18 May 1867: 274] Potter was undoubtedly the same architect who had submitted a design for St. Clement's, perhaps the young Edward Tuckerman Potter. [see entry 62] Frazer, who had submitted designs when Holy Trinity was first built, may have been John Fraser, who within two years was to form a partnership with Frank Furness and George W. Hewitt. The spire as built differs in detail, but in general closely resembles that in Notman's drawing. [F: 200, 204]

PRESENT STATUS:

Holy Trinity is still maintained in its original use.

66.

MOUNT VERNON
CEMETERY GATE

RIDGE AND LEHIGH AVENUES, PHILADELPHIA
1856–1858
Client: Mount Vernon Cemetery Company
Project: Gateway and lodge

DRAWINGS: none
OTHER EARLY ILLUSTRATIONS:
    Wood engraving on handbill, HSP and Athenaeum; photograph on postcard, HSP
DOCUMENTATION:
    Minute Book of the Mount Vernon Cemetery Company and Linten, William, Superintendent. "Mount Vernon Cemetery Company 1857." Coll. Mount Vernon Cemetery Company; StA

IN JUNE 1856 the board of Mount Vernon met to discuss building plans. Notman was not asked to lay out the grounds, G. M. Hopkins, Jr. receiving that commission [Minutes, 10], but on 11 June

It was moved by Mr. R. Buist and seconded by Dr. Mc-Calmont that the plan and drawing presented by J. Notman Esq. for gateway and tower be adopted and committee be requested to procure estimates for the erection of the same, in Pennsylvania white marble or brown stone. Adopted. [Minutes: 11]

Robert Buist, the company's treasurer, was a well-known landscape gardener and presumably an old friend of Notman, having arrived from Britain with him on the *Thames* in 1831. [see page 47, n. 17.]

On 30 June Notman was "requested to furnish complete plans and specifications for carrying out the plan already furnished by him." [Minutes: 16½] Estimates were received in July, but no decisions were made or contracts entered into. On 19 Sept. a special meeting was called "to consider an alteration for material of Gateway etc."

The subject was referred to Mr. Notman for report of expense etc. on Monday next.

... Resolved that as the architect reports that the marble can be made smooth instead of rough for $100 addition[al] expense that the same be adopted. (carried)

[Minutes: 23]

"Mount Vernon Cemetery." *Courtesy The Athenaeum*

Finally on 29 Sept. it was

Resolved that the Committee on Improvements be authorized to contract for the building of the tower. Two sides of marble and two sides of cut square stone and the remainder as proposed, provided the amount does not exceed thirty-four hundred dollars and occasion delay of more than one month. [Minutes: 25]

Work was carried on through the winter and on 26 Jan. 1857 the committee considered a proposal from Robert Wood (of the iron-casting firm of Wood and Perot) for making the gates. [Minutes, 45]

By spring a major portion of the construction was complete and payments were authorized to B. R. Marley, the carpenter, John McManimon, the mason, and John School, the marble cutter, all "as certified by Mr. Notman." [Minutes, 53] The extent of the work was reported to the board by Superintendent Linten on 1 May.

... Foundations have been dug for the circular walls by the tower and dwelling house and some grading done by the buildings.

The dwelling house has been roofed and the floors laid. The marble and stonework on the tower all done, some progress made on the gateway, and the shed finished and ready for use. [Mount Vernon, 1857]

Although the gate was satisfactory, the lodge was not. On 1 June Linten wrote

The marble work on the Gateway is progressing slowly, but steadily.... The circles ready for the marble work. The wood work on the tower up to the height, and being fast finished.

The dwelling house got ready for the plastering and there it stands, and here perhaps I may be allowed to say, that I have been very much disappointed in its not being finished long ago, and above all to the total disregard paid to comfort or convenience, in the interior arrangements. In fact with its present arrangements, it is totally unfit for anyone to live in. [Mount Vernon, 1857]

216

Evidently the original scope of the lodge had been reduced, presumably in the interest of economy. The excisions must have been made in haste, since one of the items omitted was the stair to the second floor. On 8 June the board moved to rectify the situation.

On motion resolved that the Committee on Improvements be authorized to get plans for making an addition to the Lodge with stair case etc in accordance with original plan 12 by 16 and to include a window on two sides and room over the kitchen all rough stone and rough cast. Adopted. [Minutes: 58]

However when the plans and proposals were submitted the board decided they were "inexpedient to be made at the present time" although they did "resolve to make the necessary alterations on stairway." [Minutes, 59]

By 1 Aug. Linten could report that

The work on the Tower is well on towards completion, also on the dwelling house including alteration. The marble work on the entrance goes on slowly, the two small side arches, over the footways are finished, the arch over the carriage way spring, and two of the figures ready to be put up. [Mount Vernon, 1857]

By 1 Oct. the marblework on the tower was complete, as was all the painting. By the next month the tower was paved with pressed brick. By the end of the year "blue marble jambs and sill" had been installed on the house cellar and all that remained to be done was completion of the columns terminating the "circular walls."

Notman received two payments for his services, $100 in 1857 and $300 in 1858. The total cost of the project, according to a report made by Buist on 7 Mar. 1859 was $35,330.

PRESENT STATUS:

The gateway and lodge still belong to the Mount Vernon Cemetery and still stand. However, they have been considerably altered by the removal of all but the first stage of the tower and an addition to the lodge along Lehigh Avenue.

Cathedral of St. John. *Author's photograph*

67.

CATHEDRAL OF ST. JOHN
10 CONCORD AVENUE,
WILMINGTON, DELAWARE
1857–1858
Client: Vestry of St. John's Church
Project: new church

DRAWINGS: none
DOCUMENTATION:

Cathedral of St. John, Minutes of the meetings of the Vestry of St. John's Church, Brandywine, Delaware; Treasurer's account book; *Delaware Republican*

BIBLIOGRAPHICAL REFERENCES:

F: 89-90

ON 25 Mar. 1857 contracts were made for a "large and beautiful Gothic church," designed by Notman. [Minutes: 11] The cornerstone was laid on 13 June and work progressed so rapidly that the contract to slate the roof was let on 10 Nov. [Minutes: 16, 27] A year later the church was consecrated. [*Republican*, 22 Nov. 1858: 1]

During this period Notman must have visited Wilmington frequently to supervise the work, as evidenced by a letter copied in the vestry minutes.

I have your letter of the 20th inst. and have been delayed answering it by being on a Jury. . . . The late Mr. [Alexis] DuPont and I inspected the cellar and foundation trenches with which we were satisfied, . . . as to dashing with mortar the cellar and tower Mr. A. [rmstrong, the mason] is not required to do them by the specifications. As the late Mr. DuPont made it imperative on me to keep out every item that would increase the cost of the church, unless required and necessary, therefore these were excluded by himself—you have both the cheapest and best built church I know of for the expenditure.

I wish you would remind Mr. Elliott the treasurer that my account is still unsetled, and request him to let me know if he will pay me this week.

[Minutes, 14 Feb. 1859: 46-47]

Just before its consecration the local newspaper described St. John's as

. . . purely Gothic. The walls are of Brandywine blue rock, and the roof of slate. The building is cruciform and is 116 feet long from the end of the nave to the east wall of the chancel; . . . .

The tower, very massive and well flanked with buttresses, stands in the angle formed by the transept and chancel walls.   [*Delaware Republican*, 8 Nov. 1858: 2]

PRESENT STATUS:

Originally known as St. John's, Brandywine, the church is now the Cathedral of St. John. Since its construction numerous additions have been made. Prominent among these are a vestibule on the west and an extension of the sanctuary approximately eleven feet to the east. An extensive complex of buildings has been added to the north.

68.

PARISH SCHOOLS,
ST. CLEMENT'S CHURCH
TWENTIETH AND CHERRY STREETS,
PHILADELPHIA
1864–1865
Client: Vestry of St. Clement's Church
Project: addition of meeting and classrooms, library, and chapel to existing church

DRAWING 68.1:
Title: Parish Schools for St. Clement's Church
Signature: John Notman/Architect/ Philadelphia (stamp)
Date: May 8th 1864
Scale: ⅛" : 1'
Other inscriptions: Elevation/Tower Street, Elevation/Church Yard, Elevation/ Cherry Street/Line of Cherry St.,/Plan/ First Story, Plan/Second Story
Description: measured plans and rendered elevations
Medium: ink and wash
Size: 26-13/16 x 30¼ (68.2 x 76.8)
Owner: Historical Society of Pennsylvania (AIA), S-13
DOCUMENTATION:
Minutes of the Vestry of St. Clement's Church, 1855-1878
BIBLIOGRAPHICAL REFERENCES:
D: 139; F: 179-80, 189-90

THIS IS NOTMAN'S LAST known commission, not, in fact, completed until after his death. The title and date of the drawing appear to be in Notman's hand, albeit somewhat shakily, but the rendering technique differs from his. The drawing may have been produced by George Watson Hewitt, who was associated with Notman at the time. A week after it was prepared, plans for the parish buildings were submitted to the vestry and approved. [Minutes, 15 May 1864: 103]

Work must have commenced promptly, with Notman acting as architect but not as builder, although he was intended to oversee the work. This role is made clear in two letters from Notman requesting payment of $300 on account. The arrangement was evidently that Notman was paid on a percentage basis. "I need the money," he wrote on 19 Dec. 1864, "and I know you will not refuse it remembering your promise of 5 percent on expenditures." [Minutes: 110] When the payment was not forthcoming he wrote again on 24 December, describing his services more fully. "Duplicate drawings have been provided both to the

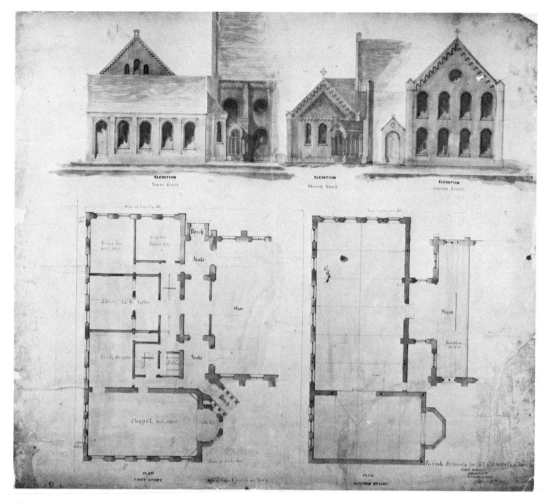

68.1

builder and Revd. Mr. Walden and every part of the building has been directed by me." [Minutes: 110] The building committee, however, felt that a payment of $100 already made was sufficient because "he had not superintended the erection of the Building, but had left the workmen to their own ingenuity and devices." [Minutes, 22 Dec. 1864: 124] A committee was appointed to negotiate with Notman, but the outcome was not recorded.

On 18 Apr. 1865, the vestry voted to resume work on the buildings, presumably after the usual winter hiatus in construction activity. Whether satisfied with Notman's performance or not, they could no longer call on him for supervision. He had died on 3 Mar. 1865.

PRESENT STATUS:

The buildings still stand, although heavily altered.

69.

JOHN T. TAITT HOUSE
1518 WALNUT STREET, PHILADELPHIA
1864–1865

DOCUMENTATION:
    AB; J
BIBLIOGRAPHICAL REFERENCES:
    D: 139

JACKSON gives no date for this house, but Notman's anonymous biographer says it was his last work, which would mean that it was designed after St. Clement's Parish School in 1864. Dallet says that Taitt occupied the house in 1865. A brownstone structure, it was later occupied by the Middle City Bank.

DRAWINGS: none
PRESENT STATUS:
    Demolished

70.

UNIDENTIFIED CHURCHES

Although the number of drawings in this category in the Historical Society of Pennsylvania's files has been reduced in the course of this study, fifteen drawings remain that cannot be identified with a specific building. The titles of some suggest that they were typical designs Notman kept "in stock" to show prospective clients. Others, however, are working drawings and must relate to executed projects. The drawings have been grouped by type rather than chronologically, since few are dated.

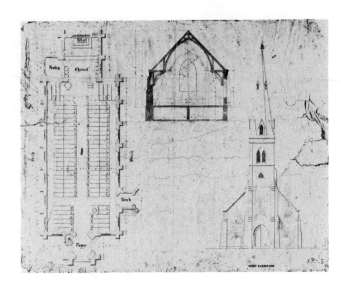

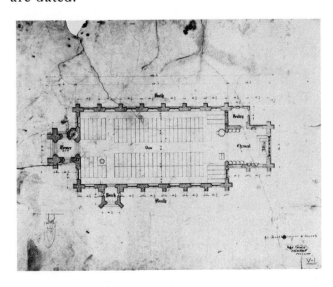

DRAWING 70.1:
   Title: Ste. Bartholomew's Church/N.Y.
(not in Notman's hand)
   Signature: John Notman/Architect/
Philada
   Date: none
   Scale: none indicated (scales ⅛″ : 1′)
   Other inscriptions: none
   Description: measured plan
   Medium: ink
   Size: 18⅛ x 24¼ (46 x 61.6)
   Owner: Historical Society of Pennsylvania
(AIA), V-1

DRAWING 70.2:
   Title: none
   Signature: none
   Date: none
   Scale: none indicated (scales ⅛″ : 1′)
   Other inscriptions: North/West Elevation
   Description: plan, section and elevation
   Medium: ink and wash,
with pencil emendations
   Size: 18 x 23¼ (46 x 59.1)
   Owner: Historical Society of Pennsylvania
(AIA), XR-15
DOCUMENTATION:
   Philadelphia *Public Ledger*; J
BIBLIOGRAPHICAL REFERENCES:
   F: 227.

JACKSON [221] lists St. Bartholomew's Church, New York, as one of Notman's works, and someone, presumably Hewitt, has pencilled the letters "N.Y." after the title on the drawing numbered V-1. However as Fairbanks has pointed out [227] neither the first St. Bartholomew's in New York, nor the second, designed by Renwick and Sands, bore any resemblance to Notman's design. It is possible that this extremely plain Early English building was the Saint Bartholomew's on the Germantown Road near 8th Street in the Kensington area of Philadelphia, of which the cornerstone was laid in 1851. [*Public Ledger*, 15 July 1851: 2]

Fairbanks [140, 227] errs in associating the drawing numbered XR-15 with St. Paul's Trenton. [see entry 38] The plan is clearly entirely identical in lay-out and dimensions with that identified as St. Bartholomew's.

PRESENT STATUS:

If executed, demolished.

DRAWING 70.3:

Title: none
Signature: John Notman Archt
Date: none
Scale: none indicated
Other inscriptions: [No] 2
Flank Elevation
Description: rendered elevation
Medium: ink and wash
Size: 16⅜ x 17⅜ (41.6 x 44.7)
Owner: Historical Society of Pennsylvania (AIA)

DRAWING 70.4:

Title: none
Signature: John Notman Archt
Date: none
Scale: none indicated
Other inscriptions: No. 5. Principal Floor
Description: plan
Medium: ink and wash
Size: 22⅛ x 17¾ (56.2 x 45.1)
Owner: Historical Society of Pennsylvania (AIA)

THE FIRST OF THESE DRAWINGS, the elevation, has been kept in a folder marked St. Stephen's, while the plan was filed with miscellaneous unidentified churches. Clearly, however, they belong together. The handling of Notman's signature is the same, as is the numbering, although the left side of the first drawing, along with its top, has been lost. More importantly, the elevation and plan coincide in all particulars. The number of bays is the same, including the blind bay of the chancel; the octagonal shape of the tower buttresses is also identical, as are the small octagonal towers at the ends of the aisles.

It is possible that these drawings represent an unexecuted project for replacing Strick-

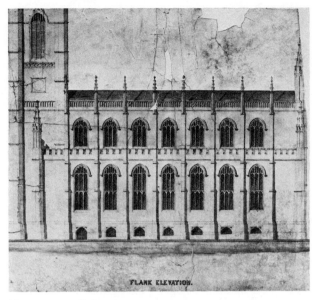

Above: 70.3; *Below:* 70.4

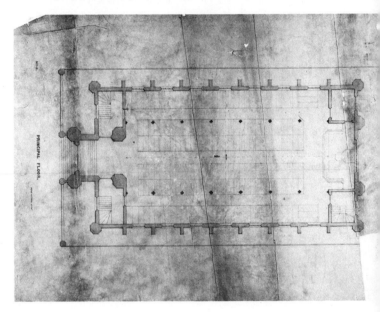

land's St. Stephen's Church on Tenth Street in Philadelphia. Extensive work was carried out at St. Stephen's in 1851, when a monument to the children of Edward S. Burd was erected.

A general refurbishing was often the solution in the mid-nineteenth century when replacement of what was thought to be an outmoded church proved too expensive. Unfortunately the vestry minutes of St. Stephen's for the relevant period are missing, so it is impossible to determine whether a more ambitious building program had been contemplated.

DRAWING 70.5:
   Title: No 5 Transept Church/Gothic Style
   Signature: John Notman/Architect/
   Philada (stamp)
   Date: 1848
   Scale: none indicated (scales ⅛″ : 1′)
   Other inscriptions: Plan/Front Elevation
   Description: measured plan and
   rendered elevation
   Medium: ink and wash
   Size: 21⅜ x 27-5/16 (54.4 x 69.4)
   Owner: Historical Society of Pennsylvania
   (AIA)

FAIRBANKS [81n] points out some resem-
blances between the facade shown in the drawing and that of the Green Hill Presbyterian
Church on Girard Avenue above Sixteenth
Street, Philadelphia.

DRAWING 70.6:
   Title: none
   Signature: John Notman/Architect/
   Philada (stamp)
   Date: Octr. 9th 1851
   Scale: ⅛″ : 1′ (stamp)
   Other inscriptions: Elevation/Elevation/
   Vertical Section/Plan
   Description: rendered front and flank
   elevations, transverse section, and plan
   Size: 23⅝ x 25⅝ (60 x 65.2)
   Owner: Historical Society of Pennsylvania
   (AIA)

FAIRBANKS [226] suggests a resemblance to
the Roxborough Presbyterian Church on
Ridge and Port Royal Avenues, Philadelphia, but adds that none of the church's records confirm such an association.

DRAWING 70.7:
   Title: none
   Signature: John Notman/Architect/
   Philada (stamp)
   Date: June 1852 (not in Notman's hand)
   Scale: none indicated (scales 1/10″ : 1′)
   Other inscriptions: Front Elevation/Plan/
   Side Elevation No 2
   Description: plan and rendered elevations
   Size: 17⅞ x 24 (45.4 x 66)
   Owner: Historical Society of Pennsylvania
   (AIA), X-R-17

FRONT ELEVATION   SIDE ELEVATION

Above: 70.7; *Below*: 70.8

DRAWING 70.8:
    Title: none
    Signature: none
    Date: none
    Scale: none indicated
    Other inscriptions: none
    Description: outline flank elevation
    Medium: ink and pencil
    Size:
    Owner: Historical Society of Pennsylvania
(AIA)

As FAIRBANKS [227] has pointed out, this design resembles, in the arrangement of tower, nave, and chancel, that of St. Mark's. The differences, however, are perhaps greater than the similarities. Most prominent is the absence of a clerestory. In addition the fenestration pattern differs greatly from that of St. Mark's. The arrangement of elements coincides with no known Notman church.

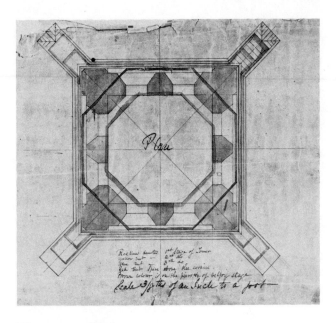

The following three drawings are possibly part of the working set for St. Mark's. Certainly the rafter system for a side aisle shown in section in the first drawing coincides with that of St. Mark's.

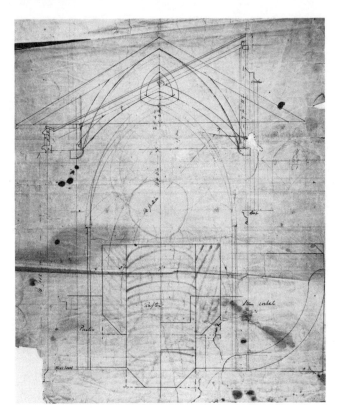

DRAWING 70.9:
Title: none
Signature: none
Date: none
Scale: ⅜″ : 1′
Other inscriptions: Plan/Red lines denotes 1st Stage of Tower/yellow line—2nd do/ blue tint—3rd do/red line Spire above the cornice/brown colour is on the piers &c of belfry stage
Description: plan of all stages of tower and spire
Medium: ink, colored ink, and wash
Size: 11⅜ x 16 (34 x 40.7)
Owner: Historical Society of Pennsylvania (AIA)

DRAWING 70.10:
Title: none
Signature: none
Date: none
Scale: none indicated
Other inscriptions: Floor level/Purlin/ Rafter/Stone corbel
Description: sketches; plans and sections, working details
Medium: ink, colored ink, and pencil
Size: 23⅛ x 18 (59.7 x 45.6)
Owner: Historical Society of Pennsylvania (AIA)

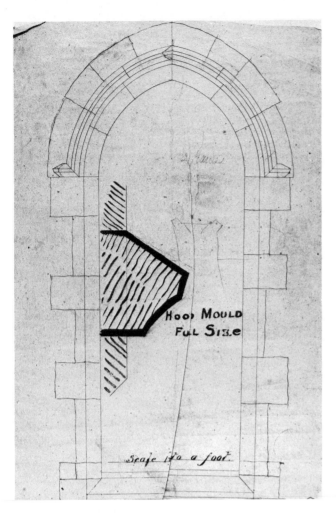

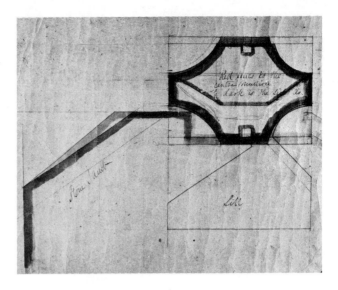

DRAWING 70.11:
Title: none
Signature: none
Date: none
Scale: 1½″ : 1′ and full
Other inscriptions: 2 Frames/Hood Mould
Description: Sketch
Medium: ink and pencil
Size: 22⅞ x 16¼ (58.1 x 41.3)
Owner: Historical Society of Pennsylvania
(AIA)

DRAWING 70.12:
Title: none
Signature: none
Date: none
Scale: none indicated (probably full)
Other inscriptions: Stone Jamb/Red lines
is the/centre Mullion/the dark is the side
do./Sill
Description: working plans of window
details
Medium: pencil, ink, and wash
Size: 15-13/16 x 19-9/16 (40.3 x 50)

THE TWO DRAWINGS below are possibly working drawings for St. Clement's. The first shows a plan for a capital that seems to relate to the capital sketched in elevation in drawing 62.11.

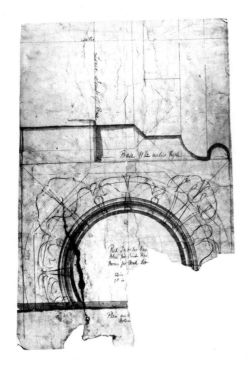

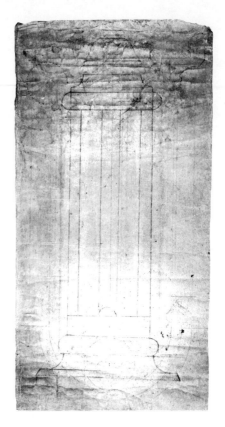

DRAWING 70.13:
   Title: Plan and [?]/Colum[n]
   Signature: none
   Date: none
   Scale: none indicated (probably full)
   Other inscriptions: Centre/Lower Joint of Base/Base 11½ inches high/Red Tint for bas[e]/Blue for Joint Ban[d] Brown for Neck dia[?]
   Description: sketch plan and section of details
   Medium: ink, pencil and wash
   Size: 26⅝ x 18⅜ (67.7 x 46.7)
   Owner: Historical Society of Pennsylvania (AIA)

DRAWING 70.14:
   Title: none
   Signature: none
   Date: none
   Scale: none indicated (probably full)
   Other inscriptions: Interior
   Description: drawn on both sides are details, probably of a window, and a columnar form on a console
   Medium: ink and pencil
   Size: 27¾ x 16-3/16 (70.5 x 36.2)
   Owner: Historical Society of Pennsylvania (AIA)

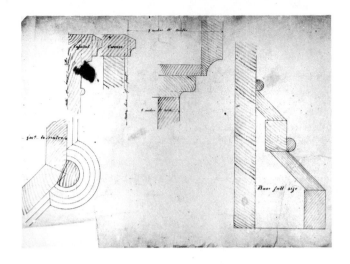

DRAWING 70.15:

  Title: none

  Signature: none

  Date: none

  Scale: Full

  Other inscriptions: centre of hanging Pillar/Capital/Cornice/centre line of front/Base full size

  Description: working plan and sections for wooden construction, perhaps a pulpit

  Medium: ink and wash

  Size: 30-15/16 x 21⅜ (78.6 x 54.4)

  Owner: Historical Society of Pennsylvania (AIA)

71.

UNIDENTIFIED HOUSES

THESE TWO WATERCOLORS of residences cannot be identified with any executed Notman commission. The first appears to be a standard design to show to clients or a design drawn for an illustration. In other instances, it is only drawings intended for illustration purpose, as opposed to architectural drawings, that Notman signed as "delr."

The second drawing, with the plants in the conservatory carefully picked out in watercolor, appears somewhat more specific. Morgan [48-49] relates this drawing to the J. W. Perry House in Brooklyn, N. Y., that appeared as Figure 79 in the 1841 edition of Downing's *Theory and Practice of Landscape Gardening*, which also has a large attached conservatory. However, according to Jane Davies, James Dakin supplied Downing with the design of the Perry House. The presence of the attached conservatory suggests a possible association with the J. P. Cushing House in Belmont, Mass. [see p. 230] A date as early as 1840 indeed seems likely for this building, which, in its conventional, symmetrical massing differs markedly from the later villas. The fenestration and detailing are also not unlike those of the 1840 project for The Athenaeum. [see entry 9] One other possibility is that this is a preliminary idea for Alverthorpe, the "plan" that Joshua Francis Fisher had obtained in 1847. Certainly the same semicircular portico carrying a balustrade, although executed in the Tuscan rather than the Ionic order, occurs on the west front of that house as executed. The flanking colonnades have been transformed into pilasters enframing triple windows in the executed design. At Alverthorpe, this Classical Revival device appears as something of an anomaly on a full-blown Tuscan villa.

Whatever their original purpose, these two well-preserved drawings were probably among those framed and hanging on the walls of the Notmans' house. [see p. 21]

NO. V. VILLA FOR

John Notman Archt. et delr.
Philadelphia May 1845

71.1

DRAWING 71.1:
   Title: No. V. Villa For
   Signature: John Notman Archt. et delr./
   Philadelphia
   Date: May 1845
   Scale: none indicated
   Other inscriptions: none
   Description: perspective rendering
   Medium: wash and watercolor
   Size: 14-9/16 x 21-9/16 (37 x 54.8)
   Owner: Historical Society of Pennsylvania
   (AIA)

DRAWING 71.2:
   Title: none
   Signature: none
   Date: none
   Scale: none indicated
   Description: rendered facade elevation
   Medium: watercolor
   Size: 11⅝ x 20¼ (29.5 x 51.5)
   Owner: Historical Society of Pennsylvania
   (AIA)

71.2

BUILDINGS LISTED BY JACKSON NOT OTHERWISE DOCUMENTED AS BY NOTMAN

MOST OF THE projects on the list provided to Joseph Jackson by William D. Hewitt can be confirmed as Notman's on the basis of other documentation. Of the remaining thirteen buildings on the list only one, the Mercantile Library, is documented as the work of another architect. Because of its general reliability, Jackson's listings merit serious consideration as part of Notman's *oeuvre*. Reliability in attribution does not extend to his dating. The entries below appear in the order in which Jackson cited them, with the dates he provided in brackets. They are followed by the actual dates, where known.

72.

MERCANTILE LIBRARY
FIFTH AND SANSOM STREETS, PHILADELPHIA
[1844] 1844–1845

ACCORDING to the Philadelphia *Public Ledger* of 2 Sept. 1845, William Johnson [actually William T. Johnston, 1811-1849] was the architect for the Mercantile Library. Tatum [176] also attributes the building to Johnston, perhaps best known as the designer of the Jayne Building.
PRESENT STATUS:
    Demolished

Gustavus A. Myers House. *Courtesy Valentine Museum*

73.

GUSTAVUS A. MYERS HOUSE
RICHMOND, VIRGINIA
[1845] c. 1849–1850

OTHER EARLY ILLUSTRATIONS:
 Early photographs in the collection of the
 Valentine Museum
BIBLIOGRAPHICAL REFERENCES:
 D: 136; Mordecai, Samuel. *Richmond in
 By-Gone Days.* Richmond (1854); Scott,
 Mary Wingfield. *Old Richmond Neigh-
 borhoods.* Richmond (1950)

JACKSON dates the house 1845, but the date of
1849 given by Dallett [136] is more probably
correct. The late 1840s were the years in
which Notman would have come into contact
with Myers in connection with his designs for
Hollywood Cemetery [see entry 34] and Capitol Square [see entry 43].

Although no documentation other than the
Jackson citation has been found for the Myers
House, the attribution to Notman is highly
credible, on the basis of its strong resemblance
to Glencairn. [see entry 40.] Like the latter,
the Myers House was built on a lot that fell
away rather abruptly at the rear. Although
the known photographs show only the front,
it is probable that the rear elevation was three
or four stories in height. Although it is impossible to tell whether there was a tower, some

construction, either a tower or a skylight over
the hall, rose above the parapets bridging the
chimneys. The most noticeable resemblance to
Glencairn is in the design of the portico and
general massing of the facade. The Richmond
house is rendered more interesting, however,
by the projecting hip-roofed bays.
PRESENT STATUS:
 Demolished

74.

J. P. CUSHING HOUSE (BELMONT PLACE)
WATERTOWN, MASSACHUSETTS
[1846] 1840

THE CUSHING estate was one of the show-
places of New England, highly praised by
Downing in both *The Theory and Practise of
Landscape Gardening* and *Rural Essays.*
There is no doubt that Asher Benjamin was
the architect of record. The contract of 10
Mar. 1840, between John P. Cushing and
Mordecai L. Wallis the builder, is now owned
by the Society for the Preservation of New
England Antiquities. It specifies that Wallis
will perform "to the satisfaction of Asher
Benjamin" and "according to the plan and
drawings made therefor by said Benjamin do
all the work mentioned in the specifications
here annexed."

According to Marjorie Blake Ross in *The
Book of Boston: The Victorian Period,* Cushing's diary at The Boston Athenaeum mentions that other architects were consulted. It is
possible that Notman was among their number.
PRESENT STATUS:
 The site of Belmont Place, now within the
 boundaries of the town of Belmont, is a
 housing tract. The house has been demolished.

Boothhurst. *Author's photograph*

75.

WILLIAM H. ROGERS HOUSE (BOOTHHURST)

NORTH OF NEW CASTLE, DELAWARE
[1847]

ALTHOUGH the house was built for James Booth, by the late nineteenth century it had passed into the hands of William H. Rogers. Adair Rogers, one of the current owners of the property, reports having seen a contract with Notman on the premises. Unfortunately, a recent search for this document was fruitless.

The mid-nineteenth century building campaign at Boothhurst consisted of major additions to a small eighteenth-century dwelling. Erection of formal rooms across the front and a service wing at the rear reduced the existing building to a slim filling for a sandwich. On the east facade an enclosed porch is flanked by open verandahs, originally covered by roofs supported by cast-iron posts. Behind this is one large formal room. The main entrance is on the south front, giving access to a hall running between the new formal room and the old house. This hall contains a statuary niche and terminates in a stair. New construction and old are united by a sheathing of stucco scored to simulate stone. The style is an austere Tudor Gothic. The ironwork, now gone, did much to enliven its severity.

The remnants of a romantic landscape with curved driveways, undulating terraces, and a pond, are still visible at Boothhurst.

PRESENT STATUS:
A plan to develop the estate would retain the house and the most significant features of the landscaping.

76.

ROBERT IREDELL HOUSE

NORRISTOWN, PENNSYLVANIA

DALLETT [139, 49n] suggests that the house, which stands at 16 West Airy Street, may date from 1864. As he points out, it has been so "colonialized" as to defy recognition.

77.

HEYL'S VILLA

6024 WAYNE AVENUE, GERMANTOWN,
PHILADELPHIA
c. 1856–1860

BIBLIOGRAPHICAL REFERENCES:
D: 139
THIS THREE-STORY stone house is a Gothic "cottage" of somewhat awkward proportions. Perhaps its extreme verticality was originally tempered by verandahs. At present its ground floor is entirely obscured by an incompatible modern addition.

Joseph Peace House. *Author's photograph*

78.

JOSEPH PEACE HOUSE
BORDENTOWN, NEW JERSEY
[1850s]

DOCUMENTATION:
Fisher, Sidney George. Diary. HSP. "Map of Bordentown, Burlington County, N. J. Surveyed and published by Thomas A. Hurley, C. E., Freehold, N. J., 1856

BIBLIOGRAPHICAL REFERENCES:
D: 131; "Morris, Tasker & Co's Illustrated Catalogue, 1860. *Architectural Elements.* Ed. by Diana S. Waite. Princeton (n.d.); Smith, Robert D. "John Notman and the Athenaeum Building." *Athenaeum Addresses.* Philadelphia (1951)

DALLETT thought Jackson in error in listing the location of the Peace House in Bordentown. He suggested that the home of Dr. Joseph Peace, Jr. in Bristol, Pa., was meant, without identifying a particular building. There is no doubt, however, that a member of the Peace family was in residence in Bordentown in 1843. Sidney George Fisher on a brief visit "Went with him [Moncure Robinson] and Mrs. Peace, to walk in the Count Joseph Bonaparte's park." [Diary, 2 July 1843] The house illustrated here is shown as the Joseph Pierce [sic] House on a map of Bordentown published in 1856.

It is a building remarkable for its combination of compactness and capaciousness. The form is basically cubical and from the streets that bound two sides of the property the building appears highly contained. The plan, however, is not symmetrical. The hall is placed off center, so that the rooms to the left of the entrance, drawing room and library, are larger than the dining room and kitchen on the right. The cube is broken, and the drawing room enlarged, by a semi-hexagonal bay fronting on Crosswicks Creek.

Most of Notman's houses were masonry; this is frame covered with flush boards. However, the interior finishes are highly sophisticated and there seems little reason to doubt that the building is by Notman.

Of great interest are surviving elements of the original heating system. Fireboxes of small furnaces remain in the basement.

79.

"CHURCH AT 70TH AND WOODLAND,"
PHILADELPHIA
1867

BIBLIOGRAPHICAL REFERENCES:
D: 137; F: 225

BOTH DALLETT AND FAIRBANKS state that the church cannot be identified. The building, however, is still standing, and still bears its original name, Siloam Methodist Church. A round stone inset over the main entrance bears the inscription "Siloam M. E. Church" and the date "1867." If the church is indeed by Notman, it was therefore not executed until after his death. The building is an extremely simple one, a nave, without tower, and with a steep gable roof. The buttressed flanks are pierced by lancet windows. No distinctive characteristics associated with Notman's work can be identified.

80.

CHURCH OF THE ANNUNCIATION, R.C.
TENTH AND DICKINSON STREETS, PHILADELPHIA
1860–1865

DOCUMENTATION:
> *North American and United States Gazette;* Westcott, Thompson. *The Official Guide Book to Philadelphia*, Philadelphia (1875)

BIBLIOGRAPHICAL REFERENCES:
> D: 137; F: 225

As FAIRBANKS notes, no manuscript material has been found to support Jackson's attribution. The corner stone of the church was laid 15 Apr. 1860. [*Gazette* 16 Apr. 1860, 1] The building was dedicated five years later on 19 Apr. 1865. [Guide, 296] It is a simple structure of boxy proportions and rather heavy-handed detailing.

PRESENT STATUS:
> Maintained in original use

Church of the Annunciation. *Author's photograph*

Church at 70th and Woodland. *Author's photograph*

81.

"CATHOLIC CONVENT"
TRENTON, NEW JERSEY
c. 1863

OTHER EARLY ILLUSTRATIONS:
> "Church of St. John the Baptist," lithograph by Packard & Butler

BIBLIOGRAPHICAL REFERENCES:
> Cleary, John J. "Catholic Pioneers of Trenton, N. J." *Historical Records and Studies of the United States Catholic Historical Society.* Joseph F. Delany *et al,* eds. New York (1917); Fox, John H. *A Century of Catholicity in Trenton, N. J.* Trenton (1900)

THE FIRST Catholic convent in Trenton was attached to the parish of St. John the Baptist, now the Church of the Sacred Heart on Broad Street. An orphan asylum was opened in 1862 and the first Sisters of Charity were brought to the city in 1863. [Fox: 5] The parish records contain no references to Notman. The lithograph, made sometime prior to the fire that destroyed the original church in 1883, shows the convent as a three-bay, three-story row house of a type ordinary in Trenton in the mid-nineteenth century. No other early views of the convent have been identified and there is at present on the site no building erected earlier than 1884.

PRESENT STATUS:
Demolished

82.

HENRY C. GIBSON HOUSE
42ND AND WALNUT STREETS, PHILADELPHIA
c. 1864
BIBLIOGRAPHICAL REFERENCES:
D: 139

DALLETT says that Gibson is first shown at this address in 1865. Unfortunately no photographs or other views of the house have been identified.

83.

ELIZA GURNEY HOUSE
BURLINGTON, NEW JERSEY

DOCUMENTATION:
Atlas of Burlington County
BIBLIOGRAPHICAL REFERENCES:
D: 131; Smith, John Jay. *Recollections of John Jay Smith*: Philadelphia (1892); Smith, Robert C. "John Notman and the Athenaeum Building." *Athenaeum Addresses*, Philadelphia (1951)

ROBERT SMITH [25, n. 38] mentions the house as demolished, without specifying its location. Dallett characterizes the attribution as vague, but places Eliza Gurney at a property called West Hill in 1872. The 1876 Atlas shows Mrs. Gurney as the owner of extensive properties on Oxmead Road in Burlington County southeast of Burlington City. These estates, West Hill on the west side of Oxmead Road and Green Hill on the east, had originally been the property of John Jay Smith's ancestors. Smith describes West Hill as the residence of Eliza Gurney in 1872. [*Recollections*, 18n] West Hill is a typical Burlington County brick Federal farmhouse built by Samuel Emlen c. 1800. [*Recollections*, 18] Its only mid-nineteenth century feature is a board-and-batten entrance lodge. Green Hill, although it too was originally constructed in the late eighteenth or early nineteenth century, shows evidence of extensive reworking in the Early Victorian era. The exterior has been covered with stucco scored to simulate ashlar, and a number of spiky gables and clustered chimney pots give it the air, if not the basic form, of a Gothic cottage. A billiard room terminating in a semi-hexagonal bay has been added and the interiors have been lavishly enriched with Gothic and rococo plaster cornices and ceiling ornaments, much of it resembling the work done at such houses as Prospect and Guernsey Hall.

OTHER BUILDINGS ATTRIBUTED TO NOTMAN

OVER THE YEARS a number of scholars, working on Notman or on topics related to him, have suggested some two score attributions for which definitive documentation is lacking. For some of the buildings once in this category—Springdale, Ellarslie, the Refectory of Princeton Theology Seminary—documentation confirming them as Notman's has been found. Others have proved to be the work of his contemporaries.

In making attributions two factors must be considered. The first is likelihood. Are the time and the place and the patrons probable? The second is the more elusive and subjective question of style. Where documentation, either visible or written, has been found, these factors are discussed briefly for the buildings listed below. For others the known surviving evidence is so slim that no conclusions can be reached. Dates have been supplied where the building history is known.

84.

CAMAC HOUSE
ELEVENTH STREET AND MONTGOMERY
  AVENUE, PHILADELPHIA
1841

OTHER EARLY ILLUSTRATIONS:
  The house is illustrated in Downing, A. J., *Cottage Residences*, New York (1842), and *A Treatise on the Theory and Practice of Landscape Gardening*. 2nd ed., New York (1844); a watercolor by David J. Kennedy is preserved at the HSP.
DOCUMENTATION:
  Letters from A. J. Downing to John Jay Smith. John Jay Smith Collection, LCP; Fisher, Sidney George. Diary. HSP; Perpetual Policy #3643, Franklin Fire Insurance Co. Papers. HSP

BIBLIOGRAPHICAL REFERENCES:
  Harbeson, William. "Mediaeval Philadelphia." *Pennsylvania Magazine of History and Biography*, LXVII, 3 (July 1943): 227-253; T

THE CAMAC HOUSE was one of Philadelphia's few examples of the "cottage orné." Tatum [180] is incorrect in dating the house c. 1825. Sidney George Fisher mentions it as a new house on 11 July 1841 and the insurance survey is dated 31 July 1841.

Harbeson [233], although he knew the Camac House only from pictures, noted the resemblance to the superintendent's cottage at Laurel Hill. While he was unaware of the authorship of either, he could not help feeling the Camac House was "the work of the same artificer as the accident in the Cemetery. There was a similar disposition of wings, a like arrangement of bow windows."

Harbeson was a sensitive observer, and further, if indirect, support for attributing the Camac House to Notman is suggested by its appearance in Downing's publications. In the fall of 1841 Downing was soliciting recommendations for new Philadelphia residences that would merit inclusion in his forthcoming books.

My publishers advise me to prepare materials for a new edition of "Landscape Gardening" which I shall do during the winter. Is there anything about Phila in the way of remarkably fine residences—not in a floral sense in which you excel, but so far as tasteful design is concerned?
  [Downing to Smith, 15 Nov. 1841]
I am preparing materials for my little vol. on "Model Cottages and Gardens" to be published in the spring....
  [Downing to Smith, 3 Dec. 1841]

In the margin of the second letter is a check mark and the name "Notman," presumably in Smith's hand. *Cottage Residences* certainly included one Notman design, the Tuscan villa illustrated as Design IX. [see entry 12] But Downing did not always credit particular architects, and it must at least be considered as a possibility that the Camac House was another Notman design suggested by Smith.
PRESENT STATUS:
  Demolished

Robert McCall House. *Courtesy Ben Whitmire*

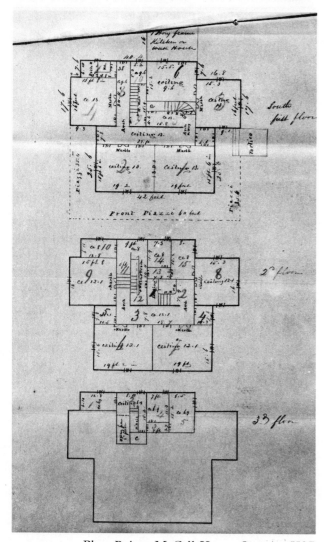

Plan. Robert McCall House. *Courtesy HSP*

85.

ROBERT McCALL HOUSE
TRENTON, NEW JERSEY
1846

OTHER EARLY ILLUSTRATIONS:

Plans of all three stories are included in the survey for Perpetual Policy #7485, Franklin Fire Insurance Co. Papers, HSP; an early photograph of the front of the building, unfortunately of too poor a quality to reproduce, appears in a newspaper clipping from the *Trenton Sunday Times-Advertiser* (no date attached), Vertical Files, Trentoniana Collection, Trenton Free Public Library.

DOCUMENTATION:

McCall, Robert. Letterbook 1849-1853. HSP; Stockton, Sarah Marks. Diary. PUL

BIBLIOGRAPHICAL REFERENCES:

Cleary, John J. "Once Lovely Montgomery Estate Yields to Prosaic 'Berryville'—Tale of West End Transformation." *Trenton Sunday Times-Advertiser*, 26 Nov. 1922; Podmore, Harry J. *Trenton Old and New.* n.p. (1927)

IT IS IMPOSSIBLE to tell from Sarah Stockton's diary whether it was this house or Ellarslie [see entry 34] that was shown to her and her husband, John P. Stockton, by Notman when they were considering plans for their own house in February 1848. However, Charles Pearson's references to Ellarslie suggest that it was a new house when he saw it in 1849. The Robert McCall House, on the other hand, was certainly there for the Stocktons to see, since the insurance survey is dated 28 Jan. 1847. Furthermore, there are strong similarities between this and the Stockton house. On the exterior both had a sturdy block to the left of the entrance, surrounded by verandahs. Both also had a projecting pavilion to the right of the entrance. The plans are also strikingly alike. They might be characterized as exploded central hall plans. Two rooms are conventionally disposed, as they would have been in a Georgian house, to the left of the hall, while to the right the equivalent rooms are pushed to the front and back by an interposed stairhall. These features combined with the similarity of the exterior detailing to that at Ellarslie, as in the extension of the window architraves below the sills to form recessed panels, support an attribution of the house to Notman.

Robert McCall was the brother of Henry McCall, Sr., who owned Ellarslie, and therefore the uncle of Henry [Harry] McCall, Jr., who occupied it. Robert McCall used the Trenton house as a summer residence, living during the winter on Chestnut Street in Philadelphia. [Letterbook, 16 July 1850]

PRESENT STATUS:

The house was added to at the west in 1864. [Insurance survey] Eventually converted to a multiple dwelling, it was demolished after World War II.

86.

CHURCH OF THE MESSIAH
2644 HUNTINGDON STREET, PORT RICHMOND,
  PHILADELPHIA
1847–1848

DOCUMENTATION:

Letter from John Notman to John Bohlen, 11 Apr. 1848, Dreer Coll., HSP; Philadelphia *Public Ledger*

BIBLIOGRAPHICAL REFERENCES:

D: 137; F: 221–223; Coolidge, John. "Gothic Revival Churches in New England and New York." Unpublished honors thesis, Department of Fine Arts, Harvard University, 1935.

THE CHURCH OF THE MESSIAH was first attributed to Notman by Coolidge. Of its date there is little question.

Consecration. The beautiful "Church of the "Messiah," at Richmond, was consecrated yesterday....

The church is a substantial edifice of the Early English Gothic style, in the form of a cross, with a beautiful rural porch at the side and a belfry. It is built of stone, the windows are painted elegantly, and it is congruous throughout, reminding the English traveller very strongly of the beautiful Parish churches of that country.... It will hold from 6 to 700 persons and 350 in the basement.

[*Public Ledger*, 25 Apr. 1848, 2]

Church of the Messiah. *Author's photograph*

Unfortunately neither the newspaper account nor the records of the church credit Notman with the design. Fairbanks [222] cites a newspaper clipping of c. 1896 in the Church of the Messiah Records at the Registrar's Library of the Diocese of Pennsylvania, that does name Notman as the architect. Notman is also linked to the church through a letter concerning its furnishings.

Dear Sirs

I send you a sketch of "Font" suited to Richmond Church—only it is something smaller than I will make seeing you have augmented the price.

Please return it this evening with approved or not as it must be hurried to get it done—it will be made most substantially.

Your Most Obdt Servt
John Notman
April 11th, 1848

PRESENT STATUS:

The building, now known as "Adriatic Hall" is still standing, although disfigured by a modern entrance. An addition has been made to the northwest almost doubling the size of the building.

87.

MORVEN
PRINCETON, NEW JERSEY
1848

DOCUMENTATION:

Stockton, Sara Marks. Diary, 1848-1854. PUL

BIBLIOGRAPHICAL REFERENCES:

Bill, Alfred Hoyt. *A House Called Morven.* 2nd ed., Princeton (1978)

EARLY IN 1848 Commodore Robert F. Stockton announced his decision "to build upon Morven," his eighteenth-century family home. [Diary, 14 Jan. 1848] If he retained an architect, it was probably Notman, who had already carried out projects for the Commodore's cousin, Richard Stockton Field, was about to design a house for one of his sons, and within a few years would design houses for another son and a brother-in-law.

Morven is a Georgian house, which already had been extensively altered in the Federal period. The mid-nineteenth century building campaign probably encompassed the verandah with its Tuscan columns; Tuscan porticos on the wings; the addition of two square appendages at the rear, one containing a bathroom said to be the first in Princeton; some interior woodwork, notably the arched doorways leading from the hall to the parlor and dining room; and an addition to the service building known as the "slave quarters" behind the main house.

PRESENT STATUS:

Still in use as official residence of the Governors of New Jersey

88.

HOLLY BUSH
GLASSBORO, NEW JERSEY
1849

BIBLIOGRAPHICAL REFERENCES:
Richardson, Herbert. "Holly Bush: A Social and Architectural History." Unpublished manuscript (1978)

THOMAS H. WHITNEY, for whom Holly Bush was built, a successful glass manufacturer and less successful politician, was the son of Mrs. Bathsheba Whitney, who had donated the land for St. Thomas's Church. In respect to location, time, and linkage through patronage, therefore, it is conceivable that Notman had a hand in the design of Holly Bush.

Hollybush. *Author's photograph*

There is no question about the date of Holly Bush. That, and the owner's name, are firmly inscribed on a stone set in the fourth stage of the tower. But otherwise documentation is sparse. Herbert Richardson, professor at Glassboro State College, suggests Notman's involvement not only on the basis of the circumstantial factors cited above, but on similarities to other documented residences, particularly Medary. Certainly there are a number of motifs employed at Holly Bush that also were part of Notman's repertory, as indeed by the late 1840s they formed part of the vocabulary of any architect or builder working in the Italianate mode. These include the square tower with hipped roof and balconies, the verandah with concave roof, the four-over-four sash, and the wide round-arched entrance.

The ensemble, however, is not totally convincing. The tower is thin in contrast to the visual robustness of this feature in Notman's villas. The roof overhangs too far, and the brackets, or rather exposed rafters, are insubstantial. The slope of the verandah roof and its intersection with the tower are awkward, as is the manner in which the bracketed hood over the entrance attempts to bridge the difference in plane between the tower and the projecting bay. Furthermore, the facade is not articulated by the fenestration. The cornices are weak and not well related to the belt course on the tower, as they are, for example, at Prospect. The gabled roofs lack an entablature, a device that Notman only omitted in such relatively informal designs as the servants' wings of Prospect and Alverthorpe or the lodge at Mount Vernon cemetery.

The plan of Holly Bush is, as Richardson has pointed out, similar to that of Medary, with an L-shaped stair hall and approximately the same disposition of rooms. Medary is the simplest of Notman's plans, lacking the subtle spatial shifts through which Notman usually directs circulation. But at Medary the space is nevertheless well controlled. This is not the case at Holly Bush. In particular the presence of two entrances of approximately the same importance, one at the end of each leg of the hall, is symptomatic of the same lack of organization that characterizes the facade. Although Notman's villas were certainly a strong influence on the design of Holly Bush, it seems doubtful that it was actually built from drawings provided by him.

PRESENT STATUS:

Holly Bush is part of the campus of Glassboro State College. It is perhaps best known as the site of a summit meeting between President Johnson and Premier Kosygin.

89.

PARISH SCHOOL OF TRINTY CHURCH
PRINCETON, NEW JERSEY
1849–1850

OTHER EARLY ILLUSTRATIONS:
Photograph in collection of PUA
DOCUMENTATION:
Minutes of Vestry Meetings, Trinity Church, 1833-1859; Princeton *Whig*
BIBLIOGRAPHICAL REFERENCES:
Greiff, Constance M., Gibbons, Mary W. and Menzies, Elizabeth G. C. *Princeton Architecture.* Princeton (1967); Hageman, John F. *Princeton and its Institutions.* Philadelphia (1879)

Parish School, Trinity Church. *Courtesy PUA*

ON 31 AUG. 1849 the vestry of Trinity Church met to consider the "propriety of building and establishing upon a permanent basis a parish school." It was reported that "a lot for the above purpose has been offered by Richard Stockton Esqr." The project meeting with approval, it was resolved that "Mesr. [W. S.] Rogers, [Commodore Robert F.] Stockton, James Potter, [?] Smith and [Charles] Ste[a]dman be a committee to obtain plans and estimates for the same." [Minutes]

No further mention appears in the church records for over a year, although the Princeton *Whig* reported on 12 Apr. 1850 that the school was almost finished and fitted with desks and seats of cast iron. Finally, at a meeting of the corporation of the church in Sept. 1850 it was simply announced that "through the liberality of a few individuals connected with this parish a building has been erected which is designed for a Parish School." [Minutes] Hageman says that the chief contributor was James Potter. [II, 93]

The most prominent men on the building committee were themselves patrons, or closely related to patrons, of Notman. Commodore Stockton was the father of John P. Stockton and had, indeed, probably paid for the building of the latter's recently completed house. It is likely that Notman had also carried out alterations to the Commodore's house. [see entry 87] He was also a first cousin of Richard Stockton Field [see entries 21, 24, and 59] James Potter was the brother of Thomas F. Potter, for whom Notman designed Prospect. It was a group that was likely to turn to Notman for the design of a new edifice.

Jonathan Fairbanks first pointed out the resemblance between this building, St. Thomas's Glassboro, and St. Paul's, Trenton. The combination of patronage and close similarity to the two documented churches makes it highly probable that Notman was responsible for the design of the parish school.

PRESENT STATUS:
Although no longer a school, the building is still utilized by Trinity Church.

Delvanside. *Courtesy Mrs. Davis Abbott*

90.

DELVANSIDE
FIFTY-FOURTH STREET AND WOODLAND AVENUE, PHILADELPHIA

ACCORDING to family tradition, this was the "country" house of John Gibson, Notman's brother-in-law. Notman and Gibson were closely associated, not only by family relationship, but professionally. Gibson, a well-known painter and decorator, and a manufacturer of stained glass, was responsible for the decorating and stained glass in many of Notman's buildings.

91.

J. B. HUTCHINSON HOUSE
BRISTOL, PENNSYLVANIA
1850–1851

DOCUMENTATION:
Estimate from Lippincott & Haines, 2 Apr. 1850, Coll. Mrs. Joseph Carson
BIBLIOGRAPHICAL REFERENCES:
Green, Doron. *A History of the Old Homes on Radcliffe Street.* Bristol (1938)

ACCORDING TO GREEN [149-152] the house was extensively remodeled and enlarged after its purchase by William H. Grundy in 1881. Its appearance thereafter, to judge by the only available photograph, was that of a three-story Queen Anne house.

The Lippincott & Haines estimate offers to build the house "as Specified" for $7,700, excluding the "plumbing, kitchen range, marble mantles and trellice work for the veranda." According to Mrs. Carson the specifications, signed by Notman, were with the estimate when she acquired the latter document, but currently cannot be found.

PRESENT STATUS:
Demolished

92.

BELVOIR
NORRISTOWN, PENNSYLVANIA
c. 1852

DALLETT [139, 49n] postulates that this large Italianate villa may be by Notman. Originally called Twesdelle, it was built for Israel Franklin Whitall, like Thomas Whitney a New Jersey glass manufacturer. In plan the house is less sophisticated than most of Notman's documented villas. An L-shaped hall is flanked by rooms on either side, that to the right being far larger, with two rooms across the back. The detailing, although generous in scale is relatively unsophisticated and even old-fashioned, with such motifs as crosseted window surrounds. No documentation connecting the building with Notman has been found.

93.

"ST. MARK'S RECTORY"

EIGHTEENTH AND LOCUST STREETS,
PHILADELPHIA
1853–1854 (?)

OTHER EARLY ILLUSTRATIONS:
Photograph published in *The Inland Architect*, XXIII, 4 (May 1894)

DOCUMENTATION:
Philadelphia *Public Ledger*

BIBLIOGRAPHICAL REFERENCES:
D: 138; Harbeson, William. "Medieval Philadelphia." *Pennsylvania Magazine of History and Biography*, LXVII, 3 (July 19 & 3): 227-253; Mortimer, Rev. Alfred. *St. Mark's Church, Philadelphia and its Lady Chapel*. New York (1909); W

WHY *The Inland Architect* published this building is something of a mystery. The style was by then old-fashioned and the architect virtually forgotten. There is no accompanying text, only the title "Residence, Northeast Corner Eighteenth and Locust Streets, Philadelphia. John Nottman [sic], Architect."

Dallett, Harbeson [243], and White [36] all refer to the building as St. Mark's Rectory and attribute it to Notman. However Mortimer [11] says the original rectory of St. Mark's was at 1620 Spruce Street and a contemporary description of what is probably the Locust Street house ascribes it to another hand.

> Splendid Residence. A commodious brown stone dwelling, for Clayton Piatt, Esq., has been nearly completed, at the corner of Eighteenth and Locust streets, opposite Rittenhouse Square. It is in the pure old Gothic style, with high gables and slate roof, and is built entirely of brown stone, the same material being used in the back building. It has a front of 40 feet, the doorway being in the centre, with a porch in keeping with the style of architecture. The plans were furnished by Charles Lacy, Architect, and the ornamental stonework executed by Charles L. Ramson.
> [*Public Ledger*, 26 Jan. 1854, 2]

Charles Lacy or Lacey was the contractor for the tower and spire of St. Mark's. [see entry 33] There is always the possibility that the newspaper was mistaken and that Notman and Lacey were again in an architect-contrac-

tor relationship. Certainly the house bore a sufficient resemblance to the Episcopal Academy to give credence to a connection with Notman.

PRESENT STATUS:
Demolished

1618-1620 Locust Street.
Author's photograph

94.

HOUSES

1602-1604 AND 1618-1620 LOCUST STREET,
PHILADELPHIA

BIBLIOGRAPHICAL REFERENCES:
D: 138

DALLETT, depending on family tradition, cites the Henry Carpenter Dallett House, number 1618, adding that the houses on either side were also by Notman. 1616 has been demolished, and 1618 and 1620 have been radically altered. However enough of the fabric remains, and exhibits enough similarity to the design of The Athenaeum, to make such an attribution highly plausible. The same holds true of the pair of decorous brownstones numbered 1602 and 1604.

PRESENT STATUS:
In mixed commercial and residential use, these buildings and their compatible neighbors are a wonderful complement to St. Mark's Church.

95.

DUNLEITH
New Castle Hundred, Delaware
Bibliographical references:
D: 133; S-PULC: 121; Wilmington *Journal Every Evening*

Dunleith has been attributed to Notman largely on the basis of its Italianate style and a coincidence of owners' surnames. Built in proximity to Boothhurst, it also belonged to a family named Rogers, the first owner being Theodore Rogers. It was undoubtedly confusion of the names that led Smith to discuss Dunleith as the Rogers House listed by Jackson, and dated by him 1847. Inherited by Theodore Roger's daughter, Helen Rogers Bradford, Dunleith is said to have been built between 1850 and 1860. [*Journal Every Evening*, 11 July 1944, 19 Aug. 1949]

Unfortunately there are no photographs of the house in the collections of the Delaware Historical Society, the New Castle Historical Society, or the Wilmington Public Library. Newspaper illustrations [*Journal Every Evening*, 11 July 1944, 13 Nov. 1958] show the house to have been large and rather pretentious, but lacking the picturesque, complex massing characteristic of Notman's major residences. Dunleith, like Guernsey Hall, had, as Smith points out, an octagonal stair hall. Although the form was the same, the architectural quality was not comparable. It is largely the massive swooping stair that defines and gives excitement to the space in the Princeton building. The graceful, but rather weak, stair at Dunleith failed to fulfill the same function.

Present status:
Burned for practice by the local fire department

96.

ROXBOROUGH PRESBYTERIAN CHURCH
Ridge and Port Royal Avenues, Philadelphia

Bibliographical references:
F: 85, 226; White, William P. and Scott, William H. *The Presbyterian Church in Philadelphia*. Philadelphia (1895)

Fairbanks suggests a resemblance between this and an unidentified drawing for a church at the Historical Society of Pennsylvania. [70.6] As he points out, however, the church is said to have been built in 1834-1835 and remodeled in the 1870s. In fact, it is probable that the central tower, which has a cornerstone dated September 1873, was not added until that date. Without the tower the resemblance to the drawing is slight indeed, confined largely to the utilization of round-headed windows. The nave has four bays rather than the five shown in the drawing and the tower itself is far blockier.

Present status:
The building still stands, although virtually overwhelmed by a twentieth-century structure, built in front of it.

97.

ANNASDALE
Near Bryn Mawr, Pennsylvania
c. 1853

Bibliographical references:
D: 131; Ashmead, Henry Graham. *History of Delaware County, Pennsylvania*. Philadelphia (1844)

The house, illustrated by Ashmead [699], appears to have been a four-square Italianate bracketed villa. It was built for Dr. Edward Peace, probably a member of the same family as Joseph Peace. [see entry 78] Because of the linkage of patronage and the use of the Italianate mode, Dallett suggests that the house may have been by Notman. From the photograph, however, it appears to have been of a simplified Tuscan type being produced by a number of architects in the Philadelphia area in the 1850s. Without further evidence, written or visual, it is impossible to judge whether Notman was its designer.

THE FOLLOWING BUILDINGS, WHICH HAVE BEEN ATTRIBUTED TO NOTMAN, HAVE PROVED TO BE THE WORK OF OTHER ARCHITECTS.

COTTAGE OF CORTLAND VAN RENSSELAER
BURLINGTON, NEW JERSEY

THIS WAS attributed by Dallett [131] who called it "remarkably similar to Riverside" on the basis of a photograph in the Library of the Department of Architecture at Harvard University. The actual house, however, which is still standing, is a Gothic cottage rather than an Italianate villa. According to Agnes Addison Gilchrist in *William Strickland Architect and Engineer, 1788-1854*, Philadelphia (1950), 88, the design was provided by Strickland. A watercolor and ink perspective signed by Strickland is now in the Karolik Collection of the Boston Museum of Fine Arts.

J. W. PERRY HOUSE
BROOKLYN, NEW YORK

MORGAN [48] suggests a relationship to a residence unidentified among the drawings at the Historical Society of Pennsylvania. According to Jane Davies, the design for the Perry House was, however, supplied by James Dakin.

CHURCH OF ST. JAMES THE LESS
PHILADELPHIA
1846–1850

DALLETT [137] ascribed the church to Notman. But as Fairbanks has indicated [217-219] neither the records of the church nor reviews of its construction in *The Ecclesiologist* support this thesis. Stanton [99-101] documents that the drawings for St. James the Less, based on the Church of St. Michael's, Long Stanton, had been brought from England by Samuel Farmar Jarvis, and prepared there by George

Gordon Place. She adds [105, 112] that further drawings were supplied by William Butterfield and that minor modifications—the addition of a bay to the nave and an added vestry—were probably the work of John E. Carver, who probably also served as contractor.

ST. MARK'S CHURCH
WEST ORANGE, NEW JERSEY
c. 1850

STANTON [305] says that the "assurance and competence of the design suggest that it was Notman, Priest, or Upjohn. . . ." According to information supplied by Mrs. George S. Yeomans, secretary of the parish, Upjohn was the architect.

ST. PAUL'S CHURCH
CAMDEN, NEW JERSEY
1834–1835

STANTON [221n], in listing a number of churches of the first non-archeological phase of the Gothic Revival, attributes St. Paul's to Notman. This may be a result of confusion with St. Paul's, Trenton, although the buildings were not alike. The first design for the much altered Camden church was by a local builder-architect named Gideon V. Stivers. According to Gail Greenberg, director of the Camden County Cultural and Heritage Commission, Stivers's "draft" for the church was adopted at an adjourned meeting of the vestry on 17 Feb. 1834.

THIRD PRESBYTERIAN CHURCH
TRENTON, NEW JERSEY
1849–1850

ROBERT C. SMITH, in correspondence with Henry L. Savage in the Princeton University Archives, suggested that this interesting Norman structure might be by Notman. However, *A Discourse Delivered on the Occasion of the Twenty-fifth Anniversary of the Organization of the Third Presbyterian Church* credits the design to "Henry Austin, of New Haven," who, according to a lithograph in the New Jersey Historical Society was also the architect for a row of Trenton houses known as "The Cottages."

Bibliography

BOOKS AND PAMPHLETS

Ashmead, Henry Graham. *History of Delaware County, Pennsylvania.* Philadelphia (1884)

Aspinwall, Marguerite. *A Hundred Years in His House, the Story of Holy Trinity on Rittenhouse Square.* Philadelphia (1956)

Baldwin, Oliver P. *Address Delivered at the Dedication of the Hollywood Cemetery.* Richmond (1849)

Bartell, Edmund, Jun. *Hints for Picturesque Improvements in Ornamented Cottages and their Scenery....* London (1804)

Bill, Alfred Hoyt. *A House Called Morven.* 2nd ed. Princeton (1978)

The Cincinnati Cemetery of Spring Grove. Report for 1857. Cincinnati (1857)

Cist, Charles. *Sketches and Statistics of Cincinnati in 1851.* Cincinnati (1851)

Cleary, John J. "Catholic Pioneers of Trenton, N. J." *Historical Records and Studies of the United States Catholic Historical Society.* Joseph F. Delany *et al.,* eds. New York (1971)

Collins, John. *Views of the City of Burlington, New Jersey.* Burlington (1847)

Collins, V[arnum] Lansing. *Princeton, past and present.* Princeton (1931)

Colvin, Howard Montagu. *A Biographical Dictionary of British Architects, 1600-1840.* London (1978)

Cooledge, Harold Norman, Jr. *Samuel Sloan (1815-1884), Architect.* University of Pennsylvania Dissertation (1963) University Microfilms, Inc.

Curl, James Stevens. *The Victorian Celebration of Death.* London (1972)

Diamonstein, Barbaralee. *The Reborn Building: New Uses, Old Places.* New York (1978)

Dearn, T. D. W. *Sketches in Architecture; Consisting of Original Designs for Cottages and Rural Dwellings....* London (1807)

Doane, George Washington. *Diocese of New Jersey: Episcopal Address to the Sixty-First Annual Convention.* Burlington (1844)

———. *Diocese of New Jersey: Episcopal Address to the Sixty-Third Annual Convention.* Burlington (1846)

———. *Diocese of New Jersey: Episcopal Address to the Sixty-Fourth Annual Convention.* Burlington (1847)

———. *Diocese of New Jersey: Episcopal Address to the Sixty-Sixth Annual Convention.* Burlington (1849)

Downing, A. J. *Cottage Residences; or, A Series of Designs for Rural Cottages and Cottage Villas, and their Gardens adapted to North America.* New York and London (1842), 2nd ed. New York (1844), 3rd ed. New York (1847), 4th ed. New York (1852), 5th ed. New York (1873)

———. *Rural Essays.* Ed., with a memoir of the author, by George William Curtis. New York (1853)

———. *A Treatise on the Theory and Practice of Landscape Gardening adapted to North America; with a view to the improvement of country residences... with remarks on rural architecture.* New York and London; Boston (1841), 2nd ed. New York (1844), 4th ed. New York (1849), 6th ed. New York (1859), 7th ed. New York (1865), 8th ed. New York (1875)

[Dunn, Nathan]. *Ten Thousand Chinese Things: A Descriptive Catalogue of the Chinese Collection.* By William B. Langdon, esq., curator of the collection. London (1842)

Elliot and Nye. *Virginia Directory* (1852)

Fox, John H. *A Century of Catholicity in Trenton, N. J.* Trenton (1900)

Freedley, Edward T. *Philadelphia and its Manufactures: A Handbook Exhibiting the Development, Variety, and Statistics of the Manufacturing Industry of Philadelphia in 1857.* Philadelphia (1859)

Freemasons, Pennsylvania Grand Lodge. *Minutes of the Grand Lodge, III, 1849-1854.* Philadelphia (1903)

Gandy, Joseph. *The Rural Architect....* London (1805)

Gardner, Edgar S., et al (eds.). *The First Two Hundred Years, 1747-1947, of the St. Andrew's Society of Philadelphia.* Philadelphia (1948)

Gebhard, David and Nevins, Deborah. *200 Years of American Architectural Drawings.* New York (1977)

Good, George. *Liberton in Ancient and Modern Times.* Edinburgh (1893)

Gowans, Alan. *Architecture in New Jersey.* Princeton (1964)

Green, Doron. *A History of the Old Homes on Radcliffe Street, Bristol, Pennsylvania.* Bristol (1938)

Greiff, Constance M. *Lost America: From the Atlantic to the Mississippi.* Princeton (1971)

Greiff, Constance M., Gibbons, Mary W., and Menzies, Elizabeth G. C. *Princeton Architecture.* Princeton (1967)

Gyfford E. *Designs for Elegant Cottages and Small Villas....* London (1806)

———. *Designs for Small Picturesque Cottages and Hunting Boxes....* London (1807)

Hageman, John Frelinghuysen. *History of Princeton and its Institutions.* Philadelphia (1879)

Hills, George Morgan. *History of the Church in Burlington, New Jersey.* Trenton (1876)

An Historical Catalogue of the St. Andrew's Society of Philadelphia 1749-1907. Philadelphia (1907)

Historical Sketch of Hollywood Cemetery. Richmond (1875)

Hitchcock, Henry-Russell. *Architecture, Nineteenth and Twentieth Centuries.* Harmondsworth (1958)

Hitchcock, Henry-Russell, and Seale, William. *Temples of Democracy*. New York (1976)

Jackson, Joseph. *Early Philadelphia Architects and Engineers*. Philadelphia (1923)

Hurd, Henry M. *et al. The Institutional Care of the Insane in the United States and Canada*. Baltimore (1916-1917)

Kendall, H. E. *Sketches of the Approved Designs of a Chapel and Gateway Entrances intended to be erected at Kensall Green for the General Cemetery Company*. London (1832)

Kirkbride, Thomas S. *Notice of Some Experiments in Heating and Ventilating Hospitals*. Philadelphia (1850)

———. *Remarks on the Construction and Arrangement of Hospitals for the Insane*. Philadelphia (1847)

———. *On the Construction, Organization, and General Arrangements of Hospitals for the Insane*. Philadelphia (1854)

Lewis, Lawrence A. *A History of the Bank of North America*. Philadelphia (1882) (Extra illustrated edition, Historical Society of Pennsylvania)

List of the Resident Members of St. Andrew's Society of Philadelphia. Philadelphia (1840)

Looney, Robert F. *Old Philadelphia in Early Photographs, 1839-1914*. New York and Philadelphia (1976)

Loth, Calder, and Sadler, Julius Trousdale, Jr. *The Only Proper Style*. Boston (1975)

Loudon, J. C., *An Encyclopedia of Cottage, Farm, and Villa Architecture and Furniture*. London (1833)

Lugar, Robert. *Architectural sketches for cottages, rural dwellings, and villas....* London (1805)

———. *Villa architecture: a collection of views, with plans of buildings executed in England, Scotland, etc. ...* London (1828)

Macaulay, James. *The Gothic Revival, 1745-1845*. Glasgow & London (1975)

Malton, James. *A Collection of Designs for Rural Retreats, as Villas principally in the Gothic and Castle Styles of Architecture*. London (n.d., prob. 1802)

Marion, John Francis. *Famous and Curious Cemeteries*. New York (1977)

Massey, James C., ed. *Two Centuries of Philadelphia Architectural Drawings*. Philadelphia (1964)

Meason, G. L. *On the Landscape Architecture of the Great Painters of Italy*. London (1828)

[Mogridge, George]. *Old Humphrey's Walks in London and its Neighborhood*. London (n.d.)

Montgomery, Rev. Henry Eglinton. *A Pastoral Letter to the Congregation of All Saints' Church, Philadelphia*. Philadelphia (1855)

Moorman, John J. *The Virginia Springs*. 2nd ed. Richmond (1854)

[Mordecai, Samuel]. *Richmond in By-Gone Days*. 2nd ed. Richmond (1860)

"Morris, Tasker and Co's Illustrated Catalogue, 1860." Waite, Diana S., ed. *Architectural Elements*. Princeton (n.d.)

Mortimer, Rev. Alfred. *St. Mark's Church, Philadelphia and its Lady Chapel*. New York (1909)

New Jersey Legislature. *Acts of the 71st Legislature of the State of New Jersey*. Trenton (1847); ... *of the 78th Legislature....* Mount Holly (1854); ... *of the 84th Legislature....* Paterson (1860)

New Jersey Legislature. *Journal of the Proceedings of the First Senate of the State of New Jersey*. Morristown (1845); ... *of the Second ...* New Brunswick (1846); ... *of the Third ...* Camden (1847); ... *of the Fourth ...* Flemington (1848)

New Jersey Legislature. General Assembly. *Minutes of the Votes and Proceedings of the Sixty-Ninth General Assembly of the State of New Jersey ...* Camden (1845); ... *of the Seventieth ...* Woodbury (1846); ... *of the Seventy-First ...* Rahway (1847); ... *of the Seventy-Second ...* Rahway (1846)

New Jersey State Hospital, Trenton. *Annual Report of the Officers of the New Jersey State Lunatic Asylum at Trenton, December 1848*. Trenton (1849)

New Jersey State Prison. *Report on the Condition of the New Jersey State Prison*. Trenton (1847)

Nicholson, Peter. *The Carpenter's New Guide*. 9th ed. Philadelphia (1827)

Notman, John. *Description and Estimate of Design Submitted by John Notman, Architect for the Smithsonian Institution*. Washington (1847)

Notman, John. *Report Accompanying Plan of Holly-Wood Cemetery, Richmond, Va.* (1848) Included in *Historical Sketch of Hollywood Cemetery*. Richmond (1875)

One Hundredth Anniversary, St. Thomas' Episcopal Church. Glassboro (1946)

Papworth, John B. *Rural residences....* London (1818)

Parker, Charles. *Villa Rustica*. London (1832-1841)

Philadelphia: Three Centuries of American Art. Philadelphia (1976)

Podmore, Harry J. *Trenton, Old and New*. Trenton (1927)

Regulations of the Laurel Hill Cemetery. Philadelphia (1837)

Reiff, Daniel D. *Washington Architecture 1791-1861*. Washington (1971)

Robinson, P. F. *Designs for Farm Buildings....* London (1830)

———. *Designs for Ornamental Villas*. 3rd ed. London (1836)

———. *A New Series of Designs for Ornamental Cottages and Villas....* London (1838)

———. *Rural Architecture....* London (1838)

Ross, Marjorie Blake. *The Book of Boston: The Victorian Period*. New York (1964)

Savage, Henry Lyttleton, ed. *Nassau Hall, 1756-1956.* Princeton (1956)

Scharf, J. Thomas and Westcott, Thompson. *History of Philadelphia, 1609-1884.* Philadelphia (1884)

Scott, Mary Wingfield, and Catterall, Louise F. *Virginia's Capitol Square.* Richmond (1957)

Scott, W. W., and Stanard, W. G. *The Capitol of Virginia and of the Confederate States.* Richmond (1894)

Smith, J[ohn] Jay. *Designs for Monuments and Mural Tablets: Adapted to Rural Cemeteries, Church Yards, Churches and Chapels on the basis of Loudon's work.* New York (1846)

——. *Guide to Laurel Hill Cemetery.* Philadelphia (1844)

——. *Statues of Old Mortality and His Pony....* Philadelphia (1838)

——. *Recollections of John Jay Smith.* Philadelphia (1892)

Smith, R. A. *Philadelphia As It Is in 1852.* Philadelphia (1852)

Smith, Robert C. "John Notman's Nassau Hall" in *Nassau Hall,* Henry Lyttleton Savage, ed. Princeton (1956)

Speedy, Tom. *Craigmillar and its Environs.* Selkirk (1892)

Stanton, Phoebe. *The Gothic Revival and American Church Architecture.* Baltimore (1968)

[Starr, Samuel]. *A Word of Self-Defense.* Trenton (1850)

The Stranger's Guide in Philadelphia. Philadelphia (1862)

[Strauch, Adolphus]. *Spring Grove Cemetery: Its History and Improvements.* Cincinnati (1869)

Tatum, George. *Penn's Great Town.* Philadelphia (1961)

Thomas, Joseph. *Universal Pronouncing Dictionary of Biography and Mythology.* Philadelphia (1870)

Thompson, Elisabeth K., ed. *Recycling Buildings: Renovations, Remodelings, Restorations, and Reuses.* New York (1977)

Trendall, E. W. *Original Designs for Cottages and Villas.* London (1837)

Tuthill, Mrs. L[ouisa] C[aroline]. *History of Architecture.* Philadelphia (1848)

Views of American Cities. New York and Paris (1848-1851)

Wainwright, Nicholas B. *Philadelphia in the Romantic Age of Lithography.* Philadelphia (1958)

Walter, Thomas U., and Smith, J[ohn] Jay. *A Guide to Workers in Metals and Stone.... From original designs, and selections made from every accessible source, American and European.* Philadelphia (1846)

Westcott, Thompson. *The Official Guide Book to Philadelphia.* Philadelphia (1875)

White, Theo B., ed. *Philadelphia Architecture in the Nineteenth Century.* 2nd rev. ed. Philadelphia (1973)

White, William P., and Scott, William H. *The Presbyterian Church in Philadelphia.* Philadelphia (1895)

PERIODICALS

The American Catholic Historical Researches, VII (July 1900), 132-133

"An American Prize—Conversion of a Classic," *House Beautiful,* 118, 5 (May 1976), 136-141

Ames, Winslow, "Alverthorpe *ex Tenebris,*" *Nineteenth Century,* III, 3 (August 1977), 66-73

Ballou's Pictorial Drawing-Room Companion, 26 May 1855, 328

Brumbaugh, Thomas B. "The Evolution of Crawford's, 'Washington,'" *The Virginia Magazine of History and Biography,* LXX, 1 (January 1962), 3-29

Cleary, John J. "Once Lovely Montgomery Estate Yields to Prosaic 'Berryville'—Tale of West End Transformation," *Trenton Sunday Times-Advertiser,* 26 Nov. 1922

"Current News and Comment: Architectural Drawings of Interest Acquired by Princeton University," *The American Architect,* CVIII, 2081 (10 Nov. 1915), 317

Dallett, Francis James, "John Notman, Architect," *Princeton University Library Chronicle,* XX, 3 (Spring 1959), 127-139

Danser, Willard S. "Trenton in Retrospect," *Trentonian,* 14 June 1961

Delanoy, Eleanor Marquand. "Guernsey Hall," *Princeton History,* 2 (1977), 4-17

The Ecclesiologist. VIII (October 1847), VIII (April 1848), IX (Aug. 1848), XII (Dec. 1851)

Frazer, Alan D. "From the Collections," *New Jersey History,* XCIII, 1-2 (Spring-Summer 1975), 58

"From Villa to Luxury Condominiums," *House and Home,* 47, 10 (Oct. 1975), 74-75

"Guernsey Hall," *The Urban Land Institute Project Reference File: Attached Residential,* 6, 11 (July-Sept. 1976)

"Guernsey Hall, Princeton," *Architectural Record,* 156, 8 (Dec. 1974), 116-117

Harbeson, John. "Philadelphia's Victorian Architecture," *Pennsylvania Magazine of History and Biography,* LXVII, 3 (July 1943), 254-271

Harbeson, William. "Mediaeval Philadelphia," *Pennsylvania Magazine of History and Biography,* LXVII, 3 (July 1943), 227-253

The Inland Architect, XXIII, 4 (May 1894)

Kent, I. J. "Art. VII On the Dwelling Rooms of a House," *The Architectural Magazine,* II (1835), 404-407

Lancaster, Clay, "Italianism in American Architecture before 1860," *American Quarterly,* IV, 2 (Summer 1952), 127-148

——. "Oriental Forms in American Architecture," *Art Bulletin,* XXIX, 3 (1947), 183-193

Meeks, Carroll. "Henry Austin and the Italian Villa," *Art Bulletin,* XXX, 2 (1949), 145-149

Mason, George C. "Professional Ancestry of the Philadelphia Chapter of the AIA," *Journal of the American Institute of Architects*, I (Sept. 1913), 370-386

"New Jersey State Asylum," *The Pennsylvania Journal of Prison Discipline and Philanthropy*, II, (1846), 57-60

"Old Landmarks Around Town," *Trenton Sunday Times*, 12 June 1910

Smith, Robert C. "John Notman and the Athenaeum Building," *Athenaeum Addresses*. Philadelphia (1951)

Smith, Robert C. "John Notman's Nassau Hall," *Princeton University Library Chronicle*, XIV, 3 (Spring 1953), 109-134

Van Trump, James, "St. Peter's, Pittsburgh by John Notman," *Journal of the Society of Architectural Historians*, XV, 2 (May 1955), 19-23

"View of the New Jersey Lunatic Asylum at Trenton,' *Gleason's Pictorial*, 5 June 1852, 361

Weaver, Bettie W. "Powhatan County's Forgotten Spa: Huguenot Springs," *Virginia Cavalcade* (Winter 1969), 13-16

Weisman, Winston. "Philadelphia Functionalism and Sullivan," *Journal of the Society of Architectural Historians*, XX, 1 (March 1961), 3-19

"Z." "Emigration of Architects to North America," *The Architectural Magazine*, I (1834), 384-386

MANUSCRIPTS

Bank of North America, Philadelphia. Minutes, Book 16. Bank of North America Records, Historical Society of Pennsylvania

Bank of North America, Philadelphia. Ledger 13. Bank of North America Records, Historical Society of Pennsylvania

Buel, Rev. D. Hillhouse to Bishop William Rollinson Whittingham. Letter, 22 May 1849. Duke University Collections

Calvary Presbyterian Church, Philadelphia. Trustees Minutes, 1851-1855. Presbyterian Historical Society

Capitol Square, Richmond. Washington Monument Funds, Boxes 16 and 17. Virginia State Library

"Capitol Square Data for Mr. W. W. Savedge." Typescript (Sept. 1931). Virginia State Library

Christ Church Hospital, Philadelphia. Minutes of the Board of Managers. Christ Church Archives

Cohan, Zara. "A comprehensive History of the State House of New Jersey and Recommendations for its Continuation as a Historic Site." Unpublished M.A. thesis, Newark State College (1969)

The College of New Jersey. Minutes of the Board of Trustees, III. Princeton University Archives

Coolidge, John. "Gothic Revival Churches in New England and New York." Unpublished honors thesis, Department of Fine Arts, Harvard University (1935)

Cooper & Hewitt Letterpress Books. New-York Historical Society

Doane, George Washington to Richard S. Field. Letter 15 Dec. 1845. Princeton University Library

Downing, A. J. to John Jay Smith. Letter, 3 Dec. 1941. John Jay Smith Collection, Library Company of Philadelphia

Downing, A. J., to John Jay Smith. Letter, 21 October 1842. John Jay Smith Collection, Library Company of Philadelphia

Emmanuel Church, Cumberland, Md. Vestry Records. Emmanuel Church

The Episcopal Academy, Philadelphia. Minutes of the Trustees of the Academy of the Protestant Episcopal Church in the City of Philadelphia, III. The Episcopal Academy

Fairbanks, Jonathan. "John Notman: Church Architect." Unpublished M.A. thesis, University of Delaware (1961)

Field, Richard S. to Elias Boudinot. Letter, 25 Apr. 1842. Princeton University Library

Fisher, Sydney George. Diary. Manuscript collection, Historical Society of Pennsylvania

Force, Debbie. "A Research Project on the Architectural History of the Pennsylvania Academy of Fine Arts." Unpublished paper, University of Pennsylvania (1977). The Pennsylvania Academy of the Fine Arts

Franklin Fire Insurance Co. Perpetual Policies Numbers 1967, 2033, 2553, 7926, 13806, 3643. Historical Society of Pennsylvania

Greiff, Constance M. "A Preliminary Report on Ellarslie." Unpublished manuscript. Trenton Museum Commission (1974)

Hodge, Charles. Letters. Hodge Collection, Princeton University Library

Immanuel Church, New Castle, Delaware. Minutes of the Vestry. Immanuel Church

Laurel Hill Cemetery Company. Cash Book I. Office, Laurel Hill Cemetery Company

Laurel Hill Cemetery Company. Minutes of the Managers, I, 1835-1898. Office, Laurel Hill Cemetery Company

Library Company of Philadelphia, Financial Records, 1836 and 1837. Library Company of Philadelphia Archives

Library Company of Philadelphia, Minutes of the Directors, VI. Library Company of Philadelphia Archives

Linten, William, Superintendent. "Mount Vernon Cemetery Company 1857." Office, Mount Vernon Cemetery Company.

Marquand, Eleanor Cross. "The Trees of Guernsey." Typescript (May 1937). Princeton University Library

McCall, Robert. Letterbook 1849-1853. Historical Society of Pennsylvania.

Meyers, Melvin. "The Architectural History of the Pennsylvania Academy of Fine Arts Before 1870." Typescript (n.d.). The Pennsylvania Academy of the Fine Arts

Morgan, Keith N. "The Landscape Gardening of John Notman, 1810-1865." Unpublished M.A. thesis, University of Delaware (1973)

Mount Vernon Cemetery Company, Philadelphia. Minute Book. Office, Mount Vernon Cemetery Company

Notman, John, to Joseph Cowperthwait. Letter, 28 March 1840. Henry F. du Pont Winterthur Museum and Library

Notman, John. Specifications for Residence of Charles L. Pearson, Esqr. (1849). Coll. of W. Houstoun Pearson

Pearson, Charles L. Diaries. Coll. of W. Houstoun Pearson

The Pennsylvania Academy of the Fine Arts. Correspondence, 1846. Pennsylvania Academy of the Fine Arts Archives

The Pennsylvania Academy of the Fine Arts, Minutes, 1805-1858. Pennsylvania Academy of the Fine Arts Archives

Philadelphia, City of. Deed Book, GS-3, 105

Playfair, W. H. Letterbook, 21 August 1830 to 5 August 1833. University of Edinburgh Library

Princeton Theological Seminary. Minutes of the Board of Trustees, 1824-1890. Speer Library, Princeton Theological Seminary

Princeton Theological Seminary. Receipt Book for moneys expended in building of New Refectory 1847. Speer Library, Princeton Theological Seminary

Report of Commissioners to sell State property, build offices, etc., made to Legislature 16th Feb. 1846. Bureau of Archives and History, New Jersey State Library

Rhoads, William B. "The Architecture of John Notman." Unpublished senior thesis, Princeton University (1966)

Richardson, Herbert. "Holly Bush: A Social and Architectural History." Unpublished manuscript (1978)

Richmond City Council Records, 12, 1848-1852. Microfilm coll., Virginia State Library

St. Anne's Church, Middletown, Del. Vestry Records, St. Anne's Appoquinimy, 1808-1883. St. Anne's Church

St. Clement's Church, Philadelphia. Minutes of the Vestry, 1855-1878. St. Clement's Church

St. John's Church, Brandywine, Del. Minutes of the meeting of the Vestry. Cathedral of St. John, Wilmington

St. John's Church, Brandywine, Del. Treasurer's account book. Cathedral of St. John, Wilmington

St. Luke's Church, Baltimore. Minutes of the Vestry. St. Luke's Church

St. Luke's and the Epiphany Church, Philadelphia. Minute Book of the Vestry. Episcopal Historical Society, Philadelphia

St. Mark's Church, Philadelphia. Minutes of the vestry of St. Mark's Church in the City of Philadelphia— A.D. MDCCCXLVIII to A.D. MDCCCLXIII. St. Mark's Church.

Shoemaker, Mary McCahon. "Thomas Somerville Stewart, Architect and Engineer." Unpublished M. Arch. History thesis, University of Virginia (1975). The Athenaeum of Philadelphia

Smith, John Jay. Papers, Ridgway Collection, Library Company of Philadelphia. Historical Society of Philadelphia

Smith, John Jay. Memoranda Respecting the Foundation of Laurel Hill Cemetery. Coll. Drayton Smith

Smithsonian Institution. Record A. Smithsonian Institution Archives

Smithsonian Institution. Report of the Board of Regents, submitted to Congress on the operations, expenditures, and condition of the Smithsonian Institution. U. S. Congress Documents, 29th Congress, S. Doc. 211, 3 Mar. 1847

Stockton, Sara Marks. Diary. Princeton University Library

Trinity Church, Princeton. Minutes of Vestry Meetings, 1833-1859. Trinity Church

Wooldridge, A. S. to William B. Phillips. Letter, 26 July 1856. Phillips mss., Virginia Historical Society

NEWSPAPERS

Delaware Republican (Wilmington), 1841-1874?

Evening Bulletin (Philadelphia), 1847-

Journal Every Evening (Wilmington), 1934-1960
Continued by *Evening Journal*

North American and United States Gazette (Philadelphia), 1847-1876

Pittsburgh Chronicle Telegraph, 1841-1927

Poulson's American Daily Advertiser (Philadelphia), 1800-1839

Princeton Whig, 1833-1854
Princeton Press, 1854-1860

Public Ledger (Philadelphia), 1836-1934

Richmond Enquirer, 1804-1877

State Gazette (Trenton)
New Jersey State Gazette, 1829-1839
State Gazette, 1840-1846
Trenton State Gazette, 1847-1928

The Trenton Sunday Times-Advertiser, 1883-

True American (Trenton), 1849-1913

Index